CASABLANCA CONFERENCE

JANUARY 1943

PAPERS
AND
MINUTES OF MEETINGS

*Edited and printed in the
Office, U. S. Secretary,
Office of the Combined Chiefs of Staff
1943*

Published by Books Express Publishing
Copyright © Books Express, 2011
ISBN 978-1-780393-97-1

Books Express publications are available from all good retail and online booksellers. For publishing proposals and direct ordering please contact us at: info@books-express.com

This volume was prepared under the auspices of the United States Chiefs of Staff who dedicate it to the memory of the late Brigadier Vivian Dykes, GBE, who served in Washington as the British Secretary of the Combined Chiefs of Staff from the time of organization, January, 1942, through the Casablanca Conference, January, 1943.

U. S. SECRET
BRITISH MOST SECRET

TABLE OF CONTENTS

PAPERS

C.C.S.		PAGE
75/3	System of Command for Combined U. S.-British Operations	1
153	Situation To Be Created In The Eastern Theater (Pacific And Burma) In 1943 (Revised)	4
153/1	Situation To Be Created In The Eastern Theater (Pacific And Burma) In 1943	8
154	Operations In Burma, 1943	11
155	Conduct Of The War In 1943	16
155/1	Conduct Of The War In 1943	18
156	Suggested Procedure For Dealing With The Agenda Of The Conference	20
157	Allied Plans Relating To Turkey	23
158	Axis Oil Position	40
159	The Bomber Offensive From North Africa (See Note 159/1)	44
159/1	The Bomber Offensive From North Africa	44
160	U-Boat War	45
161	Operation HUSKY	58
161/1	Operation HUSKY	63
162	U. S. Aid To Russia	72
162/1	U. S. Aid To Russia	75
163	System Of Air Command In The Mediterranean	78
164	Operation ANAKIM--Provision Of Forces	80
164/1	Operation ANAKIM--Provision Of Forces	82
165	Draft Telegram To Premier Stalin (See Note 165/2)	84
165/1	Draft Telegram To Premier Stalin (See Note 165/2)	84
165/2	Draft Telegram From The President Of The United States And The Prime Minister Of Great Britain To Premier Stalin	84
166	The Bomber Offensive From The United Kingdom	86
166/1/D	The Bomber Offensive From The United Kingdom	88
167	Continental Operations In 1943	90
168	Conduct Of The War In The Pacific Theater In 1943	95
169	Proposed Organization Of Command, Control, Planning And Training For Operations For A Reentry To The Continent Across The Channel, Beginning In 1943	99

U. S. SECRET
BRITISH MOST SECRET

TABLE OF CONTENTS

PAPERS

C.C.S.		PAGE
170	Report To The President And Prime Minister Draft Report On The Work Of The Conference	102
170/1	Report To The President And Prime Minister	109
170/2	Symbol--Final Report To The President And Prime Minister Summarizing Decisions By The Combined Chiefs of Staff	117
171	Directive--Operation HUSKY	125
171/1/D	Directive To Commander-In-Chief, Allied Expeditionary Force In North Africa--Operation HUSKY (See Note 171/2/D)	127
171/2/D	Directive To Commander-In-Chief, Allied Expeditionary Force In North Africa--Operation HUSKY	127
172	Shipping Capabilities For BOLERO Build-up	129

MINUTES

ANFA 1st Meeting 134
    Situation in North Africa
ANFA 2nd Meeting 142
    The General Strategic Policy for 1943
ANFA 3rd Meeting 154
    Security of Sea Communications
    Assistance to Russia
    Operations in the Mediterranean
    Operations in and from the United Kingdom
    Pacific and Far East Theater
C.C.S. 55th Meeting 169
    General Discussion of Allocation of Resources Based on Enemy Situation
C.C.S. 56th Meeting 183
    Combined Strategy Pertaining to the Pacific Situation

U. S. SECRET
BRITISH MOST SECRET

TABLE OF CONTENTS

MINUTES

	PAGE
C.C.S. 57th Meeting	195

    Antisubmarine Warfare
    Situation in North Africa
    Strategy in the European Theater

C.C.S. 58th Meeting 207
    The North African Situation
    The Strategic Concept for 1943 in the European
        Theater
    Supplies to Russia
    Employment of French Forces in North Africa

C.C.S. 59th Meeting 225
    The Eastern Theater
    Iceland
    Russian Air Assistance for P.Q. Convoys

C.C.S. 60th Meeting 232
    Operations in Burma
    The Situation to be Created in the Eastern Theater
        (the Pacific and Burma) in 1943
    Escort Vessels
    Potentialities of Polish Forces
    Raids on Berlin
    Naval Situation in the Western Mediterranean

C.C.S. 61st Meeting 248
    Conduct of the War in 1943
    Suggested Procedure for Dealing with the Agenda of
        the Conference
    Strategic Responsibility and Command Set-up for
        Dakar-French West Africa
    Publication of Results of the Conference

C.C.S. 62nd Meeting 254
    Axis Oil Position
    Allied Plans Relating to Turkey
    Meeting with General Giraud

U. S. SECRET
BRITISH MOST SECRET

TABLE OF CONTENTS

	PAGE
C.C.S. 63rd Meeting	263

    U. S. Aid to Russia

    British Responsibility for Turkey

    The Bomber Offensive from North Africa

    Command in the Mediterranean

C.C.S. 64th Meeting 272

    HUSKY

    Future Business

C.C.S. 65th Meeting 276

    The U-Boat War

    The Bomber Offensive from the United Kingdom

    Draft Telegram to M. Stalin

    ANAKIM

    BOLERO Build-up

    Report to the President and the Prime Minister

C.C.S. 66th Meeting 292

    Draft Telegram to M. Stalin

    HUSKY

C.C.S. 67th Meeting 300

    Conduct of the War in the Pacific Theater in 1943

    Press Communique

    Continental Operations in 1943

    Organization of Command, Control, Planning and
       Training for Cross-Channel Operations

    Landing Craft

    System of Command for Combined U. S. and British
       Operations

C.C.S. 68th Meeting 310

    BOLERO Build-up

    Continental Operations in 1943

    Report to the President and Prime Minister

    Operation HUSKY--Directive to General Eisenhower

    Landing Craft

C.C.S. 69th Meeting 314

    Report to the President and Prime Minister

    Operation HUSKY--Directive to General Eisenhower

    Assault Shipping

    Conclusion of the Conference

INDEX   319

U. S. SECRET
BRITISH MOST SECRET
C.C.S. 75/3   October 24, 1942

COMBINED CHIEFS OF STAFF

SYSTEM OF COMMAND FOR COMBINED U. S.-BRITISH OPERATIONS
(Previous reference: (a) C.C.S. 38th Meeting, Item 3)

Report by Combined Staff Planners

1. The enclosure, prepared by the Combined Staff Planners in accordance with reference (a), is presented for consideration by the Combined Chiefs of Staff. Annex "A", attached thereto, presents graphically the principles of unified command as contained in the report.

2. The U. S. Navy members of the Combined Staff Planners state that while this paper does not in its entirety accord with their views, it is believed that it presents the best agreement which can be reached at this time. The U. S. Navy members believe that the status of the assistants to Supreme Commander, because of the possible interpretation of their functions, may result in actually interposing an additional element in the chain of command which would limit the authority of the Supreme Commander.

ENCLOSURE

SYSTEM OF UNIFIED COMMAND FOR COMBINED OPERATIONS

DEFINITIONS:

1. Unified command is the control, exercised by a designated commander, over a force integrated from combined and joint forces allocated to him for the accomplishment of a mission or task. This force will include all the means considered necessary for the mission's successful execution. Unified command vests in the designated commander, the responsibility and authority to control the operations of all arms and services composing his force, by the organization of task forces, assignment of missions, designation of objectives, and the exercise of such control as he deems necessary to insure the success of his mission. Unified command does not authorize the commander exercising it, to control the administration and discipline of any forces of the United

U. S. SECRET
BRITISH MOST SECRET

Nations composing his command, beyond those necessary for effective control.

2. The term "joint" refers to participation of forces from two or more of the *arms* (U. S.) or *services* (British) of one nation.

3. The term "combined" refers to the participation of *forces* of two or more of the United Nations.

SUPREME COMMANDER:

4. In cases where the governments concerned so decide, a Supreme Commander will be appointed for operations when forces of more than one of the United Nations are to be employed on a specific mission or task.

5. He will be appointed by agreement between the governments concerned at the earliest possible moment after the decision to undertake an operation has been made.

6. He will exercise unified command over all forces of the United Nations allocated to his operation.

7. He will be the recipient of all major directives pertaining to the arms and services of his force.

8. Out of the means allocated to him, he will organize task forces as necessary, designate their commanders, and assign the major tasks to be performed by each.

9. He will be assisted by a small composite staff which will include in principle a Chief of Staff, a Planning Division, an Operations Division, an Intelligence Division, a Logistical Division, and a Communications Center. Each nation involved and each of the several component arms or services of the force will be represented on the staff in order to insure an understanding of the capabilities, requirements, and limitations of each component.

LAND, NAVAL AND AIR COMMANDERS:

10. The officer appointed by the Combined Chiefs of Staff as the Senior Officer of each combined arm or service not specifically allocated to task forces by the Supreme Commander, will advise the Supreme Commander on the best use of his own combined arm or service.

11. These Commanders will carry out their duties at the headquarters of the Supreme Commander unless specifically ordered otherwise by him.

TASK FORCE COMMANDERS:

12. Task Force Commanders will organize their commands as may be necessary for the execution of the tasks assigned. Sub-Task Force

U. S. SECRET
BRITISH MOST SECRET

Commanders will be designated as may be necessary for the execution of the subordinate tasks assigned. The principle of unified command will apply throughout.

13. The organization of task forces will be governed by the nature of the operations to be performed. The task forces will include all the elements--land, air and naval--necessary for the accomplishment of the task. The appointment of the Task Force Commanders, subordinate as well as major, will be governed by the nature of the task assigned, and the major arm or service involved in its performance, i.e., whether preponderantly land, air or naval.

INTEGRITY OF NATIONAL UNITS:

14. Insofar as conditions will permit, task forces will be composed of units of the same nationality. When organizations of one nation serve under the command of an officer of another, the principle will be maintained that such organizations shall be kept intact and not scattered among other units.

U. S. SECRET
BRITISH MOST SECRET

ANNEX "A"

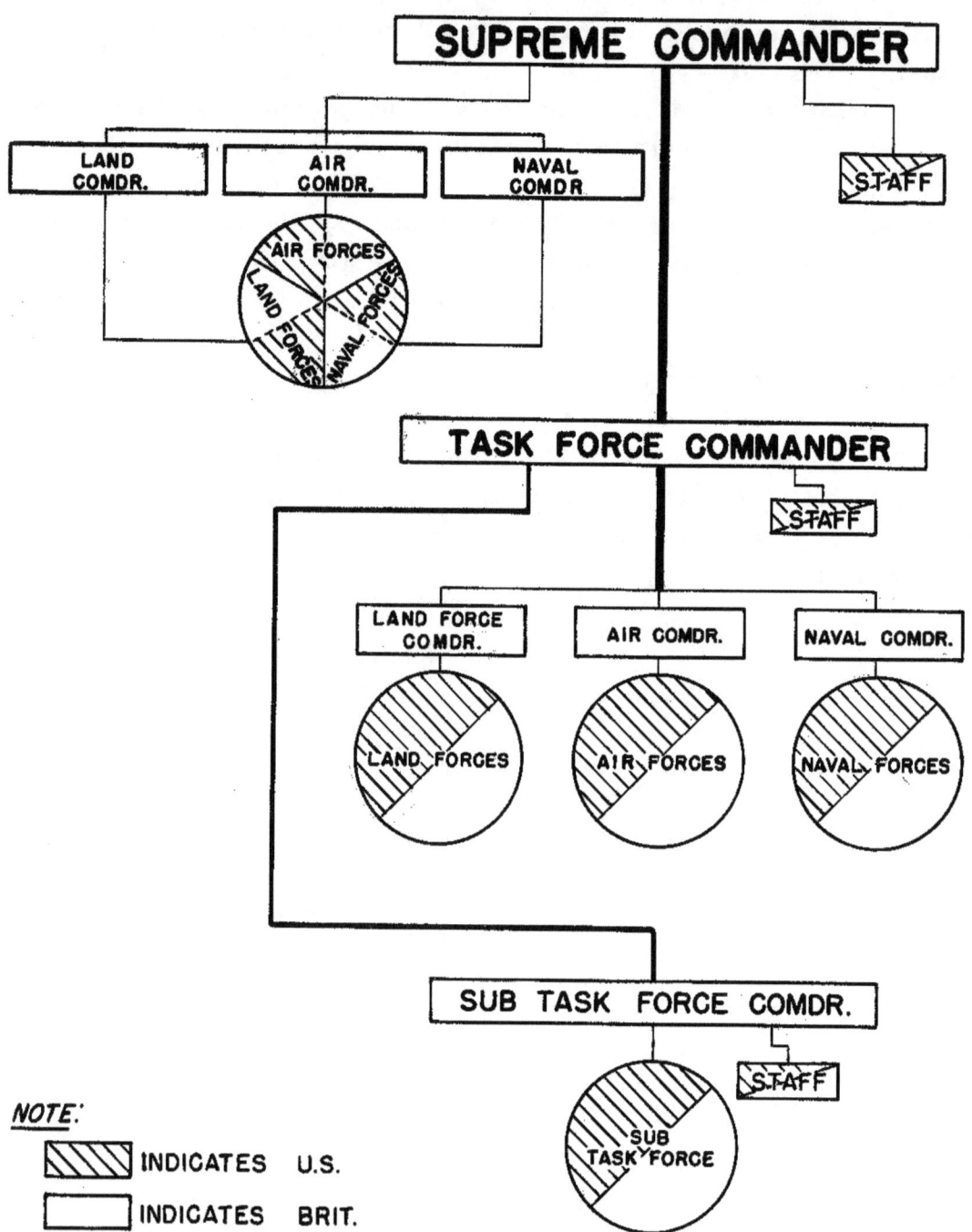

3-A

U. S. SECRET
BRITISH MOST SECRET
C.C.S. 153 (Revised)   January 17, 1943

COMBINED CHIEFS OF STAFF

SITUATION TO BE CREATED IN THE EASTERN THEATER (PACIFIC AND BURMA) IN 1943

Note by the Secretaries

At their 56th meeting, the Combined Chiefs of Staff directed the Combined Staff Planners "to report, on the basis that Germany is the primary enemy, what situation do we wish to establish in the Eastern Theater (i.e., the Pacific and Burma) in 1943 and what forces will be necessary to establish that situation."

Enclosure "A" is a partial report on the above directive prepared by the Joint U. S. Staff Planners which has been discussed at a meeting of the Combined Staff Planners.

Enclosure "B" is a continuation of the partial report given in Enclosure "A" prepared by the Joint U. S. Staff Planners.

V. DYKES,
J. R. DEANE,
Combined Secretariat.

ENCLOSURE "A"

SITUATION TO BE CREATED IN THE EASTERN THEATER (NAMELY PACIFIC AND BURMA) IN 1943

ASSUMPTIONS:

1. The Combined Planners assume

that the ultimate objective of the basic global strategy is to bring the war to a successful conclusion at the earliest practicable date;

that in gaining this objective efforts must be made toward the destruction of the economic and military power of all our adversaries at a rate exceeding their power of replacement;

that Germany is recognized as the primary or most powerful

U. S. SECRET
BRITISH MOST SECRET

and pressing enemy;

and that the major portion of the forces of the United Nations are to be directed against Germany insofar as it is consistent with the over-all objective of bringing the war to an early conclusion at the earliest possible date.

2. Tentative assumptions are made

that the present situation as between Russia and Japan will continue,

and that the Chinese will continue in the war if sufficient support is furnished by Great Britain and the United States in the way of supplies and equipment.

SITUATION TO BE CREATED:

3. We consider that the accomplishment of the over-all objective, as well as the maintenance of the security of our position in the Pacific, requires that the Japanese be kept under continual pressure sufficient in power and extent to absorb the disposable Japanese military effort.

4. The United Nations' positions in the Pacific are extended over a line roughly 12,000 miles long--from the Bering Sea, through the Hawaiian Islands, Samoa, Fiji, New Guinea and Northwest Australia, to Singapore. The Japanese, strongly established, occupy interior lines which permit offensive action by their mobile forces against any of the Allied positions--unless these mobile forces are denied freedom of action.

5. The United Nations' positions have depth at certain points, as in Alaska, Hawaii, and New Caledonia, New Guinea. The positions between Hawaii and New Caledonia have little depth and are susceptible to successful enemy attack, if these attacking forces are free to move. Some of the United Nations' positions (i.e., on the larger islands) are capable of strong defensive establishments. Other positions such as the smaller islands, like Canton, cannot be strongly defended. Economy in defensive strength of the larger islands, and security of the smaller islands, require that we maintain the initiative by offensive action. This offensive action must be directed against Japanese objectives of sufficient importance to the Japanese as to cause Japanese counteraction; they must be sufficient in power to combat successfully this Japanese counteraction.

6. By this process we intend to prevent the Japanese the opportunity

U. S. SECRET
BRITISH MOST SECRET

for consolidating (digging in), thus strengthening their positions, to an extent that would permit them to initiate offensive action at times and places of their choosing.

7. We consider that Japanese power in respect to shipping and aircraft has been getting progressively weaker; that our attacks against shipping, particularly by submarines, should be pushed to the maximum extent possible; and that our offensive action should be designed to effect a continuing decrease in Japanese naval and air power.

8. To maintain the security of our possessions in the Pacific and to contain in the Pacific area the Japanese Fleet, it is necessary to continue in that area the major portion of the United States Fleet. To give full implementation to this naval force, it is necessary that sufficient mobile ground forces, air forces, and shipping be available in that area to undertake continuing limited offensives against Japanese possessions. The character of these offensive actions envisaged for 1943 are set forth in subsequent paragraphs.

9. In planning these offensive operations in the Pacific, we take note that the ability of the United Nations to project military actions against the enemy in all areas is limited by shipping. In the Atlantic there is a further serious limitation caused by the lack of adequate numbers of escorts. Until the escort problem is improved, the amount of shipping which can be moved in the Atlantic is definitely limited. This same consideration of limitation of escort capacity does not at present apply to the Pacific, because of comparative absence of submarine menace in that area at this time.

10. The adverse situation in regard to the number of escorts available in comparison to the number of submarine packs operating in the Atlantic, and to the convoy needs in the Atlantic, will not begin to show relative improvement before October.

OPERATIONS:

11. The prospective operations to create and maintain the situation in 1943 set forth above are:

    (a) Seizure and consolidation of United Nations forces in the Solomon Islands, Eastern New Guinea up to Lae Salamaua peninsula, New Britain-New Ireland (Rabaul) area.

    (b) Seizure and occupation of Kiska-Agattu (Western Aleutians).

    (c) Seizure and occupation of Gilbert Islands, Marshall Islands,

U. S. SECRET
BRITISH MOST SECRET

  Caroline Islands, up to and including Truk. It is planned that these operations will be undertaken subsequent to Rabaul.

(d) Extension of occupation of New Guinea up to approximately the Dutch border. This will be an extension of the Truk campaign for the second part.

ENCLOSURE "B"

(3) Burma campaign. Limited operations during present favorable weather conditions such as to permit improvement of communications from India to China, to be followed by more extended operations towards the end of the year with the objective of reestablishing the communications along the lower Burma Road. The objective of this campaign is to strengthen forces in China with the view to keeping China in the war, keeping pressure on the Japanese in this area, and to the establishment and operation of air strength on Japanese shipping in Chinese and Indo-China ports as well as on the flank of Japanese sea communications along the China coast.

12. The increase of forces in the Pacific-Burma area in 1943 for the operations listed above will depend largely on the strength of Japanese dispositions. They will be of this general order:

  Ground Forces, including air personnel - 250,000 troops

  U. S. and U. K. - 500 airplanes

  Navy - The major portion of additions (by new construction) to the U. S. Fleet, while maintaining in the Atlantic present large ship strength and increasing destroyer and anti-submarine escort in the Atlantic.

  Increase in strength of the British Eastern fleet sufficent to support operations against Burma.

      Shipping 1,250,000 tons

U. S. SECRET
BRITISH MOST SECRET
C.C.S. 153/1   January 17, 1943

COMBINED CHIEFS OF STAFF

SITUATION TO BE CREATED IN THE EASTERN THEATER (PACIFIC AND BURMA) IN 1943

Memorandum by the British Joint Planning Staff

1. We have been instructed by the British Chiefs of Staff to comment on the paper by the Joint U. S. Staff Planners on the situation to be created in the Eastern Theater (Pacific and Burma) in 1943 (C.C.S. 153).

2. Our comments are as follows:

ASSUMPTIONS:

    (a) Paragraph 1:

    We feel that this should be reworded as follows:

    "The Combined Planners assume that the ultimate objective of the basic global strategy is to bring the war to a successful conclusion at the earliest practicable date. The quickest way of achieving this will be to concentrate on defeating Germany first and then to concentrate our combined resources against Japan. Meanwhile such pressure must be maintained in Japan as will prevent her from damaging interests vital to the Allies, and will hinder her from consolidating her conquests."

    (b) Paragraph 2:

    We concur.

SITUATION TO BE CREATED:

    (c) Paragraphs 3-10:

    We agree in principle with this expression of the strategy required, provided always that its application does not prejudice the earliest possible defeat of Germany.

OPERATIONS:

    (d) Paragraphs 11-12:

    We suggest the following alternative:

    The operations which are certainly required in 1943 to create and maintain the situation set forth above are:

U. S. SECRET
BRITISH MOST SECRET

      (a) Seizure of, and consolidation of United Nations forces in the Solomons, Eastern New Guinea up to the Lae-Salamaua peninsula, New Britain-New Ireland (Rabaul) area.

      (b) Burma--Limited operations during the present favorable weather period:

          (1) To recapture and establish air forces at Akyab (Cannibal).

          (2) To establish a bridgehead in the Chindwin Valley so that, when an attack on Rangoon is made, simultaneous pressure can be exerted on Mandalay (Ravenous).

          (3) To construct the Hukawng Valley road from Ledo to Mijitkyina and Lungling.

The additions to present forces in the Pacific theater required for these operations must depend upon the strength of Japanese dispositions but will be of the following general order:

      Ground forces................

      Aircraft................

      Navy................

      Amphibious forces........

      Shipping................

No forces additional to those now **present will be required** in Burma.

12. With the successful completion of the operations outlined in the preceding paragraph, a new offensive will be necessary if we are to retain the initiative and thereby contain disposable Japanese strength.

Detailed plans for undertaking the following further operations, though not necessarily in the order given, should therefore be made; but, since the timing must depend upon the speed with which the earlier operations in the Rabaul-New Guinea area are concluded, a decision whether or not to launch these further operations should be taken by the Combined Chiefs of Staff later in the year.

      (a) The seizure and occupation of Kiska-Agattu (Western Aleutians).

      (b) The seizure and occupation of the Gilbert Islands, Marshall Islands, Caroline Islands up to and including Truk.

      (c) Extension of occupation of New Guinea up to approximately the Dutch border. This will be an extension of the Truk campaign.

U. S. SECRET
BRITISH MOST SECRET

      For these operations the additional forces required will be of the order of:

           Ground forces.......
           Aircraft............
           Navy................
           Amphibious forces...
           Shipping............

13. Detailed plans for operations to reopen the Burma Road (ANAKIM) during the winter of 1943-44 will also be made. It is not possible at this stage to say by when the forces required for this operation could be provided without detracting seriously from the defeat of Germany. Orders for the completion of full administrative preparations by October 1, 1943, have, however, already been given and planning is proceeding in India.

      The forces additional to those now in the theater required for this operation must depend upon enemy strength and dispositions at the time but will be of the following order:

           Ground forces....... Nil
           Aircraft............ 18 squadrons
           Naval forces....... Covering forces as may be found necessary in the light of the naval situation at the time. As much as practicable would be found from British resources.
                           6-8 Escort Carriers
                           40 Destroyers or Escort Vessels
           Amphibious forces... Assault shipping and landing craft sufficient to lift 4 Inf. Brigade Groups and 1 Armored Brigade.
           Shipping............ 60 MT ships
                           20 Personnel ships

14. It is certain that the provision of the naval and amphibious forces required for simultaneous Truk and Anakim operations cannot but react adversely on the early defeat of Germany. It may be possible to carry out one of these operations without such a violation of our agreed strategy. The decision as to the right course of action should be taken later in the light of the development of the war.

U. S. SECRET
BRITISH MOST SECRET
C.C.S. 154   January 17, 1943

COMBINED CHIEFS OF STAFF

OPERATIONS IN BURMA, 1943

Report by British Joint Planning Staff

THE BURMA ROAD:
    1.   The reconquest of Burma should be undertaken as soon as resources within the existing strategic priorities permit.

    2.   The outstanding topographical feature governing operations in Burma is that all main communications run north from Rangoon.

        Prior to the Japanese occupation, supplies reached China by the so-called "Burma Road":

            (a) Rangoon-Mandalay-Lashio (river, rail and road).

            (b) Lashio-Lungling-Yunnanyi-Kunming-Chungking (road).

It is the only trans-Burma route by which China can receive substantial supplies. The capture of Rangoon and Mandalay must be effected before it can be reopened.

JAPANESE COMMUNICATIONS:
    3.   The Japanese rely on sea communications to Rangoon to maintain the 4 to 5 divisions they now have in Burma. They are, however, developing overland routes--rail and road--from Thailand, and these are already sufficient to enable them to maintain 3 divisions operating in Burma.

        Communications in Burma allow the Japanese to maintain larger forces in the Mandalay area than the British can maintain across the Assam frontier.

OPERATIONS JANUARY-APRIL 1943:
    4.   Field Marshal Wavell is now carrying out certain operations which are necessary preliminaries to the reconquest of Burma. These are:

            (a) Operation CANNIBAL for the recapture of, and establishment of air forces at, AKYAB. This operation has started.

            (b) Operation RAVENOUS for the establishment by IV Corps (two divisions) of a bridgehead in the Chindwin valley so that when an attack on Rangoon is made, simultaneous pressure can be exerted on Mandalay. (The routes from Assam south to the Chindwin River will not support more than two divisions.)

U. S. SECRET
BRITISH MOST SECRET

>Certain Chinese forces were to have cooperated in this operation, but their cooperation now appears uncertain. The operation by IV Corps will start in February 1943.

Both these operations should be completed before the monsoon breaks in May 1943. It is hoped that RAVENOUS will draw off some Japanese pressure from the Southwest Pacific.

OVERLAND COMMUNICATIONS WITH CHINA:

5. Neither of these preliminary operations will however reestablish land communication with China, whose retention in the war is agreed to be of great importance.

>Apart from the Burma Road proper, the only methods by which supplies might reach China appear to be:
>
>>(a) The Hukawng Valley route from Ledo via Shingbwiyang and Myitkina to Lungling--thence northeastwards by the "Burma Road" proper.
>>
>>An all-weather, one-way road has been started and the intention is to improve it to two-way as help from U.S.A. technicians and equipment become available.
>>
>>Latest advices are that the all-weather route--one or two-way--will not reach Shingbwiyang until the winter of 1943-44; although it may be possible to push through a dry-weather track as far as Myitkina after the monsoon of 1943.
>>
>>During construction it will not be possible to maintain more than one brigade group (or two Chinese divisions) on this road in addition to labor. There will therefore be great difficulty in arranging its protection, especially in the Myitkina area where Japanese forces can be maintained by rail and all-weather road.
>>
>>(b) Air transport:
>>
>>It is recommended that the air transport route should be maintained since it is the most immediate means of bringing aid to China.

RECONQUEST OF BURMA (Operation ANAKIM):

6. The reconquest of Burma will not be possible before the winter of 1943-44 at the earliest. It involves:

>(a) The recapture of Rangoon.
>
>(b) The capture of the Moulmein area with a view to blocking

U. S. SECRET
BRITISH MOST SECRET

        Japanese overland reinforcements from Thailand.
    (c) Concurrently with (a) and (b) above, pressure by British forces from Chindwin River bridgeheads, and if possible by Chinese forces from Yunnan, against Mandalay.
    (d) The defeat of the Japanese forces in Lower Burma, i.e., the Rangoon-Mandalay area.

Plans for this reconquest are known as Operation ANAKIM.

  7. The forces required for ANAKIM are approximately:

  (a) Naval   6-8 Escort Carriers
              40 Destroyers and escorts
              8 Submarines
              6 Fleet mine sweepers

in addition to such cover by heavy forces as is required by the situation at the time.

  (b) Army   8 Infantry Divisions
              1 Armored Division

  (c) Air   28 Bomber Squadrons
              17 Fighter Squadrons
              4 Coastal Squadrons

  (d) Assault Shipping and Landing Craft to lift (4 inf. bde. groups) (1 armored brigade) assault loaded.

The assault shipping and landing craft for these assaults amount to:

          9 L.S.I.(L)
         40 L.S.T.
          4 L.S.D. or L.S.G.
        100 L.C.A.
         40 L.C.P.
        120 L.C.M.
         16 L.C.S.

NOTE: (1) If L.C.T. can be made available the numbers of L.S.T. could be reduced in the proportion of one L.S.T. for every four L.C.T.

      (2) Landing craft additional to the above will probably be required for maintenance of forces ashore until it is possible to bring ports into use.

U. S. SECRET
BRITISH MOST SECRET

    (e) Shipping 60 MT ships
                   20 Personnel ships

POSSIBILITY OF CARRYING OUT "ANAKIM" IN WINTER OF 1943-44:

    Weather:

8. Operations cannot start before about November 1, 1943, and must be concluded by April 30, 1944, on account of the monsoon. To take Rangoon and Moulmein, clear the whole of Southern Burma up to Mandalay, and reopen the Burma Road from Mandalay to Lashio, it is estimated that the assault must take place at the latest in early December 1943.

To seize and consolidate the Rangoon-Moulmein area only, the initial assault might be postponed until the end of January 1944.

    Availability of British Forces:

9. (a) Naval

    The British might be able to find the capital ships and carriers required for this operation, provided no other amphibious operations were being carried out concurrently in the European or Mediterranean theaters.

    They would however require, under all circumstances, considerable help from American light naval forces.

    Subsequently, it will be necessary to keep open the sea communications to Rangoon.

(b) Army

    These will be available in India by October 1943--including the brigades required to be trained for the initial assaults.

(c) Air

    The air forces required could be made available in the Indian theater by November 1943.

(d) Assault Shipping and Landing Craft

    (1) If NO major amphibious operations are carried out elsewhere in 1943, the assault shipping and landing craft could be found by the British by October 1, 1943.

    (2) If Operation BRIMSTONE is carried out not later than the end of June 1943, and no other amphibious operation takes place, the assault shipping and landing craft could be found by the British by December 1, 1943, in Indian waters. This would permit of an assault on Rangoon about December 30, 1943.

U. S. SECRET
BRITISH MOST SECRET

    (3) If HUSKY is carried out after June 1943--or any other operation, such as the Dodecanese, in addition to BRIMSTONE--it will not be possible to provide the assault shipping and landing craft for ANAKIM from British sources until about February 1944.

    (4) If Operation ANAKIM is carried out with British assault shipping and landing craft at any time during the winter 1943-44, it would seriously curtail the British share of any cross-channel operations in the early spring of 1944.

(e) Shipping

The availability of shipping cannot be forecast now, but the U.S.A. will have to provide a part.

U. S. SECRET
BRITISH MOST SECRET
C.C.S. 155   January 18, 1943

COMBINED CHIEFS OF STAFF

CONDUCT OF THE WAR IN 1943

Note by the Secretaries

In accordance with the conclusions of the Combined Chiefs of Staff at their 60th meeting, a draft memorandum setting out the tentative agreements already reached has been prepared and is circulated herewith for consideration at the next meeting.

V. DYKES,
J. R. DEANE,
Combined Secretariat

ENCLOSURE

DRAFT MEMORANDUM

The Combined Chiefs of Staff have agreed to submit the following recommendations for the conduct of the war in 1943.

1. SECURITY:
   The defeat of the U-boat must remain a first charge on the resources of the United Nations.
2. OPERATIONS IN THE EUROPEAN THEATER:
   Operations in the European Theater will be conducted with the object of defeating Germany in 1943 with the maximum forces that can be brought to bear upon her by the United Nations.
3. The five main lines of offensive action will be:
   In the Mediterranean:
   (a) The occupation of Sicily with the object of:
      (1) Making the Mediterranean line of communications more secure.
      (2) Diverting German pressure from the Russian front.
      (3) Intensifying the pressure on Italy.
   (b) To create a situation in which Turkey can be enlisted as

U. S. SECRET
BRITISH MOST SECRET

an active ally.

In the U. K.:

(c) The heaviest possible bomber offensive against Germany.

(d) Such limited offensive operations as may be practicable with the forces available.

(e) The assembly of the strongest possible force (subject to (a) and (b) above and paragraph 5 below) to re-enter the continent as soon as German resistance is weakened to the required extent.

4. In order to insure that these operations and preparations are not prejudiced by the necessity to divert forces to retrieve an adverse situation elsewhere, adequate forces shall be allocated to the Pacific and Far Eastern Theaters.

5. OPERATIONS IN THE PACIFIC AND FAR EAST:

(a) Operations in these theaters shall continue with the forces allocated, with the object of maintaining pressure on Japan, retaining the initiative and attaining a position of readiness for the full scale offensive against Japan by the United Nations as soon as Germany is defeated.

(b) These operations must be kept within such limits as will not, in the opinion of the Combined Chiefs of Staff, prejudice the capacity of the United Nations to take advantage of any favorable opportunity that may present itself for the decisive defeat of Germany in 1943.

(c) Subject to the above reservation, plans and preparations shall be made for:

(1) The recapture of Burma (ANAKIM) beginning in 1943.

(2) Operations, after the capture of Rabaul, against the Marshalls and Carolines if time and resources allow without prejudice to ANAKIM.

6. ASSISTANCE TO RUSSIA:

The resistance of the Soviet forces must be sustained by the greatest volume of supplies that can be transported to Russia, without prohibitive cost in shipping.

U. S. SECRET
BRITISH MOST SECRET
C.C.S. 155/1   January 19, 1943

COMBINED CHIEFS OF STAFF

CONDUCT OF THE WAR IN 1943

Memorandum by the Combined Chiefs of Staff

The Combined Chiefs of Staff have agreed to submit the following recommendations for the conduct of the war in 1943.

1. SECURITY:

The defeat of the U-boat must remain a first charge on the resources of the United Nations.

2. ASSISTANCE TO RUSSIA:

The Soviet forces must be sustained by the greatest volume of supplies that can be transported to Russia without prohibitive cost in shipping.

3. OPERATIONS IN THE EUROPEAN THEATER:

Operations in the European Theater will be conducted with the object of defeating Germany in 1943 with the maximum forces that can be brought to bear upon her by the United Nations.

4. The main lines of offensive action will be:

In the Mediterranean:

(a) The occupation of Sicily with the object of:
   (1) Making the Mediterranean line of communications more secure.
   (2) Diverting German pressure from the Russian front.
   (3) Intensifying the pressure on Italy.
(b) To create a situation in which Turkey can be enlisted as an active ally.

In the U.K.:

(c) The heaviest possible bomber offensive against the German war effort.
(d) Such limited offensive operations as may be practicable with the amphibious forces available.
(e) The assembly of the strongest possible force (subject to (a) and (b) above and paragraph 6 below) in constant readiness to reenter the Continent as soon as German resistance is

U. S. SECRET

BRITISH MOST SECRET

        weakened to the required extent.

5. In order to insure that these operations and preparations are not prejudiced by the necessity to divert forces to retrieve an adverse situation elsewhere, adequate forces shall be allocated to the Pacific and Far Eastern Theaters.

6. OPERATIONS IN THE PACIFIC AND FAR EAST:

   (a) Operations in these theaters shall continue with the forces allocated, with the object of maintaining pressure on Japan, retaining the initiative and attaining a position of readiness for the full scale offensive against Japan by the United Nations as soon as Germany is defeated.

   (b) These operations must be kept within such limits as will not, in the opinion of the Combined Chiefs of Staff, jeopardize the capacity of the United Nations to take advantage of any favorable opportunity that may present itself for the decisive defeat of Germany in 1943.

   (c) Subject to the above reservation, plans and preparations shall be made for:

      (1) The recapture of Burma (ANAKIM) beginning in 1943.

      (2) Operations, after the capture of Rabaul, against the Marshalls and Carolines if time and resources allow without prejudice to ANAKIM.

U. S. SECRET
BRITISH MOST SECRET
C.C.S. 156   January 18, 1943

COMBINED CHIEFS OF STAFF

SUGGESTED PROCEDURE FOR DEALING WITH THE AGENDA OF THE CONFERENCE

Note by the Secretaries

The Combined Staffs, at an informal meeting on January 18, 1943, prepared the attached note suggesting the procedure to be followed for dealing with the major questions on the agreed Agenda of the Combined Chiefs of Staff (C.C.S. 140).

They suggest that it should be considered by the Combined Chiefs of Staff at their next meeting.

V. DYKES,
J. R. DEANE,
Combined Secretariat.

ENCLOSURE

1. The next stage of the discussions should be to examine each of the operations set out in the (C.C.S. 155) draft proposals for the conduct of the war in 1943, with a view to determining:
    (a) The resources of all kinds required for each.
    (b) How they are to be made available.
    (c) Target dates, where practicable.
2. U-BOAT WARFARE:
   The naval and air forces required to defeat the U-boat are already under examination by the Combined Staff Planners whose report should form the agenda for an early meeting.
3. MEDITERRANEAN:
    (a) Organization of Command, and establishment of spheres of responsibility in the Mediterranean.
    (b) HUSKY:
       (Reference: Paragraph 3 (a), C.C.S. 155)
       The resources required for HUSKY have been assessed by the

U. S. SECRET
BRITISH MOST SECRET

British Joint Planning Staff. A summary of this and of the outline plan will be circulated for discussion by the Combined Chiefs of Staff. Agreement should be reached as to the resources to be provided by U. S. and U. K. respectively and on the arrangements for planning and command.

(c) Air offensive from North Africa against Italy, Balkan objectives, and Axis shipping.

4. TURKEY:

(Reference: Paragraph 3 (b), C.C.S. 155)

A draft paper by the British Joint Planning Staff on Allied Plans relating to TURKEY which has not yet been considered by the British Chiefs of Staff will be circulated as a basis for discussion. British Chiefs of Staff to circulate a note on the Axis oil position for discussion in connection with this item.

5. THE BOMBER OFFENSIVE FROM THE UNITED KINGDOM:

(Reference: Paragraph 3 (c), C.C.S. 155)

British Chiefs of Staff to indicate the present and projected build-up of the R.A.F. Bomber Command and the British conception of the general plan for its employment in 1943. Agreement should be reached on the program for the build-up of U. S. Bomber forces in the United Kingdom and on the general lines of employment of Allied Bomber forces from the U. K. against Germany.

6. LIMITED OFFENSIVE OPERATIONS FROM THE U. K.:

(Reference: Paragraph 3 (d), C.C.S. 155)

British Chiefs of Staff to circulate a paper outlining their conception of the limited offensive operations possible in 1943 under the terms of C.C.S. 155 and the resources available.

7. BOLERO BUILD-UP:

(Reference: Paragraph 3 (e), C.C.S. 155)

British Chiefs of Staff to circulate a paper showing the forces which in their view could be made available for a return to the Continent in 1943 under the terms of C.C.S. 155. Agreement should be reached on the general concept of the circumstances which would make such an operation feasible.

8. ANAKIM.

(Reference: Paragraph 5 (c) (1), C.C.S. 155)

British Chiefs of Staff to circulate a paper giving the broad

U. S. SECRET
BRITISH MOST SECRET

concept for operation ANAKIM, with an indication of the forces considered necessary. Agreement should be reached as to the resources to be provided by U. S. and U. K. respectively.

9. OPERATIONS IN THE SOUTHWEST PACIFIC:

(Reference: Paragraph 5 (c) (2), C.C.S. 155)

U. S. Chiefs of Staff to circulate a paper giving the broad concept for operations in the Southwest Pacific with indications of the forces involved.

10. ASSISTANCE TO RUSSIA:

(Reference: Paragraph 6, C.C.S. 155)

Agreement should be reached on the probable effect of the operations agreed at the conference upon supplies to Russia in 1943.

11. The following items which appear in the agreed Agenda of the conference have not been dealt with above:

(a) *Strategic Responsibility and Command Set-up for Dakar-French West African Area* required to be settled as early as possible. Admiral King to be invited to make proposals.

(b) *Increased efficiency in the case of Shipping.*
Lord Leathers and General Somervell to be invited to discuss and make appropriate recommendations to the Combined Chiefs of Staff.

U. S. SECRET
BRITISH MOST SECRET
C.C.S. 157　　　　　　　　　　　　　　　　　　　　January 18, 1943

COMBINED CHIEFS OF STAFF

ALLIED PLANS RELATING TO TURKEY

Memorandum by British Joint Planning Staff

PART I

ENTRY OF TURKEY INTO THE WAR ON THE SIDE OF THE UNITED NATIONS

1. The following extract from C.C.S. 135/2 has been taken as the basis for our further examination of the problem of inducing Turkey to join the Allies and of using that country for the development of offensive operations against the Axis.

> "Our motives in inducing Turkey to join us in the war would be:
> (a) To use Turkey as a base for air attacks on important objectives, such as the Rumanian oilfields and Black Sea communications.
> (b) To close the Dardanelles to the Axis and open them to the United Nations.
> (c) To force an increased dispersal of German forces by using Turkey as a base for potential threats in the Balkans and South Russia.
> (d) To deny Turkish chrome to Germany."

INDUCEMENTS TO TURKEY:

2. The two main factors upon which Turkey's entry into the war depend are:
    (a) Her fear of Germany now;
    (b) Her fear of Russia after the war.

In order to make Turkey enter actively into the war at an early date, we must convince her that (a) is unfounded, and at the same time exploit her fear of (b)

FEAR OF GERMANY:

3. Turkey's anxieties under (a) will only be assuaged when she is satisfied either that the Allies have so stretched the Axis as to restrict the latter's ability to hurt her, or that material provision of

U. S. SECRET
BRITISH MOST SECRET

the Allies to defend her against Axis air or land attack is forthcoming in time. The former may result from a development of our existing strategy in the Mediterranean and from continued Russian successes. The latter is examined in Part II.

FEAR OF RUSSIA:

4. With regard to (b), Turkey must now appreciate that her hopes of a weak Russia are not likely to be realized. Consequently, her best chance of post-war security lies in obtaining for herself a place and support at the Peace Conference. She is particularly afraid that Russia may spread her influence through Rumania and Bulgaria and confront her with the fact of being the power in control at Turkey's western door into Europe as well as at her back door into Asia. She also fears that Russia, having secured complete control of the Black Sea, will demand unrestricted rights of passage through the Dardanelles. She would look to the Allies, and especially to the British Empire, to support her in resisting exaggerated Russian claims in regard to passage of the Straits.

5. Whether it would be wise for His Majesty's Government to oppose Russian desires regarding passage of the Straits seems a matter for urgent consideration, for if we thwarted Russia in that respect we should probably be confronted with a claim for rights of transit through Persia to a port on the Persian Gulf. This, from our point of view, would be most undesirable.

6. British and American diplomacy should be directed to exploit Turkish fears of Russia. It should be made clear that public opinion will have little sympathy, when peace comes, for a country which remained aloof when we needed her aid.

ECONOMIC AND TERRITORIAL INDUCEMENTS:

7. Guarantees of continued financial and economic assistance, of which details are given in Enclosure "A", might be a useful weapon, particularly in view of the deterioration of the Turkish position.

8. There are certain territorial adjustments by which Turkey sets store. Firstly, she is determined to have complete control of the railway which at present runs out in Syrian territory at Aleppo. Secondly, she requires some material facilities in, and some guarantees for, the Turkish population of the Dodecanese Islands. Thirdly, she desires a rectification of her frontier with Bulgaria. We can see no strategical objection to their realization after the war provided we can retain

U. S. SECRET
BRITISH MOST SECRET

certain rights to use the Aleppo-Mosul railway, but we must not lose sight of the fact that there is a strong French interest in this railway. We have also guaranteed the future integrity and independence of Syrian territory.

Greek interest would be directly affected by the realization of the second aim and it would be difficult for the Allies to encourage the appetite of an allied but still neutral country at the expense of a fighting ally.

We doubt whether these three sops would materially affect Turkey's decision on the main issue.

SUMMARY OF DIPLOMATIC POLICY:

9. We should exploit Turkish fears that she stands to lose if she remains out until the eleventh hour, making it clear through diplomatic channels that the extent of Allied support for Turkey at the Peace Conference will be conditioned by her entry into the war without delay.

PART II

INITIAL MILITARY ASSISTANCE TO TURKEY

10. An undertaking to assist Turkey against Axis aggression has already been given. This includes a plan for establishing certain forces in Turkey (Sprawl Plan) and the provision of equipment and supplies to augment Turkish resources. A summary of these measures is given as Enclosures "B", "C" and "D", from which it will be seen that a substantial quantity of material together with some aircraft have already reached Turkey.

11. The roles of the force earmarked under the Sprawl Plan were:
    (a) To gain and maintain air superiority.
    (b) Assist Turkish land and air forces in the defense of Thrace and Western Anatolia.
    (c) Provide support for Turkish forces against seaborne attack in the Izmir area.
    (d) Assist in the defense of Ankara.
    (e) Attack strategic objectives in Southeast Europe.
    (f) Protect base ports.

U. S. SECRET
BRITISH MOST SECRET

CHANGED CONDITIONS:

12. Existing plans assume that Turkey had already been attacked. The conditions under review are somewhat different. In the first place the threat we are now considering is potential rather than actual, although there is still a possibility that if the Germans believed that Turkey was about to enter the war they would try to overrun Thrace and at the same time bomb vital areas. In the second place Turkey is not compelled to fight but must be induced to come in of her own free will. As already stated, this she is unlikely to do unless she is satisfied that the general situation severely restricts German offensive potentialities in the Balkans.

THE AIR THREAT:

13. The ability of the Axis to deliver a heavy air offensive against Turkish vital areas cannot be forecast. It is certain, however, that Turkey will require the provision of air and ground defenses. The extent to which she will regard these as an inducement to fight will depend upon the rapidity with which they can be rendered effective. Should Turkey be prepared to take the plunge it would be to her advantage to augment her defenses with Allied help before she actually declares war. We can, however, undertake--provided ground equipment is installed and preparations made in Turkey beforehand--to have operational about 6 Fighter squadrons with limited antiaircraft defenses within three days of the Turkish invitation. To achieve this, approximately 100 transport aircraft would have to be made available.

THE THREAT THROUGH THRACE:

14. The Turks at present intend, if attacked in Thrace, to hold a forward line near the frontier until a "scorched earth" policy has been effected, and then to withdraw to the Catalja and Bulair lines. These are sound defensive positions, and we see no object in persuading the Turks to establish a main position forward, as this would be weak in defense. If, on the other hand, the attack does not develop, the forward area will remain available for the subsequent concentration of our offensive forces. The Turks will have, in any case, to rely initially on their own resources, since communications prevent any substantial Allied military assistance reaching Thrace quickly.

ALLIED MILITARY POLICY:

15. The force which we should establish in Turkey, in the first

U. S. SECRET
BRITISH MOST SECRET

place, should comprise the minimum defensive element to satisfy the Turks, and the maximum offensive element, within the limits of communications, to meet our own future requirements.

16. We consider that the following constitute a suitable defensive offer to the Turks:

AIR:

26 squadrons. Of this force, 6 Fighter squadrons would constitute the immediate air defense contingent referred to in paragraph 13 above. The types of the remaining squadrons proposed in the Sprawl plan may require adjustment in the light of changed conditions, but since a total of 26 squadrons has been offered to Turkey and the arrangements for the installation of this force are in hand, we consider that the total figure of 26 squadrons should stand. Additional aircraft for use by the Turks can be supplied from resources in the Middle East if priority over other commitments is considered to justify such a course.

LAND:

72 H.A.A. guns for defense of Istanbul, etc.

96 H.A.A. guns) for airfield defense.
215 Lt. A.A. guns)

4 Battalions for defense of the L. of C.

It is possible that the Turks will regard the provision of armored fighting vehicles as an added inducement. In view of the Turks' inability to use or maintain armored fighting vehicles we should prefer to supply complete armored formations with our own personnel, and this we should be prepared to do.

NAVAL:

A striking force of submarines, M.T.B.'s and possibly destroyers.

17. The next step is to build up forces to undertake offensive operations and to secure air bases in Turkey. This is considered in Part III.

PART III

DEVELOPMENT OF THE OFFENSIVE

18. Turkey will be of value to the Allies as an offensive base for air rather than land operations. Owing to the initial defensive needs of

U. S. SECRET
BRITISH MOST SECRET

the Turks it will be impossible to include in the first air contingent a striking force adequate for a widespread heavy and sustained offensive. Since, however, trans-Anatolian communications will be stretched to the limit of their capacity, the first step must be to open up the Aegean sufficiently to make use of Turkish ports. For our use Smyrna is of primary importance.

19. Any land offensive we may wish to mount from Turkey must be based on Thrace, but the Turks themselves will be making great demands on the limited Thracian ports and communications for their own maintenance.

PHASE I - OPENING THE AEGEAN

20. It is considered that the opening of the Aegean could be achieved by the capture of the Dodecanese. With air protection based on Turkey and the Dodecanese it should then be possible to pass sufficient shipping through to make full use of Turkish port capacities in spite of the Axis threat from Crete and Greece.

21. The capture of the Dodecanese is at present being studied by the Middle East.* We estimate that a force of some three divisions will be required, supported by 12 squadrons of aircraft operating from Southwest Anatolia. These squadrons will have to be included in the initial force sent to Turkey. Airfields in the coastal area opposite Rhodes will have to be constructed in advance and stocked with supplies so that operations can begin as early as possible. The subsequent garrisons might be found by our Balkan allies.

PROTECTION OF SHIPPING:

22. As soon as the Dodecanese have been captured it will be necessary to provide for the protection of our shipping through the Aegean. The estimated forces required for this purpose are given below.

NAVAL:

23. With Crete still in enemy hands, shipping must be routed as far east of that island as possible. It is not likely that the threat in the Aegean will exceed that of submarines, E-boats and aircraft. It is estimated that 8-knot convoys of 20 ships running every 14 days between Alexandria and Istanbul will meet requirements and would need an escort

---
* Mideast telegram CC/166 dated 29/12/42

U. S. SECRET
BRITISH MOST SECRET

group of about 8 ships.
AIR:
    24. A regrouping of the squadrons already in Turkey should suffice both for protection of shipping and general defensive requirements. The necessary airfields exist but must be developed and supplied in advance.
LAND:
    25. No additional land forces will be required other than a few L. of C. battalions and antiaircraft protection for the new ports and airfields brought into use, for which about 48 Heavy and 84 Light A.A. guns will be needed.

PHASE II SUBSEQUENT OPERATIONS

THE TASK OF OFFENSIVE FORCES
AIR:
    26. Air forces operating from Turkey will be required for:
        (a) Attacks on Rumanian oil refineries and their communications. This is the primary task.
        (b) Attacks on Balkan chrome mines and communications generally, both of which are difficult targets.
        (c) Attacks against Axis shipping in the Black Sea and the Aegean.
        (d) Support of any Allied land operations.
        (e) Assistance to the Russians in the Ukraine.
    For these purposes a force of 15-20 Heavy Bomber squadrons will be required and could be maintained through Smyrna. Existing airfields in Northwest Turkey will require development.
NAVAL:
    27. While the Black Sea should become a Russo-Turkish sphere of responsibility, British light naval forces will be required for the attack, in conjunction with the Turks, on Axis communications in the Aegean.
LAND:
    28. The object of a land offensive from Thrace would be to stretch Axis forces and to support Balkan patriots. The mounting of any offensive is dependent on the Turks holding an adequate bridgehead in Europe.
    29. There are two alternative lines of advance from Thrace into the Balkans: North into Bulgaria; or West into Macedonia.

U. S. SECRET
BRITISH MOST SECRET

NORTH INTO BULGARIA:

30. The objectives for a northward drive would be Axis communications in the Danube Basin and the oilfields of Ploesti, which are so vital to Germany that she would defend them if necessary at the expense of other areas. The line of advance would be through a hostile country, where communications, which always strongly favor the enemy, are initially so bad as probably to prevent much progress being made. This course might contain some Axis forces, but would have little effect on the Balkans generally.

WEST INTO MACEDONIA:

31. The objective for a westward drive would be Salonika. Once established there, further forces could be landed and arms for patriot forces of Greece, Albania, and Southern Yugoslavia imported. It should then be possible, in conjunction with the patriots, to sever Axis communications with Southern Greece and to gain control of the whole area.

32. This should result in the abandonment of Crete by the Axis. Alternatively, it might be desirable to capture Crete at an earlier stage to assist in operations on the Greek mainland. Such an operation would be best mounted in Africa, though some air support could be given from the Dodecanese and Southwest Anatolia.

33. The capture of Salonika from Thrace will, however, be a formidable and lengthy operation if the enemy puts up much resistance. Communications are bad, but not so greatly in the German's favor as those into Bulgaria. By supplementing road communications with coastwise shipping it should be possible to maintain 2-1/2 divisions, but in winter conditions this would be very difficult. A further 2-1/2 divisions could be maintained by rail as far forward as railhead, but the line is an easy one for the enemy to disrupt and repairs might take a very long time.

34. A further adverse factor is that while the line of advance itself is badly served with airfields, it is flanked by a limited number of indifferent airfields in enemy hands within S. E. fighter range. Therefore, airfields will have to be provided in Turkish Thrace before operations can start, and others constructed as the advance progresses. This will take time.

35. It is impossible to assess the chances of success of land operations through Macedonia without making a detailed study, and without a

U. S. SECRET
BRITISH MOST SECRET

firmer forecast than is now possible of the Axis military position as it will then be. The prize is great but the prospects are poor.

SUMMARY

COURSE OF OPERATIONS:

36. Offensive operations might take the following course:
    (a) The capture of the Dodecanese and the establishment of naval and air forces for the protection of shipping to Istanbul, in order to open the Eastern Aegean.
    (b) The assembly of air forces in Anatolia for offensive operations against the Balkans and sea communications.
    (c) A possible land offensive from Thrace directed against Salonika.
    (d) After reinforcement through Salonika, the severance of Axis communications with Southern Greece and assistance to guerrilla forces in Greece, Albania, and Southern Yugoslavia.
    (e) The elimination of the Axis from Greece and Crete.

PART IV

SUMMARY OF FORCES REQUIRED

AIR:

37. Immediate Air Defense
    6 Squadrons
    Balance of Defensive Requirements
    20 Squadrons
    Opening of the Aegean and Support of Land Offensive
    12 Squadrons (additional to those above)
    Bomber Offensive
    15-20 Heavy Bomber Squadrons

LAND:

38. Defensive Requirements
    4 battalions for local defense
    168 Heavy A.A. guns) For ports, airfields and
    215 Light A.A. guns) vital areas.

U. S. SECRET
BRITISH MOST SECRET

    Opening the Aegean
        3 divisions
        3 battalions for local defense
        48 Heavy A.A. guns) For ports and airfields.
        84 Light A.A. guns)
    Operations in Greece
        2-1/2 to 5 divisions, including) With possible subsequent
        at least 1 Armored division   ) reinforcement of up to 4
                                                          divisions (to include
                                                               Crete)

NAVAL:

39. Forces as necessary to assist in the capture of the Dodecanese. A striking force of destroyers, submarines, M.T.B.'s and M.G.B.'s. A commitment of about 8 escort vessels for shipping in the Aegean.

PART V

CONCLUSIONS

40. (a) We do not consider that Turkey will enter the war unless the general situation is such that she is satisfied that she can initially hold Thrace without Allied assistance and that immediate air defense is forthcoming.

    (b) Turkey will be of value to the Allies as an offensive base for air rather than land operations.

POLICY TO HASTEN TURKEY'S ENTRY INTO THE WAR:

41. (a) Political:
       We should make clear to Turkey that our good offices at the Peace Conference will depend upon her entry into the war without delay.

    (b) Financial and Economic:
       Turkey should be assured of the continuance of our present economic and financial assistance. This might be extended to the provisions of wheat and sugar in the near future, but our commitments elsewhere in the Middle East may prevent this.

U. S. SECRET
BRITISH MOST SECRET

    (c) Military:

    We should offer:

      (1) An "immediate air defense" contingent for the protection of vital centers in Western Turkey (paragraph 16).

      (2) The balance of forces up to the limit of trans-Anatolian communications (paragraph 16).

      (3) Military equipment to bring all Turkish infantry formations in Thrace up to a satisfactory scale of weapons.

      (4) Armored fighting vehicles only if these are considered necessary from the psychological point of view. We should prefer to send armored formations since the Turks cannot be relied upon to operate or maintain armored fighting vehicles efficiently.

ALLIED MILITARY POLICY:

42. (a) The provision of assistance to Turkey as in paragraph 41 (c) above.

    (b) Opening of the Aegean by the capture of the Dodecanese.

    (c) Development of the air offensive from Turkey.

    (d) If practicable, to open up and rearm the Balkans by an advance westwards from Thrace with limited forces directed on Salonika.

PREPARATORY MEASURES IN TURKEY:

43. (a) Airfield Development.

    Certain airfield developments are already included in the Sprawl Plan. We should press for further development of air fields and supplies in the following areas:

      (1) In the Istanbul and Ankara areas to operate fighters for the defense of those sites.

      (2) In the Southwest of Turkey to assist our capture of the Dodecanese.

      (3) In Anatolia and Armenia to operate bombers against Rumanian oil, Balkan communications, and in support of the Russian southern front.

    We must insure that the air defense equipment, including A.A. guns, ammunition and R.D.F., necessary for the defense of at least those airfields which will be used by our initial air contingent, is ready in Turkey for immediate operation.

U. S. SECRET
BRITISH MOST SECRET

    (b) Personnel:

    We should send in to Turkey under cover the following personnel:

        (1) Such specialists as are acceptable by the Turks to insure proper instruction in the maintenance and use of the Allied military equipment.

        (2) Reconnaissance parties for preparing the layout of airfield defenses and for studying the administrative and transportation problems.

    A number of Turkish-speaking liaison officers should be collected in the Middle East.

    (c) Communications:

    We should continue and, where necessary, augment supplies of locomotives, rolling stock and port facilities. The provision of coal dumps at strategic centers is important for the operation of communications.

RECOMMENDATIONS

44. We recommend that:

    (a) The Foreign Office be invited to examine the possibilities of diplomatic action in the light of the suggestions contained in this paper. We particularly urge that a firm policy should be decided with regard to our post-war attitude on the Dardanelles question and other matters of a primary interest to the Turks.

    (b) A copy of this paper should be sent to the Commanders-in-Chief, Middle East, in reply to their telegram (C.C./166 dated December 29, 1942) and that they should be invited to comment on the proposals contained herein.

ENCLOSURE "A"

FINANCIAL AND ECONOMIC ASSISTANCE FOR TURKEY

FINANCIAL:

1. Under the Agreements made after the collapse of France in 1940

U. S. SECRET
BRITISH MOST SECRET

the United Kingdom assumed liability for the unutilized French share of the 25 million Pound credit for the purchase of war material, which was agreed under the Special Agreement of 1939. Under this credit we are now supplying Turkey with all the arms, etc., which are available.

2. As regards non-military supplies, we have offered to lend Turkey sterling to enable her to pay for her essential needs from the sterling area. She is at present availing herself of these facilities to the extent of approximately 2 million Pounds.

3. Turkey's existing financial difficulties are those of internal finance. In regard to this we can give no real help.

ECONOMIC:

4. Our economic assistance is as great as our shipping resources and the limitations of available points of entry into Turkey will permit. There is, however, one form of assistance which is now under active consideration, namely, the supply of wheat, of which Turkey is in urgent need to the extent of 150,000-200,000 tons for 1943. Sugar is also a vital necessity and she has asked for about 20,000 tons. Success in providing these two essentials would do much to bind Turkey to us.

5. A form of assistance which would prove of great value in the future would be the supply of locomotives and rolling stock, of which the Turks are in great need. We are doing the best we can to supply Turkey's needs, but our own demands for military purposes are naturally making this difficult. (See Enclosure "D", paragraphs 3 and 4.)

ENCLOSURE "B"

OUR MILITARY COMMITMENTS TO TURKEY

1. As a result of the staff conversations in Ankara in October, 1941, we have promised to assist the Turks with the following force should Turkey be attacked:

      2 Armored Divisions
      2 Army Tank Brigades
      4 Infantry Divisions
      26 Squadrons R.A.F.

With the exception of four squadrons R.A.F., which are to be dispatched to Western Turkey immediately the Turkish frontier is crossed,

U. S. SECRET
BRITISH MOST SECRET

this offer was made subject to our operational requirements elsewhere and the provision of adequate maintenance facilities.

2. A plan (Sprawl Plan) has already been worked out for the move of this air contingent of 26 squadrons to airfields in Turkey south of a line Sea of Marmara-Alexandretta (See Map "C"), accompanied by an Army component of four brigade groups for the protection of airfields. The maintenance of this force is equivalent to that of 2-1/2 divisions. The air force consists of:

  12 Short-range Fighter Squadrons
  1 Long-range Fighter Squadron
  6 Light Bomber Squadrons
  2 Medium Bomber Squadrons
  3 Army Cooperation Squadrons
  1 General Reconnaissance Squadron
  1 Torpedo Bomber Squadron

3. It is estimated that moving by road and rail in summer the whole Sprawl force could be established in about 45 days, while the first group of 6 fighter squadrons with accompanying units would be in position at Bandirma and Balekesir in about twelve days.

4. This plan was designed to assist in the Turkish defense of Thrace and Western Anatolia. It was not intended to be a prelude for offensive operations which we ourselves might wish to undertake in the Balkans.

U. S. SECRET
BRITISH MOST SECRET

ENCLOSURE "C"

R.A.F. AND ARMY STORES ALREADY DUMPED INTO TURKEY

	R.A.F. (in tons)				Army (in tons)			
	P.O.L.	Bombs	Amn.	Sups.	P.O.L.	Amn.	R.E. Stores	Sups.
Balikesir Area	483	...	18.2	455	322	326	...	112
Kutahya Area	1,785.1	181	24.9	...	1,288	1,047	...	658
Afyon Area	5,466.7	773.2	83	3,367.3	728	457	...	224
Adana Area	357	...	...	...	1,022	366	...	392
Ulukisla Area	231	...	9	639.9	735	284	5,000	280
	8,322.8	954.2	135.1	4,462.2	4,095	2,480	5,000	1,666

Total R.A.F. -- 13,874.3 tons
Total Army -- 13,241   tons
              27,115.3 tons

U. S. SECRET
BRITISH MOST SECRET

ENCLOSURE "D"

SUPPLY OF EQUIPMENT

1. The following table shows the number of certain main items of equipment which had been shipped to Turkey up to November 20, 1942 (column (b)), and the number allocated or ordered to be sent to Turkey up to date (column (c)). Column (d) gives an indication of the quantities which might be allocated to Turkey if her priority vis-a-vis other theaters remains unchanged.

2.

Item (a)	Shipped (b)	Allocated up to end of 1942 but not yet shipped (c)	Possible future allocation (d)
Stuart light tanks	40	121	
Valentines		200	
37-mm. A/Tk. guns	416	292	50 per month
3.7-in. A.A. guns	208	12	3 per month
40-mm A.A. guns	...	169	48 per month
Searchlights	111	...	
Field guns	104	28	
Medium hows.	60	...	
Medium machine guns	1,075	205	50 per month
Light machine guns	5,450	...	Middle East told to supply 150 per month
Sub-machine guns	6,500	2,500	
Anti-tank rifles	653	225	50 per month
81-mm mortars	300	...	Order completed
R.D.F. light warning sets	...	25	

This additional allocation (in column (c) above) includes the following special offer made by the Prime Minister in September:

Stuart light tanks	40
Infantry tanks	200
37-mm. anti-tank guns	136
40-mm. Bofors	25

38

U. S. SECRET
BRITISH MOST SECRET

3. The following items have been promised to Turkey by the United Kingdom:

(a) Aircraft

	Promises	Fulfilled
Tomahawks	36 + Wastage	42
Blenheim IV's	4	4
Dominie	4 by end of March 1943	..
Hurricanes IIB or IIC	10 November 10 December	..

(b) P.D.F. Sets

Twelve mobile sets are now being packed in United Kingdom for dispatch to Turkey by sea via Middle East, and a further thirteen have been promised.

(c) Petrol

Middle East have undertaken to maintain six months' supply for the Turkish Air Force. To implement this about 3,000 tons are sent each quarter.

4. The following locomotives and rolling stock have been ordered and shipped, as shown, for Turkey:

(a) Locomotives

Shipped 25

(b) Wagons

Ordered 1,318 of which

723 have been shipped

5. If full benefit is to be gained by the entry of Turkey into the war, the supply of locomotives and rolling stock must keep pace with the development of railways. The commitment would be considerable and might have to be at the expense of other theaters.

U. S. SECRET
BRITISH MOST SECRET
C.C.S. 158   January 19, 1943

COMBINED CHIEFS OF STAFF

AXIS OIL POSITION

Note by Assistant Chief of the British Air Staff (Intelligence)

1. Reproduced below are statements from:
   (a) "The Axis Oil Position in Europe, November 1942," by the Hartley Committee.
   (b) "German Strategy in 1943," by the Joint Intelligence Sub-committee in London, December 3rd, 1942.
2. Extracts from the Hartley Committee's Report:

Statistical Review of the Position from May 1st to October 1st, 1942.

	Tons
Production during period:	7,895,000
Consumption by Armed Forces:	4,540,000
Balance available for civilian consumption:	3,355,000

According to previous estimates, the non-military requirements for the period should have amounted to 4,334,000 tons, if industrial efficiency was to be maintained. To this should be added, say, 150,000 for Occupied Russia making an apparent total deficiency of about 1,150,000 tons.

This deficiency might have been met by:

	Tons
Reduction of consumption in Germany and Occupied Territories	650,000
Withdrawal from stocks	500,000
TOTAL	1,150,000

Evidence confirms that stocks have already been so reduced that distribution is becoming difficult and that the danger level has been reached. A reduction by 500,000 below this level would impose a great strain on the distribution system which consequently is likely to be exceptionally sensitive to dislocation.

Future Trend of Oil Position:

During the six months November 1942 to May 1943 the situation

U. S. SECRET
BRITISH MOST SECRET

may improve by:

    (a) Increased production: Tons

	Tons
Increase from Synthetic Plants	100,000
Exploitation of Maikop oil field	100,000
(b) Reduced consumption:	
Military - by reduced activity in Russia	500,000
Civil - by use of producer gas	180,000
TOTAL	880,000

Balance Sheet November 1942 - May 1943

The approximate balance sheet for the next six months on the basis of the above figures would therefore be:

	Tons
Production	8,100,000
Less Service consumption	4,040,000
Leaving balance for civilian consumption	4,060,000
Estimated minimum civilian requirements (assuming restrictions continued and producer gas further exploited)	3,654,000
SURPLUS:	406,000

Assuming, therefore, reduced activity on the Eastern Front, exploitation of Maikop, continuance of present restrictions and increased use of producer gas, Germany might be able to replenish her stocks by some 400,000 tons during the next six months. She would be unlikely, however, to be in a position to restore the cuts in civilian consumption or to undertake the mechanized exploitation of Russia for the 1943 harvest. In the meantime, the Rumanian oil fields, which contribute 33 per cent of total Axis supplies, would remain of vital importance to her.

    The production trend is increasing. By the middle of 1943, additional production at the rate of one million tons per year may be expected from synthetic oil plants now in course of erection. This will possibly be increased by a further 500,000 tons annual capacity by the end of 1943.

3.   Extracts from Joint Intelligence Subcommittee's Report:

    Germany's oil situation is critical. She cannot hope to obtain any substantial additional supplies from her present resources before the middle of 1943, even if she retains Maikop. Despite ruthless economies in service and civilian use, there are already distributional

U. S. SECRET
BRITISH MOST SECRET

breakdowns which are beginning to affect military operations. During the next six months at least her oil situation will continue to embarrass her operations and restrict her plans. It will prevent her from providing the oil necessary for the 1943 Ukrainian harvest, without which her food position will remain precarious, and will continue to depress her industrial capacity. If, in these circumstances, she is forced this winter to consume oil for military purposes at the same rate as in the winter of 1941-42, she will be increasingly handicapped in holding her present position and will be unable to undertake an offensive against South or even North Caucasia in the summer of 1943. In these circumstances she may be forced or may decide to shorten her line. On the other hand, if she is allowed to remain inactive during the winter, the resultant saving in oil, plus the new source of domestic supply that will become available to her in the middle of 1943, should enable her to undertake the military effort necessary at least to complete the occupation of North Caucasia.

If Germany is given the opportunity to complete next year the occupation of North Caucasia and secures the sea passage across the Black Sea, she should command enough oil (including increased domestic supplies, which are expected in mid-1943) to meet her future military commitments, to insure a substantial grain surplus from the Ukraine in the 1944 harvest and to provide her industry with the minimum requirements for her war effort. If, on the other hand, she has shortened her line and abandoned hope of Caucasian oil and is heavily engaged by the Allies, her supplies will be so limited as to deprive her of all power of undertaking major offensive operations.

4. Since the two above papers were written, there have been the following developments:

The Russian counteroffensive is forcing the Germans to retreat on almost every section of the Eastern Front, including the Caucasus. Not only, therefore, are the chances of Germany obtaining oil from Maikop during 1943 remote, but it now appears unlikely that any respite will be given to the Germans this winter to remain inactive in order to conserve their oil supplies for a new offensive in the North Caucasus during the summer of the year. Even a withdrawal to a shorter line will result in a heavy expenditure of oil resources.

Germany in her campaigns in 1943 will, therefore, have to rely

U. S. SECRET
BRITISH MOST SECRET

on:
      (a) The Rumanian Oil Fields
      (b) Synthetic Production
      (c) Producer Gas

She will be unable up to May 1943 to make the saving of 500,000 tons by a reduced activity on the Russian Front, nor will she have available the 100,000 tons from the Caucasus. Her assets during this period will, therefore, be 600,000 tons less than those estimated in the Hartley report.

5.   It is of interest that instances have already occurred of flying training being disorganized and curtailed by shortage of fuel.

U. S. SECRET
BRITISH MOST SECRET
C.C.S. 159/1   January 20, 1943

COMBINED CHIEFS OF STAFF

THE BOMBER OFFENSIVE FROM NORTH AFRICA

Memorandum by the Combined Chiefs of Staff

1. The objects of the bomber offensive from North Africa will be, in order to time:
    (a) The furtherance of operations for the eviction of all Axis forces from Africa.
    (b) When (a) has been achieved, infliction of the heaviest possible losses on the Axis Air and Naval forces in preparation for "HUSKY", including bombing required by cover plans.
    (c) The direct furtherance of operation "HUSKY".
    (d) The destruction of the oil refineries at Ploesti.

2. So far as is possible without prejudice to the achievement of objects (a), (b) and (c) above, bombing objectives will be chosen with a view to weakening the Italian will to continue the war.

NOTE: This paper is identical to C.C.S. 159 except for deletion of "The proposals of the British Chiefs of Staff are as follows," at heading of paper; and addition of "including bombing required by cover plans," following "HUSKY" at close of paragraph 1(b).

U. S. SECRET
BRITISH MOST SECRET

C.C.S. 160

January 19, 1943

COMBINED CHIEFS OF STAFF

MINIMUM ESCORT REQUIREMENTS TO MAINTAIN THE SEA COMMUNICATIONS OF THE UNITED NATIONS

Report by the Combined Staff Planners

PART I - ATLANTIC

U. K. DRY CARGO IMPORT SITUATION:

1. The minimum import requirements for the United Kingdom during 1943 are 27 million tons. It is estimated that with U. S. assistance on the scale envisaged it should be possible to import 12 million tons during the first six months leaving a balance of 15 million tons to be imported in the second half of the year.

2. It is of primary importance that U. K. imports in the first half of the year should not fall short of the target figure of 12 million tons, since any deficit will be carried into the second half of the year, and will thus impose an even more severe strain on United Nations resources, which will be severely taxed in order to achieve the balance of 15 million tons. An additional reason for maintaining the rate of imports is that a decision to remount BOLERO would involve the movement of an additional 100-200 ships a month in the latter half of the year, which will still further increase our escort requirements

3. If, by the provision of improved protection, the average rate of loss in the North Atlantic were reduced by 25 percent, from February it is estimated that by the end of June the gain in U. K. imports would be 450,000 tons. A further gain could be obtained by closing the trans-Atlantic convoy cycle in February from 10 to 8 days. This would amount to 150,000 tons, making a total of 600,000 tons. Further, the 25 percent reduction referred to above would preserve 3/4 million d.w.t. of shipping in the whole North Atlantic which will otherwise be lost.

U. K. AND NORTH AFRICAN OIL IMPORT SITUATION:

4. The measures recently agreed to remedy the serious oil position in the U. K. include the running of (a) a direct tanker convoy from the Dutch West Indies to U. K. on a 20 day cycle; (b) a direct fast tanker

U. S. SECRET
BRITISH MOST SECRET

convoy from the Dutch West Indies to the TORCH area. These commitments will continue throughout the year since they do not suffice to build up stocks but merely to meet consumption.

CONVOYS TO NORTH RUSSIA:

5. With the increasing hours of daylight and the more southerly limit reached by the ice in the spring, it is essential to increase the scale of escort to convoys to North Russia, in order to deal with the threat of attack from German surface and air forces. It is considered that in the circumstances prevailing, a minimum striking force of 15 Fleet destroyers is required in addition to the convoy escort.

U. S. EAST COAST:

6. Although U-boat activity on the east coast of the United States and Canada has recently been much reduced, the volume of shipping in this area presents such a vulnerable target that it is essential to provide for its protection against a renewal of heavy attack.

CARIBBEAN AREA AND GULF OF MEXICO:

7. The protection of shipping employed in the transport of vital oil supplies from the oil ports to the eastern seaboard is one for which adequate provisions must be made.

TRINIDAD SOUTH ATLANTIC SHIPPING:

8. We have suffered heavy loss in this area through which a large volume of shipping to and from the United States, South America and South Africa must pass. Adequate provision must be made to safeguard this vital route, which carries among others the important bauxite supplies.

UNITED KINGDOM-WEST AFRICAN CONVOYS:

9. These convoys were temporarily suspended in order to provide escorts for TORCH. It was not, however, practicable to suspend the flow of shipping to and from West and South Africa and South America since this shipping carries military supplies to the Middle East and brings back about one-third of the United Kingdom imports. The experiment of sailing such outward bound shipping in southerly routed trans-Atlantic convoys and breaking it off in mid-Atlantic has proved too costly and has been discontinued. Similarly the necessity for homeward bound shipping to return via the east coast of the United States, has resulted in a most uneconomical use of tonnage and heavy losses in the Cape San Roque area. It is therefore necessary to reconstitute these convoys on a

U.S. SECRET
BRITISH MOST SECRET

minimum cycle of 20 days.

REOPENING THE MEDITERRANEAN:

10. The shipping running to the Middle East has already been reduced considerably.

It is proposed, when the Mediterranean route is reopened, to run a convoy of thirty cargo ships every ten days to supply and replenish the Middle East and India. The escort commitments involved can be met by the forces available locally supplemented by small savings which will be available from the reduced scale of escort required on the Freetown route when the Mediterranean is opened to cargo ships.

PART II - THE PACIFIC

11. Although the protection of shipping in the Pacific has not yet become a problem of great magnitude, it may be expected to develop. The expanding campaign will require increased shipping to sustain it. The submarine and air threat against this increased shipping will grow in intensity in proportion to the progress of the campaign. Escort requirements for protection will increase correspondingly.

PART III - THE U-BOAT THREAT

12. The scale of U-boat threat against which North Atlantic convoys require to be protected is steadily increasing. U-boats are now operating in groups of 12-18; hence the scale of attack against any convoy may be taken as about 15 U-boats.

13. The scale of surface escort required to secure convoys against attack of this intensity is greater than we can hope to meet by the provision of surface escorts alone. Further, it has been proved that a combination of air and surface escort is more economical and efficient than surface escort alone. It is, therefore, necessary to make provision for air cover to all ocean convoys. Since neither shore base nor carrier borne aircraft can be relied upon to be always operable, both forms of air cover are required.

A program of construction of escort carriers to meet our needs is already in hand and cannot be greatly accelerated. For the immediate future, therefore, air escort can only be insured by the provision of

U. S. SECRET
BRITISH MOST SECRET

shore based aircraft.

14. In assessing the scale of escort required for the various convoys account must be taken of:
- (a) The distance of the convoy route from the U-boat bases.
- (b) The availability of shore based air cover.
- (c) The availability of escort carriers.

The following scales of ocean-going escort vessels (over 200 feet in length) are considered to be the minimum acceptable:

    (1) For convoys operating in areas where packs of U-boats are likely to be encountered and assuming adequate air cover the minimum escort is assessed as 3 plus 1 for every 10 ships in the convoy.

    (2) For convoys operating in areas where pack tactics are unlikely and assuming adequate air escort is available minimum escort 1 plus 1 for every 10 ships in the convoy.

    (3) For convoys operating in areas where pack tactics are unlikely, strong air support is normally available and escorts can be strengthened by vessels under 200 feet in length. Minimum escort 1 plus 1 for every 20 ships in convoy.

    (4) The tables have been prepared on the basis that adequate air cover is available. The minimum escort given above should be doubled if adequate air cover is not available. In other words, escort strength (with particular regard to (1)) is dependent upon visibility and weather conditions in which air coverage can be considered effective. During the winter months in North Atlantic, with long nights and unfavorable weather conditions, it is to be anticipated that the effective use of escort carriers will be very much restricted, and that shore based Air will not fully provide for air escort in the Middle Atlantic. Under such conditions escort strength as calculated under (1) must be increased.

15. The above assumptions in regard to escort strength contemplate, as stated, the minimum acceptable. Operating with this minimum it is not felt that measures can be taken to accomplish destruction of submarines at the desired rate (i.e., in excess of the production rate).

U. S. SECRET
BRITISH MOST SECRET

16. If convoys are operated with escorts in strengths less than that given in paragraph 14, increased losses are to be expected. The acceptance of increased losses must be balanced against the importance of other activities that necessitate the interference.

17. Taking into account all the points discussed, the scale of escorts required for the major convoys has been calculated in Enclosure "A".

In Enclosure "B" we have presented these same assessments as part of a world-wide estimate of the Fleet Destroyers and ocean-going escort vessels required to operate with the major naval forces, secure important focal points outside the general convoy system and conduct coastal traffic.

In Enclosure "C" the forces available are compared with the requirements calculated from Enclosure "B".

In Enclosure "D" the requirements and availability of escort carriers is considered.

In Enclosure "E" consideration is given to the world-wide requirements of shore based aircraft for the protection of trade communications.

18. CONCLUSION:

On the basis of the tables included in the enclosures it will be seen that minimum acceptable requirements as to escort craft will be met approximately in August and September. We will not be in a position, however, to give fully adequate protection to ocean-going convoys to the extent of sinking attacking submarines at a rate even comparable to their production output before the end of the year.

U. S. SECRET
BRITISH MOST SECRET

ENCLOSURE "A"

DETAILED ESTIMATE OF CONVOY ESCORT REQUIREMENTS
(Vessels over 200 feet in length)

	Average Number of Ships	Interval Between Sailings (Days)	Scale of Escort	Strength of Escort (Operational)	Strength of Group (Incl. those Refitting)	No. of Groups Required	Total Escorts
North Russian U.S.-U.K.	30		Special	1	6	3	18
	(Note: Russian convoys are supported by fleet destroyer striking forces)						
S.C. & H.X. Mid-Ocean	40	4	A	7	11	10	110
S.C. & H.X. Western Local	40	4	B	5	8	8	64
Canadian Local Convoys	..	..	..	..	..	..	24
D.W.I.-U.K. Tanker	40	20	A	8	10	3	30
D.W.I.-TORCH Tanker	6 to 10	24	A	3	4	2	8
U.K.-Gibraltar (OG/HG)	30	30	A	6	9	1	9
U.K. TORCH (KMF/WS)	30	16	A	6	9	2	18
(KMS)	60	16	A	9	12	3	36
U.K.-Freetown	40	20	A	7	11	3	33
U.S.-TORCH (Troop)	20	25	Special	7	9	2	18
U.S.-TORCH (Cargo)	45	25	A	7	10	3	30
New York-Key West	18	8	C	2	3	3	9
Guantanamo-New York	30	4	C	2	3	5	15
Guantanamo-Key West	10	8	C	1	..	2	3
Guantanamo-Trinidad	23	4	C	2	3	5	15
Guantanamo-Panama	14	8	Special	1	..	2	3
Key West-Galveston & Pilottown	24	4	Special	1	..	4	6
Trinidad-Baia	38	10	C	3	4	5	20
U.S.-Iceland Shuttle Service	6	..	Special	..	..	..	6
U.S. Pacific Convoys	..	..	..	..	..	..	36
							511

U. S. SECRET
BRITISH MOST SECRET

ENCLOSURE "B"

WORLD-WIDE ESTIMATE OF REQUIREMENTS OF FLEET DESTROYERS AND OCEAN-GOING ESCORT VESSELS
(Over 200 feet in length)

	Fleet Destroyers	Escort Vessels
PRESENT BRITISH RESPONSIBILITIES:		
Home Fleet	30	–
North Russian Convoys	–	18
Transatlantic Convoys	–	–
Mid-ocean escorts	–	110
Western Local escorts	–	64
Canadian Local Convoys	–	24
Freetown Convoys	–	33
DWI-UK Tanker Convoys	–	30
UK-Gibraltar Convoys	–	0
UK-Torch and W.S. Convoys	–	54
UK-Local Escorts		
East Coast Convoys	–	52
Local Home Commands	–	28
Minelaying Squadron	–	7
Eastern Mediterranean Squadron	15	–
Gibraltar Local Escorts & Inshore Sq.	–	39
Freetown Local escorts	–	18
South Atlantic Local escorts	–	6
Eastern Fleet	18	–
East Indies Local Escorts	–	20
East Mediterranean	9	28
Red Sea	–	3
Australia & Pacific	2	3
Total	74	546
PRESENT U. S. RESPONSIBILITIES:		
Pacific Fleet	125	–
U. S. Pacific Convoys	36	–
Atlantic Fleet	48	–
U. S.-Torch Troop Convoys	18	–

U. S. SECRET
BRITISH MOST SECRET

	Fleet Destroyers	Escort Vessels
U. S. Torch Cargo Convoys	–	30
IWI--Torch Tanker Convoys	8	–
New York--Key West	–	9
Guantanamo--New York	–	15
Guantanamo--Key West	–	3
Guantanamo--Trinidad	–	15
Guantanamo--Panama	–	3
Key West--Galveston and Pilottown	–	6
Trinidad--Baia	–	20
U. S.--Iceland Shuttle Service	–	6
Total	235	107

ENCLOSURE "C"

FLEET DESTROYERS AND OCEAN-GOING ESCORT VESSELS
(Over 200 feet in length)

COMPARISON OF MINIMUM REQUIREMENTS AND AVAILABILITY

The sum of minimum requirements shown in Enclosure "B" is:

	Fleet Destroyers	Ocean Going Escort Vessels
Presently under British responsibility	74	546
Presently under U. S. responsibility	235	107
Total	309	653

The forces *available* during each month of 1943 have been estimated in the table hereunder:

 (a) Allowance is made for a period of one months working up between completion and ready for service.

 (b) Allowance is made for a number of vessels being withdrawn from operational commands for extensive repairs or modernization (U.S.-33. BR.-21)

 (c) Attrition rates are based on previous experience, namely:
   Fleet Destroyers - 5 per month
   Escort Vessels - 5 per month

U. S. SECRET
BRITISH MOST SECRET

	Fleet Destroyers				Ocean-Going Escort Vessels (over 200 ft.)		
	US	BR	Accumulated total less attrition available to United Nations		US	BR	Accumulated total less attrition available to United Nations
To service 1 Jan 1943	186	72		To service 1 Jan 1943	63	437	
	US Constr	BR Constr			US Constr	BR Constr	
January	10	1	264	January	–	5	500
February	10	1	270	February	–	1	496
March	10	1	276	March	–	5	496
April	12	3	286	April	5	3	499
May	10	1	292	May	8	8	510
June	12	1	300	June	16	17	538
July	11	3	309	July	26	9	568
August	13	1	318	August	32	12	607
September	10	2	325	September	38	11	651
October	3	3	326	October	37	13	696
November	11	5	337	November	49	18	758
December	10	1	343	December	56	20	829

ENCLOSURE "D"

UNITED NATIONS REQUIREMENTS OF ESCORT CARRIERS

REQUIREMENTS FOR CONVOY ESCORT:

It is considered that every ocean convoy escort should include an escort carrier in areas where attacks by packs of U-boats may be expected. On this basis the following is the estimated number required.

North Atlantic:

Transatlantic convoys	10
Freetown convoys	3
DWI-UK Tanker convoys	3
DWI-Torch Tanker convoys	3

The North Russian convoys have to be fought through a heavy scale of air attack during the months when hours of daylight are long. It can be assumed that such attack will be concentrated largely on the

U. S. SECRET
BRITISH MOST SECRET

escort carrier. The probable loss of all fighter protection if only one escort carrier were sent with each convoy would have such consequences that it is considered that two escort carriers should be provided for each convoy. The requirement is therefore:

    North Russian convoys   6
    Total Requirements of Convoy
      escort   25

AVAILABILITY:

After allowance is made for working up and attrition it is estimated that the following number of escort carriers will be available for service:

	U. S.	BRITISH	TOTAL
End January	7	4	11
End February	8	5	13
End March	8	5	13
End April	11	8	19
End May	18	8	26
End June	21	11	32
End July	24	13	37
End August	28	14	42

Apart from offensive operations allowance must be made for a number of these carriers being employed on training, anti-raider duties and aircraft transporting, while 20 percent will be undergoing refit at any one time.

ENCLOSURE "E"

UNITED NATIONS REQUIREMENTS OF SHORE BASED AIRCRAFT FOR THE DEFENSE OF TRADE COMMUNICATIONS

SECTION 1 - THE NORTH ATLANTIC:
1. The V.L.R. Area:

Very long range aircraft are required to escort convoys and operate against U-boats in the North Atlantic at ranges greater than 500 miles from airdromes in Great Britain, Iceland (C) and Newfoundland. This area is known as the V.L.R. Area.

They are also required to escort convoys as far south as 52° N.

U. S. SECRET
BRITISH MOST SECRET

so that flexibility may be given to routing.

It must be assumed that any convoy passing through this area is liable to be picked up and shadowed by a U-boat. It is essential to make the shadower dive. We should therefore be able to escort every convoy during daylight hours. Within the V.L.R. area this probably means about three convoys daily.

The operation of three strong packs of U-boats simultaneously in the North Atlantic is well within the enemy's resources. We must be prepared for two convoys to be attacked simultaneously and should be able to reinforce each of these with long range aircraft to harass and sink the U-boats. These aircraft would also be used for sweeps for the same purpose.

For these tasks it is estimated that 80 V.L.R. aircraft are required, of which 60 might be based in the United Kingdom and 20 in North America.

2. The Bay of Biscay Area:

The requirements in the Bay area are based on the development of a strong offensive against U-boats on passage to and from their bases, the escort of convoys passing in that area and fleet reconnaissance duty.

3. Northern Approaches:

It is necessary to have enough air activity to the approaches to the Minches and St. George's Channel to insure that U-boats cannot close in and operate in our focal points with impunity. The passage of new U-boats around the North of the Faroes provides opportunities for interception. Fleet operations in the Northern area require reconnaissance and escort aircraft. An aircraft striking force for the North Sea and Northern waters is also necessary.

4. East Coast:

One M.R. Squadron is required in the East Coast to assist in the protection of our convoys against U-boat attack.

5. Gibraltar:

The defense of the focal points in the approaches to the Mediterranean requires the allocation of suitable reconnaissance and anti-submarine aircraft able to undertake day and night operations.

SECTION 2   EAST COAST OF U.S. AND CANADA:

The focal points of trade routes on the U.S. Atlantic seaboard require a large scale of air protection. Practically all Atlantic convoy

U. S. SECRET
BRITISH MOST SECRET

routes converge in this area.

SECTION 3 - THE CARIBBEAN:

The shipping routes to the oil fields of Venezuela and Trinidad and to the Panama Canal cross this area. These same routes converge in the various passages through the West Indies, producing many focal points which require air coverage.

SECTION 4 - NORTHWEST AND WEST AFRICA:

Shore based aircraft are required to secure the focal areas off the Northwest and West African ports, to escort the convoys moving in the Atlantic in these latitudes and to maintain control of the narrows.

SECTION 5 - SOUTH AMERICAN EAST COAST AND ASCENSION ISLAND:

Due to distances, the submarine menace here is considerably reduced. However, surface raiders operate continuously in this area and air patrols are required to guard against them.

SECTION 6 - THE MEDITERRANEAN (EXCLUDING GIBRALTAR):

In the Mediterranean the sea communications are controlled to a major degree by shore based aircraft. Requirements for all types of aircraft for cooperation over the sea are considerable.

SECTION 7 - INDIAN OCEAN:

The situation in the Indian Ocean has generally improved. We are however faced with:

 (a) A surface and submarine threat in the Bay of Bengal.
 (b) A submarine threat in the Indian Ocean generally but particularly in the Mozambique Channel and in the oil route from the Persian Gulf.

SECTION 8 - THE SOUTH PACIFIC:

No figures available.

SECTION 9 - THE SOUTHWEST PACIFIC:

No figures available.

SECTION 10 - THE WEST COAST OF NORTH AMERICA:

The submarine menace off the three major ports in this area has been relieved by active operations in the Far East. However, these areas must be patrolled particularly against surface raids on large convoys.

SECTION 11 - ALASKA:

No figures available.

SCHEDULE OF REQUIREMENTS:

The shore based aircraft required to meet the commitments stated

U. S. SECRET
BRITISH MOST SECRET

in the above sections are set out in the following schedule:

SCHEDULE V

SCHEDULE OF REQUIREMENTS OF SHORE-BASED AIRCRAFT FOR THE PROTECTION OF TRADE COMMUNICATIONS

Section	Area	FB	VLR	LR	MR	MR/TB	SR	T/F
1	North Atlantic to 26°N. and European (incl. Gib) & 24 in North Africa	108,	140	.	180	.	.	200
2	North Atlantic, East Coast U.S. & Canada	96	72	.	150	250	.	.
3	Caribbean	120	48	.	72	180	.	.
4	West Africa 26°N. to Portuguese West Africa	45	.	12	32	.	.	.
5	East Coast South America	48	24	.	.	80	.	.
6	Mediterranean	18	.	.	80	.	80	96
7	Indian Ocean	117	.	24	.	96	.	96
8	South Pacific			No data available				
9	Southwest Pacific			No data available				
10	West Coast of America	72	36	.	.	110	.	.
11	Alaska			No data available				
12	South Africa	.	.	.	.	.	120	.

Flying Boats)
Very Long Range) Estimated for convoy coverages at sea.
Long Range)

All other planes required for coverage of harbors, straits and focal points of trade routes.

U. S. SECRET
BRITISH MOST SECRET
C.C.S. 161   January 20, 1943

COMBINED CHIEFS OF STAFF

OPERATION "HUSKY"

Memorandum by the British Joint Planning Staff

OUTLINE PLAN:
1. The main features of the plan are:
   (a) British assaults:
      (1) On the southeast corner of the island by three divisions on D day to secure the airfields in that area and the ports of Syracuse and Augusta. These airfields are required to enable the assault on Catania to be protected.
      (2) On Catania by one division on D 3 to secure the port and airfields.
   (b) American assaults:
      (1) On the southwest shore by one division on D day to secure the airfields in that area. These airfields are required to cover the assaults on Palermo.
      (2) On the Palermo area by two divisions on D 2 to capture the port of Palermo and adjacent ports and airfields. Escort carriers will provide additional support for the assault.
   (c) Follow-up:
      One British division will be landed through Catania and one American division through Palermo.

FORCES REQUIRED:
2. The forces required are shown in Enclosure subdivided into American and British commitments.

MOUNTING OF BRITISH PORTION:
3. It is assumed that the U.S.A. will require French North African ports for the mounting of their share of the operation. Such part of the British expedition as is mounted inside the Mediterranean must therefore be mounted from Middle East ports, e.g., Haifa, Alexandria, Port Said, Malta. Limitations of port capacity make it impossible to mount the whole of the British share from the Middle East under any conditions.

U. S. SECRET
BRITISH MOST SECRET

4. In order to use battle-experienced troops of the Eighth Army, they would have to be moved back to Egypt for training and loading after the conclusion of operations in Tunisia. If the expedition is to be mounted within reasonable time, it will not be possible to employ more than about one battle-experienced division in HUSKY.

PROVISION OF ARMY FORCES:

5. There are two alternative methods:
   A. To find the three division assault from the U. K. and the Catania assault (one division) and the follow-up (one division) from the Middle East.
   B. To find the three division assault and the follow-up (one division) from the Middle East and the Catania assault (one division) from the U. K.

ALTERNATIVE A

6. (a) Advantages:
   (1) Provided North Africa is cleared of the enemy by April 30th, it enables the British assaults to be carried out in late July.
   (2) It is more economical in shipping.
   (b) Disadvantages:
   (1) It does not use forces in the Middle East which are available over and above security commitments.
   (2) It involves the passage of a large assault convoy through the Sicilian narrows in mineable waters and under air attack. This is an unacceptable risk to the spearhead of the attack.

ALTERNATIVE B

7. (a) Advantages:
   (1) It permits a slight reduction in escort.
   (2) It obviates the disadvantages of A, and, therefore, gives the operation greater chances of tactical success.
   (b) Disadvantages:
   (1) Provided North Africa is cleared of the enemy on April

U. S. SECRET
BRITISH MOST SECRET

30th, the British assaults could take place at the end of September. This is near the time when the weather breaks.

(2) It involves the dispatch of 16 personnel ships to the Middle East which are not otherwise required in that area.

(3) It is wasteful of shipping and will prevent us making any appreciable British cargo shipping contribution to Bolero.

(4) Without reference to the Middle East we cannot state whether the port and transportation facilities in the Middle East are capable of mounting an assault of this size.

PROVISION OF NAVAL FORCES:

8. The British Naval forces can be provided.

9. In the case of escorts, by the end of August the United Nations expect to be at least 46 escorts below our minimum escort requirements. Thus they can only provide the escort required if the increased risk involved in taking them off convoy protection for the period of the operation can be accepted.

10. Even if it were possible, the mounting of all assaults from North Africa would not result in any further reduction of escorts, as the limiting factor is the number required for the protection of shipping and craft off beaches.

PROVISION OF AIR FORCES:

11. The British air forces required will be available in North Africa and the Middle East.

PROVISION OF LANDING CRAFT:

12. British landing craft requirements can be made available provided expected deliveries from the U. S. are punctual. There may, however, be difficulty in getting the required number shipped to the Middle East in time. This will require detailed examination.

13. Any large increase in the use of L.C.I.(L) and L.S.T. for the American assault will probably have to be at the expense of the present British allotment. This would prevent our assaults being undertaken as proposed.

U. S. SECRET
BRITISH MOST SECRET

PROVISION OF SHIPPING:

14. The shipping can be provided.

AMERICAN SHARE OF THE OPERATION:

15. The American share of the operation is shown in the Enclosure. We have not attempted to estimate whether this can be met but must point out that if the Italian Fleet is not driven up the Adriatic, the United States will have to provide a heavy naval covering force in addition to the forces shown.

C. E. LAMBE,
G. M. STEWART,
W. ELLIOT.

ENCLOSURE
FORCES REQUIRED
NAVAL

	British	U.S.	Total
Battleships	4	0	4
Fleet Carriers	2	0	2
Escort Carriers	0	8	8
Cruisers	10	4	14
Destroyers	30	20	50
Escorts	69	55	124
Minesweepers & small craft	–	–	–

ARMY

	British	U.S.	Total
(a) *Assault.*			
Infantry Divisions	4-1/3	3	7-1/3
Armored Regiments	1	1	2
Parachute Brigades	3	2	5
(b) *Follow-Up.*			
Infantry Divisions	1	1	2

U. S. SECRET
BRITISH MOST SECRET

AIR FORCES

	British	American	Total
S.E.F.	24	27	51
T.E.F. (day)	2	–	2
T.E.F. (P-38)	–	12	12
T.E.F. (Night)	3	–	3
Light-Medium Bombers	2	18	20
Heavy Bombers (Day)	–	10	10
G.R.	3	–	3
Fighter Recce.	2	–	2
P.R.U.	1	–	1
Transport		312 a/c.	
Torpedo Bombers	2	–	2

SHIPS AND LANDING CRAFT

	British	American	Total
H. Q. Ship	3	2	5
L.S.I.(L)	8	13	21
L.S.I.(M)	3	2	5
L.S.D.	5	0	5
L.S.T.	56	44	100
L.C.A.	98	52	150
L.C.P.	100	190	290
L.C.S.	14	12	26
L.C.M.	200	71	271
L.C.I.(L)	90	30	120
L.C.T.	72	0	72
Personnel Ships	20	20	40
M.T. Ships	94	77	171

U. S. SECRET
BRITISH MOST SECRET
C.C.S. 161/1 January 21, 1943

COMBINED CHIEFS OF STAFF

OPERATION "HUSKY"

Report by British Joint Planning Staff

EARLIEST DATE FOR THE ASSAULT:

1. After further examination we have concluded* that the earliest safe date on which we can rely for the British assaults is August 30th and do not consider that this date can be advanced unless operations in Tunisia conclude considerably earlier than anticipated.

The use of air transport to move the leading brigade of the division from Tunisia to Egypt for training might enable us to advance the assault date from August 30th to about August 15th. This is, however, the date of full moon.

2. If the British could use Algiers and a sector of the east coast of Tunisia for the training and loading of one of their divisions, the earliest date by which the British could assault could be advanced by one month. Further examination by the U. S. Planning Staffs may, however, show that Tunisia is essential for the Americans to mount their two shore to shore assaults. In this event the ship-borne portion of the British assault (about 40 ships) would have to pass the Sicilian Narrows on D day.

3. The U. S. Planning Staff have not had time to assess in detail how their portion of the operation will be carried out and in consequence the types and numbers of landing craft they will use, or the date on which they can mount the operation. The limiting factors are the provision of training establishments and organization and early provision of landing craft, and not the availability of army forces. Landing craft must in any case be delivered in North Africa in advance of present scheduled dates.

PROVISION OF RESOURCES:

4. The U. S. Planners consider from preliminary examination that the first flight of the American assaults should be in armored craft

---

* Vide Enclosure "A"

U. S. SECRET
BRITISH MOST SECRET

other than L.C.I. (L) supported by L.C.S. No craft of this type exist except British L.C.A. and L.C.S., but sufficient could probably be made available for the British and American assaults at the cost of cross-Channel operations.

IMMEDIATE ACTION:

5. Beach reconnaissance, expansion of training facilities in North Africa and Middle East, and a comprehensive program of airfield construction must be put in hand at once.

ORGANIZATION OF COMMAND:

6. We consider that a Supreme Commander must at once be appointed for Operation HUSKY.

7. Navy, Army and Air Commanders should also be appointed subordinate to the Supreme Commander. Under these Commanders will be two Task Forces--a Western and an Eastern. The appointments of these Commanders and their Staffs should be made at once.

8. The operation should in the main be planned from North Africa.

9. The Joint U. S. Staff Planners have informed us that they agree with paragraphs 6 to 8 above.

                (signed)   C. E. LAMBE
                                   G. M. STEWART
                                   W. ELLIOT

ENCLOSURE "A"

OPERATION HUSKY

OUTLINE PLAN:

1. The main features of the plan are:

    (a) British assaults:

        (1) On the southeast corner of the island by three divisions on D. day to secure the airfields in that area and the ports of Syracuse and Augusta. These airfields are required to enable the assault on Catania to be protected.

        (2) On Catania by one division on D 3 to secure the port and airfields.

U. S. SECRET
BRITISH MOST SECRET

      (b) American assaults:
          (1) On the southwest shore by one division on D day to secure the airfields in that area. These airfields are required to cover the assaults on Palermo.
          (2) On the Palermo area by two divisions on D 2 to capture the port of Palermo and adjacent ports and airfields. Escort carriers will provide additional support for the assault.
      (c) Follow up:
        One British division will be landed through Catania and one American division through Palermo.

FORCES REQUIRED:

    2. The forces required are shown in Enclosure "B" subdivided into American and British commitments.

MOUNTING OF BRITISH PORTION:

    3. It is assumed that the U.S.A. will require French North African ports for the mounting of their share of the operation. Such part of the British expedition as is mounted inside the Mediterranean must therefore be mounted from Middle East ports, e.g., Haifa, Alexandria, Port Said, Tripoli and Malta. Limitations of port capacity make it impossible to mount the *whole* of the British share from the Middle East under any conditions.

PROVISION OF ARMY FORCES:

    4. The risk involved in passing a large convoy (some 90 ships) from the U. K. through Sicilian narrows in mineable waters and under air attack is unacceptable for the initial assaults. The three division assault on D day on to the S.E. corner of the island *must* therefore be mounted in the Middle East. The follow up must be mounted from TRIPOLI or nearby ports if landing craft are to be used and economy of shipping is to be effected.

    Thus the Catania D + 3 assault (one division) can only be mounted from the U. K. and we must accept the risk of passing this assault convoy through the Sicilian narrows on about D + 2.

    It might be possible to train and mount one of the above British divisions in Algeria and Tunisia, but this will seriously curtail the American facilities for mounting their share of the operations, and will complicate the organization of the assault.

U S, SECRET
BRITISH MOST SECRET

This alternative of mounting two divisions from the Middle East and four divisions from North Africa would result in the British share of the assault being ready by August 1st. It may, however, well result in the American share of the assault being delayed beyond August 31st. No advantage in date would therefore be gained, and considerable complications would be added.

The mounting of the British share must therefore take the following form:

        3 divisions (initial assault)   from Middle East
        1 division (D + 3 assault)   from U. K.
        1 division   (follow up)   from Tripolitania

PROVISION OF ARMY FORCES FOR INITIAL ASSAULT:

5. There are four possibilities:

    (A) Use 5th and 56th from Persia-Iraq and N.Z. division or 78th division from Tunisia.

    (B) Use 5th division from Persia-Iraq
        N.Z. division)
                         from Tunisia
        78th division)

    (C) Use 5th Division from Persia-Iraq
        1 division)
                   from U. K. shipped round Cape to Egypt
        4 division)

    (D) Use 5th Division from Persia-Iraq
        1 Division or 4 Division from U. K. shipped round Cape to Egypt. 56th, N.Z. or 78th division.

ESTIMATED TIME TABLE:

6. The limiting factors in deciding the earliest date of the assault are the time required for training and in the case of alternatives (C) and (D) the time needed to move the formations to the Middle East. These are examined in Enclosure "C" from which we conclude that the earliest dates of assault are:

    (A) August 30th
    (B) August 30th
    (C) September 25th
    (D) September 10th

7. There is no advantage in moving formations from U. K. to Middle East via the Cape. Thus, we must adopt case (A) or (B). Although Case (B) employs two seasoned formations, we recommend Case (A) because:

U. S. SECRET
BRITISH MOST SECRET

    (a) Only one instead of two brigades must be back from Tunisia in time to start training on June 1st. It may be possible to withdraw one brigade in time to do this.

    (b) Only one instead of two divisions will have to be refitted in Egypt after return from Tunisia.

    (c) Two out of three instead of one division will be available for planning from March onwards. With Case (B) two division staffs could not arrive in Egypt more than about one month before the detailed plan must be completed.

8. We, therefore, recommend Case (A) be adopted and the target date for the assault be fixed at August 30th. This will mean the three division D. day assault should be mounted with:

    5th and 56th Divisions from Persia-Iraq.

    N.Z. and 78th Divisions from Tunisia.

PROVISION OF NAVAL FORCES:

9. The British Naval forces can be provided.

10. In the case of escorts, by the end of August the United Nations expect to be at least 46 escorts below our minimum escort requirements. Thus they can only provide the escort required if the increased risk involved in taking them off convoy protection for the period of the operation can be accepted.

11. Even if it were possible, the mounting of all assaults from North Africa would not result in any further reduction of escorts, as the limiting factor is the number required for the protection of shipping and craft off beaches.

PROVISION OF AIR FORCES:

12. The British air forces required will be available in North Africa and the Middle East.

PROVISION OF LANDING CRAFT:

13. British landing craft requirements can be made available provided expected deliveries from the U.S. are punctual. There may, however, be difficulty in getting the required number shipped to the Middle East in time. This will require detailed examination.

14. Any large increase in the use of L.C.I.(L) and L.S.T. for the American assault will probably have to be at the expense of the present British allotment. This would prevent our assaults being undertaken as proposed.

U. S. SECRET
BRITISH MOST SECRET

PROVISION OF SHIPPING:

15. The shipping can be provided.

AMERICAN SHARE OF THE OPERATION:

16. The American share of the operation is shown in Enclosure "B". We have not attempted to estimate whether this can be met but must point out that if the Italian Fleet is not driven up the Adriatic, the United States will have to provide a heavy naval covering force in addition to the forces shown.

                                  (Signed) C.E. LAMBE
                                                  G.M. STEWART
                                                  W. ELLIOT

ENCLOSURE "B"

FORCES REQUIRED

NAVAL

	British	U.S.	Total
Battleships	4	0	4
Fleet Carriers	2	0	2
Escort carriers	0	8	8
Cruisers	10	4	14
Destroyers	30	20	50
Escorts	60	55	124
Minesweepers & small craft			

ARMY

	British	U.S.	Total
(a) Assault:			
Infantry Divisions	4-1/3	3	7-1/3
Armored Regiments	1	1	2
Parachute Brigades	3	2	5
(b) Follow-up:			
Infantry Divisions	1	1	2

U. S. SECRET
BRITISH MOST SECRET

AIR FORCES *

	British Squadrons	U.E.	U. S. Groups	U.E.	
S.E.F.	24	432	6	480	
T.E.F. day	3	54	3	240	U. S. Groups P-38.
T.E.F. night	3	54	-	-	Excluding defense North Africa.
Light Bombers	6	108	1	57	Includes observation & Army support Squadrons.
Medium Bombers	5	90	5	285	
Heavy Bombers	2	36	7	245	
G.R. (V.P.B.)	3	48	-	-	
Torpedo	4	80	1	57	B-26 Torpedo Bombers.
PRU	3	36	-	12	
Total Combat	-	938	-	1,376	
Transport	5	80	6	312	

* These figures are for all Allied aircraft concentrated in the Central Mediterranean for offensive operations preparatory to and during HUSKY. They exclude aircraft for defense, protection of shipping, reserves for Turkey, etc., elsewhere in the Mediterranean.

SHIPS AND LANDING CRAFT

	British	American**	Total
H.Q. Ship	3	2	5
L.S.I. (L)	8	13	21
L.S.I. (M)	3	2	5
L.S.D.	5	0	5
L.S.T.	56	44	100

U. S. SECRET
BRITISH MOST SECRET

SHIPS AND LANDING CRAFT
(Continued)

	British	American**	Total
L.C.A.	89	52	150
L.C.P.	100	190	290
L.C.S	14	12	26
L.C.M.	200	170	370
L.C.I. (L)	90	30	120
L.C.T.	72	0	72
Personnel Ships	20	20	40
M.T. Ships	94	77	171

**American figures are given in terms of British types of landing cra

ENCLOSURE "C"

EXAMINATION OF EARLIEST DATE OF ASSAULT

ALTERNATIVES:

1.

	Persia-Iraq	Divisions from: Tunisia	U.K. via Cape
A.	2	1 (N.Z. or 78th)	0
B.	1	2 (N.Z. & 78th)	0
C.	1	0	2
D.	1	1	1

2. (a) The Overseas Assault Force cannot arrive in the Middle East before May 15th.

   (b) Training facilities in the Middle East can if necessary be expanded by May 1st to deal with the basic training of two brigade groups at a time.

   (c) Final rehearsal can if necessary be carried out by two brigade groups at a time in the Overseas assault Force.

   (d) Priority must be given for the shipment of landing craft to the Middle East from both U. K. and U.S.A.

   (e) We have assumed that the New Zealand and 78th divisions in

U. S. SECRET
BRITISH MOST SECRET

        Tunisia can be released in time to start training in Egypt by June 1st.

(f) We have assumed that none of the shipping saved as a result of the recent cut on Middle East and Indian maintenance can be used for transporting the U. K. divisions round the Cape. In consequence, the sailing date of these divisions is dependent upon the completion of the Torch build up.

CASE A

March 1–April 30 (a) Basic training first division from P.A.I.C.
May 1–June 30   (b) Basic training second division from P.A.I.C.

U. S. SECRET
BRITISH MOST SECRET
C.C.S. 162   January 19, 1943

COMBINED CHIEFS OF STAFF

U. S. AID TO RUSSIA

Joint Memorandum agreed by Lord Leathers and Lieutenant General Somervell

1. Existing U. S. estimates on the availability of shipping and the possibility of moving troops, naval forces, supplies and equipment during 1943 allow for the following U. S. sailings for Russian aid.

TABLE I

	Jan	Feb	Mar	Apr	May	June	Total
(a) To North Russia	0	0	0	0	0	0	0
(b) To Persian Gulf	15	15	15	15	15	15	90
(c) In Pacific (Average from U. S. and Russian Pool)	31	31	31	31	31	31	186
	46	46	46	46	46	46	276

Shipments beyond June are estimated at the same rate

2. Owing to limited capacity of Persian Gulf ports and the discontinuance of the North Atlantic route, U. S. commitments under the existing Protocol have been only about 50 percent of requirements for the last six months, necessitating the shipment of three-fourths of the year's total during the first half of the year 1943. This will require a total of 432 sailings from the U. S. to Russia prior to July 1, 1943. If Protocol commitments after July 1 are at the same rate as for the year prior to that time, two-thirds this number, or 288 sailings, will be required.

3. As the route through the Pacific is subject to interruption by the Japanese at any moment and as arms and ammunition do not move via that route, it cannot be relied on for any great increase above the present sailings.

4. It is expected that the capacity of Persian Gulf ports can be expanded to handle a total of 26 ships per month by June 1943.

5. For the northern route on the basis of 12 British cargo ships and two tankers there would remain available 16 sailings from the U. S.

U. S. SECRET
BRITISH MOST SECRET

every convoy. Owing to the restricted supply of escorts, it seems that the convoy interval will not be reduced below 42 days. With ice hazards and the menace of submarines and air attacks, it is hardly possible that total sailings will exceed this rate.

6. The total sailings for the year could therefore be on the following order:

TABLE II
NORTH RUSSIA

Jan	Feb	Mar	Apr	May	June	July	Aug	Sep	Oct	Nov	Dec	Total
16	16	–	16	16	–	16	16	–	16	16	–	128

PERSIAN ROUTE

Jan	Feb	Mar	Apr	May	June	July	Aug	Sep	Oct	Nov	Dec	Total
16	18	20	22	24	26	16	16	16	16	16	16	222

PACIFIC ROUTE

Jan	Feb	Mar	Apr	May	June	July	Aug	Sep	Oct	Nov	Dec	Total
31	31	31	31	31	31	31	31	31	31	31	31	372

TOTAL

Jan	Feb	Mar	Apr	May	June	July	Aug	Sep	Oct	Nov	Dec	Total
63	65	51	69	71	57	63	63	47	63	63	47	722

Sailings on this order would fail to meet Protocol requirements in July by 56 ships, but would permit meeting full commitments by the end of the calendar year.

7. It will be noted from Tables I and II that the following additional sailings would be required for such a program resulting in the necessity for the use of additional cargo ships for the period of a year.

TABLE III
ADDITIONAL SAILINGS REQUIRED

Jan	Feb	Mar	Apr	May	June	July	Aug	Sep	Oct	Nov	Dec	Total
17	19	5	23	25	11	17	17	1	17	17	1	170

8. The effect of meeting the Russian Protocol on the movement of U. S. troops overseas and maintaining them thereafter would be on the following order:

TABLE IV

1943	No. of troops
1st Quarter	46,000
2nd Quarter	82,000
3rd Quarter	55,000
4th Quarter	4,000
TOTAL	187,000

U. S. SECRET
BRITISH MOST SECRET

9. As requirements for other theaters are more or less fixed, the blow would fall on movements to the U. K. Some adjustment might be necessary in timing of Russian shipment to avoid interference with special requirements.

10. Additional tonnage above that assumed in existing estimates might be made available: (a) by reduction in the rate of submarine losses below the 2.6 percent assumed in these calculations; (b) by eliminating conversion of 100 EC 2's into transports; (c) by savings through the use of the Mediterranean route; (d) release of U. S. from obligation to replace British losses in like amount.

11. A reduction in rate of loss of United Nations shipping from 2.6 percent per month to only 2.0 percent per month would increase the troop carrying capacity in 1943 by 500,000 men. Even a third of this, or a reduction of the loss rate to 2.4 percent, would make these shipments to Russia possible, without lessening troop movements. With the measures projected by the Joint Chiefs of Staff, such an improvement is a possibility.

12. If conversion of EC 2's were stopped at the end of February, a gain in transport capacity of 153,000 would be possible. If losses are not reduced or no assistance from British sources for this purpose can be obtained, such a course would be desirable.

13. The British have already discounted the estimated gain in the Mediterranean by diverting this tonnage to British imports.

14. Supplement British assistance, as previously agreed, up to 300,000 tons per month, cumulative. Even on this basis, with a reduction in sinkings, there may be some relief on this score.

15. It is concluded from the above that the possibility exists of meeting Russian Protocol deliveries on the present scale during 1943 without reducing tentative schedules, but that the possibility exists that movements to the U. K. may be reduced by as much as 100,000 men. The advantages of furnishing aid to Russia are such that this hazard should be accepted. Owing to the scarcity of shipping, there should be a general agreement that all tonnage above minimum requirements should be assigned to U. S. troop movements.

U. S. SECRET
BRITISH MOST SECRET
C.C.S. 162/1

January 20, 1943

COMBINED CHIEFS OF STAFF

U. S. AID TO RUSSIA

Memorandum prepared by Lieutenant General Somervell

1. Existing U. S. estimates on the availability of shipping and the possibility of moving troops, naval forces, supplies and equipment during 1943 allow for the following U. S. sailings for Russian aid.

TABLE I

	Jan	Feb	Mar	Apr	May	June	Total
(a) To North Russia	0	0	0	0	0	0	0
(b) To Persian Gulf	15	15	15	15	15	15	90
(c) In Pacific (Average from U. S. and Russian Pool)	31	31	31	31	31	31	186
	46	46	46	46	46	46	276

Shipments beyond June are estimated at the same rate.

2. Owing to limited capacity of Persian Gulf ports and the discontinuance of the North Atlantic route, U. S. commitments under the existing Protocol have been only about 50 percent of requirements for the last six months, necessitating the shipment of three-fourths of the year's total during the first half of the year 1943. This will require a total of 432 sailings from the U. S. to Russia prior to July 1, 1943. If Protocol commitments after July 1 are at the same rate as for the year prior to that time, two-thirds this number, or 288 sailings, will be required.

3. As the route through the pacific is subject to interruption by the Japanese at any moment and as arms and ammunition do not move via that route, it cannot be relied on for any great increase above the present sailings.

4. It is expected that the capacity of Persian Gulf ports can be expanded to handle a total of 26 ships per month by June 1943.

5. For the northern route on the basis of 12 British cargo ships and two tankers there would remain available 16 sailings from the U. S.

every convoy. Owing to the restricted supply of escorts, it seems that the convoy interval will not be reduced below 42 days. With ice hazards and the menace of submarines and air attacks, it is hardly possible that total sailings will exceed this rate.

6. The total sailings for the year could therefore be on the following order:

TABLE II

NORTH RUSSIA

Jan	Feb	Mar	Apr	May	June	July	Aug	Sep	Oct	Nov	Dec	Total
16	16	-	16	16	-	16	16	-	16	16	-	128

PERSIAN ROUTE

Jan	Feb	Mar	Apr	May	June	July	Aug	Sep	Oct	Nov	Dec	Total
16	18	20	22	24	26	16	16	16	16	16	16	222

PACIFIC ROUTE

Jan	Feb	Mar	Apr	May	June	July	Aug	Sep	Oct	Nov	Dec	Total
31	31	31	31	31	31	31	31	31	31	31	31	372

TOTAL

Jan	Feb	Mar	Apr	May	June	July	Aug	Sep	Oct	Nov	Dec	Total
63	65	51	69	71	57	63	63	47	63	63	47	722

Sailings on this order would fail to meet Protocol requirements in July by 56 ships, but would permit meeting full commitments by the end of the calendar year.

7. It will be noted from Tables I and II that the following additional sailings would be required for such a program resulting in the necessity for the use of additional cargo ships for the period of a year.

TABLE III

ADDITIONAL SAILINGS REQUIRED

Jan	Feb	Mar	Apr	May	June	July	Aug	Sep	Oct	Nov	Dec	Total
17	19	5	23	25	11	17	17	1	17	17	1	170

8. The effect of meeting the Russian Protocol on the movement of U. S. troops overseas and maintaining them thereafter would be on the following order:

TABLE IV

1943	No. of troops
1st Quarter	46,000
2nd Quarter	82,000
3rd Quarter	55,000
4th Quarter	4,000
TOTAL	187,000

U. S. SECRET
BRITISH MOST SECRET

9. As requirements for other theaters are more or less fixed, the blow would fall on movements to the U. K. Some adjustment might be necessary in timing of Russian shipment to avoid interference with special requirements.

10. Additional tonnage above that assumed in existing estimates might be made available: (a) by reduction in the rate of submarine losses below the 2.6 percent assumed in these calculations; (b) by eliminating conversion of 100 EC 2's into transports; (c) by savings through the use of the Mediterranean route; (d) release of U. S. from obligation to replace British losses in like amount.

11. A reduction in rate of loss of United Nations shipping from 2.6 percent per month to only 2.0 percent per month would increase the troop carrying capacity in 1943 by 500,000 men. Even a third of this, or a reduction of the loss rate to 2.4 percent, would make these shipments to Russia possible, without lessening troop movements. With the measures projected by the Joint Chiefs of Staff, such an improvement is a possibility.

12. If conversion of EC 2's were stopped at the end of February, a gain in transport capacity of 153,000 would be possible. If losses are not reduced or no assistance from British sources for this purpose can be obtained, such a course would be desirable.

13. The British have already discounted the estimated gain in the Mediterranean by diverting this tonnage to British imports.

14. The U. S. is committed to replace losses in British tonnage in accordance with an agreement dated November 30, 1942. If there is a reduction in the number of sinkings the assistance required will be reduced. As a reduction is expected in some measure there will be a credit on this account.

15. It is concluded from the above that the possibility exists of meeting Russian Protocol deliveries on the present scale during 1943 without reducing tentative schedules, but that the possibility exists that movements to the U. K. may be reduced by as much as 100,000 men. The advantages of furnishing aid to Russia are such that this hazard should be accepted. Owing to the scarcity of shipping, there should be a general agreement that all tonnage above minimum requirements should be assigned to combined troop movements.

U. S. SECRET
BRITISH MOST SECRET
C.C.S. 163   January 20, 1943

COMBINED CHIEFS OF STAFF

SYSTEM OF AIR COMMAND IN THE MEDITERRANEAN

Proposals of the British Chiefs of Staff

1. There shall be appointed an Air Commander-in-Chief of the whole Mediterranean Theater with his headquarters at Algiers under whom will be the A.O.C. in C. Northwest Africa (General Spaatz), the A.O.C. in C. Middle East (Air Chief Marshal Douglas) and A.O.C. Malta.

2. The relationship and mutual responsibilities of the Air Commander-in-Chief, Mediterranean, and the Commander-in-Chief, Northwest African Theater, are defined as follows:

   (a) The Air Commander-in-Chief is subordinate to the Commander-in-Chief, Allied Expeditionary Force in Northwest Africa, in respect of:

   (1) The air forces stationed from time to time in the Northwest African Theater and their operations.

   (2) The operations of other Mediterranean air forces in conjunction with operations conducted in or from the Northwest African Theater.

   (b) The Commander-in-Chief, A.E.F. in Northwest Africa, will afford to the Air Commander-in-Chief, Mediterranean, all possible support and facilities in the Northwest African Theater for the operation of the Mediterranean air forces and for their efficient cooperation with the land and sea forces in the theater.

3. NORTHWEST AFRICA:

   This will be divided into three subcommands:

   (a) Heavy and medium bombers and appropriate escort fighters.

   (b) General reconnaissance and fighters for the defense of shipping, ports and back areas.

   (c) An Air Support Command, which is dealt with in detail in paragraph 4 below.

   The detailed organization of the Command must, however, be left to the decision of the Air Commander-in-Chief when he is appointed.

U. S. SECRET
BRITISH MOST SECRET

Air Force supply, maintenance, and repair arrangements in the whole of Northwest Africa shall be centralized under one control, direct under the A.O.C. in C. Northwest Africa.

4. In order that land operations may be effectively supported by the Combined air forces there must be one Army Commander or Deputy Commander-in-Chief appointed to coordinate the operations of all three armies in the Tunisian Theater--the British 1st Army, the American-French Army under General Fredendall, and the British 8th Army. The Air Officer Commanding the Air Support Command must similarly coordinate the operations of the Air Forces supporting all three armies, and will share an advanced headquarters with the Deputy Commander-in-Chief, whence he can direct the operations of the Air Forces to the best advantage of the land battle.

Army Support Wings will be attached to each of the three armies. The Wing Commanders will act as Air Advisers to the Army Commanders and will command such air forces as may from time to time be assigned to them by the A.O.C. Army Support Command in consultation with the Deputy Supreme Commander.

5. MIDDLE EAST:

The organization of Middle East will remain as it is at present, except that Malta will be detached and come direct under Air Commander-in-Chief, Mediterranean. Further, certain air forces employed in close support of the 8th Army will pass under the command of the A.O.C. Air Support under A.O.C. in C. Northwest Africa.

U. S. SECRET
BRITISH MOST SECRET
C.C.S. 164   January 20, 1943

COMBINED CHIEFS OF STAFF

OPERATION ANAKIM--PROVISION OF FORCES

Report by British Joint Planning Staff

1. The general conception of Operation ANAKIM has already been set out in C.C.S. 154.

ASSUMPTION:

2. It is assumed that Operation ANAKIM will be launched in November 1943, so giving five to six months of dry weather in which to reopen the Burma Road.

AVAILABILITY OF FORCES:

3. Until an outline plan is received from India no accurate estimate can be made. The forces required and their availability, as now forecast, are:

REQUIRED	AVAILABLE FROM BRITISH RESOURCES	REMARKS
(a) Naval Forces:		
6-8 Escort carriers	Submarines and minesweepers will probably be available. Of the remainder, the British are unlikely to be able to provide more than half.	The provision of naval forces must be decided upon at a later date.
40 Destroyers and escorts		
8 Submarines		
6 Fleet minesweepers and cover by heavy forces depending on the situation at the time.		
(b) Army:		Will be available in India by October 1, including sufficient assault trained troops.
8 Infantry divisions	Yes	
1 Armored division		
(c) Air:		Will be found from air forces already in India, raised to requisite strength by transfer from Middle East.
28 Bomber squadrons	Yes	
17 Fighter squadrons		
4 Coastal squadrons		

U. S. SECRET
BRITISH MOST SECRET

REQUIRED	AVAILABLE FROM BRITISH RESOURCES	REMARKS
(d) Assault shipping and Landing Craft:		
1 H.Q. Ship	Yes	⎰ Ex Husky or other Mediterranean Operations.
9 L.S.I. (L)	Yes	⎱
40 L.S.T. (2)	From 7-13	⎧ Balance not available from British resources will require to be provided and manned by U.S.A.
5 L.S.D.	No	
10 L.C.T. (5)	No	
120 L.C.M.	100 only	⎩
40 L.C.P.	Yes	
100 L.C.A.	Yes	
16 L.C.S.	10	This deficiency will have to be met by improvisation.
(e) Shipping:		
20 Personnel ships	No estimate	This requirement has not yet been confirmed by C-in-C India.
60 M.T. ships	yet possible	

CONCLUSION:

4. The Combined Chiefs of Staff are asked to:
    (a) Approve November 15, 1943, as provisional date for ANAKIM assault.
    (b) Approve provisional schedule of forces laid out in paragraph 3 above, it being recognized that actual provision of naval forces, assault shipping, landing craft and shipping must depend on situation in late summer of 1943.
    (c) Agree to confirm in July 1943 decision to undertake or to postpone Operation ANAKIM.

U. S. SECRET
BRITISH MOST SECRET
C.C.S. 164/1   January 21, 1943

COMBINED CHIEFS OF STAFF

OPERATION ANAKIM--PROVISION OF FORCES

Report by British Joint Planning Staff

1. The general conception of Operation ANAKIM has already been set out in C.C.S. 154.

ASSUMPTION:

2. It is assumed that Operation ANAKIM will be launched in November 1943, so giving five to six months of dry weather in which to reopen the Burma Road.

AVAILABILITY OF FORCES:

3. Until an outline plan is received from India no accurate estimate can be made. The forces required and their availability, as now forecast, are:

REQUIRED	AVAILABLE FROM BRITISH RESOURCES	REMARKS
(a) Naval Forces:		
6 Escort carriers	Submarines and minesweepers will probably be available. Of the remainder, the British are unlikely to be able to provide more than half.	The provision of naval forces must be decided upon at a later date.
40 Destroyers and escorts		
8 Submarines		
6 Fleet minesweepers and cover by heavy forces depending on the situation at the time.		
(b) Army:		Will be available in India by October 1, including sufficient assault trained troops.
8 Infantry divisions	Yes	
1 Armored division		
(c) Air:		Will be found from air forces already in India, raised to requisite strength by transfer from the Mediterranean.
28 Bomber squadrons	Yes	
17 Fighter squadrons		
4 Coastal squadrons		

U. S. SECRET
BRITISH MOST SECRET

REQUIRED	AVAILABLE FROM BRITISH RESOURCES	REMARKS
(d) Assault shipping and Landing Craft:		
1 H.Q. Ship	Yes	Ex Husky or other Mediterranean Operations.
9 L.S.I. (L)	Yes	
40 L.S.T. (2)	From 7-13	Balance not available from British resources will require to be provided and manned by U.S.A.
5 L.S.D.	No	
10 L.C.T. (5)	No	
120 L.C.M.	100 only	
40 L.C.P.	Yes	
100 L.C.A.	Yes	
16 L.C.S.	10	This deficiency will have to be met by improvisation.
(e) Shipping:		
20 Personnel ships	No estimate yet possible	This requirement has not yet been confirmed by C-in-C India.
60 M.T. ships		

CONCLUSION:

4. The Combined Chiefs of Staff are asked to:
   (a) Approve November 15, 1943, as provisional date for ANAKIM assault.
   (b) Approve provisional schedule of forces laid out in paragraph 3 above, it being recognized that actual provision of naval forces, assault shipping, landing craft and shipping must depend on situation in late summer of 1943.
   (c) Agree to confirm in July 1943 decision to undertake or to postpone Operation ANAKIM.

U. S. SECRET
BRITISH MOST SECRET
C.C.S. 165/2　　　　　　　　　　　　　　　　　　　　January 22, 1943

COMBINED CHIEFS OF STAFF

DRAFT TELEGRAM
FROM THE PRESIDENT OF THE UNITED STATES
AND THE PRIME MINISTER OF GREAT BRITAIN TO PREMIER STALIN

Prepared by the Combined Chiefs of Staff

1. We have been in conference with our Military Advisers for the past ten days, and we have decided the operations which are to be undertaken by American and British forces in 1943. We think that you would wish to know our intentions at once.

2. We are in no doubt that our correct strategy is to concentrate on the defeat of Germany, with a view to achieving early and decisive victory in the European Theater. At the same time, we must maintain sufficient pressure on Japan to retain the initiative in the Pacific and Far East, sustain China, and prevent the Japanese from extending their aggression to other theaters such as your Maritime Provinces.

3. A constant consideration has been the necessity of diverting strong German land and air forces from the Russian front and of sending to Russia the maximum flow of supplies, consistent with equally urgent requirements in other theaters. We shall spare no exertion to send you material assistance by every available route, but it would be no more in your interest than ours to do so at a cost which would cripple our capacity to relieve pressure on you by continuing an intensified offensive effort on our part.

4. Our immediate intention is to clear the Axis out of North Africa and set up the naval and air installations to open:

　　(a) An effective passage through the Mediterranean for military traffic, and

　　(b) An intensive bombardment of important Axis installations in Southern Europe.

5. We have made the decision to launch large scale amphibious operations in the Mediterranean at the earliest possible moment. The preparation for these operations is now under way and will involve a considerable concentration of forces, particularly landing craft and shipping

U. S. SECRET
BRITISH MOST SECRET

in Egyptian and North African ports. This concentration will certainly be known to our enemies, but they will not know where or when, or in what strength, we propose to strike. They will, therefore, be compelled to reinforce with both land and air forces the South of France, Corsica, Sardinia, Sicily, the heel of Italy, Yugoslavia, Greece, Crete, and the Dodecanese.

6. These operations may result in the collapse of Italy. The defection of other German satellite states would probably follow. Germany would then be faced with the choice of shortening her eastern line by a major withdrawal on your front, or of accepting a shortage of some fifty divisions and 2,000 aircraft in her global requirements.

7. In Europe we shall increase the Allied Bomber offensive from the U. K. against Germany at a rapid rate and, by midsummer, it should be more than double its present strength. Our experiences to date have shown that the day bombing attacks result in destruction and damage to large numbers of German Fighter Aircraft. We believe that an increased tempo and weight of daylight and night attacks will lead to greatly increased material and morale damage in Germany and rapidly deplete German fighter strength in Germany and occupied Western Europe. As you are aware, we are already containing more than half the German Air Force in Western Europe and the Mediterranean. We have no doubt that our greatly intensified bombing offensive, together with the other operations which we are undertaking, will compel further withdrawals of German air and other forces from the Russian front.

8. We shall also concentrate in the United Kingdom the maximum American land and air forces that shipping will permit. These, combined with the British forces in the United Kingdom, will be held in constant readiness to reenter the Continent of Europe as soon as this operation offers reasonable prospect of success.

9. In the Pacific it is our intention to eject the Japanese from Rabaul within the next few months and thereafter to exploit in the general direction of Japan. We also intend to increase the scale of our operations in Burma in order to reopen our channel of supply to China. We shall not, however, allow our operations against Japan to jeopardize our capacity to take advantage of any favorable opportunity that may present itself for the decisive defeat of Germany in 1943.

> *NOTE:* C.C.S. 165 and C.C.S. 165/1 were withdrawn inasmuch as the information contained in these papers was included in C.C.S. 165/2.

U. S. SECRET
BRITISH MOST SECRET
C.C.S. 166   January 20, 1943

COMBINED CHIEFS OF STAFF

THE BOMBER OFFENSIVE FROM THE UNITED KINGDOM

Memorandum by the British Chiefs of Staff

It is suggested that the following directive be issued by the Combined Chiefs of Staff to the appropriate British and U. S. Air Force Commanders to govern the operations of the British and American Bomber Commands in the United Kingdom.

DRAFT DIRECTIVE

1. Your object will be the progressive destruction and dislocation of the German military, industrial and economic system, and the undermining of the morale of the German people to a point where their capacity for armed resistance is fatally weakened.

2. Within that general concept, your primary objectives, subject to the exigencies of weather and of tactical feasibility, will for the present be in the order of priority set out below. This order of priority may be varied from time to time according to developments in the strategic situation. It is not to be taken to preclude attacks on Berlin when conditions are suitable for the attainment of specially valuable results unfavorable to the morale of the enemy or favorable to that of Russia.

    (a) German submarine operational bases and construction yards.
    (b) The German aircraft industry.
    (c) Transportation.
    (d) Synthetic oil plants.
    (e) Other targets in enemy war industry.

3. There may be certain other objectives of great but fleeting importance for the attack of which all necessary plans and preparations should be made. Of these, an example would be important units of the German Fleet in harbor or at sea.

4. You should take every opportunity to attack Germany by day, to destroy objectives that are unsuitable for night attack, to sustain

U. S. SECRET
BRITISH MOST SECRET

continuous pressure on German morale, to impose heavy losses on the German day fighter force, and to contain German fighter strength away from the Russian and Mediterranean theaters of war.

5. If and when it is decided that the Allied armies should reenter the Continent, you will afford them all possible support in the manner most effective.

6. In attacking objectives in occupied territories, you will conform to such instructions as may be issued from time to time by His Majesty's Government through the British Chiefs of Staff.

U. S. SECRET
BRITISH MOST SECRET
C.C.S. 166/1/D   January 21, 1943

COMBINED CHIEFS OF STAFF

THE BOMBER OFFENSIVE FROM THE UNITED KINGDOM

Directive to the appropriate British and U. S.
Air Force Commanders, to govern the operation of the
British and U. S. Bomber Commands in the United Kingdom
(Approved by the Combined Chiefs of Staff at their
65th Meeting on January 21, 1943)

1. Your primary object will be the progressive destruction and dislocation of the German military, industrial and economic system, and the undermining of the morale of the German people to a point where their capacity for armed resistance is fatally weakened.

2. Within that general concept, your primary objectives, subject to the exigencies of weather and of tactical feasibility, will for the present be in the following order of priority:

    (a) German submarine construction yards.

    (b) The German aircraft industry.

    (c) Transportation.

    (d) Oil plants.

    (e) Other targets in enemy war industry.

The above order of priority may be varied from time to time according to developments in the strategical situation. Moreover, other objectives of great importance either from the political or military point of view must be attacked. Examples of these are:

    (1) Submarine operating bases on the Biscay coast. If these can be put out of action, a great step forward will have been taken in the U-boat war which the C.C.S. have agreed to be a first charge on our resources. Day and night attacks on these bases have been inaugurated and should be continued so that an assessment of their effects can be made as soon as possible. If it is found that successful results can be achieved, these attacks should continue whenever conditions are favorable for as long and as often as is necessary. These objectives have not been included in the order of priority,

U. S. SECRET
BRITISH MOST SECRET

        which covers long-term operations, particularly as the bases are not situated in Germany.

    (2) Berlin, which should be attacked when conditions are suitable for the attainment of specially valuable results unfavorable to the morale of the enemy or favorable to that of Russia.

3. You may also be required, at the appropriate time, to attack objectives in Northern Italy in connection with amphibious operations in the Mediterranean theater.

4. There may be certain other objectives of great but fleeting importance for the attack of which all necessary plans and preparations should be made. Of these, an example would be the important units of the German Fleet in harbor or at sea.

5. You should take every opportunity to attack Germany by day, to destroy objectives that are unsuitable for night attack, to sustain continuous pressure on German morale, to impose heavy losses on the German day fighter force, and to contain German fighter strength away from the Russian and Mediterranean theaters of war.

6. When the Allied armies reenter the Continent, you will afford them all possible support in the manner most effective.

7. In attacking objectives in occupied territories, you will conform to such instructions as may be issued from time to time for political reasons by His Majesty's Government through the British Chiefs of Staff.

U. S. SECRET
BRITISH MOST SECRET
C.C.S. 167

January 22, 1943

COMBINED CHIEFS OF STAFF

CONTINENTAL OPERATIONS IN 1943

Report by British Joint Planning Staff

1. In view of the recommendations approved by the Combined Chiefs of Staff in C.C.S. 155/1, for the "Conduct of the War in 1943," we examine below the possibilities of cross-channel operations in 1943.

OBJECT OF OPERATIONS:

2. The objects of cross-channel operations in 1943 may be set down as:
   (a) Raids with the primary object of provoking a major air battle and causing the enemy loss.
   (b) Operations with the object of seizing and holding a bridgehead and, if the state of German morale and strength of her resources permit, of exploiting success.
   (c) Operations on a larger scale to take advantage of German disintegration.

ASSUMPTION AS TO DATE:

3. Where figures are quoted, we have assumed a target date of August 1st.

RESOURCES:

4. The number of divisions available will be twelve British, including one airborne, and about four American.

5. Training of naval crews will be the limiting factor in the provision of landing craft for the initial assaults. It is estimated that, without U. S. assistance, the maximum lift which can be provided will be:

Initial assault force:	Two brigade groups, with proportion of armor and commandos.
Total lift including initial assault force:	Two infantry divisions and one armored brigade on light scales, of which two brigade groups and a proportion of armor can be mounted in the initial assault.

NOTE: This is on the assumption that the British are not required to provide the U. S. with armored landing craft for Mediterranean operations.

U. S. SECRET
BRITISH MOST SECRET

6. There will by August 1943 be sufficient air forces, British and American, to support a limited cross-channel operation either against the Pas de Calais or the COTENTIN PENINSULA, provided operations in the Mediterranean have not drawn too heavily on our Fighter reserves. The decision to carry out such an operation would, however, entail a reorganization of part of the Metropolitan Air Force with a consequent brake on its expansion and operational effort.

ESTIMATED SCALE OF GERMAN RESISTANCE:

7. It may be assumed that the Germans will continue to develop their system of coast defenses, but it is fair to expect that the formations holding these defenses will be of poorer quality than at present.

8. The reserves which the Germans will be able to bring against us must depend entirely on the progress of operations elsewhere in Europe.

In the worst case, if they succeeded without heavy losses in stabilizing their Eastern front on the shortened line of R. DNIEPER, and in checking our operations in the Mediterranean, they might rebuild their reserves in Northwest Europe to approximately the level of November 1942, i.e., 41 divisions.

It is possible, however, that they may be forced to make further substantial reductions in the number of their reserve formations in Northwest Europe, and that their capacity to reinforce Northwest France rapidly may be decreased.

9. It is improbable that the strength of the German Air Force on the Western Front will be less than it has been during the last six months, i.e., about 1,000 first line aircraft of all types. In the event of a clear threat of a large scale landing by our forces in North France or in the Low Countries, the G.A.F. might be prepared to withdraw forces both from the Mediterranean and Russia to increase this strength to 1,500.

POSSIBLE AREAS FOR RAIDS:

10. Raids of which the primary object is to provoke an air battle would best be conducted against the Pas de Calais, but the nature of the defenses would be extremely costly to the assault forces.

POSSIBLE AREA FOR A LIMITED BRIDGEHEAD OPERATION:

11. The COTENTIN PENINSULA is the only possible objective for offensive operations of which the object is to remain on the Continent, as it is the only area with a short and easily defensible line within

U. S. SECRET
BRITISH MOST SECRET

reasonable distance of the beaches, and one which, at the same time, permits reasonable air support.

COMBINED COMMANDERS' PLAN FOR ASSAULT OF THE COTENTIN PENINSULA (OPERATION HADRIAN):

12. In November 1942 the Combined Commanders in London made a detailed study of the problems involved in an assault to seize and hold the COTENTIN PENINSULA, on the assumption that the Germans could bring up to 15 reserve divisions against the assaulting force during the first fourteen days. They concluded that the minimum requirements for success were:

    (a) Initial assault to be made by 5 brigade groups.

    (b) Assault to be supported by 10 parachute battalions and an airborne division, less one parachute brigade, for lifting which 847 transport aircraft would be required.

    (c) The total force, including assault forces, to be approximately 8 divisions.

    (d) The build-up of fighting troops to be substantially complete by evening of D + 1.

General Eisenhower did not himself see the plan, but his representatives collaborated in its preparation and fully concurred in the conclusion as to minimum requirements.

PRACTICABILITY OF OPERATION WITH FORCES SET OUT IN PARAGRAPH 5:

13. With the resources available in 1943, neither the size of the seaborne and airborne assault forces nor the rate of build up can approach the requirements of the Combined Commanders. It is clear, therefore, that no operation to seize and hold a footing in the COTENTIN PENINSULA has any prospect of success unless the German reserves have been very greatly reduced. Similar considerations would apply to a limited operation anywhere on the French coast.

14. There is, however, a good prospect that the German reserves will in fact be greatly reduced by August. It will, therefore, be necessary to make a detailed examination to determine:

    (a) Whether with the small assault forces available, it is possible successfully to assault the COTENTIN PENINSULA

    (b) If such an assault is practicable, to what level German reserves in Northwest France must be reduced in order to give our forces a reasonable chance of holding the PENINSULA.

15. It can, however, be said at once, without further examination, that:

(a) A minimum of four brigade groups in the initial assault will almost certainly be necessary.

(b) Shortage of seaborne assault troops will make provision of airborne troops the more necessary.

(c) To insure the success of the initial assault against the strong defenses of the French coast, and to reduce casualties among the assaulting troops, maximum allotment of support craft will be necessary.

(d) The limiting factor in the rate of subsequent build-up is availability of vehicle-carrying craft.

POSSIBILITY OF EXPLOITING A LIMITED OPERATION:

16. In view of the limited capacity of the port of CHERBOURG, operations to exploit success must be designed to secure additional port facilities so as to permit the maintenance of larger forces. Such operations might take the form of an advance by a mobile force, supported by seaborne and airborne assaults, either eastwards to capture the SEINE ports or southwestwards to secure the BRETON ports. In either instance, preliminary operations would be necessary to expand the bridgehead so as to obtain the use of the port of CAEN and the group of airfields in that area.

17. The practicability of undertaking such subsequent operations will, however, depend entirely on the state of German morale and on the extent to which they are able to concentrate reserves to oppose our further advance. The rapidity with which such operations can be undertaken will in any case depend on the rate at which we are able to reconstruct the ports and to build up our own forces and reserves. Even if German opposition is negligible, progress will be slow on account of our limited resources in vehicle-carrying craft suitable for landing over beaches.

OPERATIONS ON A LARGER SCALE TO TAKE
ADVANTAGE OF GERMAN DISINTEGRATION:

18. The return to the Continent in the case of German disintegration will be primarily an administrative problem. The Combined Commanders in London should therefore be instructed to make the necessary plans.

CONCLUSIONS:

19. (a) Unless the Germans are forced to reduce their reserves and

U. S. SECRET
BRITISH MOST SECRET

      their beach defenses in Northwest Europe substantially, no limited operation to seize and hold a footing in France is practicable with the resources likely to be available in 1943.

(b) A detailed plan for an operation to seize and hold the COTENTIN PENINSULA should be made on the basis of resources likely to be available.

(c) An examination should be made to determine to what level German reserves in Northwest Europe must sink in order to give such an operation a reasonable chance if success.

(d) Preparations should be made to mount the operation by August 1st, but the decision to put this plan into execution should be deferred until a reasonably firm estimate of the German reserves on that date can be made.

(e) Outline plans should be made for further operations to exploit success in the event of a breakdown in German morale, e.g., to extend the bridgehead to include CAEN and subsequently to secure either the NORTH SEINE or BRETON group of ports.

(f) The Combined Commanders in London should be instructed to draw up plans for a return to the Continent in the case of German disintegration.

(g) U. S. Government will have to provide:
    (1) Assault shipping and landing craft, manned by U. S. crews, to carry at least two brigade groups at assault scales.
    (2) Such additional parachute battalions and transport aircraft as may be necessary.

(h) All possible steps should be taken to provide:
    (1) Support craft for the assault.
    (2) The maximum number of improvised craft for carriage of vehicles.

                                        (Signed) C. E. LAMBE
                                                    G. M. STEWART
                                                      W. ELLIOT

U S SECRET
BRITISH MOST SECRET
C.C.S. 168   January 22, 1943

COMBINED CHIEFS OF STAFF

CONDUCT OF THE WAR IN THE PACIFIC THEATER IN 1943

Memorandum by Joint U. S. Chiefs of Staff

1. Japan has expanded the scope of her occupation so that it includes not only her former holdings of (1) Korea and Manchuria on the mainland of Asia and (2) a considerable part of China (including all of the coast), but in the past year, (3) all of Indo-China, Malaysia, Thailand, most of Burma, and as well, (4) all of the Philippines and (5) the Dutch East Indies.

2. The ultimate defeat of Japan proper will be accomplished by measures which greatly resemble those which would be effective against the British Isles—blockade (attack on ships and shipping), bombing (attack on forces, defenses, industries, and morale), and assault (attack via the sea). Of these measures, attacks on ships and shipping along enemy lines of communications are inherent in all offensive operations; it is our purpose during 1943 to work toward positions from which Japan can be attacked by land based air; assault on Japan is remote and may well not be found necessary. Allied offensive measures in 1943 comprise continued and intensified attacks on enemy ships and shipping, in the cutting or threatening to cut enemy lines of communication between Japan and Japanese holdings, and in attacks on enemy sea, air, and ground forces by obliging them to fight to retain their holdings and to maintain their lines of communication.

3. The scope and intensity of the Allied war effort in the Pacific during 1943, while conditioned on the premise that Germany is the principal enemy, requires that sufficient means be in hand surely to counter enemy potentialities (paragraph 4 to follow) and, further, must take care that the means in hand are actively employed to best advantage. The general capabilities of the Allied effort in the Pacific in 1943 comprise:

    (a) Keep Japan from further expansion, and from consolidating and exploiting her current holdings.

    (b) Maintain the vital Midway-Hawaii line (key to the Pacific).

    (c) Secure the line of communications to Australia and New Zealand.

U. S. SECRET
BRITISH MOST SECRET

 (d) Block enemy approaches to Australia (1) from the Northward via Rabaul; (2) from the Northwestward via the Malay barrier.

 (e) Attain positions which menace enemy line of communication with the Dutch East Indies, the Philippines, and the South China Sea.

 (f) Open the line of communications with China via Burma--in order to make use of Chinese geographical position (as to attack enemy line of communication in Formosa Straits and along the coast of China, perhaps to bomb Japan).

 (g) Make ready to support Russia in case of war with Japan.

 (h) Continue and intensify attrition of enemy strength by land, air, and sea (including submarine) action.

4. *Japan's potentialities* for offensive action during 1943 embrace:

 (a) The Maritime Provinces (Eastern Siberia)--Russia.

 (b) Alaska via the Aleutians.

 (c) The Midway-Hawaii line--key to the Pacific.

 (d) The Hawaii-Samoa-Fiji-New Caledonia line, which covers the line of communications to Australia and New Zealand.

 (e) Australia and New Zealand--via the Bismark Archipelago and/or the Solomons.

 (f) Australia--via the Malay barrier.

 (g) India--via Burma.

 (h) China.

 (i) *Of the above* (a) is static unless and until war takes place between Russia and Japan; (b) has proved, and will continue, unprofitable to Japan; (c) has been tried and may be tried again but is unlikely to succeed; (d) is now unprofitable except via the Gilbert and Ellice Islands toward Samoa (the Jaluit-Samoa line); (e) is now under contest by United Nations forces; (f) is unprofitable except to forestall Allied advance from Northwest Australia; (g) is feasible except that enemy position is already well extended; (h) same as (g)--profitable chiefly to forestall Allied action.

5. Allied seizure and occupation, now in progress, of the New Caledonia-New Guinea line has for objectives:

 (a) Security of the line of communications from U. S. to Australia and New Zealand;

U. S. SECRET
BRITISH MOST SECRET

    (b) Blocking of enemy approaches to Eastern Australia;

    (c) Points d'appui for further action;

    (d) Attrition of enemy forces which oppose our occupation.

6. Additional to the objectives attained by the seizure and occupation of the New Caledonia-New Guinea line (paragraph 5 above), the other feasible objectives for us appear to be:

    (a) Japan via the Maritime Provinces (Eastern Siberia) noted only for record to offset 4 (a) above.

    (b) Japan via the Aleutians and Kuriles--from Alaska.

    (c) Advance from Midway towards Truk-Guam line via Wake and Northwesterly Marshall Islands.

    (d) Advance on the Samoa-Jaluit line via Ellice and Gilbert Islands.

    (e) Advance from Rabaul area on Truk-Guam line.

    (f) Dutch East Indies via Malay barrier (as Timor).

    (g) Participation in ANAKIM.

    (h) *Of the above* (which are set down to match the items of paragraph 4 above):

        (a) Is merely potential unless and until war takes place between Japan and Russia;

        (b) Is unprofitable with means in sight in 1943 and is best undertaken, if at all, in connection with (a);

        (c) Is most useful, not only as to

            (1) Retention of initiative;

            (2) Partial counter to enemy potentialities of paragraph 4 (c); and, particularly,

            (3) To draw off enemy forces involved in holding Rabaul area;

        (d) Is effective

            (1) To forestall enemy potentialities in paragraph 4 (d);

            (2) To make the line of communications to Australia and New Zealand fully secure; and

            (3) To draw off enemy forces involved in Rabaul area;

        (e) Cannot be done until after consolidation of the Rabaul area upon completion of operations now in hand--see paragraph 5 above--but should, perhaps must, eventually be undertaken;

(f) Useful on limited scale
   (1) To counter enemy potentialities of paragraph 4 (f);
   (2) To draw off enemy forces elsewhere in the Pacific;
   (3) To employ forces available in Australia (after completion of paragraph 5) which would not otherwise be employable;
   N.B. - Attacks are not to be developed fully, as this might lead to extensive operations of the nature of frontal attacks.
(g) Not effective before November though forces contributed would likely have to be made available in October--but ANAKIM is of such importance in respect of its objective (bringing Chinese manpower and geographic position to bear on Japanese forces and positions) as to merit that priority which may be found indispensable to mount it.

7. Referring now to the general capabilities of Allied action listed in paragraph 3 above, set off against enemy potentialities in paragraph 4 above, we intend, as to the feasible objectives of paragraph 6 above-- additional to those of paragraph 5 above--to:
   (a) and (b) Make the Aleutians as secure as may be, which will implement 3 (a), (g), (h);
   N.B. - Germany can be expected to intensify pressure on Japan to attack Russia in Siberia (Maritime Provinces)
   (c) Undertake advance from Midway towards Truk-Guam line as practicable--to implement 3 (a), (b), (e), (h) and, particularly, when 6 (e) is undertaken;
   (d) Undertake advance along Samoa-Jaluit line to implement 3 (a), (c), (h);
   (e) Refrain from advance from Rabaul area towards Truk-Guam line unless and until forces are in hand to enable it to be carried through and followed up. Noted that it implements 3 (a), (b), (d) (1), (e), (h);
   (f) Undertake advance on the Malay barrier (as Timor) on limited scale to counter enemy capabilities and divert his forces-- to implement 3 (a), (d) (2), (e), (h);
   (g) Participate in ANAKIM as may be found indispensable to mounting it.

U. S. SECRET
BRITISH MOST SECRET
C.C.S. 169   January 22, 1943

COMBINED CHIEFS OF STAFF

PROPOSED ORGANIZATION OF COMMAND, CONTROL, PLANNING
AND TRAINING FOR OPERATIONS FOR A REENTRY TO THE
CONTINENT ACROSS THE CHANNEL, BEGINNING IN 1943

(Note by the Combined Staffs)

1. Strategic Basis: The Combined Chiefs of Staff agree that there is no chance of our being able to stage a large scale invasion of the Continent against unbroken opposition during 1943. Their policy is, however, that we should:
- (a) Undertake such limited operations as may be practicable with the forces available and
- (b) Assemble the strongest possible force (subject to certain prior commitments in other theaters) in constant readiness to reenter the Continent as soon as German resistance is weakened to the required extent.

2. The organization should therefore provide for:
- (a) Small scale amphibious operations, such as the progressive reoccupation of the Channel Islands.
  (Note: Raids are already adequately taken care of by the existing organization.)
- (b) The need to reenter the Continent with all available forces at the shortest possible notice in the event of a sudden and unexpected collapse of German resistance. The aim would be to seize critical political and military centers in Germany in the shortest possible time.
- (c) Operations to seize a bridgehead late in 1943, leading up to a rapid exploitation or
- (d) An invasion in force in 1944.

3. Need for a Directive: The first thing that is essential, whatever organization is set up, is a clear directive from the Combined Chiefs of Staff setting out the objects of the plans and the resources likely to be available. In this latter connection some inevitable difficulty arises from the fact that—except for the operation in paragraph

U. S. SECRET
BRITISH MOST SECRET

2 (a) – preparations for the other possible operations must be based, not on any given strength of forces available nor on any fixed estimate of enemy opposition to be encountered, but on the maximum forces that are likely to be available in the U. K. at any given time. Moreover, it is virtually impossible to fix a date, because that must depend entirely on the state of enemy resistance on the Continent.

All plans and preparations must therefore be extremely flexible.

4. Training: In order that training and preparation of the forces may not be unduly hampered by the maintenance of an unnecessarily high state of readiness, the Combined Chiefs of Staff should issue instructions on this point. In the first instance, the degree of notice might be fixed at three months. But planning for the operation described in paragraph 2 (b) above must be on the basis of immediate reentry into the Continent at the shortest possible notice with whatever resources are available at the time.

5. Principles of Command and Planning: It is suggested that 2 (a), small scale operations, such as the Channel Islands, should they be considered desirable either separately or as part of a larger operation, could adequately be dealt with by C.C.O.'s organization on the same lines as was the Dieppe raid.

6. As regards the larger operations in 2 (b), (c), and (d), the governing principle should be that the responsibility for planning and training should rest with, or under the direction of, the Commanders who will have to carry out the plans, who will be the same Commanders for all three operations. These should be designated at once.

7. Supreme Command: This raises the question of a Supreme Commander. It is considered that when the operations in 2 (b) to (d) become reasonably imminent, a Supreme Commander must be appointed. He should have a small combined staff of British and American officers of all three services, and under him will be subordinate commanders, air, land and sea, corresponding to the organization just approved for the operations in the Mediterranean.

It is considered desirable that the Supreme Commander should be appointed at once. If this is not feasible, his Chief of Staff or Deputy and a nucleus of the combined staff should be appointed immediately to give the necessary impetus and cohesion to planning.

8. The present "Round-up" Planning Staff: For some months a special

U. S. SECRET
BRITISH MOST SECRET

inter-Allied staff drawn from all three services has been in existence working together in one building in London, studying the problem and planning for a return to the Continent. In this way much specialized experience has been gained and planning has progressed far beyond the staff study stage. In particular, a great deal of administrative work has been done and measures--such as the acquisition and preparation of airfields--actually put in hand.

9. This special planning staff should be adapted to the new conditions and strengthened by the addition of American personnel. They should work, under the direction of the Supreme Commander (or his deputy until he is appointed), in conjunction with the nucleus of his combined staff in London.

Administrative planning will have to be done very largely by the normal administrative staffs in the Service Departments and in H.Q. E.T.O. U.S.A. These Headquarters should, however, appoint representatives to form, together with the Administrative Staff in Norfolk House, a joint administrative planning staff for the reentry to the Continent.

One of the first tasks of the Supreme Commander (or his deputy) should be to simplify the existing system of interdepartmental administrative planning which, at present, is unduly cumbersome.

U. S. SECRET
BRITISH MOST SECRET
C.C.S. 170   January 22, 1943

COMBINED CHIEFS OF STAFF

REPORT TO THE PRESIDENT AND PRIME MINISTER

Note by the Secretaries

In accordance with the directions of the Combined Chiefs of Staff at their 65th Meeting (Item 6), a draft report to the President and Prime Minister of the decisions reached subsequent to the submission of C.C.S. 153/1 is circulated herewith for approval.

V. DYKES,
J. R. DEANE,
Combined Secretariat

ENCLOSURE

DRAFT REPORT ON THE WORK OF THE CONFERENCE

In a previous memorandum (C.C.S. 155/1) the Combined Chiefs of Staff presented their proposals for the Conduct of the War in 1943. These proposals were in broad outline, and we have subsequently examined them and reached certain conclusions on points of detail. We have also studied a number of matters closely related to these proposals. The present memorandum contains a summary of what has been accomplished.

1. SECURITY OF SEA COMMUNICATIONS:

A close examination of the minimum escort requirements to maintain the sea communications of the United Nations has been completed (C.C.S. 160). In the course of this examination we have laid down certain scales of ocean-going escort vessels as the minimum acceptable. Our broad conclusion is that the minimum acceptable requirements of escort craft will not be met until about August or September 1943. We shall not be in a position to accomplish the destruction of submarines at a rate in excess of the production rate before the end of the year. If it is desired to provide escorts for offensive operations, the acceptance of increased losses must be balanced against the importance of the operations

U. S. SECRET
BRITISH MOST SECRET

in question. We have adopted the following resolutions on measures necessary to intensify the anti-U-boat war. (C.C.S. 65th Meeting, Item 1)

2. ASSISTANCE TO RUSSIA IN RELATION TO OTHER COMMITMENTS:

We have examined the extent of the shipments to Russia required to fulfill United States and British obligations throughout 1943 with a view to estimating the effect of these shipments on other commitments. Our conclusion is that, provided a shipping loss rate of not more than 2.4% per month can be relied on, it will be possible to meet full commitments by the end of the calendar year 1943; and we have approved a program of shipments on this basis subject to the proviso that supplies to Russia shall not be continued at prohibitive cost to the United Nations effort.

An essential point is that an agreed loss rate for 1943 shall be established so that all British and American calculations can be made on the same basis. We have accordingly directed the Combined Military Transportation Committee to make an agreed estimate.

We are agreed that in the preparation of the next Protocol with Russia (should this be necessary) to cover the period after July 1, 1943, a clause should be inserted to the effect that the commitments included in the Protocol may be reduced if the shipping losses or the necessities of other operations render their fulfillment prohibitive (C.C.S. 63rd Meeting, Item 1, and C.C.S. 162)

3. OPERATIONS IN THE MEDITERRANEAN:

(a) Operations for the Capture of Sicily.

We have carefully examined possible operations in the Mediterranean theater and we have recorded the following conclusions: (C.C.S. 66th Meeting, Item 2, and C.C.S. 161/1)

(1) To attack Sicily in 1943 with the favorable July moon as the target date.

(2) To instruct General Eisenhower to report not later than March 1: first, whether any insurmountable difficulty as to resources and training will cause the date of the assault to be delayed beyond the favorable July moon; and, secondly, in that event to confirm that the date will not be later than the favorable August moon.

(3) That the following should be the Command set-up for the operation:

U. S. SECRET
BRITISH MOST SECRET

> > a. General Eisenhower to be in Supreme Command with General Alexander as Deputy Commander-in-Chief, responsible for the detailed planning and preparation and for the execution of the actual operation when launched.
> > b. Admiral Cunningham to be Naval Commander, and Air Chief Marshal Tedder the Air Commander.
> > c. Recommendations for the officers to be appointed Western and Eastern Task Force Commanders to be submitted in due course by General Eisenhower
>
> (4) That General Eisenhower should be instructed to set up forthwith, after consultation with General Alexander, a special operational and administrative staff, with its own Chief of Staff, for planning and preparing the operation.
>
> The necessary directive to General Eisenhower conveying the above decisions has been drafted.

(b) Cover Plans:

We intend to instruct the appropriate agencies in Washington and London and the Commander-in-Chief, Allied Expeditionary Force in North Africa, to draw up a comprehensive cover plan for the Mediterranean. The possibility of carrying out feints or minor operations in the Eastern Mediterranean will be examined.

(c) Command in the Mediterranean Theater:

We have agreed to the following Command arrangements in the Mediterranean: (C.C.S. 63rd Meeting, Item 4 and C.C.S. 163)

> (1) Sea:
>
> For Operation HUSKY the Naval Commander Force X will assume the title of Commander-in-Chief, Mediterranean. The present Commander-in-Chief, Mediterranean, will be designated Commander-in-Chief, Levant. The boundary between the two Commands will be drawn from Zanti to Bardia. The Commander-in-Chief, Mediterranean, will, however, be responsible for naval matters which affect the Mediterranean as a whole.

U. S. SECRET
BRITISH MOST SECRET

    (2) Land:

    At a moment to be determined after the British 8th Army has crossed the Tunisian border, General Alexander will become Deputy Commander-in-Chief to General Eisenhower, the 8th Army at the same time being transferred to General Eisenhower's command. Subject to the concurrence of General Eisenhower, General Alexander's primary task will be to command the Allied forces on the Tunisian front with a small Headquarters of his own provided from the Middle East. After the conclusion of these operations, he will take charge of Operation HUSKY. The boundary between the North African and Middle East Commands will be the Tunisian-Tripolitania frontier.

    (3) Air:

    We have agreed that Air Chief Marshal Sir Arthur Tedder shall be appointed Air Commander-in-Chief of the whole Mediterranean theater with his Headquarters at Algiers. Under him will be the Air Officer Commanding in Chief, Northwest Africa (General Spaatz), and the Air Officer Commanding in Chief, Middle East (Air Chief Marshal Sir Sholto Douglas). We have defined the relationship and mutual responsibilities of the Air Commander-in-Chief, Mediterranean, and the Commander-in-Chief, Allied Expeditionary Forces in Northwest Africa, and we have laid down certain principles for the organization of the Mediterranean Air Command subject to any minor changes which the Air Commander-in-Chief may find necessary after his appointment.

(d) The Bomber Offensive from North Africa:

We have laid down the following as the objects of the bomber offensive from North Africa in order of time: (C.C.S. 159/1)

    (1) The furtherance of operations for the eviction of all Axis Forces from Africa.

    (2) When (1) has been achieved, infliction of the heaviest possible losses on the Axis Air and Naval Forces in preparation for HUSKY, including bombing required by cover plans.

    (3) The direct furtherance of Operation HUSKY.

U. S. SECRET
BRITISH MOST SECRET

(4) The destruction of the oil refineries at Ploesti.

So far as is possible without prejudice to the achievement of objects (1), (2), and (3) above, bombing objectives will be chosen with a view to weakening the Italian will to continue the war

4. OPERATIONS IN AND FROM THE UNITED KINGDOM:

(a) The Operation of Air Forces from the United Kingdom:

We have agreed that the United States Heavy Bombardment Units in the United Kingdom shall operate under the strategical direction of the British Chief of the Air Staff. Under this general direction the United States Commanding General will decide upon the technique and method to be employed (C.C.S. 65th Meeting, Item 2)

We have agreed upon a directive to be issued to the British Commander-in-Chief Bomber Command and to the Commanding General United States Air Forces in the United Kingdom to govern the bomber offensive from the United Kingdom; a copy of this directive is at Annex 'A' (C.C.S. 166/1/D)

(b) BOLERO

(c) Amphibious Operations in 1943 from the United Kingdom: (C.C.S. 167 and 169 and C.C.S. 68th Meeting, Item 2)

We have examined the problem of amphibious operations from the United Kingdom in 1943 There are three types of operation for which plans and preparations must now be made:

(1) Raids with the primary object of provoking an air battle and causing enemy losses

(2) Operations with the object of seizing and holding a bridgehead and, if the state of German morale and the strength of her resources permit, of exploiting successes

(3) A return to the Continent to take advantage of German disintegration

Plans and preparations for (1) above will proceed as at present An attack on the Channel Islands is an example of the type of operation which we have in mind

We propose to prepare for an operation against the Cotentin Peninsula with resources which will be available, the target date being set at August 1, 1943. This operation comes under

U. S. SECRET
BRITISH MOST SECRET

type (2) above.

We have agreed to establish forthwith a Combined Staff under a British Chief of Staff until such time as a Supreme Commander is appointed. A directive to govern the planning is in course of preparation. We intend to include in this directive provision for a return to the Continent under (3) above with the forces which will be available for the purpose in the United Kingdom month by month. The directive will also make provision for the planning of an invasion of the Continent in force in 1944

5. PACIFIC AND FAR EAST THEATER:

   (a) Operations in the Pacific Theater:

   (C.C.S. 168 and C.C.S 67th Meeting, Item 1)

   The following is an outline of the operations which it is intended to carry out in the Pacific in conformity with the provisions of our previous report (C.C.S. 155/1):

   (1) Operations to make the Aleutians as secure as may be.
   (2) An advance from Midway towards Truk Guam as practicable and particularly in conjunction with the operations now in hand for the capture of Rabaul.
   (3) An advance along the line Samoa-Jaluit.
   (4) An advance on the Malay Barrier (as Timor) on a limited scale to counter enemy capabilities and divert his forces.
   (5) It is not intended to advance from the Rabaul area towards the Truk-Guam line unless and until forces are in hand to enable the advance to be carried through and followed up.

   (b) Reconquest of Burma:

   We have approved November 15, 1943, as the provisional date for the ANAKIM assault. It will be necessary to decide in July 1943 whether to undertake or to postpone the operation. (C.C.S. 65th Meeting, Item 4)

   We have prepared a provisional schedule of the forces required for the operation and have investigated the possibility of their provision. The land and sea forces can be provided. The provision of naval forces, assault shipping, landing craft and shipping cannot be guaranteed so far in advance and must

U. S. SECRET
BRITISH MOST SECRET

        depend upon the situation existing in the late summer of 1943. (C.C.S. 164)

6.   THE AXIS OIL POSITION:

We have had laid before us certain information from British sources on the Axis oil position (C.C.S. 158). It is believed that additional information available in Washington may modify the conclusions which have been drawn by the British. We have accordingly directed the Combined Intelligence Committee to submit as early as possible an agreed assessment of the Axis oil situation based on the latest information available from both British and United States sources. In the meanwhile, we have taken note that the Axis oil situation is so restricted that it is decidedly advantageous that bombing attacks on the sources of Axis oil, namely, the Rumanian oil fields and oil traffic via the Danube, and the synthetic and producer gas plants in Germany, be undertaken as soon as other commitments allow (C.C.S. 62nd Meeting, Item 1).

7.   NAVAL AND AIR COMMAND IN WEST AFRICA:

We have agreed upon the following naval and air arrangements to cover the French West African Coast (C.C.S. 61st Meeting, Item 3):

   (a) That the West African Coast (offshore) from Cape Bojador (Rio d'Oro) southward shall be an area under command of a British Naval Officer for naval operations and of a British Air Officer for air operations in cooperation with naval forces.

   (b) That subject to (a) a sub-area extending from Cape Bojador to the western boundary of Sierra Leone and all forces operating therein shall be under French Command.

   (c) That in the French sub-area the intention will be to enable French air units to take over air duties as rapidly as equipment and training permit.

8.   TURKEY:

We have agreed upon the administrative measures necessary to give effect to the decision that all matters connected with Turkey should be handled by the British (C.C.S. 63rd Meeting, Item 2).

U. S. SECRET
BRITISH MOST SECRET
C.C.S. 170/1								January 23, 1943

COMBINED CHIEFS OF STAFF

REPORT TO THE PRESIDENT AND PRIME MINISTER

Memorandum by the Combined Chiefs of Staff

In a previous memorandum (C.C.S. 155/1) the Combined Chiefs of Staff presented their proposals for the Conduct of the War in 1943. These proposals were in broad outline and we have subsequently examined them and reached certain conclusions on points of detail. We have also studied a number of matters closely related to these proposals. The present memorandum contains a summary of what has been accomplished.

1. SECURITY OF SEA COMMUNICATIONS:

A close examination of the minimum escort requirements to maintain the sea communications of the United Nations has been completed (C.C.S. 160). In the course of this examination we have laid down certain scales of ocean-going escort vessels as the minimum acceptable. Our broad conclusion is that the minimum acceptable requirements of escort craft will not be met until about August or September 1943. We ought not to count on the destruction of submarines at a rate in excess of the production rate before the end of the year. If it is desired to provide escorts for offensive operations, the acceptance of increased losses must be balanced against the importance of the operations in question. We have adopted certain resolutions on measures necessary to intensify the anti U-boat war (C.C.S. 65th Meeting, Item 1).

2. ASSISTANCE TO RUSSIA IN RELATION TO OTHER COMMITMENTS:

We have examined the extent of the shipments to Russia required to fulfill United States and British obligations throughout 1943 with a view to estimating the effect of these shipments on other commitments. Our conclusion is that, provided a shipping loss rate of not more than 2.4 percent per month can be relied on, it will be possible to meet full commitments by the end of the calendar year 1943, and we have approved a program of shipments on this basis subject to the proviso that supplies to Russia shall not be continued at prohibitive cost to the United Nations effort.

An essential point is that an agreed loss rate for 1943 shall be

U. S. SECRET
BRITISH MOST SECRET

established so that all British and American calculations can be made on the same basis. We have accordingly directed the Combined Military Transportation Committee to make an agreed estimate.

We are agreed that in the preparation of the next Protocol with Russia (should this be necessary) to cover the period after July 1, 1943, a clause should be inserted to the effect that the commitments included in the Protocol may be reduced if the shipping losses or the necessities of other operations render their fulfilment prohibitive (C.C.S. 63rd Meeting, Item 1, and C.C.S. 162).

3. OPERATIONS IN THE MEDITERRANEAN:
   (a) Operations for the Capture of Sicily:
   We have carefully examined possible operations in the Mediterranean theater and we have recorded the following conclusions: (C.C.S. 66th Meeting, Item 2, and C.C.S. 161/1.)
   (1) To attack Sicily in 1943 with the favorable July moon as the target date.
   (2) To instruct General Eisenhower to report not later than March 1st: firstly, whether any insurmountable difficulty as to resources and training will cause the date of the assault to be delayed beyond the favorable July moon; and, secondly, in that event to confirm that the date will not be later than the favorable August moon.
   (3) That the following should be the Command set-up for the operation:
      <u>a</u>. General Eisenhower to be in Supreme Command with General Alexander as Deputy Commander-in-Chief, responsible for the detailed planning and preparation and for the execution of the actual operation when launched.
      <u>b</u>. Admiral Cunningham to be Naval Commander, and Air Chief Marshal Tedder the Air Commander.
      <u>c</u>. Recommendations for the officers to be appointed Western and Eastern Task Force Commanders to be submitted in due course by General Eisenhower.
   (4) That General Eisenhower should be instructed to set up forthwith, after consultation with General Alexander, a special operational and administrative staff, with its own Chief of Staff, for planning and preparing the operation.

U. S. SECRET
BRITISH MOST SECRET

> The necessary directive to General Eisenhower conveying the above decisions has been drafted.
>
> (b) Cover Plans:
>
> We intend to instruct the appropriate agencies in Washington and London and the Commander-in-Chief, Allied Expeditionary Force in North Africa, to draw up a comprehensive cover plan for the Mediterranean. The possibility of carrying out feints or minor operations in the Eastern Mediterranean will be examined.
>
> (c) Command in the Mediterranean Theater:
>
> We have agreed to the following Command arrangements in the Mediterranean: (C.C.S. 63rd Meeting, Item 4, and C.C.S. 163)
>
> (1) Sea:
>
> For operation HUSKY the Naval Commander Force X will assume the title of Commander-in-Chief, Mediterranean. The present Commander-in-Chief, Mediterranean, will be designated Commander-in-Chief, Levant. The boundary between the two Commands will be drawn from Zanti to Bardia. The Commander-in-Chief, Mediterranean, will, however, be responsible for naval matters which affect the Mediterranean as a whole.
>
> (2) Land:
>
> At a moment to be determined after the British 8th Army has crossed the Tunisian border, General Alexander will become Deputy Commander-in-Chief to General Eisenhower, the 8th Army at the same time being transferred to General Eisenhower's command. Subject to the concurrence of General Eisenhower, General Alexander's primary task will be to command the Allied forces on the Tunisian front with a small Headquarters of his own provided from the Middle East and after the conclusion of these operations to take charge of Operation HUSKY. The boundary between the North African and Middle East Commands will be the Tunisian-Tripolitania frontier.
>
> (3) Air:
>
> We have agreed that Air Chief Marshal Sir Arthur Tedder shall be appointed Air Commander-in-Chief of the whole

U. S. SECRET
BRITISH MOST SECRET

> Mediterranean theater with his headquarters at Algiers. Under him will be the Air Officer Commanding in Chief, Northwest Africa (General Spaatz), and the Air Officer Commanding in Chief, Middle East (Air Chief Marshal Sir Sholto Douglas). We have defined the relationship and mutual responsibilities of the Air Commander-in-Chief, Mediterranean, and the Commander-in-Chief Allied Expeditionary Forces in Northwest Africa, and we have laid down certain principles for the organization of the Mediterranean Air Command subject to any minor changes which the Air Commander-in-Chief may find necessary after his appointment.

> (d) The Bomber Offensive from North Africa:
> We have laid down the following as the objects of the bomber offensive from North Africa in order of time (C.C.S. 159/1):
> (1) The furtherance of operations for the eviction of all Axis Forces from Africa.
> (2) When (1) has been achieved, infliction of the heaviest possible losses on the Axis Air and Naval forces in preparation for HUSKY, including bombing required by cover plans.
> (3) The direct furtherance of Operation HUSKY.
> (4) The destruction of the oil refineries at Ploesti.
> So far as is possible without prejudice to the achievement of objects (1), (2) and (3) above, bombing objectives will be chosen with a view to weakening the Italian will to continue the war.

4. OPERATIONS IN AND FROM THE UNITED KINGDOM:
   (a) The Operation of Air Forces from the United Kingdom:
   We have agreed that the United States Heavy Bombardment Units in the United Kingdom shall operate under the strategical direction of the British Chief of the Air Staff. Under this general direction the United States Commanding General will decide upon the technique and method to be employed (C.C.S. 65th Meeting, Item 2).
   We have agreed upon a directive (C.C.S. 166/1/D) to be issued to the British Commander-in-Chief Bomber Command and to the

U. S. SECRET
BRITISH MOST SECRET

>   Commanding General United States Air Forces in the United Kingdom.

> (b) BOLERO:
>   (C.C.S. 172 and C.C.S. 68th Meeting, Item 1.)
>   A study has been made of the shipping capabilities for BOLERO build-up in 1943.
>   With the data available at the conference and making a number of assumptions which are set out in full in C.C.S. 172, Enclosure "C", we calculate that the U. S. forces as shown in the following table will be available for Continental operations in the U. K. on the dates shown. The figures given in the last column include the build-up of the air contingent to 172,000.

	Division	Total Numbers Equipped
By August 15	4	384,000
September 15	7	509,000
October 15	9	634,000
November 15	12	759,000
December 31	15	938,000

>   This is based on (1) the figures of 50,000 troops per division with supporting troops; (2) 45 days allowance between sailing date and availability date.
>   As the movement proceeds the over-all number of men per division will decrease and by the end of the year it may be down to 40,000, in which case the number of divisions available on December 31st may be 19 instead of 15. The number of divisions earlier in the year is unlikely to be increased.

> (c) Amphibious Operations in 1943 from the United Kingdom:
>   (C.C.S. 167 and C.C.S. 68th Meeting, Item 2.)
>   We have examined the problem of amphibious operations from the United Kingdom in 1943. There are three types of operation for which plans and preparations must now be made:
>   (1) Raids with the primary object of provoking air battles and causing enemy losses.
>   (2) Operations with the object of seizing and holding a bridgehead and, if the state of German morale and resources permit, of exploiting successes.

U. S. SECRET
BRITISH MOST SECRET

  (3) A return to the Continent to take advantage of German disintegration.

  Plans and preparations for (1) above will proceed as at present. An attack on the Channel Islands is an example of the type of operation which we have in mind.

  We propose to prepare for an operation against the Cotentin Peninsula with resources which will be available, the target date being set at August 1, 1943. This operation comes under type (2) above.

  We have agreed to establish forthwith a Combined Staff under a British Chief of Staff until such time as a Supreme Commander is appointed. A directive to govern the planning is in course of preparation. We intend to include in this directive provision for a return to the Continent under (3) above with the forces which will be available for the purpose in the United Kingdom month by month. The directive will also make provision for the planning of an invasion of the Continent in force in 1944.

5.   PACIFIC AND FAR EAST THEATER:

 (a) Operations in the Pacific Theater:

  (C.C.S. 168 and C.C.S. 67th Meeting, Item 1.)

  The following is an outline of the operations which it is intended to carry out in the Pacific in conformity with the provisions of our previous report (C.C.S. 155/1):

  (1) Operations to make the Aleutians as secure as may be.

  (2) An advance from Midway towards Truk-Guam as practicable and particularly in conjunction with the operations now in hand for the capture of Rabaul.

  (3) An advance along the line Samoa-Jaluit.

  (4) An advance on the Malay Barrier (as Timor) on a limited scale to counter enemy capabilities and divert his forces.

  (5) It is not intended to advance from the Rabaul area towards the Truk-Guam line unless and until forces are in hand to enable the advance to be carried through and followed up.

U. S. SECRET
BRITISH MOST SECRET

    (b) Reconquest of Burma:

        We have approved November 15, 1943, as the provisional date for the ANAKIM assault. It will be necessary to decide in July 1943 whether to undertake or postpone the operation (C.C.S. 65th Meeting, Item 4).

        We have prepared a provisional schedule of the forces required for the operation and have investigated the possibility of their provision. The land and air forces can be provided. The provision of naval forces, assault shipping, landing craft and shipping cannot be guaranteed so far in advance and must depend upon the situation existing in the late summer of 1943 (C.C.S. 164).

6. THE AXIS OIL POSITION:

    We have laid before us certain information from British sources on the Axis oil position (C.C.S. 158). It is believed that additional information available in Washington may modify the conclusions which have been drawn by the British. We have accordingly directed the Combined Intelligence Committee to submit as early as possible an agreed assessment of the Axis oil situation based on the latest information available from both British and United States sources. In the meanwhile, we have taken note that the Axis oil situation is so restricted that it is decidedly advantageous that bombing attacks on the sources of Axis oil, namely, the Rumanian oil fields and oil traffic via the Danube, and the synthetic and producer gas plants in Germany, be undertaken as soon as other commitments allow (C.C.S. 62nd Meeting, Item 1).

7. NAVAL AND AIR COMMAND IN WEST AFRICA:

    We have agreed upon the following naval and air arrangements to cover the French West African Coast (C.C.S. 61st Meeting, Item 3):

    (a) That the West African Coast (offshore) from Cape Bojador (Rio d'Oro) southward shall be an area under command of a British Naval Officer for naval operations and of a British Air Officer for air operations in cooperation with naval forces.

    (b) That subject to (1) a sub-area extending from Cape Bojardor to the western boundary of Sierra Leone and all forces operating therein shall be under French Command.

    (c) That in the French sub-area the intention will be to enable

U. S. SECRET
BRITISH MOST SECRET

French air units to take over air duties as rapidly as equipment and training permit.

8. TURKEY:

We have agreed upon the administrative measures necessary to give effect to the decision that all matters connected with Turkey should be handled by the British (C.C.S. 63rd Meeting, Item 2)

U. S. SECRET
BRITISH MOST SECRET
C.C.S. 170/2   January 23, 1943

COMBINED CHIEFS OF STAFF

SYMBOL

Final Report to the President and Prime Minister
Summarizing Decisions by the Combined Chiefs of Staff

In a previous memorandum (C.C.S. 155/1) the Combined Chiefs of Staff presented their proposals for the Conduct of the War in 1943. These proposals were in broad outline, and we have subsequently examined them and reached certain conclusions on points of detail. We have also studied a number of matters closely related to these proposals. The present memorandum contains a summary of what has been accomplished.

1. SECURITY OF SEA COMMUNICATIONS:

A close examination of the minimum escort requirements to maintain the sea communications of the United Nations has been completed (C.C.S. 160) In the course of this examination we have laid down certain scales of ocean-going escort vessels as the minimum acceptable. Our broad conclusion is that the minimum acceptable requirements of escort craft will not be met until about August or September 1943. We ought not to count on the destruction of U-boats at a rate in excess of the production rate before the end of the year. If it is desired to provide escorts for offensive operations, the acceptance of increased losses must be balanced against the importance of the operations in question. We have adopted certain resolutions on measures necessary to intensify the anti-U-boat war. (C.C.S. 65th Meeting, Item 1.)

2. ASSISTANCE TO RUSSIA IN RELATION TO OTHER COMMITMENTS:

We have examined the extent of the shipments to Russia required to fulfill United States and British obligations throughout 1943 with a view to estimating the effect of these shipments on other commitments Our conclusion is that, provided a shipping loss rate of not more than 2.4 percent per month can be relied on, it will be possible to meet full commitments by the end of the calendar year 1943; and we have approved a program of shipments on this basis subject to the proviso that supplies to Russia shall not be continued at prohibitive cost to the United Nations' effort.

An essential point is that an agreed loss rate for 1943 shall be

U S SECRET
BRITISH MOST SECRET

established so that all British and American calculations can be made on the same basis. We have accordingly directed the Combined Military Transportation Committee to make an agreed estimate.

We are agreed that in the preparation of the next Protocol with Russia (should this be necessary) to cover the period after July 1, 1943, a clause should be inserted to the effect that the commitments included in the Protocol may be reduced if the shipping losses or the necessities of other operations render their fulfilment prohibitive. (C.C.S. 63rd Meeting, Item 1, and C.C.S. 162.)

3. OPERATIONS IN THE MEDITERRANEAN:
   (a) Operations For The Capture of Sicily:
   We have carefully examined possible operations in the Mediterranean theater and we have recorded the following conclusions (C.C.S. 66th Meeting, Item 2, and C.C.S. 161/1).
   (1) To attack Sicily in 1943 with the favorable July* moon as the target date.
   (2) To instruct General Eisenhower to report not later than March 1st: firstly, whether any insurmountable difficulty as to resources and training will cause the date of the assault to be delayed beyond the favorable July moon, and, secondly, in that event to confirm that the date will not be later than the favorable August moon.
   (3) That the following should be the Command set up for the operation:
      a. General Eisenhower to be in Supreme Command with General Alexander as Deputy Commander-in-Chief, charged with the detailed planning and preparation and with the execution of the actual operation when launched.
      b. Admiral Cunningham to be Naval Commander, and Air Chief Marshal Tedder the Air Commander.

* We have agreed that without prejudicing the July date for the operation, an intense effort will be made during the next three weeks to achieve by contrivance and ingenuity the favorable June moon period as the date for the operation. If at the end of the three weeks our efforts have proved successful, the instructions to General Eisenhower will be modified accordingly.

U. S. SECRET
BRITISH MOST SECRET

<blockquote>

<blockquote>

c. Recommendations for the officers to be appointed Western and Eastern Task Force Commanders to be submitted in due course by General Eisenhower.

</blockquote>

(4) That General Eisenhower should be instructed to set up forthwith, after consultation with General Alexander, a special operational and administrative staff, with its own Chief of Staff, for planning and preparing the operation.

</blockquote>

The necessary directive to General Eisenhower conveying the above decisions has been drafted.

(b) Cover Plans:

We intend to instruct the appropriate agencies in Washington and London and the Commander-in-Chief, Allied Expeditionary Force in North Africa, to draw up a comprehensive cover plan for the Mediterranean. The possibility of carrying out feints or minor operations in the Eastern Mediterranean will be examined.

(c) Command in the Mediterranean Theater:

We have agreed to the following Command arrangements in the Mediterranean: (C.C.S. 63rd Meeting, Item 4 and C.C.S. 163).

<blockquote>

(1) Sea:

For operation HUSKY the Naval Commander Force X will assume the title of Commander-in-Chief, Mediterranean. The present Commander-in-Chief, Mediterranean, will be designated Commander-in-Chief, Levant. The boundary between the two Commands will be determined later. The Commander-in-Chief, Mediterranean, will, however, be responsible for naval matters which affect the Mediterranean as a whole.

(2) Land:

At a moment to be determined after the British 8th Army has crossed the Tunisian border, General Alexander will become Deputy Commander-in-Chief to General Eisenhower, the 8th Army at the same time being transferred to General Eisenhower's command. Subject to the concurrence of General Eisenhower, General Alexander's primary task will be to command the Allied forces on the Tunisian

</blockquote>

U. S. SECRET
BRITISH MOST SECRET

        front with a small Headquarters of his own provided from the Middle East and after the conclusion of these operations to take charge of Operation HUSKY. The boundary between the North African and Middle East Commands will be the Tunisian-Tripolitania frontier.

   (3) Air:

        We have agreed that Air Chief Marshal Sir Arthur Tedder shall be appointed Air Commander-in-Chief of the whole Mediterranean theater with his Headquarters at Algiers. Under him will be the Air Officer Commanding in Chief, Northwest Africa (General Spaatz), and the Air Officer Commanding in Chief, Middle East (Air Chief Marshal Sir Sholto Douglas). We have defined the relationship and mutual responsibilities of the Air Commander-in-Chief, Mediterranean and the Commander-in-Chief Allied Expeditionary Forces in Northwest Africa, and we have laid down certain principles for the organization of the Mediterranean Air Command subject to any minor changes which the Air Commander-in-Chief may find necessary after his appointment.

(d) The Bomber Offensive from North Africa:

We have laid down the following as the objects of the bomber offensive from North Africa in order of time (C.C.S. 159/1):

   (1) The furtherance of operations for the eviction of all Axis Forces from Africa.

   (2) When (1) has been achieved, infliction of the heaviest possible losses on the Axis Air and Naval forces in preparation for HUSKY, including bombing required by cover plans.

   (3) The direct furtherance of Operation HUSKY.

   (4) The destruction of the oil refineries at Ploesti.

So far as is possible without prejudice to the achievement of objects (1), (2), and (3) above, bombing objectives will be chosen with a view to weakening the Italian will to continue the war.

U. S. SECRET
BRITISH MOST SECRET

4. OPERATIONS IN AND FROM THE UNITED KINGDOM:
   (a) The Operation of Air Forces from the United Kingdom:
   We have agreed that the United States Heavy Bombardment Units in the United Kingdom shall operate under the strategical direction of the British Chief of the Air Staff. Under this general direction the United States Commanding General will decide upon the technique and method to be employed. (C.C.S. 65th Meeting, Item 2.)
   We have agreed upon a directive (C.C.S. 166/1/D) to be issued to the British Commander-in-Chief Bomber Command and to the Commanding General United States Air Forces in the United Kingdom.
   (b) BOLERO:
   (C.C.S. 172 and C.C.S. 68th Meeting, Item 1)
   A study has been made of the shipping capabilities for BOLERO build-up in 1943.
   With the date available at the conference and making a number of assumptions which are set out in full in C.C.S. 172, Enclosure "C", we calculate that the U. S. Forces as shown in the following table will be available for Continental operations in the U. K. on the dates shown. The figures given in the last column include the build-up of the air contingent to 172,000. They may be regarded as the minimum, and every effort will be made to increase the number of trained and equipped divisions in the United Kingdom by August 15th.

	Division	Total Numbers Equipped
By August 15	4	384,000
By September 15	7	509,000
By October 15	9	634,000
By November 15	12	759,000
By December 31	15	938,000

This is based on (1) the figures of 50,000 troops per division with supporting troops; (2) 45 days allowance between sailing date and availability date.
As the movement proceeds the over-all number of men per division will decrease and by the end of the year it may be

U. S. SECRET
BRITISH MOST SECRET

down to 40,000 in which case the number of divisions available on December 31st may be 19 instead of 15. The number of divisions earlier in the year is unlikely to be increased.

(c) Amphibious Operations in 1943 from the United Kingdom:
(C.C.S. 167 and 169 and C.C.S. 68th Meeting, Item 2.)

We have examined the problem of amphibious operations from the United Kingdom in 1943. There are three types of operation for which plans and preparations must now be made:

(1) Raids with the primary object of provoking air battles and causing enemy losses.

(2) Operations with the object of seizing and holding a bridgehead and, if the state of German morale and resources permit, of vigorously exploiting successes.

(3) A return to the Continent to take advantage of German disintegration.

Plans and preparations for (1) above will proceed as at present. An attack on the Channel Islands is an example of the type of operation which we have in mind.

We propose to prepare for an operation against the Cotentin Peninsula with resources which will be available, the target date being set at August 1, 1943. This operation comes under type (2) above.

We have agreed to establish forthwith a Combined Staff under a British Chief of Staff until such time as a British Supreme Commander, with an American Deputy Commander, is appointed. A directive to govern the planning is in course of preparation. We intend to include in this directive provision for a return to the Continent under (3) above with the forces which will be available for the purpose in the United Kingdom month by month.

9. PACIFIC AND FAR EAST THEATER:

(a) Operations in the Pacific Theater:
(C.C.S. 168 and C.C.S. 67th Meeting, Item 1.)

The following is an outline of the operations which it is intended to carry out in the Pacific in conformity with the provisions of our previous report (C.C.S. 155/1):

(1) Operations to make the Aleutians as secure as may be,

U. S. SECRET
BRITISH MOST SECRET

      (2) An advance from Midway towards Truk-Guam as practicable and particularly in conjunction with the operations now in hand for the capture of Rabaul.

      (3) An advance along the line Samoa-Jaluit.

      (4) An advance on the Malay Barrier (as Timor) on a limited scale to counter enemy capabilities and divert his forces.

      (5) It is not intended to advance from the Rabaul area towards the Truk-Guam line unless and until forces are in hand to enable the advance to be carried through and followed up.

  (b) Support of China:

      (1) Immediate Operations:

      Subsequent to the operations now in progress which are aimed at the capture of Akyab, a limited advance from Assam will be carried out to gain bridgeheads for further operations; to improve the air transport route to China by enabling aircraft to fly at lower altitudes; and, if Chinese cooperation is available, to gain ground for additional airfields and to extend the air warning system.

      (2) Operations In China:

      In order to support the Chinese war effort, to provide means for intensifying attacks on Japanese shipping, and to strike at Japan herself when opportunity offers, it is intended to improve air transportation into China by supplying additional transport aircraft, and to build up the U. S. Air Forces now operating in China to the maximum extent that logistical limitations and other important claims will permit. We hope that more sustained operations with increased Air Forces may begin in the spring, and we regard this development as of great importance in the general scheme.

      (3) Reconquest of Burma and Reopening of The Burma Road:

      We have approved November 15, 1943, as the provisional date for the ANAKIM assault. It will be necessary to decide in July 1943 whether to undertake or to postpone the operation (C.C.S. 65th Meeting, Item 4).

      We have prepared a provisional schedule of the forces

U S SECRET
BRITISH MOST SECRET

    required for the operation and have investigated the possibility of their provision. The land and air forces can be provided. The provision of naval forces, assault shipping, landing craft and shipping cannot be guaranteed so far in advance and must depend upon the situation existing in the late summer of 1943 (C.C.S. 164).

6. THE AXIS OIL POSITION:

  We have had laid before us certain information from British sources on the Axis oil position (C.C.S. 158). It is believed that additional information available in Washington may modify the conclusions which have been drawn by the British. We have accordingly directed the Combined Intelligence Committee to submit as early as possible an agreed assessment of the Axis oil situation based on the latest information available from both British and United States sources. In the meanwhile, we have taken note that the Axis oil situation is so restricted that it is decidedly advantageous that bombing attacks on the sources of Axis oil, namely, the Rumanian oil fields and oil traffic via the Danube, and the synthetic and producer gas plants in Germany, be undertaken as soon as other commitments allow (C.C.S. 62nd Meeting, Item 1).

7. NAVAL AND AIR COMMAND IN WEST AFRICA:

  We have agreed upon the following naval and air arrangements to cover the French West African Coast (C.C.S. 61st Meeting, Item 3):

  (a) That the West African Coast (offshore) from Cape Bojador (Rio d'Oro) southward shall be an area under command of a British Naval Officer for naval operations and of a British Air Officer for air operations in cooperation with naval forces.

  (b) That subject to (a) a sub-area extending from Cape Bojador to the western boundary of Sierra Leone and all forces operating therein shall be under French Command

  (c) That in the French sub-area the intention will be to enable French air units to take over air duties as rapidly as equipment and training permit

8. TURKEY:

  We have agreed upon the administrative measures necessary to give effect to the decision that all matters connected with Turkey should be handled by the British (C.C.S. 63rd Meeting, Item 2).

U. S. SECRET
BRITISH MOST SECRET

C.C.S. 171

January 22, 1943

COMBINED CHIEFS OF STAFF

DIRECTIVE

OPERATION HUSKY

Enclosed is a draft directive to General Eisenhower regarding Operation HUSKY which is submitted to the Combined Chiefs of Staff for approval.

            V. DYKES,
            J. R. DEANE,
            Combined Secretariat.

ENCLOSURE

DRAFT

The Combined Chiefs of Staff have resolved that an attack against Sicily will be launched in 1943.

The Combined Chiefs of Staff have further agreed that the following command set-up shall be established for the operation:

(a) You are to be the Supreme Commander with General Alexander as Deputy Commander-in-Chief, responsible for the detailed planning and preparation and for the execution of the actual operation when launched.

(b) Admiral of the Fleet Cunningham is to be the Naval Commander and Air Chief Marshal Tedder the Air Commander.

You will submit to the Combined Chiefs of Staff your recommendations for the Officers to be appointed Western and Eastern Task Force Commanders.

In consultation with General Alexander you will set up at once a special operational and administrative staff, with its own Chief of Staff, for planning and preparing the operation.

The provision of the necessary forces and their training in time for the assault on the target date given above have been the subject of exhaustive study by the Combined Chiefs of Staff and their Staffs. A Memorandum setting out the various considerations and the outline plan

U. S. SECRET
BRITISH MOST SECRET

for the operation which formed the basis of this study, is attached for your information (C.C.S. 161/1). Case A (vide C.C.S. 161/1, Enclosure "A," paragraph 5) was accepted by the Combined Chiefs of Staff for the provision of the British Ground Forces. The details of the additional forces which will be made available to you for the operation will be communicated separately by the United States and British Chiefs of Staff.

A copy of the Minutes of the 66th Meeting of the Combined Chiefs of Staff held at Casablanca on January 22, 1943, which led to the above decisions, is attached for your information.

You are to report to them not later than March 1st, whether any insurmountable difficulty as to resources and training will cause the date of the assault to be delayed beyond the favorable July moon. In the event of there being such a delay you will confirm that the assault date will not be later than the favorable August moon.

U. S. SECRET
BRITISH MOST SECRET
C.C.S. 171/2/D   January 23, 1943

COMBINED CHIEFS OF STAFF

OPERATION HUSKY

DIRECTIVE TO COMMANDER IN CHIEF, ALLIED EXPEDITIONARY FORCE IN NORTH AFRICA
(Approved by Combined Chiefs of Staff at their 69th Meeting)

The Combined Chiefs of Staff have resolved that an attack against Sicily will be launched in 1943, with the target date as the period of the favorable July* moon (Code designation HUSKY).

The Combined Chiefs of Staff have further agreed that the following command setup shall be established for the operation:
  (a) You are to be the Supreme Commander with General Alexander as Deputy Commander in Chief, charged with the detailed planning and preparation and with the execution of the actual operation when launched.
  (b) Admiral of the Fleet Cunningham is to be the Naval Commander and Air Chief Marshal Tedder the Air Commander.

You will submit to the Combined Chiefs of Staff your recommendations for the Officers to be appointed Western and Eastern Task Force Commanders.

In consultation with General Alexander you will set up at once a special operational and administrative staff, with its own Chief of Staff, for planning and preparing the operation, including cover plans.

The provision of the necessary forces and their training in time

---

* The Combined Chiefs of Staff have agreed that without prejudicing the July date for the operation, an intense effort will be made during the next three weeks to achieve by contrivance and ingenuity the favorable June moon period as the date for the operation. If at the end of the three weeks their efforts have proved successful, your instructions will be modified accordingly.

NOTE: This paper is identical with C.C.S. 171/1/D dated January 23, 1943, except for addition of above footnote.

U. S. SECRET
BRITISH MOST SECRET

for the assault on the target date given above have been the subject of exhaustive study by the Combined Chiefs of Staff and their staffs. A Memorandum setting out the various considerations and the outline plan for the operation which formed the basis of this study is attached for your information (C.C.S. 161/1). Case A (vide C.C.S. 161/1, Enclosure "A," paragraph 5) was accepted by the Combined Chiefs of Staff for the provision of the British Ground Forces. The details of the additional forces which will be made available to you for the operation will be communicated separately by the United States and British Chiefs of Staff.

A copy of the Minutes of the 66th Meeting of the Combined Chiefs of Staff held at Casablanca on January 22, 1943, which led to the above decisions, is attached for your information.

You are to report to them not later than March 1st whether any insurmountable difficulty as to resources and training will cause the date of the assault to be delayed beyond the favorable July moon. In the event of there being such a delay you will confirm that the assault date will not be later than the favorable August moon.

The code designation to be communicated to you later will apply to all general preparations for HUSKY in the Mediterranean Theater, including training, cover plans and preliminary air operations. Specific operations will be given special code designations.

U. S. SECRET
BRITISH MOST SECRET
C.C.S. 172   January 22, 1943

COMBINED CHIEFS OF STAFF

SHIPPING CAPABILITIES FOR BOLERO BUILD-UP

Note by Lieutenant General B. B. Somervell

1. The attached tables (Enclosures "A" and "B") show the possibilities with existing and presently projected shipping of moving troops and equipment from the U. S. to the U. K. Estimates of capability of British shipping have been prepared on the basis of ship sailings provided by the Ministry of War Transport; estimates on American shipping have been prepared by the Commanding General, Services of Supply, United States Army. The assumptions on which these tables have been prepared are shown in Enclosure "C".

2. There seems little possibility in the first half of the year to improve the situation. By conversion, increasing the capacity of troop ships and other combinations there does seem to be the possibility of some increase in the latter half of the year. This possibility is restricted in the winter months by the limitations on U. K. port and railway capacities under blackout conditions.

3. Continuing study will be given to securing such increases as may be possible.

4. In terms of divisions available for Continental operations, the U. S. Forces in the U. K. over and above the build-up of the air contingent to 172,000 are as follows:

	Division	Total Numbers Equipped
By Aug. 15	4	384,000
Sept. 15	7	509,000
Oct. 15	9	634,000
Nov. 15	12	759,000
Dec. 31	15	938,000

This is based on (1) the figure of 50,000 troops per division with supporting troops; (2) 45 days allowance between sailing date and availability date.

U. S. SECRET
BRITISH MOST SECRET

ENCLOSURE "A"

SHIPPING CAPABILITIES ON BOLERO BUILD-UP

	Present or Enroute Dec. 31, 1942	Quarterly Increments during '43				Total for 1943	Grand Total by 12/31/43
		1st Q	2d Q	3d Q	4th Q		
Capability of U. S. Cargo Ships		80,000	116,000	369,000	491,000	1,056,000	
Capability of U. K. Cargo Ships		-	53,000	15,000	63,000	131,000	
Total Capability of Cargo Shipping		80,000	169,000	384,000	554,000	1,187,000	
Capability of U. S. Troop Ships		103,000	105,000	235,000	299,000	742,000	
Capability of U. K. Troop Ships		40,000	105,000	140,000	60,000	345,000	
Total Capability of Personnel Shipping		143,000	210,000	375,000	359,000	1,087,000	
Rate of Build-up in U. K.		80,000	169,000	375,000	359,000*	983,000	
Cumulated Strength in U. K.	135,000	215,000	384,000	759,000	1,118,000		1,118,000

* It is estimated by British Ministry of War Transport that the above figures would involve approximately 150 BOLERO cargo ships per month in the last quarter of the year. Provided U. S. dock labor and locomotives are forthcoming as stipulated, this rate is possible during the summer but not during the winter months.

U.S. SECRET
BRITISH MOST SECRET

ENCLOSURE B

PROJECTED U S TROOP MOVEMENTS IN 1943

Theater	Present or Enroute Dec. 31, 1943	1st Q	2nd Q	3rd Q	4th Q	Total for 1943	Grand Total by Dec. 31, 1943
S. and S.W. Pacific	224,000	48,700	30,500	24,500	7,500	111,200	335,200
Burma	31,000	7,500	7,500	15,000	-	30,000	61,000
N. Africa and Husky	216,000	68,000	116,000*	-	-	184,000	400,000
Bases	454,000	4,000	4,000	4,000	5,400	17,400	471,400
U K.	135,000	80,000	169,000	375,000	359,000	983,000	1,118,000
Totals	1,060,000	208,200	327,000	418,500	371,900	1,325,600	2,385,600

* One division (16,000 troops) combat loaded from U. S.

U. S. SECRET
BRITISH MOST SECRET

ENCLOSURE "C"

ASSUMPTIONS FOR CALCULATIONS OF
U. S. SHIPPING CAPABILITIES
UNDER PLAN ADOPTED BY C.C.S. FOR 1943

1. Loss rate in dry cargo ships taken at 2.6% per month.

2. U. S. controlled dry cargo shipping taken at 9,185,000 DWT on October 1, 1942.

3. British controlled dry cargo shipping taken at 19,700,000 DWT on October 1, 1942.

4. U. S. construction program for 1943 as reported in Anfa No. 339, i.e., 15,440,000 DWT of dry cargo ships, of which 357,000 DWT will be converted to tankers. Construction is estimated to proceed at the following rate:

	Nov. 15 Program	Jan. 16 Program	Increase
1st Qtr.	3,265,000	3,519,000	254,000
2nd Qtr.	3,222,000	4,106,000	884,000
3rd Qtr.	3,214,000	3,745,000	531,000
4th Qtr.	3,191,000	3,717,000	526,000
Total Dry Cargo	12,892,000	15,087,000	2,195,000
Tankers	3,118,000	3,475,000	357,000
Total	16,010,000	18,562,000	2,552,000

5. British and Canadian construction programs as furnished by Munitions Assignments Board.

6. Excess of British losses over construction in U. K and Canada replaced from U. S. construction. This will permit the reestablishment of the British Import Program at a level considered as meeting their minimum requirements.

7. No EC2's converted to transports through 1943.

8. Five cargo ships converted to combat loaders by Navy each month, November to April, inclusive.

9. Shipping employed on an average turn-around of 2 1/2 months.

10. Repair rate taken at 12-1/2% of total dry cargo fleet.

11. Initial movement based on 8 ship tons per man.

12. Maintenance based on 1.3 ship tons per man per month except for U. K. where it is reduced to 1.0 ship tons per man per month.

U. S. SECRET
BRITISH MOST SECRET

13. Navy employment of dry cargo tonnage in 4th Quarter of 1942 averages 1,160,000 DWT and is increased by 300,000 DWT each quarter of 1943 as assumed in J.P.S. 57/3.

14. The transfer of vessels between oceans to meet theater requirements.

15. U. S. shipping for war economy and defense aid taken at 4,000,000 tons supplemented by 170 voyages in Russian aid according to C.C.S. 162/1.

16. Lift ratio between North Atlantic and South and Southwest Pacific taken at 1.4 to 1.

17. British aid reckoned as follows:

SHIPPING	1st Q	2nd Q	3rd Q	4th Q	TOTAL
Personnel (lift)	40,000	105,000	140,000	60,000	345,000
Cargo (1000 shpg tons)	–	500	300	800	1,600

NOTES:
- (a) The figures are based on a very rapid estimate and must, of course, be subject to check after detailed examination.
- (b) The assistance shown is dependent on the following assumptions:
    - (1) That no shipping can be taken from the U. K. Import Program.
    - (2) That TORCH build-up ceases with KMS 11 and that thereafter the British shipping released from TORCH can be employed on BOLERO assistance *except* for the demands of HUSKY and ANAKIM.
    - (3) That the Ministry of War Transport are able to continue to provide shipping to cover all other military requirements on the agreed minimum level without encroaching on the TORCH pool.
    - (4) That it is possible to find escorts for the convoy program involved.

18. Movements to U. S. bases will be restricted to 17,400 to Iran.

19. Requirements for HUSKY as decided in C.C.S. 161/1 (Plan A).

20. Any excess movements to South and Southwest Pacific and Burma over 141,200 to be by Navy tonnage.

21. U. S. movements to North Africa to cease when total of 400,000 is reached. One division (16,000 troops) to be combat loaded from the United States.

22. Escorts are not limiting factor.

CASABLANCA CONFERENCE

JANUARY 1943

MINUTES OF ANFA MEETINGS

(Presided Over By The President And The Prime Minister)

	PAGE
ANFA 1st Meeting	134
ANFA 2nd Meeting	142
ANFA 3rd Meeting	154

U. S. SECRET
BRITISH MOST SECRET

ANFA 1st Meeting

MINUTES of Meeting held at Anfa Camp,
on Friday, January 15, 1943, at 1730.

PRESENT

The President	The Rt. Hon. Winston S. Churchill (Prime Minister and Minister of Defense)
General G. C. Marshall	
Admiral E. J. King	Admiral of the Fleet Sir Dudley Pound
Lt. General H. H. Arnold	
Lt. General D. D. Eisenhower	Field Marshal Sir John Dill
Mr. Harry Hopkins	General Sir Alan F. Brooke
Lt. Colonel Elliot Roosevelt	Air Chief Marshal Sir C. Portal
Lt. Franklin D. Roosevelt, Jr., USNR	General the Hon. Sir Harold Alexander
	Air Chief Marshal Sir Arthur Tedder
	Vice-Admiral the Lord Louis Mountbatten
	Lt. General Sir Hastings L. Ismay

SECRETARIAT

Brig. General J. R. Deane
Brigadier E. I. C. Jacob

U. S. SECRET
BRITISH MOST SECRET

THE SITUATION IN NORTH AFRICA

GENERAL EISENHOWER gave a review of the situation on his front. He explained that the Allied forces which landed in French North Africa were equipped to capture three ports. They were not a mobile army and had little strength for offensive operations. This arrangement had been necessary since the attitude of the French was an unknown quantity. General Anderson had advanced with great boldness and rapidity taking every kind of risk in an attempt to get into Tunis and Bizerte in the first rush. He had finally been stopped by dive bombing when he got into the open country near Tunis, and by wet weather which hampered movement off the roads. Every effort had then been made to reinforce the forward troops, units being moved from Oran and from Casablanca. It was hoped to launch an offensive on December 22nd to capture Tunis, making use of superior gun power. The weather had turned against us and it had proved necessary to call off the offensive. A means of carrying out operations in the drier country in the south had then been sought and an operation had now been planned for the capture of Sfax which would begin on January 24th. He had been waiting, however, for a chance of coordinating action with General Alexander, as it was important that the timing should fit in with the movements of the 8th Army.

GENERAL EISENHOWER then gave details of how it was proposed to conduct the forthcoming operation and of the forces to be employed. It was intended to use the American First Armored Division (less one light battalion), a regimental combat team and additional units of artillery, and also to use the airfields in the Gafsa and Tebessa areas for supporting aircraft. The Germans had disposed their armor northeast of Pont du Fahs, and it would be necessary to guard against a counter stroke towards the rear of the forces attacking Sfax. It was hoped to put supplies into Sfax by sea from the eastward to ease the maintenance problem. It was hoped that this operation would be of real assistance to the 8th Army because the Germans were sending supplies by rail to Sfax whence they were sending small coasting vessels to Rommel. The Sfax force would be separated by 75 miles of rough country from the British 1st Army, in which there were two critical points: Pont du Fahs and Foudouk, which were held by the French. Apart from one regiment in Algiers, and part of a

U. S. SECRET
BRITISH MOST SECRET

division in Oran, there was virtually nothing between the troops in the front line and Morocco. Troops in the latter place were too far away to move up over the long and difficult line of communications. The 1st Army had 7 to 10 days' supplies of all kinds, and so if an opening were offered by the Germans they could launch an attack. In the whole theater of war there were now about 320,000 troops. Supplies were ample in the Casablanca area, but again difficulty of transportation prevented much being moved forward.

GENERAL EISENHOWER then gave a description of the various airfields being used by the Allied Air Forces, and of the difficulties of keeping them serviceable. He then referred to the political situation and pointed out that it was very closely related to the military situation in view of the very vulnerable nature of the line of communications for the guarding of which French troops were responsible. Returning to the air situation he said that Air Chief Marshal Tedder had twice visited Algiers and detailed plans had been worked out to insure the coordinated action of the Air Forces from the Middle East, Malta and French North Africa. Medium bombers based on Philippeville were now being used with effect against shipping.

GENERAL ALEXANDER then gave an account of the operations of the 8th Army. He said that the El Alamein position was about 40 miles long and was occupied by the German 15th Panzer, 21st Panzer, 90th Light and 164th Infantry Divisions which were at full strength in men and equipment, and by 10 Italian Divisions. The position had no open flank so the problem was one of punching a hole through which the armor could be launched. The attack went in under a very heavy barrage of 500 guns on October 24th. Infantry advanced through deep minefields for 4,000 to 6,000 yards. For the next ten days there was severe fighting designed to eat up the enemy's reserves and prepare the way for the final breakthrough. On November 4th, the front was broken and the opportunity came for the fine American Sherman tanks to pour through. In two weeks Tobruk was reached and by the end of a month the army was at Agheila. They had the satisfaction of advancing twice as fast as Rommel had been able to move during our retreat. The Germans had not enough transport to go round and so they had made certain that what there was was used for the German units. Our casualties in twelve days were 16,000; the enemy's

U. S. SECRET
BRITISH MOST SECRET

must have totalled between 60,000 and 70,000 and Rommel must have lost nearly 5,000 vehicles. None of this would have been possible had it not been for the air superiority gained by the Air Forces who had throughout done magnificent work.

For the further advance beyond Agheila everything depended upon the use of Benghazi. The harbor was left by the Germans in a terrible mess. However by dint of fine work on the part of the Navy, a flow of 3,000 tons per day was reached. A severe gale which again breached the mole and sank several ships interrupted the flow, but it was now back again to 2,000 tons per day. Sirte was useless but there was a small place near Agheila where 400 tons per day had been unloaded.

The plan of the operations which had now begun was an attack by the 7th Armored Division, the New Zealand Division and the 51st Highland Division who were carrying with them 10 days' supplies and 500 miles of petrol. It was hoped to reach Tripoli by January 26th.

The enemy's fighting value was hard to assess but he was believed to have at his disposal the following forces:

15th Panzer Division with 30 tanks   )   50 additional
21st Panzer Division with about 27 tanks)   tanks were be-
                                              lieved to be
                                              ready in Tunisia.

90th Light Division) both weak in strength
164th Division   ) and short of artillery.
About 9 Italian Divisions.

The total strength might be assessed at 50,000 Germans and 30,000 Italians, though only about 20,000 of the former were strictly fighting troops. The enemy's organization was much broken up and he was very short of artillery. Furthermore, his army had retreated 1,000 miles, which must have had its effect on morale. Our superiority rested in tanks and guns, of which we had ample. General LeClerc's advance through Fezzan had been a fine piece of work but would not exercise an influence on the present battle.

U. S. SECRET
BRITISH MOST SECRET

If we got to Tripoli according to plan the 8th Army would be quite immobilized until the port was open. This would take probably seven or ten days, though in the worst case it might take three months. It was hoped to work up to 3,000 tons a day and if this was achieved it would be possible to attack the Mareth Line towards the middle of March with 2 Armored and 4 Infantry Divisions. We were getting photographs of the Mareth Line, which was certainly a prepared position, though lacking in depth. It should be realized that the distances involved were very great. From Buerat to Tripoli was 248 miles and from Tripoli to Gabes was 220 miles. It would, of course, be possible, if the enemy's resistance proved weak, to advance to the Mareth Line with very light forces somewhat earlier.

Discussion then turned upon the coordination of the operations of the 8th Army and of those of General Eisenhower's command. GENERAL EISENHOWER inquired what Rommel's position would be if the 8th Army captured Tripoli and if he captured Sfax. Could the 8th Army keep Rommel engaged so that the forces at Sfax could neglect its right flank and turn all its attention towards the North?

GENERAL ALEXANDER said that Rommel was living very much from hand to mouth for supplies and if he lost all his ports he would certainly be trapped; nevertheless, it would be necessary to give very careful study to the Sfax operation. It should be realized that if a force advanced on Sfax, Rommel would react like lightning and his plan would be the best possible. Great care would be necessary to insure that undue risks were not taken.

SIR ALAN BROOKE said that a great deal depended upon the timing of the Sfax operation. It might be unfortunate if the force arrived at Sfax just at the time that the 8th Army had reached Tripoli and were immobilized for lack of supplies.

It was generally agreed that the coordination of the action of the two armies was a matter of the highest importance and the present opportunity should be utilized to the full.

U. S. SECRET
BRITISH MOST SECRET

Discussion then turned on the strength required to hold the North African shore when it had been completely cleared of the enemy. **GENERAL ALEXANDER** said that he had calculated that two divisions with a mobile reserve would be sufficient for Cyrenaica and Tripolitania. **GENERAL EISENHOWER** said that he considered four divisions should be held to watch Spanish Morocco and that one infantry and one armored division would certainly be necessary in Algeria and Tunisia. There were at present six U. S. divisions in French North Africa and three more were set up in the original plan to come. If these were shipped there would be three U. S. divisions over and above defensive requirements. He thought it would be unwise to hand over the defense of Tunisia too early to the French. The **PRIME MINISTER** agreed. He said that it appeared that there would be some thirteen divisions in the whole North African theater available for future operations.

In reply to an inquiry **SIR ARTHUR TEDDER** said that he was of the opinion that convoys could be passed through the Mediterranean when airfields had been established and when the Tunisian tip had been cleared. **SIR DUDLEY POUND** agreed. He reckoned that if thirty ships could be passed through every ten days the whole of the Cape traffic could be done away with and 225 ships would thus be released for other uses. It was hard to estimate the relative losses which might be incurred, but though the percentage of loss might be slightly higher through the Mediterranean the total would be less as fewer ships would be involved. The Mediterranean route would be more expensive in escorts, but there would be a saving in the time of voyages.

The **PRIME MINISTER** said that the opening of the Mediterranean would have its effect on the attitude of Turkey; moreover, the British 10th Army, consisting of six divisions, which had been established in Persia with the object of meeting the threat through the Caucasus, was now available to encourage and support the Turks.

In discussion it was suggested that it might be worth while calculating what specialized units would be required to round out the Turkish Army. **SIR ALAN BROOKE** pointed out that up to the present the Turks had been supplied with technical material and arms, but although their Army consisted of first-rate material, as infantry, they tended to

U S SECRET
BRITISH MOST SECRET

misuse technical equipment and allow it to deteriorate. He did not think their army would ever be fit to operate offensively outside Turkey. It might, however, serve to hold Turkey as a base from which our forces could operate.

SIR ARTHUR TEDDER said that the Turks had a small air force to which we gave a limited number of aircraft; it would never be fit to fight. Our plan was to operate initially some twenty-five fighter and bomber squadrons from airfields in Turkey which had been prepared and stocked. Further airfields would be required if we were to operate offensively and plans were all drawn up for their preparation. It was intended to move antiaircraft defenses in with the squadrons.

SIR ARTHUR TEDDER then gave an account of the part played by the Air Force in the recent victories in the Middle East. He emphasized that their task began during the British retreat from Gazala. Since that time the enemy air force had been beaten down and great efforts had been made to stop Rommel's supplies. The action of an air force in operations of this kind was difficult to explain concisely, extending as it did over great areas and diverse tasks. The Middle East Air Forces had first struck at Rommel's supplies and then at the supplies to Tunisia; for the latter purpose Malta had been reinforced to the utmost and aircraft had been transferred to Tunisia. The coordination of the Air Forces of the Middle East, Malta and Tunisia was a complicated problem and he was very glad to have the present opportunity of meeting General Eisenhower and discussing it.

GENERAL EISENHOWER explained the difficulties under which the Air Forces in Tunisia were operating in support of the Army. There were only two airfields available for fighters and even these were 100 miles from the front line. The Germans, on the other hand, had two all-weather airfields in Tunis. In the early stages U. S. units from the Western Zone had been moved up and placed under British command; Air Marshal Welch had disposed them in the Tebessa area. For the operation now contemplated the British fighter force would operate from Souk El Arba under Lawson and the U. S. fighters would operate in the South under General Crane. His own conception of the layout on this front was that the British Army Commander should control it all since there was no sound arrangement by which the front could be divided. The French, however, had refused

U. S. SECRET
BRITISH MOST SECRET

to serve under British command. This had meant that he had had to establish a Command Post from which to direct operations. He hoped to overcome this kind of difficulty in the near future.

The PRIME MINISTER inquired whether there was any danger of the Germans striking through General Anderson's left flank rather in the manner adopted by the 8th Army at El Alamein. GENERAL EISENHOWER said that the 1st Army had such superiority over the enemy in artillery that he did not think there was much fear of this. Though the enemy's specialist and tank units were good, his infantry had not seemed to be up to the same standard.

In conclusion it was emphasized that events had reached a crucial stage in the North African Theater and that the events of the next two or three weeks would be of vital importance. The present was the time at which to consider what action should be taken when the North African shore had finally been cleared.

U. S. SECRET
BRITISH MOST SECRET

ANFA 2nd Meeting

MINUTES of Meeting held at Anfa Camp,
on Monday, January 18, 1943, at 1700.

PRESENT

The President
General G.C. Marshall
Admiral E.J. King
Lt. General H.H. Arnold
Mr. Harry Hopkins

The Rt. Hon. Winston S. Churchill (Prime Minister and Minister of Defense)
Admiral of the Fleet Sir Dudley Pound
Field Marshal Sir John Dill
General Sir Alan F. Brooke
Air Chief Marshal Sir C. Portal
Vice Admiral the Lord Louis Mountbatten
Lt. General Sir Hastings L. Ismay

SECRETARIAT

Brig. General J. R. Deane
Brigadier E. I. C. Jacob

U. S. SECRET
BRITISH MOST SECRET

The PRESIDENT and the PRIME MINISTER asked the Chiefs of Staff for a report of progress regarding the current conferences.

SIR ALAN BROOKE stated that after seven days of argument he felt that definite progress had been made. A document is now being prepared setting forth the general strategic policy for 1943. This will be gone over in detail at the C.C.S. meeting on the morning of January 19th.

SIR ALAN BROOKE summarized the document as follows:

1. A statement that the measures to be taken to combat the submarine menace are a first charge on the resources of the United Nations and provide security for all of our operations.

2. A statement that we shall concentrate on the defeat of Germany first which will be followed by the defeat of Japan.

3. Our efforts in defeating Germany will be concerned first with efforts to force them to withdraw ground and air forces from the Russian front. This will be accomplished by operations from North Africa by which Southern Europe, the Dodecanese Islands, Greece, Crete, Sardinia, and Sicily will all be threatened, thus forcing Germany to deploy her forces to meet each threat. The actual operation decided upon is the capture of Sicily.

At the same time, we shall go on with preparing forces and assembling landing craft in England for a thrust across the Channel in the event that the German strength in France decreases, either through withdrawal of her troops or because of an internal collapse.

4. Operations in the Pacific are to be continued to include the capture of Rabaul and Eastern New Guinea while plans are to be prepared to extend the operations to the Marshall Islands and the capture of Truk if the situation permits.

5. Plans and preparations to undertake Operation ANAKIM late in 1943 are to be instituted at once with the understanding that the United States will assist to make up deficiencies in landing craft and naval vessels needed for this operation. The operation is to be planned for December of 1943 with the view to capturing Burma and opening the Burma road prior to the monsoon season of 1944.

U. S. SECRET
BRITISH MOST SECRET

    6. The maximum combined air offensive will be conducted against Germany from the United Kingdom. By this and every other available means, attempts will be made to undermine Germany's morale.

    7. Every effort will be made, political and otherwise, to induce Turkey to enter the war in order that we may establish air bases there for operations against Rumania.

    8. Operation RAVENOUS will be undertaken for the purpose of establishing bridgeheads over the Chindwin River, and also to prepare roads and airfields in northern Burma which will facilitate the mounting of Operation ANAKIM toward the end of the year. In this connection, Operation CANNIBAL is now being undertaken with a view to securing air bases in the Akyab area.

SIR ALAN BROOKE explained that Chiang Kai-shek wishes to postpone his part of Operation RAVENOUS until there is more naval support in the Bay of Bengal. He added that this was strategically sound as the Chinese operation would be more effective if coordinated as a part of ANAKIM. He said RAVENOUS requires no Naval support.

GENERAL MARSHALL then explained that while that part of the Chinese operation which was to consist of an advance from Yunnan could be advantageously postponed, the advance from Ramgarh could well be initiated as part of operation RAVENOUS in order to provide security for the construction of a road southward from Ledo. However, this will have to have the approval of the Generalissimo.

The PRIME MINISTER then stated that he wished it made clear that if and when Hitler breaks down, all of the British resources and effort will be turned toward the defeat of Japan. He stated that not only are British interests involved, but her honor is engaged. If it were thought well for the effect on the people of the United States of America, the British Government would enter into a treaty or convention with the U. S. Government to this effect.

The PRESIDENT stated that a formal agreement regarding British efforts against Japan was entirely unnecessary. He said, however, that efforts should be made to obtain an engagement from Russia to concentrate on the defeat of Japan after Germany had been eliminated from

U. S. SECRET
BRITISH MOST SECRET

the war. He thought that Russia would probably want to come in with the United Nations in that event, but he would like to have an expression from them as to whether they will come in and how.

MR. CHURCHILL then discussed operation SLEDGEHAMMER. He thought it should be given a "sharper point" and that plans should be made to undertake it, including the appointment of a Commander and the fixing of a target date. He had not been in favor of such an operation in 1942 but he felt that it was our duty to engage the enemy on as wide a front and as continuously as possible, and as the only way of stopping an operation with the full force of the British Metropolitan air forces and the U. S. air forces in Great Britain is to do a SLEDGEHAMMER, he thought we should do everything we could to make the operation possible this summer.

The PRESIDENT agreed with the Prime Minister and further suggested that we join together to build up forces in the United Kingdom. He said that it would be desirable to prepare a schedule of the build-up of forces by month in order that we would know what the potential effort might be at any time, and plans should be made for utilizing this potential at any time that there are signs of Germany's deterioration.

The PRIME MINISTER then discussed possible operations from the Mediterranean against the Dodecanese. He considered that these might be developed either as feints in order to conceal the location of the main effort against Sicily, or perhaps as a real attack. He had received a message from the three Commanders-in-Chief in the Middle East informing him that plans to this effect were under way. He desired that the final document prepared by the Chiefs of Staff covering the strategy for 1943 should include some mention of the Dodecanese.

The PRIME MINISTER said that he felt that General Chennault's air force in China should be reinforced. He stated that General Wavell concurred in this view.

The PRESIDENT stated that the effects of help to China would be largely political. A small effort to send aid would have a tremendously favorable effect on Chinese morale. The Generalissimo has been disappointed with regard to the Burma operations. He has considerable difficulty in maintaining the loyalty of some of the Chinese provinces. Anything that we can do to help China and to hurt Japan will have a heartening effect on him.

U. S. SECRET
BRITISH MOST SECRET

The PRESIDENT stated that reinforcing our air power in China would also be a severe blow to Japan. He said that the Japanese people panic easily. This was especially true at the time of their earthquake. Mr. Grew, the United States Ambassador, in reporting this incident, stated that it was necessary for the Japanese broadcast to adopt every means possible to quiet the people.

The PRESIDENT considered that we should send from 200 to 250 planes to China. This should include heavy bombers which, because of the difficulties of supply, could be based in India. They could be used to operate in raids over Japan proper by refueling in China on their way to and from such missions.

He thought that the United Nations should commit themselves to this line of action and that whoever of the Chiefs of Staff was next to see the Generalissimo, should inform him to this effect.

The PRESIDENT then discussed operations in the Mediterranean. He said we had been extremely fortunate in Operation TORCH. He was worried, however, about news concerning the operations against Sicily reaching Germany. To prevent this, he thought that we should give the operations in the Mediterranean some such name as "UNDERBELLY" and continually think of them as being aimed at any one of a number of objectives, knowing secretly all the while, that they were to be toward Sicily.

ADMIRAL KING stated that deception could be well achieved by the use of cover plans. He said that the document that is now in preparation and will be discussed on January 19th goes a long way toward establishing a policy of how we are to win the war. It has taken some days for the Chiefs of Staff to express themselves but in principle they are all agreed. He expressed the opinion that the document being prepared would be approved after a short discussion and with minor amendments. He said that he personally would like to have had it expanded to present a complete concept for concluding the war but that he was well pleased with it as it is.

GENERAL MARSHALL said that when the United States Chiefs of Staff came to the conference, they preferred to undertake Operation ROUNDUP in 1943. The decision, however, has been made to undertake Operation HUSKY because we will have in North Africa a large number of

U. S. SECRET
BRITISH MOST SECRET

troops available and because it will effect an economy of tonnage which is the major consideration. It is estimated that possession of the north coast of Africa and Sicily will release approximately 225 vessels which will facilitate operations in Burma, the Middle East, and the Pacific. He felt that the capture of Sicily would do much to improve the air coverage for our shipping in the Mediterranean. This will add considerably to the safety of the passage. He said that Admiral Cunningham and other naval officers had indicated that the capture of Sicily would not be of great benefit in the protection of our convoys, Admiral Cunningham having stated that the possession of Sicily would only make us 5 percent more effective in the protection of convoys.

SIR CHARLES PORTAL thought there had been a misunderstanding of Admiral Cunningham's views. He feels that without Sicily we will lose 15 ships out of 100, or be 85 percent effective. We will lose only 10 ships out of 100, 90 percent effective, with Sicily in our possession. The number of the ships lost is therefore 50 percent greater with Sicily in possession of the Axis.

GENERAL MARSHALL said the second consideration which brought about the decision to operate against Sicily was the possibility of eliminating Italy from the war and thus necessitating Germany's taking over the present commitments of the Italians.

GENERAL MARSHALL emphasized that ROUNDUP would be a difficult if not impossible operation to undertake once we have committed ourselves to Operation HUSKY. He said that the United Kingdom maintains a small spearhead of amphibious forces consisting of about 20,000 troops which are available at all times for an operation across the Channel. This force could be augmented by follow-up troops carried in small craft which might be available in England. Unless there is a complete crack in German morale, operations across the Channel will have to be extremely limited. It will be fully as difficult to assemble landing craft following Operation HUSKY and send them to England as it will be to assemble them after the capture of Rabaul and send them to Burma. Probably three months will be required to accomplish this in either case.

GENERAL MARSHALL said that sudden signs of deterioration of the Axis forces might take two forms; first, a collapse in the interior with

U. S. SECRET
BRITISH MOST SECRET

the troops initially holding fast; and, second, by the withdrawal of troops from France. In the latter case, we should make every effort to cross the Channel and in doing so, utilize any means that are available. He said the greatest difficulty in setting up strength for ROUNDUP in addition to Operation HUSKY is the lack of escort vessels and landing craft.

GENERAL MARSHALL then discussed increasing the air force in China. The United States now has an agreement to increase the Chinese air force to the extent to which it can be supplied. The increase will be much more than the force is now. It is contemplated sending a group of heavy bombers which may be used to shuttle back and forth from China to India. There will be 25 to 30 additional medium bombers with the appropriate aircraft to furnish them fighter protection. He emphasized that while we are committed to the build-up of the Chinese air forces, it is a tremendously expensive operation. The air transport planes which must be utilized in their supply could be utilized with great effect elsewhere.

GENERAL MARSHALL said that in the agreements reached by the Combined Chiefs of Staff, effective measures had been adopted to improve the situation in the Pacific. He said he hoped these were sufficient to insure that we would not again be threatened by a series of crises, since sufficient forces would be made available to insure our maintaining pressure on Japan.

GENERAL MARSHALL said that as summer approaches, the Combined Chiefs of Staff should meet again to make the necessary readjustments in the decisions made now.

He then discussed the use of United States bombers in England. He thought that they should be under the operational direction of the British, who should prescribe the targets and the timing of attacks. Control of operational procedure and technique should remain under the United States Commanders. The Combined Chiefs of Staff will attempt to prescribe general priorities of bombing objectives

GENERAL MARSHALL said we should coordinate and improve our methods in combating the submarine menace and that this also would be a subject of discussion during the conferences.

U. S. SECRET
BRITISH MOST SECRET

Another vital question before the Combined Chiefs of staff is how to maintain the Russian forces at their maximum effort both by forcing a withdrawal of German pressure on their front and also by insuring the flow of munitions to them. It is questionable to what extent the United Nations can take the losses of tonnage incidental to escorting the northern convoys. It may be possible to decrease the intervals between convoys or add to the strength of their escorts. However, it is entirely within the power of Germany to administer such losses as to make it necessary to discontinue this route to Russia.

GENERAL MARSHALL said that he does not believe it necessary to take excessive punishment in running these convoys simply to keep Mr. Stalin placated. In any event, he feels that it would be necessary to inform Mr. Stalin that the convoys would have to be discontinued during Operation HUSKY.

GENERAL ARNOLD said that the agreements tentatively arrived at would be very helpful from the air point of view. They will facilitate the allocation of aircraft and the development of procedure and technique.

The PRIME MINISTER said that since we have surveyed the whole field of strategy, it will now be necessary for the Chiefs of Staff to go into ways and means by which the adopted strategy can be accomplished. They must determine where risks should be incurred and where the reduction of forces is necessary. This may take several days. It will involve the broad distribution of our resources. He agreed with General Marshall that another meeting should be held before summer and expressed his pleasure to the President of the United States, and to the U. S. Chiefs of Staff, for arranging to attend this conference.

The PRESIDENT said that he particularly appreciated having Sir John Dill at the conferences since he would be the individual who would carry on the liaison between the Chiefs of Staff in London and the Chiefs of Staff in Washington between whom he constituted an indispensable link.

SIR DUDLEY POUND then said that we must go into ways and means of implementing our agreed decisions. Two problems involved are the security of the Atlantic convoys and the extent to which it will be necessary to decrease such security when Operation HUSKY is undertaken.

U S SECRET
BRITISH MOST SECRET

He said that increased pressure against the submarine menace must be maintained by adequate coverage of our convoys and by striking at places where submarines are manufactured and assembled. If this is done, the situation may be considerably improved by the time operation HUSKY is undertaken. He agreed with General Marshall that it will be necessary during Operation HUSKY to discontinue the northern convoys.

The PRIME MINISTER said that this would be an added reason for increasing the tonnage sent to Russia prior to Operation HUSKY.

SIR DUDLEY POUND replied that this could be done provided the United States would help in the escort problem.

The PRESIDENT then discussed the possibility of assembling a large number of river and lake craft available in the United States and sending them quietly to Europe in order to transport troops across the Channel in case Germany cracks.

LORD MOUNTBATTEN stated that five Great Lakes steamers had already been sent.

The PRESIDENT told Admiral King to survey the situation and see what could be done in this respect.

SIR JOHN DILL expressed his satisfaction over the progress of the present conferences.

The PRIME MINISTER then discussed the situation in Turkey. He said that the British had some right to expect Turkey to enter the war when the Balkans were invaded, but in view of our own weakness to help Turkey they did not press it. Turkey will be in a weak position at the peace table following the war if she has not participated in it. It was possible to give them a guarantee for existing territory, and for their rights over passage through the Dardanelles. The United Nations should be prepared to provide Turkey with antiaircraft, flak, tanks and other mechanized vehicles and also be prepared to send some of this equipment manned with units, since Turkish troops do not handle machinery particularly well. He feels that Turkey might be influenced to enter the war by the successes of Russian troops on the north and those of the United States-United Kingdom troops on the south. At present they are angry with the Bulgarians and it would not be surprising if they did enter the war.

U. S. SECRET
BRITISH MOST SECRET

The PRIME MINISTER said that since most of the troops which would be involved in reinforcing Turkey would be British, he asked that the British be allowed to play the Turkish hand, just as the United States is now handling the situation with reference to China. The British would keep the United States advised at all times as to the progress being made.

The PRESIDENT concurred in this view and also said that if ROUNDUP should be undertaken, he felt that it should be under British command.

The PRIME MINISTER said that he thought the question of command in ROUNDUP operation might be determined later, but he agreed that it would be advisable to designate a British commander at this time who could undertake the planning of the operation. In his view, the command of operations should as a general rule be held by an officer of the nation which furnishes the majority of the forces.

He said that in perhaps five weeks six divisions of the 8th Army would enter Tunisia, and it was understood that they would, of course, come under command of General Eisenhower. He thought, however, it would be advisable for General Alexander to be designated as the Deputy Commander of the Allied Forces.

The PRESIDENT and GENERAL MARSHALL both expressed agreement, and the latter said he thought it would be particularly desirable since there would be two British armies involved in the Tunisian front.

ADMIRAL KING suggested the possibility of unifying command prior to the 8th Army's entry into Tunisia, feeling that there were many matters common to both the Allied Expeditionary Forces and the 8th Army which should be coordinated. After discussion, it was agreed that date of appointment should be left for future decision.

GENERAL MARSHALL informed the Prime Minister and the Chiefs of Staff of the great contribution that Admiral Cunningham had made to the success of Operation TORCH. He wished to express the appreciation of the United States Chiefs of Staff not only for the skill that Admiral Cunningham had displayed, but also for his spirit of helpfulness and for his cooperation.

U. S. SECRET
BRITISH MOST SECRET

The PRIME MINISTER thanked General Marshall and directed that General Marshall's comments be included in the minutes in order that he could present them to the Cabinet.

After being informed that the agreements arrived at at the conference would be included in a paper, the PRIME MINISTER suggested that one should be drawn up for presentation to Premier Stalin. He felt that the Soviet is entitled to know what we intend to do, but that it should be made clear that the paper expressed our intentions and did not constitute promises.

The PRESIDENT brought up the subject of press releases concerning the current conferences. He said that a photograph should be made of the participants in the conference and be given out with a release date which might be set as the day that he and the Prime Minister departed.

The PRIME MINISTER suggested that at the same time we release a statement to the effect that the United Nations are resolved to pursue the war to the bitter end, neither party relaxing in its efforts until the unconditional surrender of Germany and Japan has been achieved. He said that before issuing such a statement, he would like to consult with his colleagues in London.

FIELD MARSHAL DILL then asked the President if there were any information concerning General De Gaulle.

The PRESIDENT replied that he had arranged to have General Giraud come here for a conference, but that so far the Prime Minister had been unable to effect such arrangements with General De Gaulle.

The PRIME MINISTER said that General De Gaulle had refused, saying that if the President wished to see him, he would no doubt invite him to come to Washington. De Gaulle had said that he would not meet Giraud in an atmosphere dominated by the High Command of the United Nations. The Prime Minister said that he had sent an invitation to De Gaulle to come, and the invitation had been sent in the name of the President and himself. He indicated to General De Gaulle that if he refused the invitation, it would be necessary for him and the President to consider whether or not he was a leader who merited their support.

U. S. SECRET
BRITISH MOST SECRET

The PRESIDENT stated that General Giraud had informed him that there were sufficient French officers and noncommissioned officers in North Africa to enable the French to raise an army of 250,000 men. He thought General Giraud should be instructed to raise such an army, and that we should make every effort to provide him with equipment. He said that General Giraud was desirous of being relieved of some of his civilian responsibilities.

The PRIME MINISTER said that he thought the political representatives of the United States and the United Kingdom should be at all times represented in whatever controlling machinery is set up, and that even General Eisenhower should present his demands to the French Government through civilian representatives, except in those cases where he wished to exercise his prerogatives as a military commander of an occupied country.

SIR ALAN BROOKE said that the French have a considerable number of French 75 mm. guns on hand together with ammunition. They were to receive the tanks from the British 6th Armored Division when this unit received its Sherman tanks from the United States. He said that there were also some antiaircraft weapons available which can be given to the French. GENERAL MARSHALL stated that he thought it necessary to give the French the best equipment obtainable, and that he proposed to do so from United States resources subject to shipping limitations. His idea was that if we are to equip the French, we must make good units of them.

The PRESIDENT thought it would be desirable to utilize some French units in Operation HUSKY even if only as a reserve.

The PRIME MINISTER then expressed the hope that the United States would bring to North Africa the remaining three divisions which are scheduled to come here.

GENERAL MARSHALL replied that there had been no change in schedule yet, but that after the complete details for Operation HUSKY had been worked out, a determination could be made as to what divisions should be brought or what other changes might be made.

U. S. SECRET
BRITISH MOST SECRET

ANFA 3rd Meeting

MINUTES of Meeting held at Anfa Camp,
on Saturday, January 23, 1943, at 1700.

PRESENT

The President
General G. C. Marshall
Admiral E. J. King
Lt. General H. H. Arnold
Lt. General B. B. Somervell
Mr. Harry Hopkins
Commander R. E. Libby

The Rt. Hon. Winston S. Churchill
   (Prime Minister and Minister of
   Defense)
Admiral of the Fleet Sir Dudley
   Pound
Field Marshal Sir John Dill
General Sir Alan F. Brooke
Air Chief Marshal Sir C. Portal
Vice Admiral the Lord Louis
   Mountbatten
Lt. General Sir Hastings L. Ismay

SECRETARIAT

Brig. General J. R. Deane
Brigadier E. I. C. Jacob

U. S. SECRET
BRITISH MOST SECRET

The PRESIDENT suggested discussing the report submitted to him and the Prime Minister in C.C.S. 170/1, paragraph by paragraph.

Both the President and the Prime Minister, before starting the discussion, said that they wished to congratulate the Chiefs of Staff on the character of the work which had been done during the conferences. The Prime Minister said it was the first instance he knew of when military leaders had remained together so long, free from political considerations, and had devoted their full thought to the strategic aspects of the war.

The PRESIDENT agreed to this and recalled an incident in the last war when Marshal Foch, Field Marshal Haig and General Pershing had had a similar conference which lasted but 5 hours.

1. SECURITY OF SEA COMMUNICATIONS.

In discussing the security of sea communications, the PRIME MINISTER indicated that he wished German submarines to be referred to as "U-Boats" rather than dignifying them by calling them "submarines."

2. ASSISTANCE TO RUSSIA.

A discussion regarding assistance to Russia in relation to other commitments then followed.

The PRESIDENT said that in March we will be faced with the necessity of arranging to extend the Russian Protocol. He thought the last sentence in paragraph 2 of C.C.S. 170/1 which provides that "supply to Russia will not be continued at prohibitive cost to the United Nations' efforts" should stand and asked Mr. Hopkins for his view on the subject.

MR. HOPKINS said that the present Protocol has such a clause but that, of course, it cannot be exercised without raising violent objections from Premier Stalin.

The PRIME MINISTER said that aid to Russia must be pushed, and no investment could pay a better military dividend. The United Nations cannot let Russia down. He said that the Chiefs of Staff had been considering whether or not 16 destroyers could be made available from the United States in order to reduce the length of the convoy turnaround from 40 to 27 days.

U. S. SECRET
BRITISH MOST SECRET

ADMIRAL KING said that the destroyers simply were not available. The escort vessel situation is so tight as to make it necessary to eliminate the Russian convoys starting about June 14th in order to take care of the needs of Operation HUSKY. He pointed out that there is already a shortage of 65 escorts to protect the convoys in the Atlantic service and that the HUSKY operation will make this shortage more acute.

MR HOPKINS suggested the possibility of stopping the convoys entirely if we could give Russia something that she had not previously expected and suggested that this be airplanes.

The PRESIDENT asked what new escort construction would be available by June of 1943.

ADMIRAL KING replied that there would be 100 escort vessels completed but that, if the present loss rates continued, this number would represent only a small net gain.

SIR DUDLEY POUND said there is no substitute for destroyers in protecting convoys. At the present time we are utilizing 16 destroyers and 8 ships of other types with the convoys running on a 40-day cycle. If this were to be reduced to 27 days, it would be necessary to double this force in order to have two convoys in operation.

MR HOPKINS asked whether the destroyers and escort vessels that are now with these convoys could not be released for use elsewhere if the convoys were eliminated entirely.

SIR DUDLEY POUND said the escort vessels would be released, except for the Home Fleet destroyers which must be kept available to watch for a break-out into the Atlantic of the German fleet.

MR HOPKINS repeated that some consideration should be given by the Chiefs of Staff regarding the entire elimination of the Russian convoys via the northern route. He said that it might be possible to increase the delivery of munitions to Russia over the Persian route and via Alaska although the Russians object to handling some types of munitions over these routes. At the same time, we could increase the Protocol in certain types of munitions such as aircraft. If this were done, there would be a saving in the use of the 500,000 tons of shipping from

U. S. SECRET
BRITISH MOST SECRET

the Russian convoys. The considerable losses of shipping connected with the northern convoys would be eliminated, as well as the cargoes which are lost when ships are sunk. He felt that the Chiefs of Staff have been inclined to consider aid to Russia as a political expedient and that actually the question should be viewed from the standpoint of military necessity.

The PRIME MINISTER said it would be a great thing if we could continue the Russian convoys throughout the HUSKY Operation. He thought it better to continue them on a 40-day cycle rather than attempt the 27-day cycle prior to HUSKY and then stop the convoys while HUSKY was being undertaken. He said we have never made any promises that we would take supplies to Russia. We have merely committed ourselves to making munitions available to them at our ports.

GENERAL SOMERVELL said that by July 1st we will be able to send 30 ships a month to the Persian Gulf ports, and this would offer good prospects for increasing the supply to Russia.

The PRESIDENT said that supplying Russia is a paying investment. Stopping the convoys in July and August would occur just at the time when the Russians would be engaged in their most severe fighting. He pointed out that it is difficult to say now just what the situation regarding shipping losses will be in July or August, or what the conditions will be along the route of the northern convoys. He said, for example, at the time of the last conference in June 1942, the United States was suffering great shipping losses along her eastern coast. This area has now been almost cleared of submarines, and the greatest losses are now occurring off the coast of South America.

ADMIRAL KING said that we are definitely committed to mounting Operation HUSKY and that everything must be done to insure its success, including the elimination of the Russian convoys if that be necessary.

GENERAL MARSHALL, in referring to Mr. Hopkins' opinion of the Chiefs of Staff's attitude towards aid to Russia, said that in the current conferences, it had been decided that the first charge against the United Nations was the defeat of the submarine menace and aid to Russia had to come next. He said that if we had to take the losses which had

U. S. SECRET
BRITISH MOST SECRET

been suffered in the Murmansk convoys, they would hurt Russia as much as the U. S. and U. K. Such losses make it impossible for us to attack on other fronts and thus eliminate the possibility of forcing the Germans to withdraw ground and air troops from the Russian front. He said these losses last year came just at the time that we were laboring to build up BOLERO. It must be made certain that we do not hazard the success of Operation HUSKY.

The PRIME MINISTER agreed that if passage of convoys on the northern route were prohibitive in cost, they must be stopped. He thought it would be right to have in our minds the possibility of continuing convoys through the HUSKY period, but to make no promises to Stalin.

SIR DUDLEY POUND said this must be the case because if we were committed to continuing these convoys, the Royal Navy could not play its part in Operation HUSKY.

The PRIME MINISTER said that the discussion should rest on the point that the discontinuance of these convoys will depend upon the losses that are suffered. He said we must tell Mr. Stalin the facts, that he must rely on a 40-day schedule. Also that we cannot promise the continuance of the convoys while Operation HUSKY is being undertaken. He said it should also be made clear to Mr. Stalin that the U. S. and U. K. are under no obligation to continue the convoys.

The PRESIDENT said that the draft message to Mr. Stalin would require some revision. It must be remembered that the Russian General Staff are making plans on the assumption that the munitions called for in the Protocol will be available. In justice to them, they should know just what is intended. He asked how a 2.4% per month loss rate would relate to the 700,000 tons loss of shipping per year.

ADMIRAL KING said he thought the loss rate of 2.4% would reduce the losses in shipping to less than 700,000 tons. He recalled the Prime Minister's having said before the House of Commons that if our losses could be reduced below 500,000 tons per year, the shipping situation would be satisfactory.

The PRESIDENT said that the shipping situation is bound to improve during the coming year as a result of nearly doubling the

U. S. SECRET
BRITISH MOST SECRET

construction program and by reason of the more effective antisubmarine measures which are to be taken.

ADMIRAL KING agreed with this and said that the great losses on the eastern coast of the United States were possible in large measure because of a lack of effective means to combat the submarines. He said that great improvement has been made in this respect.

The PRIME MINISTER suggested that it should be decided that if the shipping situation is better than we expect, we shall continue the 40-day convoy throughout Operation HUSKY, but that we should not commit ourselves either way. He said that, while it might be possible to continue the convoys, they must be stopped if the losses are too great.

ADMIRAL KING suggested that before deciding on discontinuing the convoys, the situation should be reviewed as of the first of May.

3. OPERATIONS IN THE MEDITERRANEAN.
The discussion then turned to Operation HUSKY.

The PRIME MINISTER said he wished to set the target date as the period of the favorable June moon rather than that of July.

GENERAL MARSHALL said that the matter of training must be considered as well as other features in connection with the preparations for Operation HUSKY. He said that all training and preparations must be scheduled, and that if an impossible or improbable target date was set and then later changed to one that was practicable, all of the schedules would be out of adjustment. This might result in compromising ourselves with regard to every aspect of the operation. The subject of the target date had been quite exhaustively studied, and it is going to be difficult to mount Operation HUSKY with properly trained forces even in July.

The PRESIDENT asked if the fixing of the target date in July was made on the assumption that the Axis forces would be driven from Tunisia by the end of April. He asked what the effect would be if they were to be eliminated from Africa by the end of March.

GENERAL MARSHALL replied that success in Tunisia at the end of March would improve the situation somewhat but was not the limiting factor. The limiting factor was on the naval side with respect to organizing

U. S. SECRET
BRITISH MOST SECRET

crews and assembling landing craft. After this has been accomplished, the naval crews and landing craft must be made available for the training of the troops. He said that the situation in Tunisia might result in delaying Operation HUSKY but that an earlier success there would not help in moving the target date forward.

ADMIRAL KING said it was a question as to whether the assault on Sicily should be made by partially or fully trained forces.

The PRESIDENT suggested that the operation might be easier than Operation TORCH in view of the better weather found in the Mediterranean.

LORD MOUNTBATTEN said that the difficulty of the HUSKY Operation was not in the weather but the excellence that might be expected in the enemy's defenses.

GENERAL MARSHALL pointed out some of the errors that had been made in the TORCH operation through lack of adequate training. Some of the landing boats went to the wrong place. One Ranger unit had the mission of taking a shore battery and clearing a certain area. It actually landed 18 miles away from its objective.

The PRESIDENT said he thought this might have been the result of poor navigation rather than a lack of adequate training.

GENERAL MARSHALL replied that while we do have divisions with amphibious training, we do not have the landing craft or crews. The craft must be built and the crews must be trained.

The PRIME MINISTER agreed that General Marshall's point that the target date for HUSKY did not depend on the Tunisian operations but rather on the necessity of training was a good one.

He said, however, that the British are to send their overseas assault force which has a capacity of 7 brigade groups to participate in Operation HUSKY. He had been told that this could not leave England until March 14th and then must undergo some training in the eastern Mediterranean. He said he felt sure that the force could be sent earlier. In this connection, LORD LOUIS MOUNTBATTEN said that he had been informed that it could be sent by the end of February.

U. S. SECRET
BRITISH MOST SECRET

The PRIME MINISTER said that this would be done. He then discussed the question of navigation. When operations of the importance of HUSKY are to be undertaken, no effort should be spared to obtain capable navigators. He suggested the possibility of combing the navy, particularly the "R" class battleships, with the purpose of setting up a special group of navigators.

SIR DUDLEY POUND said that skilled navigators could not be taken from the navy without serious effects and, in any event, they would have to be supplemented by inexperienced men and the training period could not therefore be shortened.

The PRIME MINISTER said that he feared the gap of perhaps four months during the summer when no U. S. or British troops would be in contact with the Germans.

The PRESIDENT agreed and said that this gap might have a serious effect all over the world.

SIR ALAN BROOKE said that the Combined Chiefs of Staff had examined the timing of the operation most carefully. September was the first date that had been put forward and this they had rejected. Further study had brought the date back to the end of August. The Combined Chiefs of Staff had then put on the same kind of pressure that the President and the Prime Minister were now applying, with the result that July had been tentatively fixed, though August remained a more likely date. He was in agreement with General Marshall that to try and fix too early a date would prejudice the preparations. It was impossible to shorten the loading period, and thus the only process off which time might be lopped was training. If this were curtailed, the result might be disastrous.

The PRIME MINISTER thought that by intense efforts the loading might be accelerated. Similarly if landing craft now employed in maintaining the 8th Army could be recovered forthwith, training might start earlier. All these points must be rigorously examined before the July date could be accepted.

GENERAL MARSHALL pointed out that if the date were to be made earlier, it would have to be by a complete four weeks unless the added risks of moonlight were acceptable.

U. S. SECRET
BRITISH MOST SECRET

The PRESIDENT said that the present proposals were based on a large number of factors which might well prove correct, but which were estimates. Another estimate which must be taken into account was the state of morale in Italy, which recent reports showed to be deteriorating. If this process continued, the Germans might be faced with an Italy in revolt, and it would then be essential for us to have our preparations far enough advanced to be able to act, not necessarily in Sicily but perhaps in Sardinia, or even in Italy. For this reason he would like to set the date of the operation in June, it being understood that it might have to be carried out in July if the enemy's strength remained as at present.

GENERAL MARSHALL pointed out that to bring back the date at the expense of adequate preparation would not make it any easier to stage an improvised operation during the intervening months. The troops would have been moved into place quite early in the preparatory period, so that they would be standing ready if required.

SIR ALAN BROOKE agreed and pointed out that we should probably get some advance indication of an Italian collapse which would enable us to speed up the launching of a smaller force. It would be quite wrong to risk a costly failure by unduly curtailing the period of preparation.

The PRIME MINISTER said that General Marshall was pleading for the integrity of the operation, and the arguments which he had employed were most convincing. Nevertheless, he was not himself yet convinced that the integrity of the operation could not be maintained with a June date. Some quicker methods might be found of moving troops into place.

GENERAL MARSHALL said that this also had been examined. He pointed out that the period after the fall of Tunis would not be one of inactivity, as a growing air bombardment of Italy would be launched. We ought to place ourselves in a position to do the hard operation against Sicily while being ready to improvise if the enemy weakened. The initial landing in Sicily was on a larger scale than had been envisaged for Operation ROUNDUP.

The PRESIDENT inquired whether any easement could be secured if the Spanish situation cleared still further during the Spring.

U.S. SECRET
BRITISH MOST SECRET

GENERAL MARSHALL said that in any case the troops standing ready to move into Spanish Morocco would be simultaneously training for Sicily.

ADMIRAL KING said that one of the innumerable items which had to be considered in this operation was the provision of armored landing craft, which he and Lord Louis Mountbatten agreed were essential. None of these was at present available for the U. S. forces. He agreed that the ideal method of launching the operation would be to follow in on the heels of the Germans fleeing from Tunis. He was convinced, however, that the closest we could come to this ideal was July. He would have liked June, but felt it impossible to promise such a date.

The PRESIDENT said that the important point was to retain a flexible mind in the matter so that advantage could be taken of every opportunity.

GENERAL MARSHALL said that he had felt embarrassed over the date of this operation remembering as he did the incentive which had existed for hastening TORCH in view of the U. S. elections. In spite of that, it had not proved possible to advance the date.

The PRIME MINISTER said there had been much admiration in England of the fact that the election had not been allowed to influence in the slightest the course of military events.

After some further discussion, it was agreed that:
(a) Operations for the Capture of Sicily:
The July date should stand subject to an instruction that in the next three weeks, without prejudice to the July date, there should be an intense effort made to try and achieve the favorable June moon as the date of the operation. If at the end of this three weeks, the June date could be fixed, General Eisenhower's instructions could be modified to conform.

(b) Cover Plans:
The PRIME MINISTER suggested that Norway should again play a part in the cover plans.

SIR ALAN BROOKE pointed out that it might be awkward for the Russian convoys if we gave the Germans cause for reinforcing Norway. He thought that much the best cover would be given by the active preparations

U. S. SECRET
BRITISH MOST SECRET

going on all over the North African shore. These would not only disguise the objective, but would cause dispersion of enemy forces.

The PRESIDENT thought that the creation of General Giraud's French army might also play a part in making the enemy think that the southern coast of France was our objective.

(c) Command of the Mediterranean Theater:

The PRIME MINISTER said that he thought the United States had been very generous and broad-minded in the command arrangements. He thought that the most natural method of procedure would be at the appropriate moment to announce that the 8th Army, on entering Tunisia, had passed under the command of General Eisenhower, and that General Alexander had been appointed as his deputy.

(d) The Bomber Offensive from North Africa:

The PRIME MINISTER thought that it would be advisable to maintain the threat of bombardment against Rome, but that it should not actually be carried out without further consultation.

The PRESIDENT agreed.

4. OPERATIONS IN AND FROM THE UNITED KINGDOM.

(b) BOLERO:

The PRIME MINISTER thought that it was very disappointing that there would only be 4 U. S. divisions equipped in the U. K. by August 15th. He inquired whether by using the Queens, the number for September could not be achieved in August.

GENERAL SOMERVELL said that the limiting factor in the first half of the year was cargo ships, and in the second half of the year it was personnel ships. To move more men over in the first half would only result in their arriving in England with no equipment, and thus their training would be interrupted. The Queens were all fully employed in various parts of the world.

GENERAL MARSHALL pointed out that the figures in the table were a minimum, and the 4 divisions shown for August 15th would probably be 19 rather than 15. Allowance had to be made in the early build-up for the Air Corps personnel.

U. S. SECRET
BRITISH MOST SECRET

The PRIME MINISTER inquired whether the initial equipment of 8 tons per man, and the maintenance of 1.3 tons per man per month, could not be reduced; similarly, could not savings be made on reserves and on vehicles. For the type of operations which would be undertaken in France in 1943, a big advance was not likely. Fighting men for the beaches were the prime essential.

GENERAL SOMERVELL said that the calculation of the rate of build up had been made on the basis of one ton per man per month. The other factors mentioned by the Prime Minister had also been taken into account, and everything would be done to reduce any unnecessary volume to be transported. He pointed out that there was a 45-day interval between the arrival of a division and its availability for operations; thus, the divisions which were shown as being available on August 15th would have sailed by July 1st. If the British could lend additional cargo shipping in the early part of the year, the flow of troops could be increased.

The PRIME MINISTER said that it was in the early part of the year that the British shipping shortage would be most acute. He suggested that it should be recorded that the figures shown in the report were a minimum and that every effort would be made to increase them.

(c) Amphibious Operations in 1943 from the U. K.

The PRIME MINISTER suggested that the word "vigorously" should be inserted before the word "exploiting" in subparagraph (2) of this section of the report. This was agreed to.

The PRESIDENT inquired whether an operation against the Brest Peninsula could not be staged instead of against Cherbourg. The advantages of the former were very much greater. He also inquired about the date proposed for the operations.

LORD LOUIS MOUNTBATTEN said that the date for the Channel Island operations had been chosen so as to fit in with Operation HUSKY. A difficulty had arisen in that the armored craft required by the Americans for HUSKY would have to come from the British Channel Assault Force. A telegram had been sent to the Admiralty asking that the output of these craft should be doubled so as to produce 160 more in the next four months. This might be done provided 400 additional Scripps Ford conversion

U. S. SECRET
BRITISH MOST SECRET

engines were allocated to the U. K. from the U.S.A. He understood this point was under investigation.

The PRESIDENT inquired whether some Ford tank engines could not be produced and taken by air transport from the U.S.A. to the U.K. He understood that the engine was much the same.

GENERAL SOMERVELL said that there was a difference in the engines, though the same facilities were required to produce both. He could not at present state the production possibilities.

The PRIME MINISTER suggested that some reduction of tank engine output could be accepted if necessary.

SIR ALAN BROOKE agreed.

LORD LOUIS MOUNTBATTEN said that the landing craft resources would only permit of an initial assault by 2 brigade groups with an immediate follow-up of one brigade group and some armor. This could only be increased with U. S. help.

ADMIRAL KING said that all available U. S. resources would be devoted to Operation HUSKY.

On the question of command the PRESIDENT inquired whether sufficient drive would be applied if only a Chief of Staff were appointed. He hoped there would not be a long delay before a Supreme Commander was selected.

GENERAL MARSHALL said he understood it was a question of the availability of the right man.

SIR ALAN BROOKE thought that the Chief of Staff, if a man with the right qualities were chosen, could do what was necessary in the early stages

The PRIME MINISTER suggested that in any case an American Deputy to the Supreme Commander should be appointed.

SIR ALAN BROOKE and GENERAL MARSHALL agreed.

The PRESIDENT suggested that the last sentence of this section should be omitted. This was agreed to.

U. S. SECRET
BRITISH MOST SECRET

5. PACIFIC AND FAR EAST THEATER.

The **PRESIDENT** said that he was disturbed to find that this section contained no reference to operations in or from China. Operations in Burma, though desirable, would not have the direct effect upon the Chinese which was necessary to sustain and increase their war effort. Similarly, an island-to-island advance across the Pacific would take too long to reduce the Japanese power. Some other method of striking at Japan must be found. The opportunity was presented by Japan's shipping situation. She began the war with 6,000,000 tons. In the first year of the war 1,000,000 tons net had been sunk, leaving her with 5,000,000. When this was reduced to 4,000,000, Japan would be hard pressed to maintain her garrison in the chain of islands stretching all the way from Burma to New Guinea and would have to start pulling in her lines. The most effective weapon against shipping was the submarine, and the U. S. submarines were achieving notable results. There was another method of striking at the Japanese shipping, and that was by attacking the routes running close to the Asiatic shore from Korea down to Siam. This could be done by aircraft operating from China. He thought that 200 aircraft should be operating in China by April. They could spend most of their time in attacks on shipping, but occasionally they could make a special raid on Japan. There seemed to be two methods of achieving this object: either the planes could be based and maintained in China or else they could be based in India, moving to China each time for a mission, returning to their bases in India on completion. An indication of the shortage of Japanese shipping was the fact that they were buying up junks to replace coastal steamers, so that they could employ these on their maintenance routes.

GENERAL ARNOLD said that he was fully aware of the need for reinforcing the U. S. Air Force in China. One group of aircraft was just preparing to leave the U.S.A.; and he would examine, when he got to India, the best method of operating the aircraft. He hoped that effective operations would start before April. It should be remembered, however, that there were large demands for transport aircraft in other theaters, and these could not be neglected. Nevertheless, he hoped to have 135-150 transport planes operating on the India-China route by the end of the Fall.

U. S. SECRET
BRITISH MOST SECRET

GENERAL MARSHALL said that the provision of transport planes for India competed with urgent requirements for HUSKY, and for cross-channel operations. Nevertheless, he felt it was vital to step up the effort in China, and this would be done.

The PRIME MINISTER expressed his agreement with the President's proposals. He suggested that the document should now be reconsidered by the Combined Chiefs of Staff, and amendments arising out of the present discussion should be incorporated in a final edition. The document would then fittingly embody the results of a remarkable period of sustained work.

The PRESIDENT agreed with this proposal, and expressed his congratulations to the Combined Chiefs of Staff on the results which they had achieved.

CASABLANCA CONFERENCE
JANUARY 1943

MINUTES OF THE COMBINED CHIEFS OF STAFF MEETINGS

	PAGE
C.C.S. 55th Meeting	169
C.C.S. 56th Meeting	183
C.C.S. 57th Meeting	195
C.C.S. 58th Meeting	207
C.C.S. 59th Meeting	225
C.C.S. 60th Meeting	232
C.C.S. 61st Meeting	248
C.C.S. 62nd Meeting	254
C.C.S. 63rd Meeting	263
C.C.S. 64th Meeting	272
C.C.S. 65th Meeting	276
C.C.S. 66th Meeting	292
C.C.S. 67th Meeting	300
C.C.S. 68th Meeting	310
C.C.S. 69th Meeting	314

U. S. SECRET
BRITISH MOST SECRET

C.C.S. 55th Meeting

COMBINED CHIEFS OF STAFF

MINUTES of Meeting held at Anfa Camp
on Thursday, January 14, 1943, at 1030.

PRESENT

General G. C. Marshall, USA
Admiral E. J. King, USN
Lt. General H. H. Arnold, USA

General Sir Alan F. Brooke
Admiral of the Fleet Sir Dudley Pound
Air Chief Marshal Sir Charles F. A. Portal

THE FOLLOWING WERE ALSO PRESENT

Lt. General B. B. Somervell, USA
Rear Admiral C. M. Cooke, Jr., USN
Brig. General A. C. Wedemeyer, USA

Field Marshal Sir John Dill
Vice Admiral the Lord Louis Mountbatten
Lt. General Sir Hastings L. Ismay

SECRETARIAT

Brigadier V. Dykes
Brig. General J. R. Deane, USA

U. S. SECRET
BRITISH MOST SECRET

GENERAL MARSHALL outlined the broad problem facing the Combined Chiefs of Staff as the allocation of resources between the two major theaters of war--the Atlantic (which included for this purpose the Mediterranean) and the Pacific. He suggested as a concept on which to work that this broad allocation should consist of 70 percent in the Atlantic theater and 30 percent in the Pacific theater.

ADMIRAL KING said that according to his estimates we were at present engaging only 15 percent of our total resources against the Japanese in the Pacific theater, which for this purpose included the Indian Ocean and Burma. In his view this was not sufficient to prevent Japan consolidating herself and thereby presenting ultimately too difficult a problem. The Japanese were fighting a delaying action in the Solomon Islands and digging in along the whole line of the Netherlands East Indies and the Philippines. They were shipping back raw material into Japan as fast as they could. He felt that before the Combined Chiefs of Staff turned to the discussion of particular operations they should first fix the general proportion of effort to be applied in the two main theaters.

SIR ALAN BROOKE suggested that in fixing this balance of effort between the two theaters, it would be wise first to try and weigh up the enemy situation as both the U. S. and British Chiefs of Staff saw it. The U. S. Chiefs of Staff would naturally know more of the situation in Japan than the British. He expressed the admiration of the British Chiefs of Staff on the magnificent work of the U. S. Forces during the last twelve months after the early disasters of the war against Japan. At one time it seemed as if nothing would stem the tide of the Japanese, but the position was now very different. The Japanese were definitely on a defensive basis and from intelligence received it appeared as if they were taking quite a different outlook on the war now from what they had been some months ago. They were worried about the situation of their European allies.

The security of the United States and the United Kingdom had always been basic factors in our strategy. The threat to the United Kingdom had been at one time serious, but as a result of our latest review of this danger it was felt that the forces in the United Kingdom could be reorientated from a defensive to an offensive basis. The greatest danger at the present time was to our communications. The shortage of

U. S. SECRET
BRITISH MOST SECRET

shipping was a stranglehold on all offensive operations and unless we could effectively combat the U-boat menace, we might not be able to win the war.

Germany's situation was undoubtedly developing favorably from our point of view. She was staggering under the failure of her second offensive against Russia, and feeling must be growing in that country that it was impossible for her to defeat Russia. Her successes in 1942 against Russia had been very much smaller in scale than in 1941. She had failed in her main object of the 1942 campaign, the capture of the Caucasus oil. By failing to capture even the port of Tuapse, she had failed in securing the facilities to export such oil as she had captured at Grozny. Her northern flank was in danger as also were the troops in the Caucasus salient.

The Russian offensive had been well carried out and had now reached within fifty miles of Rostov. Germany had only two courses open to her, either to push back the Russians into Stalingrad, which would be almost impossible during the winter, or to shorten her line. The latter, therefore, was the more probable course; and that would involve reverting to the 1941 line. The psychological effect of this withdrawal would be very serious in Germany.

Germany was thus on the defensive both in Russia and in North Africa. In the operations which had led to the defeat of the Germans in North Africa after the British defeat at Tobruk very great assistance had been given by the timely arrival of American Sherman tanks and S.P. guns.

Germany was already having trouble among her allies. The Rumanians had suffered severely in the Crimea but had been forced to carry on, although greatly weakened in strength. The Italian troops on the Russian front had also suffered heavy losses and the Hungarian forces, which had never had much stomach for the fight, were also in bad shape. Italy was becoming more and more shaky; and if she collapsed, Germany would not only have to bolster up Italy by sending troops into the country but would also have to replace the numerous German divisions in Yugoslavia and in Greece. Alternatively she would have to withdraw altogether from the Balkans and Italy, and leave it open to the Allies.

U. S. SECRET
BRITISH MOST SECRET

All indications showed that Germany's manpower was failing and that some cannibalization of her divisions would have to be carried out. The latest estimate was that she would lose ten divisions in this way during the first quarter of 1943. Lack of oil was another of Germany's major difficulties which would hit her particularly hard during the next six months.

Taking all these factors into account, it seemed at least possible that the precarious internal situation of Germany might make it possible to achieve a final victory in the European theater before the end of 1943. The immediate problem was how best to apply our available resources in order to take advantage of Germany's present situation.

The means we had at our disposal were broadly three in number. First there was Russia, which constituted the largest land power; her efficiency was rising and the work of moving Russian manufacturing plants to the eastward away from the German invasion had been very well carried out. Russia's oil situation was now more satisfactory than had seemed likely earlier in the year, but she was short of grain. In order to get the best value out of Russia, we must support her in every way we could. Our second main weapon was air bombardment, by U. S. and British forces. This we must exploit to the maximum. Our third means of striking at Germany was by amphibious operations which included invasion of the Continent. The possession of sea power enabled us to threaten the enemy at several points and thereby compel him to disperse his forces. Once commited to a point of entry, however, the enemy would be able to concentrate his forces against us, and it was therefore necessary to choose this point of entry with the greatest care at the place where the enemy was least able to concentrate large forces.

As a point of reentry to the Continent, France had great advantages. In the first place the sea-crossing was short, and we had better facilities for giving air support to our invasion. On the other hand the German defenses in this area were most strong and Germany's power of concentrating against us was greatest. A recent study had shown that the East-West communications across the Continent enabled Germany to move seven divisions simultaneously from the Russian front to the West in about twelve to fourteen days. The North-South communications on the Continent

U. S. SECRET
BRITISH MOST SECRET

were not nearly so good. Not more than one division at a time could be moved from the North to the Mediterranean front. The Italian railways were close to the coast and vulnerable to interruption from the sea, and in the Balkans there was only a single line of railway passing through Nish. From this point of view, therefore, the Southern front seemed to offer better prospects for amphibious operations.

TORCH operations in North Africa had been an outstanding example of successful cooperation between U. S. and British forces, and the British Chiefs of Staff wished to express their admiration of the very able manner in which General Eisenhower had overcome the extremely difficult problems with which he had been faced. North Africa would provide a valuable base from which either to threaten Southern Europe or to undertake offensive operations. By this use we could compel the Germans to disperse their forces in order to reinforce threatened points. In this way we could probably give greater assistance to Russia than if we committed ourselves definitely to Northern France. Once we had captured Bizerte, we could pass merchant ship convoys through the Mediterranean. Their very passage would compel the Germans to fight in the air, since if they let them pass through unmolested the effect of their U-boat operations against our shipping would be largely nullified. These air battles against the German Air Force would be of the greatest importance. Already more than half the German Air Force was deployed on fronts other than the Russian.

In all Mediterranean operations Spain, of course, was a most important factor. There must be always some anxiety that Spain would close the door behind us, but all recent opinion tended to show that Spain was turning away from Germany and that it was at least highly improbable that she would ever grant free access to German forces. The more successes we had in the Mediterranean the more likely it was that this favorable tendency in Spain would continue. Spain knew that from the economic point of view she must depend primarily on the Allies. Against this there was, of course, the fear of Communism in Spain if the Allies were victorious and Russia overran Germany. Generally speaking, however, the feeling of the British Chiefs of Staff was that we had no cause for anxiety about Spain at the present time.

Another important factor in the Mediterranean was Turkey. That country no doubt would either try and keep out of the war altogether or

U.S. SECRET
BRITISH MOST SECRET

at least join in on the side of the Allies only at the eleventh hour. There were, however, reasons to hope that if well handled, Turkey might be brought in earlier. As an inducement we should have to give her equipment, technical personnel and instructors. It did not seem wise to press Turkey to undertake an advance into the Balkans but rather to hold her position and afford us bases from which to attack Germany, in particular the Rumanian oil. We might also obtain a free passage to the Black Sea as another means of striking at Germany.

Summing up prospects in the European Theater, SIR ALAN BROOKE said that the British Chiefs of Staff felt that we should first expand the bomber offensive against the Axis to the maximum and that operations in the Mediterranean offered the best chance of compelling Germany to disperse her resources. With this end in view we should take as our immediate objective the knocking out of Italy. At the same time, we should try and bring in Turkey on our side. By this means we should give Germany no respite at all in 1943 and we should give the best aid to Russia, whom we must continue to supply with all the equipment which we could send. The difficulty, of course, was that many of these operations were mutually exclusive. For example, to send large supplies to Russia used up great quantities of available escort vessels. This naturally cut down our capacity to undertake amphibious operations. A balance would have to be struck between these various commitments, and we should have to face the necessity for accepting considerable losses in shipping, providing these paid a good dividend.

We must be in a position to take advantage of a crack in Germany in the late summer. There were already indications of considerable German withdrawals from France to the eastward. If Germany were compelled to withdraw considerable numbers of troops from France, the possibilities of an invasion across the Channel would be much greater. The estimate of the British Chiefs of Staff was that by August 1943 there would be available for cross channel operations some 13 British and 9 U.S. divisions whether or not we undertook limited operations in the Mediterranean. Mediterranean operations, however, would produce other shortages, notably in Assault Shipping; and it might be difficult, if not impossible, to transfer landing craft from the Mediterranean to the United Kingdom or to the Burma front in time.

U. S. SECRET
BRITISH MOST SECRET

In all amphibious operations the provision of landing craft was the critical factor. Not only had the crews to be provided but the naval crews to man them had to be trained and the land forces had to be trained to work from them. This training was a slow process.

The British landing craft resources were being formed into two main forces, one earmarked for operations on the Continent and one for operations further afield, such as Burma. As regards operations in Burma, a limited offensive was now being undertaken with the object of capturing Akyab, on which the 14th Indian Division was now closing. Operations in the North of Burma presented very difficult logistical problems owing to the absence of roads.

The complete conquest of Burma was a much bigger problem, and naval supremacy in the Bay of Bengal would be required for it. It would be necessary to undertake simultaneous offensives against Rangoon and Moulmein since Rangoon could not be taken if the Moulmein airfields were in the hands of the Japs. Rail communications between Thailand and Burma were being improved and it might be necessary to extend the occupation of Burma by going some distance into Thailand as well. For this major operation seven divisions were being prepared in India; and two African divisions, one from the East and one from the West, could be found, both composed of seasoned native troops well adapted to jungle fighting. If the Germans were compelled to abandon their Caucasus offensive, troops could also be found from Iraq and Persia. There appeared, therefore, no particular difficulty in finding the land divisions; the difficulty lay rather in the provision of the necessary naval forces. It must be realized, however, that once started operations for the recapture of Burma would develop into a full-scale campaign.

SIR DUDLEY POUND stated that in the Atlantic the greatest concerns to the Home Fleet were: first, to prevent a break-out of the German naval forces; and, second, to provide protection for convoys to North Russia.

At first, the Russian convoys did not present any great difficulty. Their early success gave everyone a false sense of security. German interference, however, has been increasing constantly, culminating with the concentration of their surface vessels on the coast of Norway;

U. S. SECRET
BRITISH MOST SECRET

namely, the TIRPITZ, LUTZOW, HIPPER, SCHARNHORST, and PRINZ EUGEN, all of which have now been completely repaired. A force of 20 U-boats was maintained in northern waters, as well as considerable air force. The security of Russian convoys is affected chiefly by the hours of darkness and the ice limit. For the next three months, the ice limit will only permit utilizing a channel about 220 miles in width which can be kept under close air reconnaissance by the Germans. The passage occupies about twelve days, and vessels are under attack all but two of them.

For the last convoy of 16 ships there were 12 escort vessels of the corvette type and 4 destroyers. Two six-inch cruisers were employed to give cover against surface attack; the Commander of the convoy had placed the cruisers between the vessels being escorted and the operational base of the German surface vessels. However, the HIPPER and LUTZOW attacked from the other side and came into contact with the 4 British destroyers. Until joined by the two cruisers, the destroyers prevented an attack on the convoy for some forty minutes and drove the enemy ships out of gun range of the convoy, although one of our destroyers and a minesweeper were sunk. As soon as the cruisers appeared, the HIPPER and LUTZOW withdrew. The Germans thus sacrificed a splendid opportunity to effect some serious damage on an inferior force.

It was first thought that the German Admiral commanding had made an error in judgment, but it was later learned that he had received orders from the German authorities ashore to expedite his withdrawal. This would seem to indicate that the Germans are following a policy of preventing their ships from receiving any damage. It can possibly be explained by their desire to keep them intact preliminary to a break-out into the Atlantic.

SIR DUDLEY POUND stated that before such a break-out into the Atlantic could be effected, the Germans must send out oilers which will enable them to refuel at sea, since he doubted if the Germans would again attempt to retire to Brest in view of their previous experience there.

During the months of long daylight, the danger of air attack precluded the use of cruisers with the Russian convoys; and their escorts consisted only of a powerful destroyer force. Convoys can then only be

U. S. SECRET
BRITISH MOST SECRET

run every thirty-six to forty-two days. Twelve days are required for the journey, three days for refueling, twelve days for the return journey, and the remainder for boiler cleaning, etc. The Royal Navy does not have sufficient destroyers to operate two convoys simultaneously. If, therefore, it is necessary to send more than thirty ships to Russia every forty days, it will be necessary for the United States to furnish some assistance in escort vessels.

SIR DUDLEY POUND then stated that there was considerable traffic between Japan and Germany, Japan sending to Germany rubber and other raw materials obtained in the Far East in return for machinery and machine parts. It was important to stop this traffic at once. There are two places from which this can be best accomplished: first, in the Bay of Biscay by air and submarine action, and second, in the Atlantic narrows. For the latter a British task force was being built up on the east side and a U. S. task force was operating from the United States on the west side.

SIR DUDLEY POUND then discussed the situation in the Indian Ocean. It had at first been hoped to create a considerable Eastern Fleet, but this has been seriously reduced in size by TORCH and other operations; and it now appears that its remaining carrier, the Illustrious, may be needed for future operations in the Mediterranean. If this is so, now would be an opportune time to withdraw it from the Indian Ocean for repairs and the installation of the most modern fighter direction devices. Without the protection of carrier aircraft, the Eastern Fleet is unable to operate in the eastern part of the Indian Ocean against Japanese naval forces accompanied by aircraft carriers.

In the Mediterranean area, Admiral Cunningham has a force of three battleships and two aircraft carriers. One of the duties of this Task Force consists in containing three modern Italian battleships which are at present unlocated. In the Eastern Mediterranean, British naval forces had been heavily engaged in the supply of the 8th Army in the Eastern North African ports. What the future redistribution of the Mediterranean naval forces will be must be based on the future strategy to be adopted.

SIR DUDLEY POUND then discussed the German U-boat situation. At the present time the Germans have one hundred and ten submarines in

U. S. SECRET
BRITISH MOST SECRET

the Atlantic in addition to those in the Mediterranean and off the coast of Norway. It is anticipated that new production will go to the Atlantic.

The Germans are apparently concentrating their submarines into large groups, each of which is responsible for a certain area. One of these has been located off the coast of Newfoundland, one in the Central Atlantic, and one off Southwest Ireland. It is possible that a convoy may at any time blunder into a pack of German submarines if our intelligence is at fault.

Recently there were two convoys from the United States, each attacked by a considerable number of German submarines, one convoy losing two vessels and the other losing none. This was accomplished by providing air coverage for the convoys with Liberator airplanes which resulted in keeping the U-boats down during the day. While they were down, the convoys were able to alter their course and, by nightfall, leave the submarines behind.

SIR DUDLEY POUND then described an experiment which had been made owing to shortage of escorts due to TORCH, in sending cargo vessels bound for Freetown out with a trans-Atlantic convoy, the vessels bound for Freetown breaking off from the convoy at a suitable moment and proceeding to their destination independently. The experiment was unsuccessful and the loss amounted to ten percent. Seventeen out of forty-four ships were lost in one convoy. The British have, therefore, found it necessary to resume the Freetown convoys.

SIR DUDLEY POUND stated that escorts to convoys must be sufficiently large to deal with a heavy attack. He said our aim must be to get a long-range air protection and additional escort vessels. He added that it would be desirable to obtain more long-range aircraft protection to escorts from the United States.

SIR DUDLEY POUND indicated that we must make special efforts to provide adequate protection in the early part of 1943 in order that we may be able to meet the great demands in the build-up of BOLERO in the latter part of the year.

SIR CHARLES PORTAL then discussed the air situation. He stated that our experience so far has been that the German operations are definitely tied up with the adequacy of their air power. He felt that this

U. S. SECRET
BRITISH MOST SECRET

will be as true with regard to the German defensive operations as it has been in their offensive operations.

The present state of the German air force is critical. The stamina of the airplane crews is decreasing; the crews lack interest and are less determined, and their training is deteriorating. One explanation for this is that training units and personnel are being used for combat purposes because of a shortage of aircraft. He felt that there is no depth behind the German front line of aircraft. The British Intelligence Service is of the opinion that if the United Nations can keep Germany fighting with aircraft, they will suffer losses from which they cannot recover.

He felt certain that they are incapable of conducting large scale operations on two fronts and that if they are kept fighting through the winter and spring they will have in the summer a shortage of from seven hundred to two thousand first-line aircraft below what will be necessary for all fronts.

He stated that German production for next year will be about twenty-three thousand aircraft; Italy will produce three or four thousand; and Japan will produce about seven thousand. On the other hand, the lowest estimates for the United Nations' aircraft production will be one hundred thousand combat airplanes or about four times that of the Axis powers.

SIR CHARLES PORTAL said that our greatest need is to force the Germans to extend the use of their aircraft to as many areas as possible and thus destroy and bleed them. The best ways to accomplish this are: (1) to engage them while they are in support of land operations. (However this is only possible at present on the Russian front.); (2) to meet them while they are attempting to stop our amphibian operations; and (3) by directing operations directly at Germany.

He stated that one of the most pressing questions was how we should accomplish our air attack against Germany. The United Kingdom is the most advantageous base for such operations and one of the most important questions before the present conference is to decide on where the United States bombers are to be used.

He indicated that daylight attacks by United States bombers should be continued, as this has a serious effect on the German Air Force,

U. S. SECRET
BRITISH MOST SECRET

on their industries, and on their morale. The question of whether to strike Italy from the United Kingdom or from North Africa is still an open question; but before deciding to build up a strong bomber force in North Africa, it is desirable to be certain that this action is more advantageous than concentrating them in the United Kingdom.

GENERAL MARSHALL stated that insofar as the estimates presented by the British Chiefs of Staff concerning Germany, Russia, and the occupied countries are concerned, the United States Chiefs of Staff are in full accord.

He also expressed concurrence in the idea that the U-boat menace is the paramount issue and that everything must be done to combat it by directing our attacks against it from the place of manufacture of submarines to the places where they are used.

He stated that the Japs are digging in, in an effort to build up a defensive front from the Solomons, through New Guinea and Timor, particularly with their air forces.

He pointed out that the United States Chiefs of Staff are anxious to find some method whereby they can strike in the rear and against the flank of the Japanese defenses. In this connection, they feel that operations in Burma will serve to weaken the Japs' defensive front and that, therefore, they are most anxious to undertake Operation RAVENOUS

They feel that a reverse in this operation would not be a calamity but that a success would bring advantages all out of proportion to the risks involved. It would have an effect not only in the South Pacific area but would enable us to furnish strong support to China. A successful Operation RAVENOUS would result in an eventual economy of tonnage by relieving the Japanese pressure in the Southwest Pacific.

GENERAL MARSHALL then stated that the United States Chiefs of Staff are concerned as to whether operations in the Mediterranean area would bring advantages commensurate with the risks involved. He said that the Joint Chiefs of Staff are inclined to look favorably on an operation from the United Kingdom because of the strong air support that can be furnished from that base as well as the relative ease with which it can be supplied from the United States.

U. S. SECRET
BRITISH MOST SECRET

He repeated that our first concern must be the defeat of Germany's submarine warfare.

SIR CHARLES PORTAL then said that the British Chiefs of Staff also felt that the defeat of the submarine menace must be given first priority in the use of air power, particularly in the protection of our line of communications.

For long range antisubmarine operations not only the provision of suitable aircraft had to be considered but also the bases from which they are to be used. The British are considering the advisability of establishing an air base in Greenland for this purpose. They were most grateful for the 21 Liberators provided by the U.S.A. for the Bay of Biscay. There are three possible methods of attack on submarines: (1) along the sea lanes; (2) against bases in the Bay of Biscay; and (3) against factories in which submarines are built. The British now propose making air attacks in sufficient force to destroy the entire port in which the submarines are based rather than confining their attacks to the submarine pens and surrounding installations. He pointed out that no one can be certain as to how much damage can be done in the port towns themselves and that the method proposed will be in the nature of an experiment, the results of which will not be known for five or six months.

ADMIRAL KING then asked whether the possibility of concentrating all air attacks on the building yards had been considered.

SIR CHARLES PORTAL replied that the building yards are not sufficiently large to be certain of hitting them at night.

ADMIRAL KING said that he felt the most favorable targets against the submarine menace were the yards at which they are assembled and at their bases. He said that he had the personal impression that there has not been a program undertaken there that has been consistently followed. He felt that the attacks had been sporadic. He thought that attacks should be aimed: first, against factories where component parts are made; secondly, at yards where the submarines are assembled; thirdly, at bases; and fourthly, at sea.

GENERAL ARNOLD said he felt we should attempt to find what component part or parts of submarines constitute a bottleneck and then strike at factories where they are made.

U. S. SECRET
BRITISH MOST SECRET

SIR CHARLES PORTAL stated that the greatest bottleneck was the ball bearings, but pointed out that it would be tactically impossible to destroy the factories.

GENERAL ARNOLD drew attention to the necessity for a decision as to where airplanes are to be utilized before they left the factory. This is so because different theaters require different equipment on aircraft.

GENERAL MARSHALL stated that the United States is now in the process of recasting its troop deployments. As an example, he indicated that it had become possible to reduce the size of the Caribbean garrison considerably. He stated that the United States is also considering reducing the size of the Iceland garrison and in that connection he thought it would be desirable to have opinions of the Combined Chiefs of Staff on the hazards that now face Iceland. The purpose of this scaling down of forces wherever it can be accomplished is for saving shipping.

U. S. SECRET
BRITISH MOST SECRET

C.C.S. 56th Meeting

COMBINED CHIEFS OF STAFF

MINUTES of Meeting held at Anfa Camp
on Thursday, January 14, 1943, at 1430.

PRESENT

General G. C. Marshall, USA	General Sir Alan F. Brooke
Admiral E. J. King, USN	Admiral of the Fleet Sir Dudley Pound
Lt. General H. H. Arnold, USA	Air Chief Marshal Sir Charles F. A. Portal

THE FOLLOWING WERE ALSO PRESENT

Lt. General B. B. Somervell, USA	Field Marshal Sir John Dill
Rear Admiral C. M. Cooke, Jr., USN	Vice Admiral the Lord Louis Mountbatten
Brig. General A. C. Wedemeyer, USA	
Commander R. E. Libby, USN	Lt. General Sir Hastings L. Ismay

SECRETARIAT

Brigadier V. Dykes
Brig. General J. R. Deane, USA

U. S. SECRET
BRITISH MOST SECRET

COMBINED STRATEGY

SIR ALLEN BROOKE said that he would like to hear the views of the United States Chiefs of Staff regarding the situation in the Pacific.

ADMIRAL KING stated that of the nine fronts on which the United Nations are now engaged, four are in the Pacific. These include the Alaska-Aleutian area, the Hawaiian-Midway area, the South and Southwest Pacific areas, and the Burma-China area.

He said that when he took office as Commander-in-Chief of the United States Fleet on December 30, 1941, he immediately sent a dispatch to the Commander-in-Chief of the Pacific Fleet stating that his mission was, first, to hold the Hawaiian-Midway line and the communications with the Pacific coast; and, secondly, to hold the remainder of the line of communications to Australia and New Zealand.

The Navy had already established a refueling point at Bora Bora which was sufficiently far to the rear to insure its being held. Marines had been sent to Samoa and there were also troops in the Fiji Islands. Steps had been taken to establish three strong points on the line of communications: Samoa, the Fiji Islands, and New Caledonia. The Joint Chiefs of Staff had then established a base for the Navy in Auckland with an advanced base at Tongatabu. As time went on, the United States forces went into the New Hebrides to Efate and Esperitu Santos.

Meanwhile, there had been engagements with the Japanese near the Marshall Islands, the Island of Wake, and in the Coral Sea.

The Japanese had advanced as far south as Tulagi with the apparent intent of using it as a base from which to operate against our line of communications.

ADMIRAL KING said that had we been set at the time of Midway, we could have made great progress in an attack on the Solomon Islands. The operation was in preparation in July and took place on August 7th but we did not have sufficient force even at that time to exploit our success beyond the occupation of Tulagi and Guadalcanal. The Japanese reaction there was more violent and sustained than had been anticipated. Another reason why we could not proceed further with the Solomon operations was

U. S. SECRET
BRITISH MOST SECRET

that Operation TORCH had been decided upon and much of our available means had to be diverted to it.

ADMIRAL KING stated, however, that we have attempted to go on with the Solomon operations. The Japanese reaction was, at first, probably designed to "save face" but eventually that became a minor consideration. The Japanese have a long line of communications, and it soon became apparent that they were fighting a delaying action to cover the Netherlands East Indies and the Philippines where the "treasures" are to be found.

He pointed out that we have had some success in the attrition of the Japanese forces but not as much as has been claimed. At present, the Tulagi area is pretty well stabilized and General MacArthur has driven the Japanese out of the Papuan Peninsula on New Guinea. The enemy is reinforcing Lae and Salamaua.

The main object of the operations has been the safety of the approaches to northeastern Australia, and the key to the situation is Rabaul.

The campaign in the Solomons was to be divided into three parts: (1) the capture of Tulagi, (2) securing the northeast coast of New Guinea, and (3) the capture of Rabaul. The process has been slow but the United States forces are going on with it. The immediate question is where to go when this campaign has been completed.

ADMIRAL KING stated that he felt the Philippines should be our objective rather than the Netherlands East Indies. The Philippines could be captured by a flank action whereas the capture of the Netherlands East Indies must of necessity be the result of a frontal attack. The most likely intermediate objective, once Rabaul is captured, is Truk and thence to the Marianas.

Prior to the war, every class at the Naval War College was required to play the game of the Pacific Islands involving the recapture of the Philippines. There are three ways in which the Philippines may be taken: first, the direct route which would constitute a frontal attack; second, the southern route which is outflanked by the enemy along much of its course; and third, the northern route through the Aleutians to

U. S. SECRET
BRITISH MOST SECRET

the northern tip of the Island of Luzon. The northern route would include establishing a base in the northwestern Marshall Islands and then proceeding to Truk and the Marianas. The Marianas are the key of the situation because of their location on the Japanese line of communications. Any line of action decided upon requires considerable force, especially air strength. All of the necessary operations are amphibious.

ADMIRAL KING said that Mr. Stalin had been good enough to say that the Solomons operations have been of considerable assistance to Russia.

He pointed out the importance to the Japanese of occupying the Maritime Provinces in order to secure the Japanese Islands. He felt that such action would be necessary and that the Japanese should attach more importance to them than holding the Netherlands East Indies.

ADMIRAL KING stated that the Japanese are now replenishing Japan with raw materials and also fortifying an inner defense ring along the line of the Netherlands East Indies and the Philippines. For these reasons, he believed that it was necessary for the United Nations to prevent the Japanese having time to consolidate their gains. He compared this situation with the present desire of the United Nations to avoid giving Germany a respite during the winter months.

ADMIRAL KING then said that the idea of utilizing 30 percent of the United Nations war effort against Japan was a concept rather than an arithmetical computation. He had caused studies to be made of how much of the total war effort is now being applied to Japan and found it to be approximately 15 percent. He said that this is not sufficient to do more than hold; it is not enough to permit maintaining pressure on the Japanese.

ADMIRAL KING stated that we are continuously exploring possibilities of an attack against Japan by the northern route and called attention to the fact that the United States forces had just captured Amchitka. All operations in the Pacific are limited by the amount of available shipping.

ADMIRAL KING pointed out that the Japanese route for a naval effort against Siberia is secure. He said that he had recently had a

U. S. SECRET
BRITISH MOST SECRET

survey made of Paramushiro Island, the northernmost of the Kurile Islands. This revealed that it would be unsatisfactory as a base for operating against Japan.

It would be desirable to have the cooperation of the Russians in this respect but there has been difficulty in obtaining any information from them. The best means of obtaining information so far has been by direct correspondence between the President and Mr. Stalin.

GENERAL MARSHALL then reviewed the deployment of the United States troops in all of the islands of the Pacific, giving the strength of each in ground and air troops and in aircraft. He pointed out the logistical difficulties of supplying these forces.

ADMIRAL KING then gave the disposition of the Marine forces which amount to approximately 60,000 men in the area from Midway to the South Pacific Islands.

GENERAL MARSHALL said that in the light of the logistical requirements in the Pacific, the United States' interest in undertaking an operation to open the Burma Road could be well understood. General Stilwell and Field Marshal Wavell would have to determine the logistical requirements of such an operation but, in any event, they would be minor in comparison to the requirements in the Operation TORCH. Any success in the Operation RAVENOUS would have a tremendous effect in the Pacific chiefly by making it necessary for the Japanese to divert forces to the Burma operations, thus lessening the pressure in the South Pacific and the consequent demands on our available shipping.

GENERAL MARSHALL stated that the peace of mind of the United States Chiefs of Staff was greater now than it had been a year ago. The Japanese are now on the defensive and must be careful of a surprise move from us. However, he pointed out that we must still worry about the locations of the Japanese aircraft carriers because they constitute a constant threat against our line of communications and for raiding purposes against our west coast.

We must not allow the Japanese any pause. They fight with no idea of surrendering and they will continue to be aggressive until attrition has defeated them. To accomplish this, we must maintain the initiative and force them to meet us.

U S SECRET
BRITISH MOST SECRET

GENERAL ARNOLD then discussed the United States efforts to obtain information concerning Russia. He stated that when the Germans threatened to capture the Caucasus, the Russians began to be fearful that the supply of airplanes from the United States via the southern route would be eliminated. They, therefore, requested the United States to start delivery of airplanes from Alaska at once. The United States agreed to this providing the Russians would demonstrate that there were sufficient facilities available to make possible the delivery of one hundred and fifty planes a month. The Russians did not have these facilities at the time but built them rapidly. At the present time, both the southern route and the Alaskan route are in use. In the coming year, the delivery to Russia amounts to four hundred airplanes a month. These will be divided over the two routes. Bombers are flown to Basra but the flight is so long that the Russians refuse to accept the engines and this necessitates replacing them. The northern route will be used for this purpose as much as possible inasmuch as it eliminates fifty hours of flying time on the journey.

GENERAL ARNOLD then stated that the U. S. Chiefs of Staff were desirous of knowing what facilities were available in southern Siberia and Vladivostok in order to see if they could be of assistance to Russia in case Russia was attacked by the Japanese.

GENERAL MARSHALL stated that Mr. Stalin had finally given General Bradley permission to make a survey. General Bradley, however, considered that it would be better to present the Russians with a specific proposal. He returned to the United States, and it was decided to offer Russia one hundred heavy bombers seventy-two days after the outbreak of war between Russia and Japan. Mr. Stalin had rejected this offer and said he would like 100 aircraft at once for use against Germany.

GENERAL MARSHALL also stated that the Russians object to the presence of "gossipy" people from the United Nations and that they were afraid that the United Nations personnel could not put up with the conditions which are imposed on Russian troops.

SIR CHARLES PORTAL stated that the British had operated successfully with the Russian navy in the Murmansk area but that they had the same experiences with the Russian army as the U. S. had.

U. S SECRET
BRITISH MOST SECRET

GENERAL MARSHALL then described the difficulties which the United States Chiefs of Staff had had concerning sending air units to the Caucasus. The Russians had stated definitely that they did not desire units but airplanes only. There had been some sentiment among the United States authorities to furnish sufficient airplanes for the purpose of placating Mr. Stalin. However, to do so, especially in the case of heavy bombers, would necessitate immobilizing these airplanes for as much as six months while the Russians were learning to operate them and establishing ground crews for their maintenance. General Marshall stated that in his opinion it was unwise to withhold this striking power against the enemy for so long a period.

ADMIRAL KING then asked the British Chiefs of Staff if they had the impression that the Russians were unwilling to help themselves. The Germans were successfully operating air forces out of the northern part of Norway and the Russians had apparently made no effort to stop them although they were well within range.

SIR DUDLEY POUND stated that the Russians do send destroyers out to meet convoys. They invariably state, however, that they have run out of fuel before completing their task and then leave the convoy for home at a rate of 28 knots, which is hardly consistent with a shortage of fuel. Their Air Force has not furnished much protection.

SIR CHARLES PORTAL stated that he felt the reason for this was that their air personnel is not properly trained. The Russians had made some attempts to strike at the German forces but had been unsuccessful

GENERAL MARSHALL asked why the Russians were willing to risk whole divisions but not their naval forces

SIR DUDLEY POUND replied that they are continental people who do not understand naval action. Their submarines have been the only effective units of their navy.

SIR ALAN BROOKE agreed with this statement and added that while they do not know what dangers are involved in escorting convoys, they are very free to offer silly advice as to how security should be attained

GENERAL MARSHALL then described the development of troops of the United States, which was proceeding very well. He added that United States

U. S. SECRET
BRITISH MOST SECRET

troops, both in this and the last war, appeared to "veteranize" quickly in the field. The young officers and non-commissioned officers had exhibited a remarkable facility for eliminating errors rapidly. We may expect their effectiveness to increase enormously in a short time.

He thought we were particularly fortunate in the deadly character of the Pacific fight, since our forces which have been engaged in the Pacific have become imbued with the idea that it is "kill or be killed"; and this attitude gives promise of tremendous power for future operations. The staffs are sound and the engineers are particularly effective. He recalled a remark that had been made in the War Department, when Field Marshal Wavell questioned the possibility of building a road which could support the Burma operations, to the effect that "Wavell does not know General Wheeler," the United States engineer in this theater.

SIR ALAN BROOKE inquired how far forward the U. S. Chiefs of Staff envisaged it would be necessary to go in order to prevent the Japanese from digging themselves in. He feared that if operations were too extended it would inevitably lead to an all-out war against Japan and it was certain that we had not sufficient resources to undertake this at the same time as a major effort against Germany. Would it be possible for the forces at present in the Pacific to hold the Japanese without incurring the additional drain on our resources which would result from pushing forward our present defensive positions?

GENERAL MARSHALL explained that it had been essential to act offensively in order to stop the Japanese advancing. For example, in New Guinea it had been necessary to push the Japanese back to prevent them capturing Port Moresby. In order to do this, every device for reinforcing the troops on the island had had to be employed. The same considerations applied in Guadalcanal. It had been essential to take offensive action to seize the island. Short of offensive action of this nature, the only way of stopping the Japanese was by complete exhaustion through attrition. It was very difficult to pause; the process of whittling away Japan had to be continuous.

SIR CHARLES PORTAL asked whether it was not possible to stand on a line and inflict heavy losses on the Japanese when they tried to break through it. From the very fact that the Japanese continued to attack, it

U. S. SECRET
BRITISH MOST SECRET

was clear that they had already been pushed back further than they cared to go. We also inquired whether the U. S. Chiefs of Staff thought it would be possible to gain a decision by air bombardment of Japan alone.

GENERAL ARNOLD pointed out that the Allied forces in the Southwest Pacific were now operating from the tips of two narrow salients. The Japanese had greater width in their line and could therefore operate on a larger scale than the forces which we could bring to bear.

GENERAL MARSHALL said that in Papua it would be possible to gain additional airfields alongside our present position, but this was not the case in Guadalcanal where only a small strip of suitable territory was available. To broaden our base there, we should have to have New Britain and New Ireland. As regards air bombardment of Japan, the U. S. view was that Japanese industries were so vulnerable to the air that heavy attack would ultimately destroy her capacity to maintain her war effort.

SIR CHARLES PORTAL suggested that it should be possible to determine what it was that we had to prevent the Japanese from doing, and what forces we should require for the purpose. We should then see what forces remained for use elsewhere in the world.

ADMIRAL KING observed that unless some effort was made to assist Chiang Kai-shek, the Chinese might pull out of the war. The 30 percent effort to which he had referred would, of course, include operations in Burma.

SIR ALAN BROOKE agreed that operation RAVENOUS might be successful but when we had reached the objective we should still have to defend our line of communication against Japanese attack from the flank. It was calculated that the route would only suffice to maintain two Divisions, and this would leave little if any capacity for the supply air forces operating in China.

ADMIRAL KING pointed out that in addition to opening the supply route to China, RAVENOUS would gain the territory necessary to secure the air supply route from India to China.

SIR ALAN BROOKE agreed that it would be well worth while taking a risk on RAVENOUS since it would not cut across the main effort against Germany, whereas ANAKIM would.

U. S. SECRET
BRITISH MOST SECRET

GENERAL MARSHALL pointed out that the Chinese only required about half the maintenance tonnage required by white troops. In any event, even a small residual tonnage for supplies to China would probably be far greater than could be transported by air. Twelve bombers in China under General Chennault had done wonderful work; and if he had even 50, the results they might achieve would be very great. For this reason the U. S. Chiefs of Staff thought that RAVENOUS was a gamble well worth while. It should also be remembered that any help given to China which would threaten Japan might have a most favorable effect on Stalin.

GENERAL ARNOLD said that General Chennault claimed he could drive the Japanese Air Force out of China if he had 175 aircraft. This might be an exaggerated claim, but there was no doubt additional air forces in China would have a very great effect. By December it was hoped to have 150 transports working from India to China, with a maximum delivery estimated at 10,000 tons per month.

ADMIRAL KING asked on whom would fall the principal burden of beating Japan once Germany had been knocked out.

SIR ALAN BROOKE said that once Germany was defeated, practically all the British naval forces would be released for the war against Japan. Forces destined for the recapture of Burma and Malaya were already forming in India. He did not think it wise, however, to embark on Operation ANAKIM unless we were quite prepared for a full-scale campaign.

SIR CHARLES PORTAL said that India had already been asked to provide airfields for double the number of air forces we were ever likely to have available before the defeat of Germany. These were intended for the campaign against Japan. He had no doubt that as soon as Germany was defeated the British Government would turn the whole of their resources against Japan.

GENERAL MARSHALL pointed out that to depend on sea operations alone against Japan was hazardous, owing to the rapidity with which the balance of sea power could change in the event of a reverse. For example, in the Midway battle the U. S. Forces had been able to get all their aircraft into the air before the Japanese attack developed. In consequence, the Japanese had lost four carriers as against one American. With a little

U. S. SECRET
BRITISH MOST SECRET

ill-fortune the reverse might have taken place; and in that case, the whole of the west coast of America would have been open to Japanese carrier-borne attack. The Japanese territories were not nearly so vulnerable in this respect.

ADMIRAL KING said that the Japanese might well strike again at Midway. They were on interior lines, and it was easier for them to take the initiative against us. At the present time it looked as if their carriers were being prepared for another attack somewhere, perhaps on Midway or Samoa. It was essential, therefore, to maintain the initiative against the Japanese and not wait for them to come against us.

GENERAL MARSHALL explained the difficulties with which he had been faced in finding even the small forces required by General Stilwell to support LAVENCIS. Shipping could not be spared for them in the absence of some definite assurance from Chiang Kai-shek and agreement with Field Marshal Wavell on the operations to be undertaken. By the time these had been obtained much time had been lost and shipping had to be found by drawing it away from other commitments in the Pacific such as Alaska and Hawaii. General MacArthur was some 20,000 men short of his requirements, and provision of these reinforcements had had to be deferred. By the most rigid economy sufficient shipping had at last been found to move 6,000 men to General Stilwell. In order to cut down numbers to the minimum, units had been stripped to the bone of all personnel which were not absolutely essential. It was certainly fortunate that losses sustained in the Pacific from submarines had been so small.

ADMIRAL KING said he was puzzled to know why these losses had been so small and what the Japanese were keeping their submarines for.

SIR DUDLEY POUND said that, in British experience, Japanese submarines were much less of a menace than the German. They were less efficiently operated, and quite small escorts were sufficient to drive them away. He pointed out that it was in a way to our advantage to allow the Japanese to dig in well in places which we did not mean to attack as this dispersed their forces. To recapture the Philippines before the defeat of Germany was impossible; and it was, therefore, all to the good if the Japanese locked up troops in these Islands. The quickest way of recapturing the Philippines would be to defeat Germany. It seemed to him that

U. S. SECRET
BRITISH MOST SECRET

the correct strategy was to establish a line where we had better air facilities than the Japanese and then to allow them to wear out their air forces by attacking us on that line. Would it be of any advantage to go as far forward as Truk in the immediate future rather than just before the main attack on the Philippines? Even if we had Truk he questioned whether we could operate surface forces against the Japanese lines of communication at the present time.

ADMIRAL KING agreed that the recapture of the Philippines must probably await the defeat of Germany. On the other hand, he would be in favor of seizing Truk and going forward to the Marianas in order to dominate the Japanese sea routes to the eastward thus freeing our submarines for the more covered Japanese supply route to the westward. He felt it was necessary to soften up the Japanese before making our main effort and not simply to allow them to do what they wanted, while we held a static position. The 30 percent allocation of resources which he had suggested would certainly suffice for the recapture of Rabaul.

After some further discussion,

THE COMMITTEE:
Agreed to direct the Combined Staff Planners to report, on the basis that Germany is the primary enemy, what situation do we wish to establish in the Eastern Theater (i.e., the Pacific and Burma) in 1943, and what forces will be necessary to establish that situation.

U. S. SECRET
BRITISH MOST SECRET

C.C.S. 57th Meeting

COMBINED CHIEFS OF STAFF

MINUTES of Meeting held at Anfa Camp
on Friday, January 15, 1943, at 1430.

PRESENT

General G.C. Marshall, USA	General Sir Alan F. Brooke
Admiral E. J. King, USN	Admiral of the Fleet Sir Dudley Pound
Lt. General H. H. Arnold, USA	Air Chief Marshal Sir Charles F. A. Portal

THE FOLLOWING WERE ALSO PRESENT

Lt. General B. B. Somervell, USA	Field Marshal Sir John Dill
Lt. General D. D. Eisenhower, USA (For Item 2)	Vice Admiral the Lord Louis Mountbatten
Rear Admiral C. M. Cooke, Jr., USN	Lt. General Sir Hastings L. Ismay
Brig. General A. C. Wedemeyer, USA	Captain C. E. Lambe, RN
	Brigadier G. M. Stewart
	Air Commodore W. Elliot

SECRETARIAT

Brigadier V Dykes
Brig. General J. R. Deane, USA

U. S. SECRET
BRITISH MOST SECRET

1. ANTISUBMARINE WARFARE.

SIR DUDLEY POUND said that the four points at which the U-boats could be attacked were the factories and building yards, the operating bases, the routes to their hunting grounds, and the hunting grounds themselves. He had sent for detailed information concerning the construction bottlenecks. As regards the operating bases, the British Government had agreed to intensify air attacks on French ports which were used as bases. The only question now at issue was that of giving some warning to the French inhabitants.

Attacks on the U-boats on passage to the hunting grounds had been successful for a time and considerable damage and delay had been inflicted on them as long as the U-boats did not know when the aircraft were detecting them with their A.S.V. equipment. This equipment was used in conjunction with the Leigh light at night. Now, however, U-boats were fitted with listening devices which detected the A.S.V. outside the range of the light. Ten-centimeter A.S.V's. were now being introduced, but no doubt in time the Germans would find a counter to them. Nevertheless, if we were successful even in compelling them to remain submerged in darkness, it would have the effect of making them surface in daylight to recharge batteries.

For dealing with the submarines on the hunting grounds, the two requirements were first: as much air cover as possible, and second: adequate escorts. A rough rule of thumb for the number of escorts was to have three ships with every convoy plus one for every ten ships in the convoy. A convoy of forty ships would thus have seven escorts. In practice, however, we were never able to supply this number of escorts, and as a general rule we never had more than six with any convoy. When escorting vessels had to be withdrawn for operations, there was no pool from which to replace them. We had now new commitments in the Sierra Leone convoys which had had to be re-started, and the convoys bringing oil from the Dutch West Indies to the United Kingdom and to North Africa. As a minimum sixty-five more escort vessels were required in the Atlantic alone. Before any decisions were taken on our strategy for 1943, it seemed essential to weigh carefully the requirements in escort vessels for any operations to be undertaken. Once an operation was launched and escorts were withdrawn from convoys, they could not be returned usually

U. S. SECRET
BRITISH MOST SECRET

for four or five months, during which an acute shortage was felt. The only relief during such a period would be the intake from new construction.

SIR CHARLES PORTAL said that the air had proved the most effective weapon against the U-boat. The estimated German output of U-boats was twenty a month. He gave the following figures for attacks on U-boats during the last two months:

		November	December
U-Boats sunk) by aircraft		8	2
U-Boats damaged)		24	9
U-Boats sunk) by other means		8	6
U-Boats damaged)		7	6

Air patrols over the U-boat routes to the hunting grounds were very costly in aircraft since it was calculated that there was only one sighting for 250 hours flying time. Nevertheless, even if a large number of U-boats were not actually destroyed by this means, aircraft patrols had a good effect in compelling U-boats to remain submerged and thereby reducing their time on the hunting grounds. A further method of attack on U-boats was the laying of mines from the air at the exits of the U-boat bases and construction yards.

GENERAL ARNOLD inquired whether it was not possible to use flying boats for anti-submarine work, both over the hunting grounds and on the routes to them. This would avoid the use of valuable long range bombers.

SIR CHARLES PORTAL said that the long range bomber was essential for work over the convoys, since flying boats, owing to their slow speed, took too long to reach them after a call for assistance. Moreover, the load of the flying boat in bombs and depth charges was less than that of the Liberator. In addition they were not processed for the 10-centimeter A.S.V. A considerable number of Catalinas were being used in spite of these disadvantages. It was estimated that the minimum requirements for the whole of the Atlantic and British Home Waters was between 120 and 135 long range bombers. New devices were being developed to combat the German listening apparatus which detected the presence of A.S.V. aircraft.

ADMIRAL KING asked whether economy in long range bombers could not be effected by using Catalinas for patrol work and reserving long

U. S. SECRET
BRITISH MOST SECRET

range bombers for emergency calls when convoys were actually attacked. The Catalina had a very long endurance and could be kept in the air for twenty-four hours if the crew was large enough to provide two watches. One advantage of the flying boat was that any sheltered water could be used for a base instead of airfields.

SIR CHARLES PORTAL said that Catalinas were being used to the maximum. A survey had been made of the West African coast and it was found that two depot ships for Catalinas would suffice on the northern part, but this did not cover the requirements of the Indian Ocean or the South Atlantic.

SIR DUDLEY POUND said that anti-submarine aircraft were essential in the area north of Freetown. The requirements in long range bombers which had been stated were an absolute minimum, even allowing for the maximum use of flying boats.

SIR CHARLES PORTAL asked whether the aircraft in the Pacific, details of which had been given at a meeting on the previous day, were available for anti-submarine work as well as local defense of the Islands themselves.

ADMIRAL KING said that fortunately the Japanese had not yet made any great use of submarines in the Pacific, and it was, therefore, possible to work with only small escorts. If the Japanese submarines became more active, aircraft would have to be used against them. The total resources available, however, were insufficient for security everywhere. When Alaska was threatened, forces had to be sent up from all quarters. The acute shortage of escort vessels was of course fully recognized.

SIR DUDLEY POUND pointed out that where long range shore based aircraft could not be employed to cover the whole passage, as for example in the direct convoys from the Dutch West Indies to the United Kingdom, auxiliary aircraft carriers had to be used with the convoys themselves. On the northern route it was hoped to establish bases for long range aircraft in Newfoundland to join up with aircraft working from the United Kingdom.

GENERAL ARNOLD said that Greenland would be of little use for this purpose owing to the long hours of darkness and the very bad weather.

U. S. SECRET
BRITISH MOST SECRET

ADMIRAL COOKE asked whether full use was being made of direction finding apparatus to pick up the short range inter-communication radio of U-boats working in packs. The Japanese had developed this technique to a high degree.

SIR DUDLEY POUND said that all destroyers and most corvettes, were fitted with the necessary apparatus for this purpose. This use was being developed to the maximum.

SIR CHARLES PORTAL suggested that it would be desirable to have an assessment made of the total resources required in escort vessels and aircraft to combat the submarine menace, in order that the Combined Chiefs of Staff should have a picture of what would be left over for offensive operations during the coming year.

THE COMMITTEE:
Agreed to direct the Combined Staff Planners to examine and report the minimum requirements of escorts (including aircraft carriers) and aircraft which should be devoted to the security of the sea communications of the United Nations during 1943.

(GENERAL EISENHOWER entered the Meeting at this point.)

2. SITUATION IN NORTH AFRICA.

GENERAL EISENHOWER gave a resume of the situation in North Africa at the present time. Operations in December had been held up by bad weather and mud which restricted the use of vehicles entirely to the roads. Since this check every effort had been made to build up for an attack in the North by increasing our air power, improving the communications to the front and re-equipping the 6th Armored Division with Sherman Tanks. By the end of December, however, it was clear that the weather conditions would compel postponement of any attack for a considerable time. Attention had then been directed to the possibility of an attack further to the south where ground conditions were better. For this purpose forces composed of the 1st U. S. Armored Division and two U. S. Regimental Combat teams with Anti-Aircraft and Anti-Tank Units were being concentrated. At first operations on the right flank had been looked upon primarily as a diversion, but it now seemed probable that it would be possible to advance on Sfax and hold it with infantry while withdrawing

U. S. SECRET
BRITISH MOST SECRET

the 1st Armored Division as a mobile reserve further to the rear, where it could be maintained more easily. This mobile reserve would be available to deal with a threat either from the North or from Rommel's forces retiring from the direction of Tripoli. The plan was to launch the attack on Sfax on January 24th. Although the road to Gabes was better, the time factor made it necessary to go direct for Sfax. There seemed, however, every reason to hope that Sfax could be successfully taken.

SIR ALAN BROOKE pointed out the need for careful coordination of the attack on Sfax with General Anderson's operations in the North and those of the 8th Army in the South. If weather conditions made it impossible for General Anderson to move forward, except on the roads, before March 15th there seemed to be a danger that the Germans would thin out in the North and defeat the Sfax forces in detail. It would take some time before the 8th Army could bring pressure to bear from the southward in support of this force, since even at the best General Montgomery did not expect to reach Tripoli before the middle of February; and before he could advance from there the port would have to be cleared in order to supply his forces with petrol for a further advance.

GENERAL EISENHOWER agreed that it was improbable that any movement off the roads would be possible in the North before March 15th, though General Anderson had seven days' reserves built up which would be kept intact for an attack whenever conditions permitted. He hoped that General Montgomery would push on through Tripoli as fast as possible. By the end of January the 46th Division would be concentrated forward under General Anderson and the 18th Regimental Combat Team would be withdrawn into reserve. As long as the 1st U. S. Armored Division was kept for counterattack, he felt that he could deal with any threat to the Sfax force. He hoped, however, to be able to discuss the whole problem with General Alexander and to make any necessary adjustments in the plan on the latter's arrival.

SIR ALAN BROOKE pointed out that after two months of "an active defensive," the 78th Division would not be in very good condition for the attack in the North and suggested that it would be better to let a fresh division form the spearhead.

GENERAL EISENHOWER said that he was faced with the dilemma of either allowing the troops in the North to deteriorate by remaining

U. S. SECRET
BRITISH MOST SECRET

inactive in the mud or suffering some losses to them through keeping them more active. In his opinion the latter was the lesser of two evils. Also that active patrolling would reveal any thinning out of the Axis force in the North.

The latest intelligence reports place the Axis strength in North Africa at about 65,000. Every effort had been made to retard their build-up but the appalling conditions of the airfields and the bad weather had largely closed down air operations against them recently. At the present time it was calculated that the Axis were getting in about 750 men a day with the necessary supplies for them, in addition to a certain amount of supplies for Rommel.

The French forces in the middle of the front were playing a most important part since they were holding the line between the British in the North and the American forces in the South. Unless they held firm, a serious situation would develop. Moreover, he was completely dependent on them for the working of his long line of communication and the ports. These considerations necessitated careful handling of the French. The French units themselves were badly equipped and some of them were poorly trained. The French troops from Tunisia were somewhat unreliable since their families were now in the German area. In one battalion there had been 132 desertions. The French Generals Barre and Juin were cooperating excellently with General Anderson and General Fredendall. Unfortunately, General Juin was not being given very much scope by General Giraud. The latter might be a good Division Commander but he had no political sense and no idea of administration. He was dictatorial by nature and seemed to suffer from megalomania. In addition he was very sensitive and always ready to take offense. He did not seem to be a big enough man to carry the burden of civil government in any way. It had been far easier to deal with Admiral Darlan.

Civil affairs, which included economic as well as political matters, had of course, given a great deal of anxiety. There were many agencies involved but the necessary organization to deal with all these problems was being improved.

Rail communications forward were very limited in capacity at present. East of Algiers the daily tonnage which could be carried amounted

U S. SECRET
BRITISH MOST SECRET

to about 2,200 tons but with additional rolling stock and locomotives which were being sent from the United States, it was hoped to increase this to 4,400. From Casablanca to Oran the daily tonnage was only about 900. Port clearance was improving. At Oran it averaged 5,000 tons a day. At Algiers the daily clearance was not so great and initially it had been much reduced by the presence of French ships lying at many of the berths. Losses of shipping had been sustained by air attack at Bougie and Bone. Air defense of the ports was being steadily improved. All available French antiaircraft weapons had been brought into action and night fighters had been sent from the United Kingdom. Radar had been installed to cover the stretch from Bone to Algiers and some had also been provided at Oran and Casablanca. Passive air defense measures in the ports were being improved and assistance had been given by an expert sent from the United Kingdom who had done very good work at Algiers. One difficulty was that there was no rigid control over the French civil population.

SIR CHARLES PORTAL said that the Radar cover between Bond and Algiers was not yet effective below 10,000 feet. He had made arrangements for additional equipment to be provided to make good this deficiency. He inquired what air defense could be provided for Sfax.

GENERAL EISENHOWER said that there was good natural cover for the troops in Sfax. One airfield there was practically complete and there was another at Gabes. The improvement of airfields had been one of the greatest problems. Approximately 2,000 tons of steel matting were required for a single runway and this quantity used up the complete capacity of railroads in the forward areas for a whole day. Every possible expedient had been tried to use local material but broken stone merely sank into the mud. Once the weather improved all these difficulties would vanish since there were large areas in the forward zone which could be used as airfields with little or no preparation at all.

(GENERAL EISENHOWER withdrew at this point.)

3. STRATEGY IN THE EUROPEAN THEATER.

SIR ALAN BROOKE outlined two broad policies which should be followed in the European Theater during 1943. The first was to close down in the Mediterranean as soon as the North African coast had been cleared and the sea route through the Mediterranean had been opened, and to devote

U. S. SECRET
BRITISH MOST SECRET

every effort to building up in the United Kingdom for an invasion of the North of France at the earliest possible moment. The British Chiefs of Staff had examined the possibilities and calculated that 21 to 23 divisions could be made available for this purpose by September 15th. It had at first been thought that port and railway capacity would be the limiting factor on the build-up of American troops' expansion but it looked as if these difficulties could be overcome if the expansion of receiving depots for supplies were pushed ahead. As a basis of calculation, a monthly movement of 120 merchant vessels from the U. K. to the U.S.A. had been taken, the corresponding troop lift being 120,000. This would allow 9 to 12 U. S. divisions to be transported to the U. K. by September 1st. The number of troops which could be put into France was severely limited, however, by the availability of landing craft and of administrative facilities in France.

Three possible areas for invasion had been considered:
(a) The Calais-Boulogne area which, although heavily defended, was within fighter cover of the United Kingdom;
(b) Cherbourg Peninsula, which could be seized by a comparatively small force;
(c) Brest Peninsula, which was a more worth while objective, would require a much larger force, say, at least 15 divisions to hold the 150 kilometers of front.

One of the objections to operations against the North of France was the excellent railway connections across Europe which would enable the Germans rapidly to reinforce the invaded area. Moreover, it would not be possible to begin the operation until the early autumn and no support would therefore be given to Russia throughout the summer. This last factor seemed to be the principal objection. A land invasion on a small scale would have little more than a local effect except for the air fighting which would inevitably ensue from it.

The other broad possibility was to maintain activity in the Mediterranean while building up the maximum air offensive against Germany from the U. K. and putting in as many troops as could be spared with a view to undertaking a comparatively small operation such as seizing Cherbourg Peninsula.

U. S. SECRET
BRITISH MOST SECRET

The Mediterranean offered many choices: Sardinia, Sicily, Crete, and the Dodecanese. Our amphibious power enabled us to threaten all these points simultaneously and thereby cause the Germans to disperse their forces. Unless they were to risk the loss of these islands, they would be compelled to reinforce them as well as the coasts of Italy, Greece, and France. If Italy could be knocked out, Germany would be involved in large new commitments in an attempt to bolster her up and replacing Italian troops in the Balkans. Other German satellites might also fall out. The British Chiefs of Staff considered that our best policy would be to threaten Germany everywhere in the Mediterranean, to try to knock out Italy, and to bring in Turkey on our side. It was not, of course, certain that we could bring Turkey in but by a combination of inducements and pressure we might be successful. With Turkey as a base, we could attack the Rumanian oil fields and open up the Black Sea Route to Russia.

If this policy was adopted, we shall have to make a careful choice of our objective. The main choice seemed to lie between the capture of Sardinia and Corsica and the capture of Sicily. Sicily would be the bigger prize but would be a bigger undertaking and the operation could not be staged until late in the summer. The threat, however, would compel dispersion on Germany long before the operation itself was launched. As for Sardinia and Corsica, these increased the possibilities of air attack against Italy by providing bases for fighter escorted bombers. The operation might be combined with operations from the Middle East against the Dodecanese.

One of the great advantages of adopting the Mediterranean policy was that a larger force of heavy bombers could be built up in the United Kingdom for the attack on Germany than if we concentrated for an invasion of France. For the latter purpose, a much larger proportion of the lighter type of bomber and ground support planes would be needed and the number of heavy bombers would suffer accordingly.

ADMIRAL KING pointed out that the more troops that we concentrated in the Mediterranean, the more likely Germany was to move into Spain in order to cut our line of communications through the straits of Gibraltar. An invasion of Northern France such as the seizure of the Brest Peninsula would not nearly so likely precipitate such an event. He doubted whether

U. S. SECRET
BRITISH MOST SECRET

the Spaniards could be relied upon to offer anything more than guerilla resistance to a German invasion.

SIR ALAN BROOKE said that the British Chiefs of Staff did not consider it was at all probable that Spain would permit free passage to the German forces. It was calculated that some 20 divisions would be necessary to occupy the country if the Spaniards resisted at all. This would be a very large commitment for Germany. In any event, we would be able to secure the south side of the Straits of Gibraltar by occupying Spanish Morocco and this would prevent the complete closure of the sea route. He did not think it would be possible for Germany to seize the Spanish airfields in the South by parachute troops. The problem of supplying them by air would be extremely difficult.

SIR CHARLES PORTAL pointed out that if the Spaniards allowed the Germans free passage we should declare war on Spain which was depending on us for many of the necessities of life. Even if the Germans did go in, we should be better able to afford aircraft for the protection of shipping through the Straits of Gibraltar than could the Germans for its attack. It would be much more advantageous for the Germans if we built up against France and left the Mediterranean alone. They would then be able to withdraw large numbers of air forces from the Mediterranean and reinforce the Russian Front, relying on the strong defenses of Northern France to resist an invasion. On the other hand if we kept the Mediterranean active, they would be compelled to keep large air forces there the whole time. This was of the greatest importance since Germany's main shortages were air forces and oil.

Considerable discussion followed on the details and timings of operations against Sicily and Sardinia in which the following were the principal points made:

(a) If the capture of Sicily was mounted from the United Kingdom and the United States, it could be carried out early in August, but would require some 190 escort vessels. If it was mounted from North Africa some 65 escorts would be saved, but its launching would be delayed about one month. This delay was due to the time required for amphibious training in North Africa where facilities were extremely limited.

U S SECRET
BRITISH MOST SECRET

      (b) The capture of Sardinia could be undertaken in about May, i.e., three months earlier than Sicily. Air cover for the Sardinia operation, however, would be more difficult owing to its greater distance from North Africa.

      (c) The total coastline of Sicily was about 500 miles and it was anticipated that some 7 to 8 enemy divisions would be defending the island. This compared very favorably with the coastline of Northern France which was the same length, more strongly fortified and would be defended by 15 divisions.

      (d) Part of the air cover for operations against Sicily could be provided from Malta from which about 300 fighters could be operated. Additional fighter protection could be given if Pantellaria was seized in a preliminary operation. The troops required for the operation amounted to some 9 divisions, 10 to 12 brigade groups being employed as assaulting troops.

      (e) It was doubtful whether the whole operation against Sicily could be undertaken by troops already in the Mediterranean owing to the difficulties of training them in time in North Africa. Assembly and repair of landing craft was another bottleneck.

SIR DUDLEY POUND estimated that once the North African Coast had been cleared, even without having Sicily in our possession, it would be possible to run a convoy of thirty ships once every ten days through the Mediterranean, in substitution for the present shipping to the Middle East, Persian Gulf and India, which moved via the Cape. This would effect a saving of some 225 ships. The average losses per month on the Cape route are at present about 15 ships. The estimated losses if the Mediterranean route were used should only be about 9 a month even allowing a higher percentage of loss. He understood, however, that the United States estimate was 18.

U. S. SECRET
BRITISH MOST SECRET

C.C.S. 58th Meeting

COMBINED CHIEFS OF STAFF

MINUTES of Meeting held at Anfa Camp
on Saturday, January 16, 1943, at 1030.

PRESENT

General G. C. Marshall, USA	General Sir Alan F. Brooke
Admiral E. J. King, USN	Admiral of the Fleet Sir Dudley Pound
Lt. General H. H. Arnold, USA	Air Chief Marshal Sir Charles F. A. Portal

THE FOLLOWING WERE ALSO PRESENT

Lt. General B. B. Somervell, USA	Field Marshal Sir John Dill
Rear Admiral C. M. Cooke, Jr., USN (For first half of meeting)	Vice Admiral the Lord Louis Mountbatten
Brig. General A. C. Wedemeyer, USA (For first half of meeting)	Lt. General Sir Hastings L. Ismay
Colonel J. E. Smart, USA (For first half of meeting)	Major General J. N. Kennedy
Commander R. E. Libby, USN	Air Vice Marshal J. C. Slessor

SECRETARIAT

Brigadier V. Dykes
Brig. General J. R. Deane, USA

(The meeting adjourned from 1300 to 1530)

U. S. SECRET
BRITISH MOST SECRET

1. THE NORTH AFRICAN SITUATION.

SIR ALAN BROOKE gave an account of a conference between General Alexander and General Eisenhower regarding the coming operations in Tunisia and Libya. General Eisenhower had planned an offensive against Sfax to be launched on January 24th. The plan presented some difficulties. The 1st Army cannot attack prior to March 15th. The British 8th Army expects to take Tripoli by January 24th. At that time they will be out of fuel for their vehicles and a certain amount of reorganizing will be necessary. It is probable that the 8th Army will not be able to attack Rommel's forces on the Mareth line prior to February 15th. Thus they will be too late to take advantage of the favorable situation created by General Eisenhower's attack on Sfax and consequently Rommel will be free for a period of time to operate against General Eisenhower's southern forces and perhaps force him to withdraw from Sfax. This might be coupled with a German attack from the north which would place General Eisenhower's southern forces in an extremely precarious position.

SIR ALAN BROOKE stated that it had been decided that the Sfax attack would be canceled. Instead, raids would be conducted against the German line of communications from Sfax but the bulk of General Eisenhower's forces consisting of the 1st Armored Division, reinforced, would be held in the vicinity of Tebessa prepared to assist General Alexancer in his attack on Rommel's forces or to assist the 1st Army to the north. The Sfax attack might be accomplished later and, if so, it would be timed by agreement between General Alexander and General Eisenhower who will confer frequently.

2. THE STRATEGIC CONCEPT FOR 1943 IN THE EUROPEAN THEATER.

GENERAL MARSHALL stated that the United States Chiefs of Staff were anxious to learn the British concept as to how Germany is to be defeated. It has been the conception of the United States Chiefs of Staff that Germany must be defeated by a powerful effort on the continent, carrying out the BOLERO-ROUNDUP plans. Aid to Russia is regarded as being of paramount importance in order to assist the Russian Army to absorb the strength of the German ground and air forces.

He said we must devise means to enable Russia to continue aggressively through 1943 by providing them with supplies. The amount of such supplies and the methods of delivering them must be determined upon. The

U. S. SECRET
BRITISH MOST SECRET

German air and ground forces brought to bear against Russia must be reduced. Any method of accomplishing this other than on the Continent is a deviation from the basic plan. The question is then to what extent must the United Nations adhere to the general concept and to what extent do they undertake diversions for the purpose of assisting Russia, improving the tonnage situation, and maintaining momentum.

In commenting on the British presentation of their plans for the Mediterranean, GENERAL MARSHALL stated that the United States Chiefs of Staff would like to have further information on the following points:

(a) Were not the East-West communications in northern Europe, which the British consider capable of moving seven divisions every twelve days, subject to severe interference by heavy air attacks from England?

(b) If the Mediterranean operations were undertaken and there were a break in the German strength, might it occur so rapidly that full advantage could not be taken of it? It was, therefore, desired that the British Chiefs of Staff expand on what the tonnage savings from the Mediterranean operations might be in order to determine if they were worth the costs involved.

(c) What would be the effects of Mediterranean operations on the timing of the United Nations concentrations in England? In General Eisenhower's opinion, it was unwise to count on further use of landing craft used in the initial landings for any other operation. A fifty or seventy-five percent loss should be anticipated. General Eisenhower also thought that operations on the Continent to establish a bridgehead would require more divisions than had originally been thought necessary.

(d) What were the relative merits of undertaking an operation against Sicily or Sardinia, particularly in regard to the effects on tonnage, and the development of forces in the United Kingdom?

(e) Was an operation against Sicily merely a means towards an end or an end in itself? Is it to be a part of an integrated plan to win the war or simply taking advantage of an opportunity?

GENERAL MARSHALL said the United States Chiefs of Staff agreed that every effort must be made to build up forces to support Turkey in order to be able to reinforce her for resistance against the Axis powers

U. S. SECRET
BRITISH MOST SECRET

and to secure the use of her airfields for bombing operations by the United Nations.

He thought that if operations are to be undertaken in the Mediterranean, they should be financed by the troops now in North Africa. One of the strongest arguments for undertaking such an operation is that there will be an excess of troops in North Africa once Tunisia has been cleared of the Axis forces.

ADMIRAL KING stated that he thought it most important to determine how the war is to be conducted. The percentage of the war effort to be applied to Germany and to Japan must be determined as well as over-all plans for the defeat of each. He asked if Russia is to carry the burden as far as the ground forces are concerned; also, if the United Nations were to invade the Continent, and when. He said that since Europe is in the British area of strategic responsibility, he would like to hear their views on these questions. He thought it should be decided whether a planned step-by-step policy was to be pursued or whether we should rely on seizing opportunities.

GENERAL ARNOLD stated that he was interested to know whether an attack on Sicily was to be a means to an end or an end in itself and what relation such an attack would have to the whole strategic conception.

GENERAL MARSHALL said that, when planning for GYMNAST, we were attempting to undertake an operation "on a shoe string." He said we then changed to the BOLERO-ROUNDUP concept and had to prepare for SLEDGEHAMMER because of the strong possibility of a Russian collapse last autumn. Troop concentrations had been started and production programs rearranged for BOLERO. This created difficult complications. The naval program was upset because of the necessity to undertake the construction of landing craft. It was then decided to undertake Operation TORCH in which great risks were involved but in which we have been abnormally fortunate.

GENERAL MARSHALL described the difficulties with which the United States Chiefs of Staff were faced over questions of priorities in production. It was essential to fix our strategic policy as carefully as possible in order to avoid production difficulties.

GENERAL MARSHALL thought it important that we now reorient ourselves and decide what the "main plot" is to be. Every diversion or side

U.S. SECRET
BRITISH MOST SECRET

issue from the main plot acts as a "suction pump." He stated that the operations against Sicily appeared to be advantageous because of the excess number of troops in North Africa brought about by the splendid efforts of the British 8th Army. However, before deciding to undertake such an operation, he thought it necessary to determine just what part it would play in the over-all strategic plan.

SIR ALAN BROOKE said that on the Continent Russia is the only ally having large land forces in action. Any effort of the other allies must necessarily be so small as to be unimportant in the over-all picture. He felt that ground operations by the United States and the United Kingdom would not exert any great influence until there were definite signs that Germany was weakening.

GENERAL MARSHALL stated that it was desirable to force the enemy to meet us in air combat. He asked Sir Alan Brooke to discuss the effects of air superiority of the United Nations on the operations of ground troops of the Continent. He felt that if a bridgehead were established and Germany did not attempt to meet our air superiority, the bridgehead could be expanded. On the other hand, if they did meet our air superiority, it would necessitate withdrawing large air forces from the Russian front.

He referred to a suggestion by Mr. Molotov that we send a ground force to the Continent sufficient to divert forty German divisions from the Russian front. He said that this was out of the question and that our aim should be to weaken the German air power in the Russian theater rather than the ground forces.

SIR ALAN BROOKE stated that with limited ground forces, he did not believe that we could constitute sufficient threat in Northern France to the Germans to force them to withdraw much of their air power from the Russian front. The Germans have forty-four divisions in France, some of which have been moved south as a result of Operation TORCH. However, the Germans still have sufficient strength to overwhelm us on the ground and perhaps hem us in with wire or concrete to such an extent that any expansion of the bridgehead would be extremely difficult. Moreover, we cannot undertake any operation in Northern France until very late in the summer of 1943. Since, therefore, we cannot go into the Continent in

U. S. SECRET
BRITISH MOST SECRET

force until Germany weakens, we should try to make the Germans disperse their forces as much as possible. This can be accomplished by attacking the German allies, Italy in particular. This would result in a considerable shortage of German troops on the Russian front. An effort should be made to put Italy out of the war, largely by bombing attacks on the north from the United Kingdom and in the south from North Africa and Sicily.

Our policy should be to force Italy out of the war and bring Turkey in. If Italy were out of the war, Germany would be forced to occupy that country with a considerable number of divisions and also would be forced to replace Italian divisions in other Axis occupied countries such as Yugoslavia and Greece.

Preparations for an attack against Sicily would be known to the Germans and would necessitate the dispersing of their forces to meet any of the capabilities of our amphibious forces. They would have to be prepared to meet us in Sardinia, Sicily, Crete, Greece and the Dodecanese, and this would give great opportunity for deception plans. He felt that this would cause a much greater withdrawal of strength from the Russian front than any operations which we might undertake across the channel. The protection of the sea route alone would bring on a considerable air battle in the Mediterranean which will give relief to the Russian front. Airplanes which normally leave Russia during the winter months and participate in operations in the Mediterranean would be unable to return to the Russian front in the spring.

SIR ALAN BROOKE said that at the same time as operations against Sicily were being undertaken, there must be a continued build-up of the United Nations forces in the United Kingdom. These must be prepared to undertake the final action of the war as soon as Germany gives definite signs of weakness.

SIR ALAN BROOKE did not believe we could undertake any further operations in Italy from Sicily in 1943, unless Italy collapsed completely. We should be very careful of accepting any invitation to support an anti-Fascist insurrection. To do so might only immobilize a considerable force to no useful purpose.

SIR ALAN BROOKE did not feel that air operations against the German and French railway systems in the north would be particularly

U. S. SECRET
BRITISH MOST SECRET

effective or do anything more than impose delay. There were so many alternative routes. On the other hand, operations against the north-south railway lines, particularly those in Italy, could be made effective because of the close proximity of the lines to the shore which makes them vulnerable to commando raids as well as to air action.

SIR DUDLEY POUND discussed the effects that taking Sardinia and Sicily would have on the passage of convoys. He said that securing either of these islands will not have as much effect as securing Tunisia. He anticipated that when Tunisia is gained, we shall be able to convoy thirty cargo ships through the Mediterranean every ten days which will result in the release of two hundred and twenty five ships for other purposes. The route would not be safe for personnel ships or tankers. The capture of Sardinia would have little effect on the movements of shipping. On the other hand, the capture of Sicily would enable us to move troop convoys as well as cargo convoys through the Mediterranean with relative safety. The troop convoys, however, will, in the future, be limited almost entirely to replacement troops for the Middle East.

He stated that there will also be a saving in tankers because of the possibility of supplying the necessities for oil in the Mediterranean from Haifa rather than bringing oil from the United States.

SIR ALAN BROOKE recapitulated the comparative merits of an attack on Sardinia and Sicily as follows. The loss of Sicily would be a much heavier blow to Italy than Sardinia and would effectively secure the sea route through the Mediterranean. On the other hand, it was a much more ambitious operation and would have to be mounted later. Sardinia was a smaller undertaking, and could be mounted earlier. It would provide an excellent air base for attack on Industrial Italy, particularly if Corsica were taken as well.

SIR CHARLES PORTAL pointed out that if Sicily had to be taken later in the year and if the Germans in consequence were able to reinforce it more strongly, it would be a much tougher nut to crack. On the other hand, once in possession of the Sicilian airfields we could make it very difficult indeed for the Axis to reinforce the island. The railways along the Italian coasts in the two were vulnerable to air attack and raiding; and there were narrow defiles leading from the port of Messina in the island itself.

U. S. SECRET
BRITISH MOST SECRET

SIR CHARLES PORTAL referred to the suggestion that we might be able to offset inferiority in land forces in Northern France by the greatly superior air forces which could be operated from the United Kingdom. So far as the Brest Peninsula was concerned, no fighter support could be given from the United Kingdom, since it was out of range. The Cherbourg Peninsula was better from this point of view and offered some possibilities as a preliminary operation. Nevertheless, with the limited air facilities in the Peninsula we should probably find ourselves pinned down at the neck of the Peninsula by ground forces whose superiority we should be unable to offset by the use of air. We should certainly be opposed by strong German air forces there. Once we were committed in Northern France the Germans would quickly bring up their air forces from the Mediterranean, realizing that we could not undertake amphibious operations on a considerable scale both across the channel and in the Mediterranean. On the other hand, by threatening in the Mediterranean we should cause a far greater dispersion of German air forces.

SIR CHARLES PORTAL said that in his view it was impossible to map out a detailed plan for winning the war, but Germany's position, if we knocked out Italy, would undoubtedly be most serious. Her ability to continue the fight depended on (a) the possession of the necessary resources and (b) the will to fight on. As regards resources, her main shortages at present were oil and air power. We had no exact knowledge of her oil position, but if she had not succeeded in gaining the Caucasus oil, and if her synthetic oil plants were attacked by precision bombing in daylight, there could be little doubt that her forces would rapidly become immobilized from lack of oil.

As regards her air forces, calculations had been made by the British Air Intelligence Staffs of German deficiencies under the following hypotheses:

- Case A - Italy fighting and Germany continuing the offensive in Caucasia.
- Case B - As for A, but Italy knocked out.
- Case C - Italy fighting and Germany holding a shortened line in Russia by withdrawing to Rostov.
- Case D - As for C, but Italy not fighting.

U. S. SECRET
BRITISH MOST SECRET

German deficiencies in June 1943 were calculated as follows:

Case	Deficiencies in First Line Aircraft	Deficiencies in Divisions.
A	1700	34
B	2250	54
C	700	9
D	1250	30

Germany's will to fight depended largely on her confidence in ultimate success. If we and the Russians began to score continual successes against Germany, which she could not defeat owing to her lack of means, she would begin to realize that the prospects were hopeless. She might be faced with the dilemma of withdrawing all her troops from France and concentrating in the East against Russia. The way to defeat Germany, therefore, seemed to be to take every chance of attacking her oil supplies; to increase the air bombardment of Germany itself with its inevitable results on German morale, and on industrial capacity and its effect in producing heavy casualties in her population and great misery by the destruction of their dwellings. If we could achieve as well a series of successes, even though these might be comparatively small in extent, it seemed fairly certain that a point would be reached at which Germany would suddenly crack. No one, however, could say precisely when or how the collapse would come.

ADMIRAL KING said he understood the general concept of the British Chiefs of Staff was to make use of Russia's geographical position and her reserves of manpower to make the main effort on land against Germany and to support Russia by diverting as many German forces as possible from the Eastern front. This raised the question as to whether we should not give Russia larger supplies of equipment.

Once the North African coast had been cleared it seemed that we should have a surplus of troops in North Africa and the Mediterranean whom we could not readily move elsewhere. It seemed therefore economical to use them in that area if possible. Sicily seemed undoubtedly to offer a greater dividend though its cost would be higher than Sardinia. The question was whether we could afford to delay so long before taking further offensive action against Germany and whether the Russians would be satisfied unless a "second front" was opened in France. The chief bottleneck seemed to be the provision of landing craft. Operations in Norway

U. S. SECRET
BRITISH MOST SECRET

seemed to be worth examining though they would almost inevitably lead to a demand from Sweden for assistance and equipment.

As regards the Brest Peninsula, it was worth noting that once we were established there, U. S. troops could be moved in direct from America without the need for trans-shipment in the United Kingdom. The effect of capturing Brest on the U-boat war needed careful consideration.

SIR CHARLES PORTAL said that Brest was one of the four Biscay ports used by the Germans as U-boat bases, but he doubted whether the possession of the peninsula would greatly assist the proposed heavy bomber attacks on Lorient, La Pallice and Bordeaux. All these were within easy range of the United Kingdom and to operate against them from the Brest Peninsula would involve putting in additional facilities there. The airfields in the peninsula were likely to be fully employed in the air defense of the area and direct support of the army, leaving nothing to spare for fighter escorts for daylight bombing attacks on the Biscay ports.

The next point discussed was the effect of Mediterranean operations on BOLERO. SIR ALAN BROOKE said that the number of divisions which the British Chiefs of Staff calculated could be made available by September 15th for operations from the United Kingdom into Northern France were:

21-24 if the Mediterranean were closed down.
16-18 if Mediterranean operations were undertaken.

If the capture of Sicily were undertaken, the number of landing craft left available for operations in Northern France would be less. SIR DUDLEY POUND observed that all calculations of the number of divisions available for operations in Northern France were based on the date of September 15th. In his view this was too late since the weather was liable to break in the third week in September and it was essential to have a port by then. The first assault should not be later than August 15th.

GENERAL MARSHALL inquired whether considerable numbers of landing craft would not be required for the maintenance of Sicily after it was taken.

SIR CHARLES PORTAL said that once Sicily had been occupied the air defense of the ports should present no particular difficulty. We were able to put large ships into Malta which was very exposed to air attack.

U. S. SECRET
BRITISH MOST SECRET

The number of enemy airfields in the toe of Italy was small, and fighters on the Sicilian airdromes should be able to deal with dive bombers.

LORD LOUIS MOUNTBATTEN then reviewed the British landing craft situation. Available landing craft were being allocated broadly as follows:

(a) A group in the United Kingdom of the smaller types of cross-channel craft sufficient to lift 4 brigade groups with their vehicles, or 7 brigade groups loaded for raids when very few motor vehicles would be taken.

(b) A group in the Western Mediterranean sufficient to lift 1 brigade group complete.

(c) A similar group in the Eastern Mediterranean.

(d) A group in India sufficient to train 1 brigade group, but not enough to lift the brigade group if it had to undertake actual operations.

(e) An oversea assault force, as a strategic reserve, sufficient to lift 6 brigade groups. The personnel would be carried in combat loaders but they could not all be put ashore in the first flight as the ships could not carry sufficient landing craft for the purpose.

Every attempt was being made to organize landing craft bases in the U. K. so as to give the maximum flexibility and thus allow for a change of plan. The switch over from ROUNDUP to TORCH had caused great difficulties owing to the fact that bases prepared for ROUNDUP were in the South of England whereas Scottish bases had to be used for TORCH.

LORD LOUIS MOUNTBATTEN observed that he was working on the assumption that any U. S. troops would be carried in landing craft manned by the U. S. In the TORCH landings the majority of U. S. forces at Oran and Algiers had been landed in British manned craft. He emphasized the need for working out allocations of landing craft well ahead owing to the long time involved in training the necessary crews.

GENERAL SOMERVELL said that the introduction of the L.S.T. and the L.C.I. necessitated considerable change in our ideas about landing craft; the former carried some 150 infantry as well as tanks, and the latter 250 infantry. He calculated that if all the available landing craft were concentrated in North Africa we should be able to lift a total of some 80,000 men by April. Allowing for the use of 105-foot and 50-foot

U. S. SECRET
BRITISH MOST SECRET

craft as well, this lift would probably increase to about 90,000 in June. If this force of landing craft were used for a second and third ferrying flight, on a short sea crossing, their lift would probably be about 60,000 in the second flight and 45,000 in the third flight, allowing for inevitable casualties in craft. He considered the use of these landing craft, working to beaches, a sounder proposition than the risking of large ships under air attack. The latter should be reserved for the long ocean hauls.

To transfer landing craft from the Mediterranean to the United Kingdom for a subsequent operation later in the year presented considerable problems. It was certainly essential to have considerable numbers of landing craft in the United Kingdom well in advance for training purposes.

SIR ALAN BROOKE said that the British Joint Planners had calculated August as the earliest date for the attack on Sicily. If the whole operation were mounted from North Africa in order to save escorts, the date would be postponed until the end of August. His own view was that, even under the latter condition, the date might be advanced to July. Assuming that the attack be launched about July 20th, he expected that we might gain control of the Island within about six weeks.

GENERAL MARSHALL inquired when, on the above assumptions, there would be sufficient landing craft in the United Kingdom to take advantage of a crack in Germany.

LORD LOUIS MOUNTBATTEN said that three months would have to be allowed from the time when the landing craft could be dispensed with to the time when they would be ready for action again in the United Kingdom. The large types of sea-going landing vessels presented no difficulty but small 50-foot craft were essential for the assault landing. Both the United States and British Planners were agreed that it was not possible to use the large craft for the first flights. These small craft had to be collected from the site of operations, transported to Scotland, distributed for repair, reassembled and then again transported by ship to the South of England for a Continental operation.

There would be in England, however, at all times the assault force to which he had previously referred which could lift 4 Brigade Groups with their transport for an assault against heavy opposition.

U. S. SECRET
BRITISH MOST SECRET

In addition, for the follow-up troops, a great number of landing barges and small coasting vessels were being prepared. The spearhead would not be affected at all by operations in the Mediterranean and would always be kept intact. Any landing craft recovered from the Mediterranean would therefore be in the nature of a bonus.

ADMIRAL KING said that the intended use of combat loaders for an assault on Sicily greatly disturbed him. He had hoped that it would be possible to use the larger types of landing craft instead. He feared that a large number of these valuable combat loaders would be lost in the operation.

LORD LOUIS MOUNTBATTEN said that in the HUSKY plan all available L.S.T.'s and L.C.I.'s would be used, but in addition, 26 combat loaders were required for the assault troops. Of these, the British could provide half.

ADMIRAL KING pointed out that the two main factors in winning the war were manpower and munitions. In respect to military manpower, the British Commonwealth had presumably mobilized practically up to the limit. The United States at the present time had reached about 60% of their contemplated strength in military manpower though the position had not yet completely stabilized. His own guess at Russia's position was that she had mobilized about 80% of available military manpower. China's resources in manpower were still relatively untouched, and India likewise was scarcely tapped.

As regards munitions, the greatest potential lay in the United States. Next came Great Britain, but she could not supply the full needs of the British Commonwealth forces. Russia was more self-supporting than at first appeared likely but had to receive a considerable amount of assistance from the Allies. From the munitions point of view, China and India were liabilities since their available manpower enormously exceeded their industrial production.

In the European theater Russia was most advantageously placed for dealing with Germany in view of her geographical position and manpower; in the Pacific, China bore a similar relation to the Japanese. It should be our basic policy to provide the manpower resources of Russia and China with the necessary equipment to enable them to fight. With this in mind, the United States Chiefs of Staff set great store by Operation

U. S. SECRET
BRITISH MOST SECRET

RAVENOUS. It seemed likely that one of the major British contributions to the defeat of Japan would be to complete the reconquest of Burma and the opening of the Burma Road.

GENERAL MARSHALL observed that, with regard to Operation RAVENOUS, Chiang Kai-shek had now withdrawn from his undertaking to move in from Yunnan on the grounds that Field Marshal Wavell could only provide very limited British forces and there would be no British naval strength in the Bay of Bengal to cut the Japanese reinforcements route to Rangoon. General Stilwell was certainly placed in a very difficult position at the present time.

Discussion then turned on the need for long-range planning in order that production policy could be coordinated with strategy.

GENERAL ARNOLD pointed out that if operations in the Mediterranean were undertaken, the seizure of Brest, in the British view, would not be possible this year. Further, that even if Cherbourg or Brest were taken, our forces would not be able to break out for a further invasion of the Continent. It looked very much as if no Continental operations on any scale were in prospect before the spring of 1944. We should have to decide not only what we were going to do in 1943 but also in 1944 since otherwise, owing to the time lag, our priorities in production might be wrongly decided.

SIR ALAN BROOKE expressed the view that we should definitely count on reentering the Continent in 1944 on a large scale.

SIR CHARLES PORTAL pointed out that production plans could never follow strategy precisely since the situation changed so frequently in war. The best that could be hoped for was to take broad decisions on major questions and these would always be in the nature of compromises. For example, when considering the possibility of reentering the Continent, it had been decided that we must treat it as a fortress and that heavy initial bombardment would be required to break into it. It had therefore been decided to give very high priority to the production of heavy bombers which would be used to soften up Germany before the invasion of the Continent.

U. S. SECRET
BRITISH MOST SECRET

Further discussion then followed on the possibility of a German crack in 1943.

SIR JOHN DILL felt that there was quite a possibility of beating Germany this year. We should therefore strain every nerve to effect this since the sooner we beat Germany the sooner we could turn on Japan. We must not let Japan consolidate her position for too long. Japan certainly could not be beaten this year, but Germany might.

ADMIRAL KING doubted whether Germany could be defeated before 1944. He felt that her defeat could only be effected by direct military action rather than by a failure in her morale. Was it necessary, however, to accept that we could do nothing in Northern France before April 1944?

SIR CHARLES PORTAL said that this depended entirely on Germany's power of resistance. If we concentrated everything we could on Germany this year, it was possible that we might cause her to crumble and thus be able to move into Germany with comparatively small forces. Until this condition had been produced, however, some 20 divisions would get us nowhere on the Continent. A factor which must not be forgotten was the terrific latent power of the oppressed people which could only come into play when the crumbling process started. At that moment, however, their efforts might contribute greatly to the final collapse. He did not see Germany fighting on and on, completely surrounded by the armed forces of the Allies. A point would come at which the whole structure of Germany and the Nazi Party would collapse, and this moment might well come during the current year. It was essential therefore to have ready a plan and some resources in the United Kingdom to take advantage of a crack. In order to produce the crack, however, we must keep up the maximum pressure on Germany by land operations; air bombardment alone was not sufficient

In further discussion the importance of deciding the requirements and availability of escort vessels was emphasized. These appeared to be one of the principal limiting factors.

ADMIRAL KING said that there was no reserve of escort vessels but if Operation HUSKY were decided upon, the United States and British Navies would have to find the escort vessels somehow just as they had in the case of TORCH.

U. S. SECRET
BRITISH MOST SECRET

After some further discussion,

THE COMMITTEE:
Agreed to direct the Combined Staff Planners to reexamine the British plan for HUSKY in the light of the American and British resources of all kinds that can be made available for it, and to calculate the earliest date by which the Operation could be mounted.

3. SUPPLIES TO RUSSIA.

SIR DUDLEY POUND recapitulated the factors governing PQ convoys to North Russia. With the present resources of the Home Fleet not more than one 30-ship convoy could be run every 40 to 42 days. Each convoy had to contain two oilers, leaving a net total of 28 cargo ships. With more destroyers it would be possible to "double-end" the convoys, reducing cycle to 27 days instead of 40-42. For this purpose about 12 destroyers would be required from the U. S. Navy. He wished to emphasize, however, that if the Germans employed their surface ships boldly and kept up the same amount of air and U-boats as last year, it was within their power to stop the PQ convoys altogether.

GENERAL SOMERVELL reviewed the general problem of supplying Russia. The northern route was at present the best since the turn-round was shortest. The turn-round on the Persian Gulf route was about five months. Some fifteen ships a month are now being used on this route but the flow was restricted by port and inland transportation deficiencies. Once the Mediterranean was opened some relief might be given by the use of HAIFA and the overland route from there to Bagdad. For this purpose additional heavy trucks for the road haul would be needed. U. S. Technical troops were being dispatched to Persia to improve the trans-Persian transportation facilities, and it was hoped to increase these to about 10,000 tons per day. If this could be achieved, 40 ships a month instead of 15 could be sent into the Persian Gulf.

The sea route from Seattle to Vladivostok was also being used for non-military supplies and raw materials. Twelve ships manned by the Russians were now working this route, and it was hoped to add 10 ships a month in the future. The use of this route naturally depended on non-interference by the Japanese.

U. S. SECRET
BRITISH MOST SECRET

All these potential increases in shipping to Russia naturally would have to be found by cutting down elsewhere. If the opening of the Mediterranean saved some million and a half tons of shipping, this would provide a surplus for the purpose; but there appears to be no other sources. It should be possible for Great Britain and the United States to keep the pipeline full even if these potential increases were made. The maximum tonnage might be as high as 10 million tons per annum; the target for the current year was 4 million but it was doubtful if it would be reached. One million deadweight tons of supplies for Russia were awaiting shipment now in U. S. ports.

SIR ALAN BROOKE observed that one unsatisfactory feature of the whole business of supplying Russia was their refusal to put their cards on the table. It might well be that we were straining ourselves unduly and taking great risks when there was no real necessity to do so.

4. EMPLOYMENT OF FRENCH FORCES IN NORTH AFRICA.

GENERAL MARSHALL asked for the views of the British Chiefs of Staff on the employment of French divisions. The United States Chiefs of Staff felt that they can be effectively used and that their use will effect a considerable economy of force. The French divisions regarded as being the best must be reequipped as soon as practical. This, however, has political complications which must be resolved.

SIR ALAN BROOKE agreed that we should exploit the use of French troops in North Africa to the maximum, particularly for garrison work. We should have to provide them with a considerable quantity of antiaircraft weapons. Their usefulness would depend greatly on whether we could establish a satisfactory French government. Good leadership was required to rekindle in them the desire to fight. Too many of the French were only waiting for the end of the war.

GENERAL MARSHALL asked what the effect would be on Spain if French troops were stationed opposite the border of Spanish Morocco. There seemed no doubt that some very useful French divisions could be formed in North Africa.

SIR ALAN BROOKE thought that it would be wise to keep U. S. forces on the Spanish border as well as French troops. This would tend

U. S. SECRET
BRITISH MOST SECRET

to allay Spanish suspicions of the French intentions and at the same time remove any temptation from the Spanish to cross the frontier if they thought the French troops of inferior quality.

U. S. SECRET
BRITISH MOST SECRET

C.C.S. **59**th Meeting

COMBINED CHIEFS OF STAFF

MINUTES of Meeting held at Anfa Camp
on Sunday, January 17, 1943, at 1030

PRESENT

General G. C. Marshall, USA
Admiral E. J. King, USN
Lt. General H. H. Arnold, USA

General Sir Alan F. Brooke
Admiral of the Fleet Sir Dudley
   Pound
Air Chief Marshal Sir Charles
   F. A. Portal

THE FOLLOWING WERE ALSO PRESENT

Lt. General B. B. Somervell, USA
Rear Admiral C. M. Cooke, Jr., USN
Brig. General A. C. Wedemeyer, USA
Commander R. E. Libby, USN

Field Marshal Sir John Dill
Vice Admiral the Lord Louis
   Mountbatten
Lt. General Sir Hastings L. Ismay
Major General J. N. Kennedy
Air Vice Marshall J. C. Slessor

SECRETARIAT

Brigadier V. Dykes
Brig. General J. R. Deane, USA

U. S. SECRET
BRITISH MOST SECRET

1. THE EASTERN THEATER.

GENERAL MARSHALL proposed discussing a paper prepared by the United States Joint Staff Planners regarding the forces needed in the Pacific Theater in 1943.

The British Chiefs of Staff stated that they would like to have an opportunity to study the paper before discussing it in detail.

GENERAL MARSHALL pointed out that in their discussions with the British Planners, the United States Planners were told that the British did not feel that ANAKIM was possible of accomplishment during the dry season of 1943-1944. He said that the United States Chiefs of Staff are particularly concerned about the timing of this operation because of the seriousness of the situation regarding China.

ADMIRAL KING added that Operation ANAKIM was also of importance with regard to our strategy in defeating Japan.

SIR ALAN BROOKE said that there were two stumbling blocks to Operation ANAKIM in 1943. These are naval cover and the assemblage of landing craft in sufficient time to permit adequate training. He felt the land forces could be found but that it would be difficult to assemble the landing craft following Operation HUSKY.

SIR DUDLEY POUND said that in order to do Operation TORCH, it had been necessary to withdraw a considerable force from the Eastern Fleet and that it was probable the same conditions would pertain in operations undertaken in other theaters in 1943.

ADMIRAL KING said that ANAKIM was at least ten months off. He added that to postpone the date would put us in a critical situation. It is absolutely essential that we utilize China's geographical position and their manpower and ANAKIM is a step in this direction.

ADMIRAL COOKE said that he felt the operation could be started in November or December of 1943 and the actual landings be made in January. He said that there would be considerable landing craft available from production between April of 1943 and January of 1944. Some of this additional landing craft will be available for Burma in October. Therefore, the requirements for landing craft could probably be met. As for the naval force, he considered that we would only need carriers,

U. S. SECRET
BRITISH MOST SECRET

destroyers, and cruisers. He did not feel that battleships would be necessary if the Japanese were being contained by the United States Fleet in the Pacific. The real bottleneck is the availability of shipping.

ADMIRAL KING said that he definitely considered that Operation ANAKIM must be aimed at in 1943 and carried through if the situation permits.

SIR DUDLEY POUND considered in such an important operation that battleship cover would be necessary.

ADMIRAL KING again pointed out that the operation would not be undertaken for at least ten months. By this time the destroyer program should be well along, the submarine menace should be reduced, and the shipping situation much improved through increased production and the opening of the Mediterranean. To postpone the operation in 1943 would result in not undertaking it for almost two years.

GENERAL MARSHALL then informed the Chiefs of Staff of a message which Generalissimo Chiang Kai-shek had sent to the President in which he regretted that Chinese troops would not be able to participate in Operation RAVENOUS, the reasons being that the British ground forces are inadequate and that the British will not agree to engage the Eastern Fleet in the Bay of Bengal to interrupt the Japanese line of communications.

LORD LOUIS MOUNTBATTEN stated that the British Chiefs of Staff agree that the Burma road must be opened and that the entire question is one of the availability of resources.

ADMIRAL KING said that the United States Chiefs of Staff recognize Germany is our prime enemy and that their strategy does not envisage a complete defeat of Japan before defeating Germany. He added, however, that every effort must be applied which will put us in a position of readiness from which we can operate against Japan after Germany has been defeated.

SIR ALAN BROOKE agreed to this unless the attainment of such positions of readiness would delay or jeopardize the defeat of Germany.

GENERAL MARSHALL said that he felt it was a question of creating more than positions of readiness as far as the Japanese are concerned.

U. S. SECRET
BRITISH MOST SECRET

We must maintain the initiative against them by offensive moves on our part. The present operations in the South Pacific are tremendously expensive in merchant vessels, naval vessels, and escorts. The situation is also fraught with the possibility of a sudden reverse and the consequent loss of sea power. He said that he is most anxious to open the Burma Road, not so much for the morale effect on China as for the need to provide air support to China for operations against Japan and Japanese shipping. He said the expensive operations in which we are now engaged in the South Pacific react on everything else the United Nations attempt to do whether it be in the Mediterranean, the United Kingdom, or elsewhere. He discussed the situation in the Pacific as being so critical as to make it appear at one time that Operation TORCH would have to be called off. He also stated that unless Operation ANAKIM could be undertaken, he felt that a situation might arise in the Pacific at any time that would necessitate the United States regretfully withdrawing from the commitments in the European theater.

GENERAL MARSHALL spoke of our commitments in the Pacific, of our responsibilities, with particular reference to the number of garrisons we have on small islands and the impossibility of letting any of them down. He insisted that the United States could not stand for another Bataan. He said that he is desirous of undertaking the Burma operation in order to reduce our hazards in the Pacific and thus undertake the campaign against Germany.

GENERAL MARSHALL spoke of other commitments in the Pacific that are serious but in which we have been willing to accept the hazards. In this connection he pointed to the Japanese operation in the Aleutians and the necessity of protecting the Hawaiian-Midway line of communications. In these instances he felt that, while we were vulnerable to Japanese attack, support from the United States could be furnished quickly because of the relatively short distances involved.

GENERAL MARSHALL informed the Chiefs of Staff that the President is desirous of giving additional air support to China. This will be done because of the psychological results to be achieved despite the fact that it is a tremendously expensive operation.

ADMIRAL KING pointed out that the demands in the Pacific are enormous and continuous. Many of the demands are made by Australia,

U. S. SECRET
BRITISH MOST SECRET

a Dominion of the British Commonwealth. Australia is in the area of the United States strategic responsibility and most of our efforts have been devoted to protecting its line of communications. He said, in this connection, that the political and military situations are interlocked and these factors must be considered together when deciding what operations are to be undertaken. He repeated that we must place ourselves in positions of readiness for the time when all the resources of the United Nations will be brought against Japan.

2. ICELAND.

GENERAL MARSHALL asked for the views of the British Chiefs of Staff on the size of the garrison which should be maintained in Iceland. At the present time there were some 40,000 United States' ground troops in the island and two squadrons of fighter aircraft, together with a squadron of naval patrol craft. He was anxious to cut down these numbers.

SIR DUDLEY POUND said that the British garrison had been about 22,000 men. In his view an invasion of Iceland by the Germans was quite out of the question. Taking into account the general attitude of the Germans and their unwillingness to risk their ships without heavy air cover in Northern waters, he did not think even a tip and run raid was at all likely. It was possible, of course, that they might change their policy, but the only object of a German attempt to seize the island would be to deny it to us as an air base. Our possession of it made our control of the Northern exit to the Atlantic more secure. It seemed much more likely that if the Germans wished to adopt a more active policy, they would use their surface ships against our convoys rather than for a hazardous expedition against Iceland. These were his first thoughts and he would like to have a more considered opinion prepared for the United States Chiefs of Staff.

ADMIRAL KING was in general agreement with the views of Sir Dudley Pound. He pointed out that the German situation had greatly changed during the last six months.

THE COMMITTEE:
Took note that the British Chiefs of Staff would prepare for the information of the United States Chiefs of Staff a memorandum setting out their views on the defense of Iceland.

U. S. SECRET
BRITISH MOST SECRET

3.   RUSSIAN AIR ASSISTANCE FOR P. Q. CONVOYS.

ADMIRAL KING suggested that more should be done to induce the Russians to attack the German air forces in Northern Norway which were such a menace to the Murmansk convoys. The German air bases were out of range from the United Kingdom but the Russians could undoubtedly do something if they wished to. The Murmansk route was the most important of the four routes for Russian supplies, and he felt we ought to press the Russians to give us more assistance.

SIR DUDLEY POUND said that the British had pressed the Russians in 1942 to assist with escorts and with air attack. They did provide some assistance with escorts, but always found some reason for not sending their surface ships out as far as Bear Island where the danger was greatest. Whatever they might undertake to do, however, it would be quite unsafe to rely on their promises, and reduce the scale of our own protection.

As regards air, the British Mission had pressed the Russians hard for assistance, and the Prime Minister had also communicated with Mr. Stalin. In the end some Russian Army bombers had been sent North to attack the German airdromes. Such action, however, was only of very limited value. It would be no use asking them to attack the German ships since they were untrained in this work. Two British squadrons of Hampdens had been sent up to North Russia last year. At the beginning of the winter the British personnel had been withdrawn, and these were now manned by the Russians. Recently, however, when the Lutzow and Hipper came out, the Russians failed to take any action against them with these aircraft, although asked to do so.

SIR CHARLES PORTAL said that the Germans had some seven airfields between Bodo and Petsamo, all well defended. The Russians had three airfields in the Murmansk-Archangel area. Bombing of airfields was very unprofitable. For example, Malta had only three airfields within 100 miles of Sicily but a very large force of German bombers had been quite unable to prevent us using them. Whatever they did, the Russians would not be able to stop the German air reconnaissance. Medium bombers and long range fighters for their escorts would be required for the purpose; German fields were out of range of dive bombing attack.

U. S. SECRET
BRITISH MOST SECRET

SIR ALAN BROOKE said that the possibility of amphibious operations to capture the German airfields had been most exhaustively examined by the British Staffs, but they had not been found practicable. The effect of TORCH, however, had been very great in causing withdrawals of German aircraft from Norway. Their present strength was only about 53 aircraft all told, whereas they had had up to 300 previously.

SIR DUDLEY POUND pointed out that one of the greatest difficulties was that the convoys were open to attack for about ten days. This enabled the Germans to reinforce their airfields in Northern Norway from elsewhere before the convoy was out of the danger zone.

U. S. SECRET
BRITISH MOST SECRET

C.C.S. 60th Meeting

COMBINED CHIEFS OF STAFF

MINUTES of Meeting held at Anfa Camp
on Monday, January 18, 1943, at 1030.

PRESENT

General G. C. Marshall, USA	General Sir Alan F. Brooke
Admiral E. J. King, USN	Admiral of the Fleet Sir Dudley Pound
Lt. General H. H. Arnold, USA	Air Chief Marshal Sir Charles F. A. Portal

THE FOLLOWING WERE ALSO PRESENT

Lt. General B. B. Somervell, USA	Field Marshal Sir John Dill
Rear Admiral C. M. Cooke, Jr., USN	Admiral Sir Andrew B. Cunningham (for the last item)
Brig. General A. C. Wedemeyer, USA	Vice Admiral the Lord Louis Mountbatten
Brig. General J. E. Hull, USA	Lt. General Sir Hastings L. Ismay
Colonel J. E. Smart, USA	Major General J. N. Kennedy
Commander R. E. Libby, USN	Air Vice Marshal J. C. Slessor
	Captain C. E. Lambe, RN*
	Brigadier G. M. Stewart*
	Air Commodore W. Elliott*
	Brigadier M. W. M. Macleod*
	Lt. Colonel W. A. Howkins*
	Brigadier E. I. C. Jacob**

SECRETARIAT

Brigadier V. Dykes
Brig. General J. R. Deane, USA

(The meeting adjourned from 1300 to 1500)
* For part of the meeting   ** For second part of the meeting

U. S. SECRET
BRITISH MOST SECRET

1. OPERATIONS IN BURMA.
   (C.C.S. 154)

At the request of GENERAL MARSHALL, ADMIRAL COOKE discussed the landing craft situation in regard to Operation ANAKIM. He said the United States Planners had estimated the number of landing craft of types built by the United States which would be required for Operation ANAKIM would be available in November 1943. These requirements can be made available from United States production and they will be in addition to allocations of landing craft already made. There has been uncertainty as to what the production of landing craft would be because of the necessity of revising the whole production program in the United States.

SIR ALAN BROOKE asked if this number of landing craft would be available over and above those needed in all other operations under consideration, including ROUNDUP.

ADMIRAL COOKE replied that the landing craft which would be made available for ANAKIM would be from United States production that will be too late for other operations in 1943 which are being considered.

LORD LOUIS MOUNTBATTEN stated that the British will be unable to man additional landing craft beyond those for which they are asking.

SIR ALAN BROOKE then described the proposed Operation ANAKIM. The operation must start by the middle of December in order to clear up the communications to the north after the capture of Rangoon. To protect the flank it would be necessary to occupy Moulmein and the airports on the west coast of Thailand. It will be necessary to protect the east flank to prevent the Japanese from coming in from Thailand by routes that are capable of sustaining a maximum of five divisions, in order to insure that once in Burma, our forces remain there. Thereafter, it will also be necessary to maintain adequate air and naval cover to keep open the lines of communication to Rangoon.

SIR ALAN BROOKE pointed out that naval forces must be built up for the operation. As far as air power is concerned, 18 squadrons will be available and can be provided. The landing craft is the most ticklish question. Landing craft training establishments have now been provided for two brigade groups in the Mediterranean and one in India. There is also a mobile overseas reserve but it will take three months to move

U. S. SECRET
BRITISH MOST SECRET

this after it completes operations either in the Mediterranean or operations from the United Kingdom. He believed that the necessary shipping could be made available but that the two main bottlenecks were naval coverage and landing craft.

ADMIRAL KING stated that we can count on shipping some landing craft from the Southwest Pacific to Burma together with operating crews. These could probably be made available in Burma in November. While the operation was at least ten months off, he did not see why necessary naval coverage could not be assembled, either by having the United States relieve the British from naval missions elsewhere so that they could furnish the Burma coverage, or by supplying the deficiency from the United States naval units to participate in the Burma operation. He stated that he was willing to commit himself to assisting the British in these operations.

ADMIRAL KING stated that our use of landing craft in the Pacific would be in the Rabaul operations primarily. Operations beyond Rabaul would not require landing craft of the types needed for Rabaul. The Rabaul operations would be completed long before ANAKIM would be mounted. He added that even though we had gone beyond Rabaul in the Pacific, the operations could be curtailed or lessened in order to insure the success of ANAKIM in view of its importance.

LORD LOUIS MOUNTBATTEN said that the possibility of securing help from the Pacific altered the whole situation as far as the British were concerned and that with the assistance of the United States, he thought that the necessary landing craft could be assembled.

GENERAL MARSHALL then asked Sir Alan Brooke to discuss the relation between Operation RAVENOUS and Operation ANAKIM.

SIR ALAN BROOKE said that Operation CANNIBAL now being undertaken was for the purpose of securing the airport in Akyab. This is necessary in order to furnish air support for future operations. He described Akyab as a locality in no man's land lightly garrisoned by both sides.

He described Operation RAVENOUS as one to improve the line of communications preparatory to Operation ANAKIM, in order to drive in from the North at the same time as the offensive from the South. A British

U. S. SECRET
BRITISH MOST SECRET

corps is to secure bridgeheads over the Chindwin River and improve the road between Imphal and Kalewa, to connect it with the Chindwin River for use as a supply line to the South. The Ramgarh force was to advance on Myitkyna from Ledo which will also enable us to build a road between these two points. This road will be of value in supplying our forces in Operation ANAKIM and also will be used as a connecting road to join with the main Burma road into China.

SIR ALAN BROOKE gave a resume' of the present conditions of roads in Burma which indicated that all are badly in need of improvement. He said that all of the component operations of RAVENOUS are independent of each other. The operation of the British 2nd Corps from Imphal is thus independent of the action taken by the Chinese Ramgarh and Yunnan forces. The improvement of the road from Ledo was only possible to the extent of the advance made by the Ramgarh force.

SIR ALAN BROOKE said that ANAKIM is now definitely on the books, is being planned, and should be put to the front. With the assistance from the United States Navy in providing landing craft, the operation would be feasible.

LORD LOUIS MOUNTBATTEN then discussed again the question of landing craft with particular reference to paragraph 9 (d) of C.C.S. 154. In reply to a question from GENERAL MARSHALL, he stated that the assault force in England would remain there as a permanent spearhead in case of a crack in German morale. The overseas assault force contains sufficient landing craft to undertake the operation in Burma by October 1st provided that they had not been used in operations elsewhere. If they had been so used, their use in Burma would be delayed for a period of three months following the termination of the operation in which they had been engaged. He added, however, that with the assistance promised by Admiral King from the South Pacific, he felt that sufficient landing craft could be assembled to mount ANAKIM.

SIR CHARLES PORTAL pointed out that the amphibious operations in ANAKIM would have to be supported by aircraft based on carriers.

ADMIRAL KING said the main point was that we should plan to do ANAKIM in 1943.

U S SECRET
BRITISH MOST SECRET

THE COMMITTEE:

(a) Agreed that all plans and necessary preparations should be made for the purpose of mounting ANAKIM in 1943.

(b) Agreed that the actual mounting of Operation ANAKIM would be determined by the Combined Chiefs of Staff in the summer of 1943 (preferably not later than July) in the light of the situation then existing.

(c) Took note that if ANAKIM is mounted in 1943, the United States will assist in making up deficiencies in the necessary landing craft and naval forces by diversion from the Pacific Theater, and in merchant shipping, if necessary.

2. THE SITUATION TO BE CREATED IN THE EASTERN THEATER (THE PACIFIC AND BURMA) IN 1943.
(C.C.S. 153 and 153/1)

SIR ALAN BROOKE stated that the British Chiefs of Staff took exception to paragraph 1 of C.C.S. 153 in that it did not provide that Germany must be defeated before undertaking the defeat of the Japanese.

GENERAL MARSHALL stated that, in his opinion, the British Chiefs of Staff wished to be certain that we keep the enemy engaged in the Mediterranean and that at the same time maintain a sufficient force in the United Kingdom to take advantage of a crack in the German strength either from the withdrawal of their forces in France or because of lowered morale. He inferred that the British Chiefs of Staff would prefer to maintain such a force in the United Kingdom dormant and awaiting an opportunity rather than have it utilized in a sustained attack elsewhere. The United States Chiefs of Staff know that they can use these forces offensively in the Pacific Theater. He felt that the question resolved itself into whether we would maintain a large force in the United Kingdom awaiting an opportunity or keep the force engaged in an active offensive in the Pacific.

GENERAL MARSHALL said that the number of troops used in the Pacific would not have much effect on the build-up of forces in the United Kingdom. The conflict arises chiefly in the use of landing craft and shipping. He said that to a large measure the shipping used in the Pacific is already committed and, therefore, could not be made available for a build-up of forces in the United Kingdom and the necessity of

U. S. SECRET
BRITISH MOST SECRET

maintaining them. These forces are at the end of a long line of communications and the question arises as to whether we should let them remain there precariously or do something to improve their situation.

SIR ALAN BROOKE stated that we have reached a stage in the war where we must review the correctness of our basic strategic concept which calls for the defeat of Germany first. He was convinced that we cannot defeat Germany and Japan simultaneously. The British Chiefs of Staff have arrived at the conclusion that it will be better to concentrate on Germany. Because of the distances involved, the British Chiefs of Staff believe that the defeat of Japan first is impossible and that if we attempt to do so, we shall lose the war.

He said that having decided that it is necessary to defeat Germany first, the immediate question is whether to attempt to do so by an invasion of Northern France or to exploit our successes in North Africa. The British Chiefs of Staff consider that an all-out Mediterranean effort is best but that it must be "all-out."

He said the British Chiefs of Staff appreciate the position in the Pacific and that they will do everything they can to meet it but that they feel we must give first consideration to the defeat of Germany. This can be done by finishing Tunisia and then operating in the Mediterranean so as to draw the maximum number of German ground and air forces from the Russian front. In undertaking operations in the Mediterranean, assistance from the United States is necessary. He felt that if we do not maintain constant pressure on Germany, they will be given an opportunity to recover and thus prolong the war.

GENERAL MARSHALL said the United States Chiefs of Staff do not propose doing nothing in the Mediterranean or in France; they have no idea that we should not concentrate first on defeating Germany. The question that is to be decided is how this can best be accomplished. On the other hand, it is the view of the United States Chiefs of Staff that the war should be ended as quickly as possible, which cannot be accomplished if we neglect the Pacific theater entirely and leave the Japanese to consolidate their gains and unnecessarily strengthen their position.

GENERAL MARSHALL said that he advocated an attack on the Continent but that he was opposed to immobilizing a large force in the United

U. S. SECRET
BRITISH MOST SECRET

Kingdom, awaiting an uncertain prospect, when they might be better engaged in offensive operations which are possible.

GENERAL MARSHALL stated that it was apparently agreed by the Combined Chiefs of Staff to give Russia every possible assistance and to endeavor to bring Turkey into the war. His primary concern with the operations in the Pacific was to insure that our positions would be so strengthened as to provide us with the means for necessary operations rather than to continue conducting them on a "shoe string." He felt that this would ultimately reduce the necessity for tonnage in the Pacific and this was his chief reason for advocating operations in Burma.

SIR ALAN BROOKE said that the British Chiefs of Staff certainly did not want to keep forces tied up in Europe doing nothing. During the build-up period, however, the first forces to arrive from America could not be used actively against the enemy; a certain minimum concentration had to be effected before they could be employed. His point was that we should direct our resources to the defeat of Germany first. He agreed as to the desirability of ANAKIM since it appeared that for this operation we could use forces available in the theater without detracting from the earliest possible defeat of Germany. This conception was focused in paragraph 2 (c) of the British Joint Planning Staff's paper (C.C.S. 153/1) in which it was stated that we agreed in principle with the U. S. strategy in the Pacific "provided always that its application does not prejudice the earliest possible defeat of Germany."

ADMIRAL KING pointed out that this expression might be read as meaning that *anything* which was done in the Pacific interfered with the earliest possible defeat of Germany and that the Pacific theater should therefore remain totally inactive.

SIR CHARLES PORTAL said that this was certainly not the understanding of the British Chiefs of Staff who had always accepted that pressure should be maintained on Japan. They had, perhaps, misunderstood the U. S. Chiefs of Staff and thought that the point at issue was whether the main effort should be in the Pacific or in the United Kingdom. The British view was that for getting at Germany in the immediate future, the Mediterranean offered better prospects than Northern France. For this purpose they were advocating Mediterranean operations with amphibious forces while concentrating, so far as the United Kingdom was

U. S. SECRET
BRITISH MOST SECRET

concerned, on building up a large heavy bomber force, which was the only form of force that could operate continuously against Germany.

GENERAL MARSHALL said that he was most anxious not to become committed to interminable operations in the Mediterranean. He wished Northern France to be the scene of the main effort against Germany-- that had always been his conception.

SIR CHARLES PORTAL said that it was impossible to say exactly where we should stop in the Mediterranean since we hoped to knock Italy out altogether. This action would give the greatest support to Russia and might open the door to an invasion of France.

GENERAL MARSHALL pointed out that extended operations in the Mediterranean as well as the concentration of forces in England for the invasion of Northern France might well prevent us from undertaking operations in Burma; he was not at all in favor of this. Moreover, American forces at present in the Southwest Pacific were desperately short at present of their immediate requirements.

ADMIRAL KING said that we had on many occasions been close to a disaster in the Pacific. The real point at issue was to determine the balance between the effort to be put against Germany and against Japan, but we must have enough in the Pacific to maintain the initiative against the Japanese. The U. S. intentions were not to plan for anything beyond gaining positions in readiness for the final offensive against Japan. He felt very strongly, however, that the details of such operations must be left to the U. S. Chiefs of Staff, who were strategically responsible for the Pacific theater. He did not feel this was a question for a decision of the Combined Chiefs of Staff. The U. S. Chiefs of Staff had not been consulted before the British undertook operations in Madagascar and French Somaliland--nor did they expect to be; but the same considerations applied to the details of operations in the Pacific.

In his view there would be plenty of forces in the theater for all necessary operations in the Mediterranean and it was now determined that such operations should be undertaken. The operations contemplated in the Pacific, however, would have no effect on what could be done in the Mediterranean or from the United Kingdom.

SIR CHARLES PORTAL said that the British Chiefs of Staff would be satisfied if they could be assured of this point. Their fear was that

U. S. SECRET
BRITISH MOST SECRET

the result of extended operations in the Pacific might be an insufficient concentration in the United Kingdom to take advantage of a crack in Germany.

GENERAL MARSHALL pointed out that the whole concept of defeating Germany first had been jeopardized by the lack of resources in the Pacific. Heavy bombers set up to go to the United Kingdom had had to be diverted to the South Pacific to avoid disaster there. Fortunately disaster had been avoided; but if it had occurred, there would have been a huge diversion of U. S. effort to the Pacific theater. The U. S. had nearly been compelled to pull out of TORCH and the decision to spare the necessary naval forces from the Pacific had been a most courageous one on the part of Admiral King. A hand-to-mouth policy of this nature was most uneconomical. He was anxious to get a secure position in the Pacific so that we knew where we were. The reconquest of Burma would be an enormous contribution to this and would effect ultimately a great economy of forces.

Discussion then turned on the operations proposed to secure the Pacific theater, which were set out in C.C.S. 153

SIR ALAN BROOKE said that in the British view it would be sufficient to stop at Rabaul and ANAKIM and that to go on to Truk would take up too much force. There would inevitably be large shipping losses in the course of such operations, which would be a continuous drain on our resources.

ADMIRAL KING pointed out that the proposed operations would be carried out one after the other. After Rabaul had been captured, the same forces might be employed to go on to the Marshalls. Rabaul might be taken by May and ANAKIM could not start before November. During the intervening months, surely the troops in the theater should not be allowed to remain idle but should be employed to keep up pressure on the Japanese and maintain the initiative. Only by this means could we offset the advantage which the Japanese had in their possession of interior lines. Operations into the Marshalls could be stopped at any point desired and were not an unlimited commitment which had to be seen through to the end. It might well be that Truk would, after all, be found impossible to capture this year.

U. S. SECRET
BRITISH MOST SECRET

GENERAL MARSHALL said that there seemed general agreement as to the need for the capture of Rabaul and the desirability of ANAKIM. Could it not be agreed that operations should be continued as far as Truk if it were possible with the forces available at that time? There should be no question of sacrificing ANAKIM for Truk.

SIR CHARLES PORTAL said he would not like to be committed to ANAKIM, even with forces released after the capture of Rabaul, without first reviewing whether some other operation more profitable to the war as a whole might not be desirable. For example, to take an extreme case, suppose after the capture of Rabaul a good opportunity arose, owing to a crack in Germany, of breaking into France. Should we refuse to take advantage of it because we were already committed to ANAKIM?

GENERAL MARSHALL felt that if such a situation arose we should certainly seize the opportunity. He agreed that a further meeting of the Combined Chiefs of Staff might be necessary in the summer to decide these questions.

SIR ALAN BROOKE proposed that at the present time we should limit our outlook in the Pacific to Rabaul, which should certainly be undertaken, and to preparations for ANAKIM, the decision to launch this being taken later. Similarly, any decision on Truk should be deferred.

ADMIRAL KING pointed out that the effect of this would be strictly to limit commitments in the Pacific, although the British Chiefs of Staff apparently contemplated an unlimited commitment in the European theater.

GENERAL MARSHALL agreed that a decision on ANAKIM and Truk could be left until later. He pointed out that C.C.S. 153 merely proposed a series of operations which might be carried out in 1943 with the means available.

ADMIRAL KING said that on logistic grounds alone it would be impossible to bring forces from the Pacific theater to the European theater. ANAKIM was not therefore an alternative to operations in the European theater.

GENERAL SOMERVELL supported this view. He pointed out that, once Rabaul had been seized, ships would be required to maintain the garrison

U. S. SECRET
BRITISH MOST SECRET

there and these could be employed to exploit success by minor operations against other islands.

As regards landing craft, the U. S. Chiefs of Staff had committed themselves to supply a large proportion of the craft needed for ANAKIM. Operations against the Pacific Islands required combat loaders and not the tank-landing ships and tank-landing craft which were needed elsewhere.

ADMIRAL COOKE said that a very large proportion of the U. S. shipping in the Pacific was needed for the maintenance of the Fleet, which was operating 7,000 miles from its home bases. This requirement would continue whether or not operations against Truk were undertaken. U. S. production of L.S.T.'s would shortly amount to about fifteen per month. These could not be ready in time for Mediterranean operations in the summer, but would be available for ANAKIM. As regards land forces, the figure of 250,000 put down in C.C.S. 153 included 150,000 men now in movement or set up to move, and another two divisions which he understood were already earmarked for operations in Burma this year from India. This left a total of only some 50,000 men additional for the whole Pacific theater.

SIR CHARLES PORTAL reiterated that it would be unwise to accept a definite commitment for ANAKIM now since a favorable situation might arise in Europe during the year which would make operations in the European theater more profitable than anything in the Pacific.

ADMIRAL KING said that forces set out in C.C.S. 153 constituted the minimum necessary to maintain pressure on the Japanese. Although the forces in the Pacific were primarily for defensive purposes, many of them could be used simultaneously for minor offensives, such as air bombardment of Japanese bases. Favorable opportunities might then be seized for exploitation.

GENERAL MARSHALL suggested that paragraph 11 (c) of C.C.S. 153 could be revised to read "seizure and occupation of Gilbert Islands, Marshall Islands, Caroline Islands up to and including Truk *with the resources available in the theater.*"

(The meeting adjourned at this point.)

On the resumption of their meeting the Combined Chiefs of Staff had before them a draft note setting out tentative agreements which appeared to have been reached in the preceding discussion.

U. S. SECRET
BRITISH MOST SECRET

After some further discussion,

THE COMMITTEE:

(a) Invited General Ismay and General Hull to redraft this note to include further points which had been raised.

(b) Instructed the Secretaries to circulate this draft for discussion at the next meeting.

3. ESCORT VESSELS.

SIR DUDLEY POUND emphasized the need for the Combined Chiefs of Staff having before them a proper survey of the escort vessel position before taking any final decision on operations during the coming year. He recapitulated the British needs for additional escorts in the Atlantic and pointed out that considerable U. S. assistance would be required not only in the Atlantic but also for HUSKY if that operation were undertaken When escorts were withdrawn for an operation such as TORCH or HUSKY, they were absent from their normal duties for about four months. It took at least one month to collect them beforehand from the various convoys on which they were working and a similar period to redistribute them after the operation. Experience in TORCH had shown that it was not possible to release them from the operation itself under about two months

ADMIRAL KING said that with the U. S. and U. K. construction coming out during the next six months, the position should be easier by July, when HUSKY was to be launched. He thought it should be possible to find additional escorts for the Atlantic as well as those required for HUSKY. If the use of combat loaders for HUSKY could be cut to the minimum, escort requirements would be correspondingly reduced.

SIR DUDLEY POUND said that new construction in the U. K. was comparatively small during the first half of 1943 and would do little more than make good recent heavy losses.

ADMIRAL COOKE said that the examination of the escort position by the British Joint Planning Staff was progressing well but it appeared that the total number of U. S. and British escort vessels would not be sufficient to provide any surplus after providing for normal convoy work. Any operations undertaken would therefore involve accepting increased losses in normal convoys. The Combined Chiefs of Staff would have to decide what losses would be acceptable.

U. S. SECRET
BRITISH MOST SECRET

The discussion then turned on the relation of P.Q. convoys to Mediterranean operations.

SIR DUDLEY POUND said that one problem was whether a 30-ship convoy every forty days would be considered sufficient for Russia or whether we should be pressed, as we had been in the past, to increase Russian deliveries. The worst three months were from February to the middle of May when daylight hours were increasing and the channel was restricted by ice. Later in the year the ice retreated and although the days were longer, the passage of convoys became less dangerous.

GENERAL MARSHALL felt that we should not again risk the same heavy losses which had been sustained on the Russian convoys in 1942. Such losses were likely to cripple our whole offensive effort against the enemy. He suggested that the Combined Chiefs of Staff should include a reference to this effect in the note which was being drafted. One alleviating factor was the improvement in the Persian Gulf route which would offset reductions on the Murmansk route.

SIR DUDLEY POUND said that the Prime Minister had made it clear to Mr. Stalin that we might have to call off P.Q. convoys if the scale of German attack became too heavy. If warning was given of our intention to stop the convoys, there was likely to be heavy pressure to increase deliveries during the early part of the year, when, as he had previously explained, conditions were most difficult. This meant either increasing the size of the convoys or reducing the cycle. The dangers which we were likely to face this year were much greater than last year.

4. POTENTIALITIES OF POLISH FORCES.

SIR ALAN BROOKE, in answer to a question by GENERAL MARSHALL, said that the Polish forces consisted (1) of a "secret" army inside Poland and (2) of regular Polish troops outside the country. As regards the first, there was a definite organization of determined men; with leaders, though they were almost entirely unarmed. Their intelligence service had been good, but recently many of their agents had been caught by the Germans and less information about German forces was now coming out from Poland. General Sikorski claimed that by the use of this organization he could do great damage on the Polish railways to interrupt German communications at a critical moment. There could be no doubt that

U. S. SECRET
BRITISH MOST SECRET

this secret army would play a valuable part in the final rising against Germany, particularly if combined with similar action in adjacent Balkan countries. There was always a danger of a premature rising, however.

The Polish forces outside Poland consisted of an armored division and a parachute brigade with certain other units in the United Kingdom and 2 divisions and 2 brigade groups in the Middle East. General Sikorski's conception was to get some of these troops into Poland to supplement the secret army. The difficulty was the method of transport, on which General Sikorski was rather vague. He envisaged the use of air transport and parachutes, but there were obvious limitations in this.

GENERAL MARSHALL inquired whether any steps had been taken to meet a request of General Sikorski for the bombing of an area in Poland from which the Germans were clearing out all Polish inhabitants under circumstances of great brutality.

SIR CHARLES PORTAL said the Poles had been informed that this operation was impracticable, but steps would be taken to publicize the presence of Polish air forces in the raids on Berlin which might be considered partly as a reprisal on behalf of Poland.

5. RAIDS ON BERLIN.

SIR CHARLES PORTAL gave details of the recent raids on Berlin, and estimated that, making all allowance for the comparative sizes of London and Berlin and the time interval, the two raids on Berlin on successive nights had hit Berlin about twice as hard as London had been hit in the two heaviest raids of April and May 1941. The aggregate losses in the two Berlin raids amounted to 6 percent, the figure expected being 10 percent. The effect of the raids would be largely morale though there were important electrical works in the area attacked. They would be a great encouragement to the Russians as well as the Poles.

(SIR ANDREW CUNNINGHAM entered the meeting at this point.)

6. NAVAL SITUATION IN THE WESTERN MEDITERRANEAN.

ADMIRAL CUNNINGHAM said that the Germans might threaten our shipping passing through the Straits of Gibraltar by U-boats and by aircraft and coast defense guns from Southern Spain. He considered the risk from U-boats was comparatively small. The Germans had never been

U. S. SECRET
BRITISH MOST SECRET

able to maintain many U-boats in the Straits where currents made their operation difficult. The danger from aircraft would be no less than to coastal convoys along the east coast of England. Provided we had fighters established in the airfields of Spanish Morocco, we should be able to deal with this threat. Coast defense guns constituted the greatest danger, but only experience would show how bad this would be. The guns were supposed to have radar range-finding apparatus but we had means of jamming this which would probably be effective. The guns would have to be neutralized by counter-battery from the southern shore and by air bombardment.

He thought that ships with a speed of 11 knots and upwards would get through the Straits without heavy losses even with the Germans in Southern Spain provided we held Spanish Morocco. Even without it, we should be able to get some convoys through by night. The Planning Staffs at Algiers had been examining the problem and their preliminary conclusions were that if we seized Majorca we should be able to prevent the Germans building up a large air strength in Southern Spain.

SIR DUDLEY POUND said that in spite of the German coast defense guns on the French shore of the Straits of Dover, we had not lost a ship from them. The range, however, was some 38,000 yards, whereas the distance across the Straits of Gibraltar was only about half that.

SIR ALAN BROOKE said that a plan had been prepared for seizing Southern Spain with a force of about six divisions. It would not be possible, however, to do this at the same time as HUSKY. It must be remembered that even if the Spaniards offered no resistance at all it would take some time for the Germans to become fully established in Southern Spain.

ADMIRAL CUNNINGHAM, referring to the possibility of capturing Sicily, said that he did not anticipate very heavy shipping losses in the operation but the actual assault of the beaches would be a very expensive operation. He did not consider that the possession of the island would very greatly add to the security of the sea route through the Mediterranean. If we were in Sicily, he would estimate this route as being 90 percent or more secure; without Sicily, it would be about 85 percent secure, once we held the whole of the North African coast.

U. S. SECRET
BRITISH MOST SECRET

SIR CHARLES PORTAL pointed out that from the air point of view the possession of Sicily would make a very considerable difference. If the Germans were not in the island, it would be difficult for them to operate against our shipping at all; they would have to use bases in Sardinia and the mainland of Italy, which were a considerable distance from the Narrows.

ADMIRAL CUNNINGHAM then described the naval situation in the Tunisia area. The Germans had made heavy attacks on Bone on three successive days damaging four merchant ships and a cruiser, but the defenses were now much improved and our cruisers were still operating from the port. We had at first sunk about one ship a day, but the Germans were getting far too many ships into Tunisia now. We should be able to inflict much greater damage on them as soon as we had fully organized our arrangements. Steps were now being taken to block the channel between the Italian minefields with our own mines.

U. S. SECRET
BRITISH MOST SECRET

C.C.S. 61st Meeting

COMBINED CHIEFS OF STAFF

MINUTES of Meeting held at Anfa Camp
on Tuesday, January 19, 1943, at 1000.

PRESENT

General G. C. Marshall, USA	General Sir Alan F. Brooke
Admiral E. J. King, USN	Admiral of the Fleet Sir Dudley Pound
Lt. General H. H. Arnold, USA	Air Chief Marshal Sir Charles F. A. Portal

THE FOLLOWING WERE ALSO PRESENT

Lt General B. B. Somervell, USA	Field Marshal Sir John Dill
Rear Admiral C. M. Cooke, Jr., USN	Vice Admiral the Lord Louis Mountbatten
Brig. General J. E. Hull, USA	Lt. General Sir Hastings L. Ismay
Brig. General A. C. Wedemeyer, USA	Major General J. N. Kennedy
Colonel J. E. Smart, USA	Air Vice Marshal J. C. Slessor
Commander R. E. Libby, USN	

SECRETARIAT

Brigadier V. Dykes
Brig. General J. R. Deane, USA
Brigadier E. I. C. Jacob
Lt. Colonel L. T. Grove, USA

U. S. SECRET
BRITISH MOST SECRET

1. CONDUCT OF THE WAR IN 1943.
   (C.C.S. 155)

   The Combined Chiefs of Staff considered a draft memorandum prepared as a result of their meeting the previous day. Certain amendments were suggested and agreed.

   THE COMMITTEE:
   Approved the memorandum* as amended.

2. SUGGESTED PROCEDURE FOR DEALING WITH THE AGENDA OF THE CONFERENCE.
   (C.C.S. 155/1)

   The Combined Chiefs of Staff considered a note, prepared by the Combined Staffs suggesting the procedure to be followed for dealing with the major questions on the agreed Agenda of the Combined Chiefs of Staff (C.C.S. 140). Certain alterations were suggested to the tentative program of meetings set out in the annex to these minutes.

   THE COMMITTEE:
   Approved the suggested procedure subject to the Annex being revised as agreed at their meeting.**

3. STRATEGIC RESPONSIBILITY AND COMMAND SET UP FOR DAKAR FRENCH WEST AFRICA.

   ADMIRAL KING said that no question of land forces was involved in West Africa. Admiral Glassford had proposed that the West African Coast from Cape Bojador to the Western boundary of Sierra Leone should be placed under French naval command. The French naval forces should be responsible for such operations off shore as might be necessary in that area. He understood that M. Boisson and Admiral Collinet were both agreeable to this suggestion.

   The proposed arrangement would include the air cover for off shore operations. The difficulty would be the lack of equipment of the French air forces. He suggested that to overcome this difficulty we should set out to familiarize the French with modern aircraft. To do this it would be necessary to give them up-to-date equipment and adequate

   * Subsequently issued as C C S. 155/1.
   ** Annex.

U. S. SECRET
BRITISH MOST SECRET

training and to include them, so far as possible, in actual operations. He said that the West African coast from Cape Bojador southwards was a British sphere, and his proposal was that the French in their area should work under Admiral Pegram. We should have to decide whether to deal with the French as full allies or whether it would be necessary to exercise some degree of control over them.

SIR DUDLEY POUND said that he had formed the impression that Admiral Collinet was all out to help and that the arrangement which Admiral Glassford proposed was based on the assumption that the French would fully cooperate.

SIR CHARLES PORTAL said that he was in general agreement with the suggestions put forward by Admiral King.

It was essential that all coastal air operations in West Africa should be coordinated by the British Air Commander who would be working in cooperation with the British Naval Commander. He was fully alive to the importance of giving the French airmen at Dakar some equipment to enable them immediately to take a share in air operations in the proposed French sub-area. For this purpose he proposed, subject to the agreement of the Combined Chiefs of Staff, to allot them 2 Sunderland Flying Boats and 4 Hudson patrol bombers which, to begin with, would be operated by British crews with the more experienced French crews alongside them until they were fit to take over themselves.

He was less anxious about the reliability of the French than about their technical ability and training. So far, they had neither the equipment, training or experience of coastal air operations in modern war. He proposed, therefore, that the less experienced French air crews, together with the appropriate maintenance personnel, should be withdrawn to British training establishments, with the object of forming them, if they turned out to be any good and as soon as the equipment could be made available into two squadrons, one of Catalinas and one of Wellington patrol bombers. He agreed that the equipment of these coastal squadrons in West Africa should be a British responsibility, but pointed out that, owing to present shortage of suitable aircraft and the necessity for adequate training of crews, the formation of the proposed two squadrons was not likely to be practicable in the immediate future.

U. S. SECRET
BRITISH MOST SECRET

GENERAL ARNOLD said that the United States concept was gradually to draw in French air force personnel as they became trained and equipped for operational work over a period of about a year. He agreed that in French West Africa this would be a British responsibility.

GENERAL MARSHALL said that he was in favor of proceeding with a definite program for reequipping the French forces. This would, of course, imply French acceptance of our organization and training methods, and would inevitably delay the progress of equipping our own forces. He thought, however, that we should do the thing whole-heartedly; and he was prepared, subject to General Eisenhower's views, to modify the United States program in order to equip French forces up to a strength of 250,000. All the equipment provided for the French would be at the expense of United States troops forming in America. He proposed to make use of French shipping to bring it over.

GENERAL SOMERVELL said that General Giraud had agreed to turn over 160,000 tons of French shipping to the Allied pool. Out of this tonnage General Giraud proposed that 85,000 tons should be allocated to meet French civil requirements, leaving 75,000 tons for shipping equipment for the French forces. General Somervell calculated that this would enable them to be equipped at the rate of about one division a month. No allowance was made in this program for the carriage of coal and oil which was at present being shipped by the British.

THE COMMITTEE:
Agreed:
(a) That the West African Coast (offshore) from Cape Bojador (Rio d'Oro) southward shall be an area under command of a British Naval Officer for naval operations and of a British Air Officer for air operations in cooperation with naval forces.
(b) That subject to (a), a sub-area extending from Cape Bojador to the western boundary of Sierra Leone and all forces operating therein shall be under French Command.
(c) That in the French sub-area the intention will be to enable French air units to take over air duties as rapidly as equipment and training permit.

U. S. SECRET
BRITISH MOST SECRET

4. PUBLICATION OF RESULTS OF THE CONFERENCE.

SIR ALAN BROOKE drew the attention of the Committee to the decision which the President and the Prime Minister had made at their meeting the previous day that:

(a) The results of this conference should be communicated to Stalin in the form of a document setting out our intentions for 1943.

(b) A communique should be prepared for issue to the Press when the conference is finished.

SIR ALAN BROOKE suggested that a small subcommittee should be appointed to draft a suitable document for approval by the Committee at the end of the conference.

THE COMMITTEE:

Agreed:

To appoint a subcommittee for this purpose consisting of:
United States Representatives:
Brigadier General Hull
Colonel Smart
Commander Libby
British Representatives:
Lt. General Ismay
Major General Kennedy
Air Vice Marshal Slessor

U S SECRET
BRITISH MOST SECRET

ANNEX TO MINUTES 61ST MEETING
REVISED PROGRAM OF MEETINGS

TUESDAY, 19th:
    Discussion of future procedure.
    System of command in French West Africa.
    Turkey and Axis oil.

WEDNESDAY, 20th:
    Organization of command and allocation of spheres of responsibility
        in the Mediterranean.
    Assistance to Russia in relation to other commitments.
    HUSKY
    Bomber Offensive from North Africa.

THURSDAY, 21st:
    U Boat War.
    Landing Craft.

FRIDAY, 22nd:
    Bomber Offensive from U. K.
    BOLERO Build-up
    1943 Limited Operations from U. K.

SATURDAY, 23rd:
    ANAKIM.
    SOUTHWEST PACIFIC.

U. S. SECRET
BRITISH MOST SECRET

C.C.S. 62nd Meeting

COMBINED CHIEFS OF STAFF

MINUTES of Meeting held at Anfa Camp
on Tuesday, January 19, 1943, at 1600.

PRESENT

General G. C. Marshall, USA	General Sir Alan F. Brooke
Admiral E. J. King, USN	Admiral of the Fleet Sir Dudley Pound
Lt. General H. H. Arnold, USA	Air Chief Marshal Sir Charles F. A. Portal

THE FOLLOWING WERE ALSO PRESENT

Lt. General B. B. Somervell, USA	Field Marshal Sir John Dill
Rear Admiral C. M. Cooke, Jr., USN	Vice Admiral the Lord Louis Mountbatten
Brig. General J. E. Hull, USA	
Brig. General A. C. Wedemeyer, USA	Lt. General Sir Hastings L. Ismay
Colonel J. E. Smart, USA	Major General J. N. Kennedy
Commander R. E. Libby, USN	Air Vice Marshal J. C. Slessor
Major C. R. Codman, USA **	Air Vice Marshal F. F. Inglis *
	Lt. Colonel C. E. R. Hirsch *
	General Henri Giraud **

SECRETARIAT

Brigadier V. Dykes
Brig. General J. R. Deane, USA
Brigadier E. I. C. Jacob

* For Item 1
** For Item 3

U. S. SECRET
BRITISH MOST SECRET

1. AXIS OIL POSITION.
   (C.C.S. 158)

THE COMBINED CHIEFS OF STAFF had before them a note by the Assistant Chief of British Air Staff (Intelligence) summarizing the latest British views on the Axis oil position (C.C.S. 158).

SIR CHARLES PORTAL said that the British had fully realized the great strategical importance of oil targets in Germany, but for tactical reasons these were extremely difficult to attack. The most important targets were the synthetic oil plants and the Rumanian oil refineries. Unfortunately the latter, from bases at present available, were at extreme range of our bombers; and he felt that it would be a mistake to make light and sporadic attacks on Ploesti, which would do little harm and only result in an increase of the German air defenses. It would be better to wait until we had the Turkish air bases before starting our attacks. The synthetic oil plants were in the Ruhr and elsewhere, but they were very small targets which needed precision bombing to put out of action. Recent developments in radio navigation increased the chances of success on these targets, and great hopes were placed on the possibility of daylight precision bombing by the U. S. Air Forces. When a sufficient force had been built up in a few months' time, it might be possible to resume attacks on these targets more effectively, provided of course that this could be achieved without prejudice to the U-boat warfare.

GENERAL ARNOLD pointed out that the Ploesti fields--which were roughly equidistant from Sicily, Benghazi, Cairo, and Aleppo--were within range of the B-24 with a load of 4,000 pounds of bombs or under.

SIR CHARLES PORTAL pointed out that one of the chief difficulties was getting the necessary meteorological information, without which long-distance attacks of this nature were unlikely to be successful. It was becoming increasingly difficult to obtain information from secret radio stations in the Balkans owing to the activities of the Gestapo.

AIR VICE MARSHAL INGLIS confirmed that in the British view the Rumanian oil supplies were vital to Germany. Her stocks were so low that she depended on Rumanian oil for about thirty-three percent of her total need.

GENERAL SOMERVELL said that the latest American estimate was less

U. S. SECRET
BRITISH MOST SECRET

optimistic about the shortage of oil in Germany than the British. It was believed that Germany would have a surplus of about 40,000,000 barrels at the end of 1943 instead of the 10,000,000 barrels which she had at the end of 1942, owing to the opening up of new sources in Hungary and elsewhere. It was, therefore, calculated that even if the whole of the Rumanian production were knocked out early in the year, she would still have enough for operations in 1944. There were two tetraethyl lead factories however, the destruction of which would hamstring the production of German aviation fuel.

SIR CHARLES PORTAL suggested that this latest American information should be immediately given to the British intelligence Staffs with a view to the production of an agreed estimate.

GENERAL MARSHALL emphasized the importance of making great efforts against German oil if we could be sure that it formed a really critical target. U. S. aircraft in the Southwest Pacific were bombing targets at a greater distance from their base than Rumania from the present bases available. We might have to wait a long time before the Turkish bases could be used.

SIR CHARLES PORTAL said that we must be sure our bombing would be really effective. The value of attacks on German oil had to be balanced against the needs of HUSKY, for which we should try to cause the maximum loss to the German air forces in the Mediterranean during the coming months. Only by this means could we hope to obtain the necessary air superiority on which depended the success of the operation.

After some discussion,

THE COMMITTEE:
(a) Took note that the Axis oil situation is so restricted that it is decidedly advantageous that bombing attacks on the sources of Axis oil--namely, the Rumanian oilfields and oil traffic via the Danube, and the synthetic and producer gas plants in Germany--be undertaken as soon as other commitments allow.
(b) Directed the Combined Intelligence Committee to submit as early as possible an agreed assessment of the Axis oil

U. S. SECRET
BRITISH MOST SECRET

situation based on the latest information available from both British and U. S. sources.

2. ALLIED PLANS RELATING TO TURKEY.
   (C.C.S. 157)

In discussing C.C.S. 157, SIR ALAN BROOKE said that the plans for inducing Turkey to enter the war on the side of the United Nations were largely political and that the military efforts were designed to further the political negotiations.

He said that Turkey is in need of specialized equipment and that it would be preferable to furnish operating units rather than the equipment alone. The Turkish people are not particularly adept in handling mechanized equipment, but they seem to have a strong desire to attempt it. As a result, we shall probably have to furnish the equipment with certain personnel to train Turkish troops in its use.

SIR ALAN BROOKE then presented the following draft resolution which he recommended be approved by the Combined Chiefs of Staff:

"The Combined Chiefs of Staff recognize that Turkey lies within a theater of British responsibility, and that all matters connected with Turkey should be handled by the British in the same way that all matters connected with China are handled by the United States of America.

"In particular, the British should be responsible for framing and presenting to both Assignment Boards all bids for equipment for Turkey. The onward despatch to Turkey from the Middle East of such equipment will be a function of command of the British Commanders-in-Chief in the Middle East. They will not divert much equipment to other uses except for urgent operational reasons, and will report such diversions to the appropriate Munitions Assignment Board."

GENERAL SOMERVELL stated that just prior to his departure from Washington, an agreement had been reached between the State Department and the British Joint Staff Mission as to methods by which munitions should be supplied to Turkey.

U. S. SECRET
BRITISH MOST SECRET

SIR ALAN BROOKE said that this agreement was not acceptable in London. He pointed out that any agreements previously made were superseded by the agreement arrived at on January 18th between the Prime Minister and the President which provided that all matters connected with Turkey should be handled by the British in the same way that all matters connected with China are handled by the United States.

GENERAL MARSHALL stated that he desired more time to study the resolution referred to above and requested that action with regard to it be postponed until the meeting of January 20th. He said that there was some confusion in his mind as to just what was intended with regard to Turkey. The President had said that he had hoped to arrange for Turkey's permission for the passage of munitions en route to Russia through Turkish territory. C.C.S. 157 indicates that certain arrangements have already been made regarding the supply of munitions to Russia. In addition, the decision has been reached to make certain troop concentrations available to assist Turkey in the event that she enters into the war on the side of the United Nations. He asked Sir Alan Brooke what he considered the probabilities with regard to Turkey would be.

SIR ALAN BROOKE said that the British had an agreement to assist Turkey if she were attacked. The agreement includes furnishing Turkey 26 squadrons of pursuit aviation. In order that these squadrons might be able to operate quickly, certain necessary equipment had already been sent there. This had been a defensive agreement, but the intention is now to operate an offensive from Turkey. The present plan is that Turkey should merely hold the Axis forces beyond her frontier and thus secure air bases from which the United Nations could operate against Rumania.

He said it was hoped that we could induce Turkey to come into the war. This might be accomplished by political moves. Certain territorial promises might be made to Turkey at this time. For example, they might be promised the "Duck's Bill" in Syria, control of the Dodecanese, certain parts of Bulgaria, and assurance that her communications in the Bosphorus will be unhampered. The more apparent a victory by the United Nations becomes, the more will Turkey desire to have a place at the peace table. This might be sufficient inducement for her to join the United Nations. In any event, our efforts with regard to Turkey will not be very costly, but they may provide an opportunity for appreciable gains.

U. S. SECRET
BRITISH MOST SECRET

GENERAL MARSHALL said that he had no doubt about the value of bringing Turkey into the war. He thought that if she could be induced to join us at the right moment, the results might play a determining part in the conclusion of the war. He asked Sir Alan Brooke what he thought Turkey's reaction might be if we effected a large concentration in the rear of her borders.

SIR ALAN BROOKE said it would strengthen the United Nations in the eyes of Turkey and give tangible evidence that we are ready to assist her. He said that the capture of the Dodecanese by the United Nations would give Turkey a feeling of confidence in their power but that these islands could be much more easily captured by an operation from Turkey, once she had joined in with us. He added that there is no possibility of doing operation HUSKY and capturing the Dodecanese simultaneously.

SIR CHARLES PORTAL said that holding the Dodecanese would facilitate operations in Turkey by insuring the use of the port of Smyrna.

THE COMMITTEE:
(a) Agreed to consider the proposed resolution on Turkey, quoted above, at the meeting on January 20th.
(b) Took note of the paper under consideration.

3. MEETING WITH GENERAL GIRAUD.

GENERAL MARSHALL said that the Combined Chiefs of Staff were much honored by the presence of General Giraud and were very pleased that it had been possible to arrange the meeting. He hoped that General Giraud would express his views, and in particular that he would indicate the present status of the French forces and the rapidity with which they could be built up.

GENERAL GIRAUD said that he was proud at being able to participate in the work of the Combined Chiefs of Staff. The French army had now reentered the war and had not only the will to fight but also the experience and knowledge. As an example, he might mention a message which he had that morning received on the telephone from his Chief of Staff; this was to the effect that the Germans had yesterday attacked the junction of the British and French armies between Medjes el Bab and Pont du Fahs with 80 tanks supported by infantry. On the British front the attack had completely broken down and 10 tanks had been knocked out.

U. S. SECRET
BRITISH MOST SECRET

On the French front an attack by 50 tanks had been made against a battalion locality. The battalion had held its ground all day, and it was not until the evening that certain advanced posts were evacuated by order of the battalion commander. He had not had any further news but he understood that the situation was in hand. The action showed the quality of the French troops. They had not been able to knock out any tanks as they had no antitank guns. They had, however, prevented the German infantry from supporting their tanks and had held their ground. Similar examples had occurred on the whole front during the last two months. Such troops were worthy of modern arms.

On the existing cadres, the French army could form three armored divisions and ten mobile infantry divisions. It would also be possible to raise the following air forces:

    50 fighter squadrons with 500 aircraft
    30 light bomber squadrons with 300 aircraft.
    200 transport aircraft.

Such a force was an indispensable accompaniment for a modern army. The French pilots had already given proof of what they could do. One squadron of the Groupe Lafayette, armed with 12 P-40 aircraft, had been fighting for the last six days; they had shot down five enemy aircraft for the loss of one. He was particularly anxious to receive: first, fighter aircraft in the supply of which he hoped the British would participate; and, subsequently, light bombers so that he could equip the pilots of whose quality he had intimate knowledge and who would quickly master the new equipment. He realized that there were considerable difficulties due to the shortage of shipping and the needs of the Allied forces. Some of the aircraft, however, could fly from America, and possibly the fighters might be flown in from aircraft carriers. He felt confident that the French army could make a great contribution to the European campaign if it were properly equipped. He estimated that the campaign in North Africa would be over in two months' time; and in this campaign he included the capture of Sicily, Sardinia and Corsica, which he regarded as forming a direct prolongation of Africa and as bases for further action.

GENERAL MARSHALL said that he was very glad to have heard General Giraud's views. Speaking on behalf of the U. S. Army, air and ground, he explained that he was going into the details of how quickly modern

U. S. SECRET
BRITISH MOST SECRET

equipment could be provided for the French Army. He knew that the shipping question was under detailed consideration by Admiral King and French Naval officers. General Somervell, the Head of the Services of Supply, had already called on General Giraud to discuss these matters and had reported thereon to him. The question of priority of delivery of items and the method to be adopted in equipping French Units would be taken up with General Giraud. General Arnold had been conferring with French officers to see what could be done to provide air equipment. It was in the interests of the U.S.A. to bring the French forces to a high state of efficiency, and everything possible would be done to obviate the difficulties of distance. It was not a question of whether to equip the French Army, but rather of how to carry it out. Availability of equipment was not the limiting factor, but transport.

SIR ALAN BROOKE expressed, on behalf of the British Chiefs of Staff, great pleasure at the report which General Giraud had given of the state of the French Army. With the more limited resources at the disposal of the British, they would do what they could to help in providing modern equipment. He fully realized the important part which the French forces would play in bringing the war to a successful conclusion.

ADMIRAL KING said that arrangements were well in hand for the rehabilitation in rotation of the French warships. Resources would not permit of them being dealt with all at once. He welcomed the officers and men of the French Navy who were now joining in the struggle for victory.

SIR DUDLEY POUND said that the navies of the Allies were now fighting in every ocean of the world and the U-boats were extending their activities further and further afield. The combined British and American naval forces were less than we should like to have to meet this menace, and the help of the French naval forces would be most welcome. From his experience at the beginning of the war, he knew the value of French naval assistance, and he knew also that this help would be of the same quality now as then.

SIR CHARLES PORTAL said that he had the clearest recollection from two wars of the skill and high performance of the French air forces. He, therefore, hoped that they could be equipped as soon as possible to

U. S. SECRET
BRITISH MOST SECRET

fight once more alongside the Allies. Within the limit of British resources, which were considerably strained, everything would be done to hasten the day of this collaboration.

GENERAL ARNOLD said that he had been trying for some time to find the most effective use for the French pilots, who had proved their ability to take over and operate skillfully American equipment. He hoped that this study would soon be completed.

SIR JOHN DILL said that he felt inspired by the presence of General Giraud, knowing as he did how much General Giraud had suffered for France. It was a matter of great pleasure, therefore, to have the General back to lead France to victory.

GENERAL GIRAUD said that in the early days of the war he had worked in the closest touch with the British Army. The cooperation between all arms at that time, and particularly between the 1st French Army and the Second Corps, of which Sir John Dill was the distinguished Commander, had showed how close such contact could be. Now once more cooperation had been resumed. In September 1940, when he was in a German prison camp, he had told the German generals that they had lost the war. Their attempt to invade Great Britain had failed, and though he could not prophesy how long the war would last, Germany could never win. Sooner or later the U. S. would come to the help of Great Britain. The Germans had asked him to sign a paper to say that he would not escape during the period of two hours each day when the French generals were allowed outside. He had said that he refused to sign any paper in German. They had asked him whether he was planning to escape as he had done in 1915. He had said, "Never mind what I am thinking. You are my jailers, I am your prisoner. It is your duty to guard me; it is my duty to escape. Let us see who can carry out his duty best. It took a year to get away, but now I am here amongst you once more."

The Combined Chiefs of Staff expressed with applause their warm approval of the statement made by General Giraud who then withdrew from the meeting.

U. S. SECRET
BRITISH MOST SECRET

C.C.S. 63rd Meeting

COMBINED CHIEFS OF STAFF

MINUTES of Meeting held at Anfa Camp
on Wednesday, January 20, 1943, at 1000.

PRESENT

General G. C. Marshall, USA	General Sir Alan F. Brooke
Admiral E. J. King, USN	Admiral of the Fleet Sir Dudley Pound
Lt. General H. H. Arnold, USA	Air Chief Marshal Sir Charles F. A. Portal

THE FOLLOWING WERE ALSO PRESENT

Lt. General B. B. Somervell, USA	Lord Leathers (For Item 1)
Rear Admiral C. M. Cooke, Jr., USN	Field Marshal Sir John Dill
Brig. General J. E. Hull, USA	Vice Admiral the Lord Louis Mountbatten
Brig. General A. C. Wedemeyer, USA	
Colonel J. E. Smart, USA	Lt. General Sir Hastings L. Ismay
Commander R. E. Libby, USN	

SECRETARIAT

Brigadier V. Dykes
Brig. General J. R. Deane, USA
Brigadier E. I. C. Jacob
Lt. Colonel L. T. Grove, USA

U. S. SECRET
BRITISH MOST SECRET

1. U. S. AID TO RUSSIA.
    (C.C.S. 162)

GENERAL MARSHALL requested Lord Leathers to give his comments on C.C.S. 162.

LORD LEATHERS stated that the bulk of the munitions sent to Russia under the Protocol are from the United States. He said that C.C.S. 162 does not constitute a paper with which he is in full agreement as is indicated in its heading. He cannot be certain of the basic figures presented because he does not know the backlog of munitions to Russia that are now in the United States. He did, however, concur in General Somervell's conclusions of the paper.

LORD LEATHERS stated that an agreement had been arrived at between the United States and British authorities in Washington, including representatives of both Navies, that all calculations for the allocation of shipping in 1943 should be based on a loss rate of 1.9% per month, whereas General Somervell used a rate of 2.6% in his preparation of C.C.S. 162. He said that if the 1.9% figure works out correctly, more shipping will be available than is indicated in this paper.

ADMIRAL KING said he had no knowledge of such an agreement and thought that 1.9% was optimistic. This was the figure for December 1942 which was particularly favorable.

GENERAL SOMERVELL agreed that if we are able to reduce the losses in shipping from 2.6% to 2% per month, an additional troop lift of 500,000 men to England would be possible in 1943. If it were further reduced to 1.9%, an additional 50,000 could be lifted.

GENERAL MARSHALL said that if we accept General Somervell's loss rate, the question as to what can be sent to Russia must be reexamined. It must also be determined whether we should undertake such a program considering its effects on troop lift.

GENERAL SOMERVELL added that he recognized that there should be an improvement in the loss rate in 1943 over that which was sustained in 1942 because of the more effective anti-submarine measures which are contemplated. He felt it safer, however, to plan on the continuance of the 1942 rate until it could be effectively demonstrated that the losses

U. S. SECRET
BRITISH MOST SECRET

would decrease. He said that it was reasonably certain that the loss rate would drop as low as 2.4% per month. In this case, all of the commitments under the Russian Protocol could be fulfilled. If the rate improves beyond 2.4%, an additional troop lift for BOLERO will become available.

LORD LEATHERS stated that it is particularly important to establish an agreed estimated loss rate for planning purposes. This will insure that all those concerned with shipping problems will be speaking and thinking in the same terms when planning troop or cargo movements.

SIR DUDLEY POUND said that the figures in the paper apparently are based on the assumption that the northern route to Russia will be open throughout the year. He stated that this will not be the case, particularly during the period of Operation HUSKY. He further thought that the paper should include some statement indicating that commitments to Russia will only be fulfilled provided they will not entail prohibitive losses in shipping.

GENERAL SOMERVELL said that stopping the northern convoys during the period of Operation HUSKY would eliminate 64 sailings for which the capacity was available on the Persian route. In reply to a question by Admiral King as to why the shipments to the Persian Gulf dropped off in June, General Somervell said that the commitments to Russia would not require the total capacity of all routes and that, therefore, a reduced rate had been applied to the Persian route which had the longest turn-around. This will provide a safety margin to take care of contingencies such as stopping the northern route during Operation HUSKY.

LORD LEATHERS pointed out that C.C.S. 162 applies only to aid from the United States. He said that the British can overtake their backlog of deliveries about the end of June; a relatively small number of British shipments is involved. Assuming a convoy every 27 days, there will be 11 or 12 ships in each, whereas if they were to be run every 40 days, each convoy must include 15 British ships.

GENERAL SOMERVELL proposed an amendment to clarify paragraph 14 of C.C.S. 162.* He then asked for a careful consideration of the conclusions contained in Paragraph 15 of the paper.

* Corrected version circulated as C.C.S. 162/1.

U. S. SECRET
BRITISH MOST SECRET

LORD LEATHERS suggested that in the last sentence the phrase "assigned to United States troop movements" be changed to "assigned to combined troop movements."

SIR CHARLES PORTAL asked if it would be possible to frame our commitment to Russia so as to make it clear that some curtailment in the delivery of munitions might be required because of operational necessities. He felt that the Combined Chiefs of Staff were taking a big step in making a firm commitment regarding the delivery of munitions to Russia at the expense of all operational requirements.

LORD LEATHERS stated that we have reserved the right in the past to curtail shipments of munitions to Russia but that Russia did not like to have such reservations made and always objected when an actual curtailment became necessary. A notable exception to this was that they agreed that the northern convoys be discontinued during Operation TORCH.

GENERAL SOMERVELL pointed out that the current Protocol which expires in June of 1943 does include such a resolution. The new Protocol will be framed by the State Department and the Foreign Office, but actually there will be ample opportunity for the Combined Chiefs of Staff to review it before the negotiations between governments are initiated. It will thus be possible to insure that a safety clause is included in the basic document.

THE COMMITTEE:
(a) Agreed that a loss rate of not more than 2.4% per month could be relied on with sufficient certainty to warrant the Combined Chiefs of Staff giving their approval to the total shipping commitments set forth in Paragraph 6, Table II of C.C.S. 162, subject to the proviso that supplies to Russia shall not be continued at prohibitive cost to the United Nations' effort.
(b) Took note that the Persian Gulf route could make good the loss of 64 North Russian sailings if these had to be eliminated in the latter part of the year owing to other operations.

U. S. SECRET
BRITISH MOST SECRET

    (c) Agreed to direct the Combined Military Transportation Committee to make an agreed estimate of the rate of United Nations' shipping losses in 1943 which can be used by all United Nations' Agencies for planning purposes.

    (d) Agreed to amend* paragraph 15 of C.C.S. 162 so as to delete the words "United States" in the last sentence and substitute the word "Combined" therefor.

    (e) Agreed that, in the preparation of the next Protocol with Russia, a clause should be included to the effect that the commitments included in the Protocol may be reduced if shipping losses or the necessities of other operations render their fulfillment prohibitive.

2.   BRITISH RESPONSIBILITY FOR TURKEY.
    (C.C.S. 62nd Meeting, Item 2)

GENERAL MARSHALL suggested the addition of the words "through the Combined Chiefs of Staff" after "Assignment Boards" in the first sentence of the second paragraph of the draft resolution proposed by the British Chiefs of Staff at their previous meeting.

BRIGADIER JACOB explained the procedure for the submission of Turkish bids to the Munitions Assignments Boards in London and Washington. Turkish requirements were, in the first instance, scrutinized and coordinated by a Committee in Ankara containing U. S., British and Turkish representatives. This Committee transmitted requirements to London. The London Munitions Assignments Board passed on to the Washington Board bids for all material which could not be supplied from the U. K. The bids were presented by the British representatives of the Washington Munitions Assignments Board. Difficulty was caused, however, by the fact that the Turkish Embassy in Washington was apt to approach the War Department simultaneously with requests for equipment and, as a result, duplication took place. The object of the proposal of the British Chiefs of Staff was to canalize all Turkish demands for munitions through London where the majority of these demands were met. Turkey was only one of a large number of claimants for material, and the general principle followed was that all the small European nations dealt with the London Board in the first instance, whereas the South American Republics and China dealt with

---

* Corrected version circulated as C.C.S. 162/1.

U. S. SECRET
BRITISH MOST SECRET

Washington. For example, any demands made by the Chinese in London were refused, and the Chinese were told to present them direct to Washington. He feared that if all bids had to be passed through the Combined Chiefs of Staff, they would be smothered in a mass of detail.

ADMIRAL KING said his only concern was to insure that the Combined Chiefs of Staff had an opportunity to exercise control over the actions of the Munitions Assignments Boards in connection with Turkish bids.

> THE COMMITTEE:
> (a) Agreed that Turkey lies within a theater of British responsibility, and that all matters connected with Turkey should be handled by the British in the same way that all matters connected with China are handled by the United States of America.
> (b) Agreed that, in particular, under the general direction of the Combined Chiefs of Staff, the British should be responsible for framing and presenting to both Assignments Boards all bids for equipment for Turkey. The onward dispatch to Turkey from the Middle East of such equipment will be a function of command of the British Commanders-in-Chief in the Middle East. They will not divert such equipment to other uses except for urgent operational reasons, and will report such diversions to the appropriate Munitions Assignments Board.

3. THE BOMBER OFFENSIVE FROM NORTH AFRICA.
   (C.C.S. 159)

The Committee had before them a memorandum by the British Chiefs of Staff setting out in order of time the proposed objectives for the bomber offensive from North Africa.

In discussion certain amendments were suggested and agreed.

THE COMMITTEE:
Approved the British Chiefs of Staff memorandum as amended in the discussion.*

* Subsequently circulated as C.C.S. 159/1

U. S. SECRET
BRITISH MOST SECRET

4. COMMAND IN THE MEDITERRANEAN.
(C.C.S. 163)

The Committee had before them a memorandum by the British Chiefs of Staff giving their recommendations for the set-up of air command in the Mediterranean.

SIR ALAN BROOKE said that with the 8th Army approaching Tunisia the time was near when it would be necessary to place it under General Eisenhower's command. It was, therefore, proposed that General Alexander should come in as Deputy Commander-in-Chief under General Eisenhower with the primary task of commanding the group of armies on the Tunisian front. He would be accompanied by a small nucleus staff with the necessary signals. This proposal, if accepted, would leave General Eisenhower in supreme command over:

(a) The group of armies on the Tunisian front.
(b) The U. S. 5th Army in Morocco.
(c) French forces under General Juin.

He would still have, in addition, his political responsibilities in North Africa.

The position was slightly complicated by the fact that the 8th Army must still be supplied from the East. This could, however, be arranged and the organization in the Middle East was quite adequate for the task.

SIR ALAN BROOKE then pointed out that responsibility for planning HUSKY, or whatever operation in the Mediterranean might be decided upon, must soon be fixed. It would probably be thought that General Eisenhower was the appropriate man to assume this responsibility. If that were decided, he would have General Alexander available to take charge of the necessary work.

SIR CHARLES PORTAL said that intensive air operations in the Eastern Mediterranean were coming to an end, but that many of the bases, such as Malta, in that area as well as the very large maintenance organization which had been established there, would still be available. It was essential that the action of all operational air forces in the Mediterranean area should be coordinated by one Commander.

GENERAL ARNOLD said that certain minor changes in the proposed organization would almost certainly be necessary, but the general set-up was acceptable to him.

U. S. SECRET
BRITISH MOST SECRET

SIR CHARLES PORTAL agreed and said that such changes could most easily be made by the Air Commander-in-Chief once he had been appointed.

ADMIRAL KING asked what dividing line was proposed between the Middle East and Northwest African theaters.

SIR ALAN BROOKE replied that the British Chiefs of Staff when considering this matter had thought that a line from the Tunisia-Tripolitania frontier to Corfu would be most suitable.

SIR DUDLEY POUND then referred to the question of the naval command which would be necessary for HUSKY. His proposal was that Admiral Cunningham should become Commander-in-Chief, Mediterranean, and that Admiral Harwood should adopt the title of Commander-in-Chief, Levant. The boundary might be the line Bardia-Zanti. Thus Malta would come under Admiral Cunningham who would be responsible for coordinating all movements and matters which affect the Mediterranean as a whole. He would also be responsible for the distribution of forces between the Mediterranean and Levant Commands.

THE COMMITTEE:

(a) Accepted the proposals contained in C.C.S. 163, subject to any minor changes which might be found necessary by the Air Commander-in-Chief after his appointment.
(b) Took note with approval that it had been agreed that, at a time to be determined after the British 8th Army had crossed the Tunisian border, General Alexander should become Deputy Commander-in-Chief to General Eisenhower, and that the British 8th Army should at the same time be transferred to the command of General Eisenhower, although it would continue to be based on the Middle East.
(c) Agreed that, subject to the concurrence of General Eisenhower, General Alexander's primary task would be to command the Allied forces on the Tunisian front with a small headquarters of his own, provided from the Middle East, and that after the conclusion of these operations he should take charge of Operation HUSKY.

U. S. SECRET
BRITISH MOST SECRET

(d) Took note of the proposals of the First Sea Lord as set out above for Naval command in the Mediterranean during HUSKY, i.e., Western and Eastern Commands under Commander-in-Chief Mediterranean and Commander-in-Chief Levant, respectively, with Commander-in-Chief Mediterranean responsible for general coordination.

(e) Agreed that General Eisenhower should be informed of the above decisions.

U. S. SECRET
BRITISH MOST SECRET

C.C.S. 64th Meeting

COMBINED CHIEFS OF STAFF

MINUTES of Meeting held at Anfa Camp
on Wednesday, January 20, 1943, at 1430.

PRESENT

General G. C. Marshall, USA	General Sir Alan F. Brooke
Admiral E. J. King, USN	Admiral of the Fleet Sir Dudley Pound
Lt. General H. H. Arnold, USA	Air Chief Marshal Sir Charles F. A. Portal

THE FOLLOWING WERE ALSO PRESENT

Lt. General B. B. Somervell, USA	Field Marshal Sir John Dill
Rear Admiral C. M. Cooke, Jr., USN	Vice Admiral the Lord Louis Mountbatten
Brig. General J. E. Hull, USA	Lt. General Sir Hastings L. Ismay
Brig. General A. C. Wedemeyer, USA	Major General J. N. Kennedy
Colonel J. E. Smart, USA	Air Vice Marshal J. C. Slessor
Commander R. E. Libby, USN	

SECRETARIAT

Brigadier V. Dykes
Brig. General J. R. Deane, USA
Lt. Colonel L. T. Grove, USA

U S SECRET
BRITISH MOST SECRET

1.   HUSKY.

   (C.C.S. 161)

The Committee had before them a memorandum by the British Joint Planning Staff.

SIR ALAN BROOKE outlined the British proposals for undertaking this operation. He said that there were two broad alternatives for carrying out the British portion of the assault—either to mount the assaulting force in the U.K. and bring the follow-up from the Middle East, or to mount the major part of the operation from the Middle East. The former would enable us to start at an earlier date but, it involved a grave risk in passing the spearhead of the assault forces through the Sicilian narrows in mineable waters and under air attack. For this reason the British Chiefs of Staff considered that the second alternative should be adopted.

If the major portion of the assault was to be mounted from North Africa, it seemed that training would be the bottleneck.

LORD LOUIS MOUNTBATTEN said that a Brigade required three weeks training before it was fit to take part in the assault. A Brigade which had had previous training could be "brushed up" in about ten days. In either case, a further two weeks' training was necessary for final rehearsals. Time could only be saved by arranging for two or more Brigades to be trained simultaneously. It was not possible to reduce the training periods below the figures he had given.

SIR ALAN BROOKE agreed that these training times could not be further reduced. He thought, however, that we could not accept the end of September as the earliest date for the operation. Various devices were being examined, such as the setting up of additional training establishments and making use of a wider range of ports in the Middle East; and it was hoped to bring forward this date to about the end of August. It was assumed that Tunisia would have been cleared by the end of April.

ADMIRAL KING asked what divisions were now with the 8th Army and whether any divisions were available in the Middle East which could start training at once.

SIR ALAN BROOKE said that, although there were some divisions

U. S. SECRET
BRITISH MOST SECRET

not actively engaged in the present battle, they would all be required for operations after the capture of Tripoli.

BRIGADIER GENERAL WEDEMEYER said that no difficulty was foreseen in finding the land forces required for the U. S. portion of the operation. It was assumed that the divisions required would be taken from Morocco and not from Tunisia. The Airborne Division would have to come from the U.S.A. Certain types of aircraft would also have to be brought over, but the majority were already available in North Africa. All could certainly be provided. He felt that some date at the end of July or the beginning of August should be possible.

REAR ADMIRAL COOKE said that a great deal of research into the capacity of Northwest African ports and the provision of landing craft would be necessary. This was already in hand. On the question of timing, his view was about two months before a planning staff could be assembled and detailed plans could be produced. He agreed that it might be possible to start the operation in July.

SIR CHARLES PORTAL pointed out that the operation must depend on when the British could be ready and when the Americans could be ready and the later date set as D-day. He suggested that these should be worked out separately. It might be found that the later date was too late to be acceptable. He thought that if Tunisia were cleared by the end of April, a further two months should be sufficient for the preparation of airfields in the Tunisian tip.

GENERAL MARSHALL referred to the transport by air of 20,000 Chinese to Ramgarh and asked whether time might not be saved by making use of air transport to carry personnel from Northwest Africa to the Middle East. He suggested that, rather than transport troops to the Middle East via the Cape, they might be shipped to North Africa, carry out their training there, and then be taken by air to the Middle East. By that time the passage of the necessary landing craft should have been completed. He said that Sicily was our goal and that we ought not to be diverted from it by the apparent difficulties of the undertaking.

ADMIRAL KING agreed that, although for the assault the capacity of the Northwest African ports might be barely sufficient, it should be possible to find room for training British as well as American formations

U.S. SECRET
BRITISH MOST SECRET

in this area. He asked whether the Tunisian ports were being used for the assault.

BRIGADIER GENERAL WEDEMEYER said that it was intended to make use of Bizerte, Tunis, and Sousse for the U. S. portion of the assault. For training he agreed that it might be possible to squeeze up further west and so leave some of these ports for training British formations if required.

SIR ALAN BROOKE said that every possible permutation must be examined and that we should aim at arriving at a starting date in July. Two points called for early decision--first, the set up of an organization to plan the whole operation; and, second, the preparation of a cover plan which would need to be integrated between the U.S.A., U.K., Northwest Africa, and the Middle East and put into effect at an early date. He pointed out that the Germans would be forced to divert troops from the Russian front as soon as our preparations made it clear that an offensive was impending somewhere. The effect of the operation would, therefore, be felt long before the actual assault was launched.

THE COMMITTEE:
(A) Directed the U. S. and British Planning Staffs to:
(1) Examine all possible expedients for speeding up the preparations for HUSKY and to report on the earliest possible date by which the operation could be mounted
(2) Recommend how the organization for planning HUSKY should be set up

2. FUTURE BUSINESS

SIR ALAN BROOKE suggested that it might be possible to bring forward certain items on the Agenda so as to complete the conference as early as possible. After a short discussion,

THE COMMITTEE:
Agreed on the following program:

THURSDAY	FRIDAY
U boat War.	HUSKY.
Bomber Offensive from Great Britain.	Landing Craft.
	Limited Operations
ANAKIM.	S. W. Pacific.
BOLERO (if time permits).	

U. S. SECRET
BRITISH MOST SECRET

C.C.S. 65th Meeting

COMBINED CHIEFS OF STAFF

MINUTES of Meeting held at Anfa Camp
on Thursday, January 21, 1943, at 1000.

PRESENT

General G.C. Marshall, USA	General Sir Alan F. Brooke
Admiral E.J. King, USN	Admiral of the Fleet Sir Dudley Pound
Lt. General H.H. Arnold, USA	Air Chief Marshal Sir Charles F. A. Portal

THE FOLLOWING WERE ALSO PRESENT

Lt. General B. B. Somervell, USA	Field Marshal Sir John Dill
Rear Admiral C. M. Cooke, Jr., USN	Vice Admiral the Lord Louis Mountbatten
Brig. General A. C. Wedemeyer, USA	Lt. General Sir Hastings L. Ismay
Colonel J. E. Smart, USA	Major General J. N. Kennedy
Commander R. E. Libby, USN	Air Vice Marshal J. C. Slessor

SECRETARIAT

Brigadier V. Dykes
Brig. General J. R. Deane, USA
Brigadier E. I. C. Jacob

U S SECRET
BRITISH MOST SECRET

1. THE U-BOAT WAR.
   (C.C.S. 160)

The Combined Chiefs of Staff had before them a report by the Combined Staff Planners on minimum escort requirements to maintain the sea communications of the United Nations (C.C.S. 160).

SIR DUDLEY POUND said that most of the points in the body of the paper had been touched on in the course of previous discussions, but he drew particular attention to paragraph 14 emphasizing the need for adequate air cover if the number of escorts was to be kept to a minimum. Schedule V on the last page of the paper showed the large number of escorts required for this purpose. The table in Enclosure "C" showed the small numbers of escort vessels which would be coming out of production during the first half of 1943.

SIR CHARLES PORTAL explained that the categories of aircraft in this Schedule were as follows:

- V.L.R. – Aircraft with a range over 2,000 miles, such as Liberators, and specially prepared Halifaxes with a range of about 2,100 miles which were temporarily assigned to antisubmarine work.
- L.R. – Aircraft with a range between 1,200 and 2,000 miles.
- M.R. – Aircraft with a range between 600 and 1,200 miles.

He inquired whether it could be taken that the requirements of Section 2 in Schedule V (North Atlantic, East Coast U. S. and Canada) involved no commitments for the United Kingdom.

ADMIRAL KING said that he had not the exact figures, but he had no reason to doubt that this commitment would be fulfilled by the U. S. and Canada entirely. The Caribbean and the East Coast of South America were also, of course, entirely U. S. commitments. The full details of the U. S figures were not available at the present time, but he suggested that the report should be accepted as a working basis.

ADMIRAL KING said that the report of the Combined Staff Planners on the U-boat war, which had been ordered by the Combined Chiefs of Staff at a recent meeting in Washington, should be ready very shortly. This would contain the full U. S. figures.

U. S. SECRET
BRITISH MOST SECRET

SIR DUDLEY POUND pointed out that in their agreed policy for the conduct of the war in 1943 (C.C.S. 155/1), the Combined Chiefs of Staff had said that the defeat of the U-boat must remain the first charge on the resources of the United Nations. Nevertheless, it had been decided that the Rabaul and HUSKY operations were to be carried out, and these would inevitably detract from the anti-submarine effort. He felt that the Combined Chiefs of Staff should clearly record their reasons for thus diverging from the anti-submarine effort as a first objective. He passed around draft conclusions on the Combined Staff Planners' report, which he had discussed with Admiral King, but suggested that since the first two of these were bound up with the directive for the bomber offensive from the U. K., which was to be discussed next, these should be taken up after that item.

After an adjournment,

THE COMMITTEE:
(a) Took note of C.C.S. 160.
(b) Agreed that:
 (1) Intensified bombing of U-boat operating bases should be carried out.
 (2) Intensified bombing of U-boat constructional yards should be carried out.
 (3) U. S. and British Naval Staffs should:
  a. Scrutinize the dispositions of all existing destroyers and escort craft;
  b. Allocate as much new construction, or vessels released by new construction, as possible to convoy protection.
 The above with a view to each nation providing, to the greatest extent possible, half of the present deficiency of sixty-five escorts for the protection of Atlantic convoys.
 (4) U. S. and British Naval Staffs should provide auxiliary escort carriers for working with Atlantic convoys at the earliest practicable moment.
 (5) Long distance shore-based air cover should be provided over the following convoy routes as a matter of urgency:
  a. North Atlantic convoys (U. S.-U. K.)--from both sides of the Atlantic.

U. S. SECRET
BRITISH MOST SECRET

        <u>b</u>. D.W.I. oil convoys from the West Indies and U. K.
        <u>c</u>. TORCH oil convoys from the West Indies and Gibraltar.
        <u>d</u>. U. K.-Freetown convoys from Northwest and West Africa.

    (6) Greenland airdromes should be developed for use by L.R. or V.L.R. aircraft.

    (7) Non-ocean-going escorts should be used for HUSKY to the maximum possible extent.

2. THE BOMBER OFFENSIVE FROM THE UNITED KINGDOM.
(C.C.S. 166)

The Combined Chiefs of Staff had before them a draft directive for the bomber offensive from the United Kingdom submitted by the British Chiefs of Staff (C.C.S. 166)

SIR CHARLES PORTAL, in answer to a question by General Marshall on the precise implications of paragraph 6, said that political considerations often override military expediency in the case of objectives in the occupied countries. The British Government, on representations from one of the exiled Governments, sometimes placed a political embargo on some excellent military target. In such cases decisions had often to be taken very quickly, and it would not be practicable to deal with the matter through the Combined Chiefs of Staff in Washington.

GENERAL MARSHALL suggested, and the Committee agreed, that the words "for political reasons" should be inserted in paragraph 6 in order to make this clear.

In discussion it was also agreed that the word "synthetic" should be deleted from paragraph 2 (d).

SIR CHARLES PORTAL referred to the difficulty which always arose in such directives over the precise interpretation of placing the German submarine bases and construction yards first in order of priority. This might be held to preclude attacks on any other targets. At the present time the U. S. 8th Bomber Command had U-boat targets at the top of their list and attacked them on every possible occasion with good results. There had been, however, considerable criticism in the U. K. because they never attacked targets in Germany. If too literal an interpretation of the order of priority were taken and the entire weight of our bomber effort were placed on the German submarine bases, to the exclusion of

U. S. SECRET
BRITISH MOST SECRET

targets in Germany, there would be very serious criticism indeed. His own view was that other targets besides the submarine bases and yards should not be excluded and that paragraph 2 of the paper required some redrafting to make it clear that there was no intention to concentrate on what were strategically defensive operations to the exclusion of the offensive.

GENERAL MARSHALL said that he fully appreciated this difficulty.

SIR DUDLEY POUND pointed out that the acceptance of large-scale amphibious operations for 1943 must inevitably detract from the anti-submarine effort and every endeavor should, therefore, be made to offset this by a higher concentration of the air effort against U-boat targets. He believed that if we put the maximum effort onto the Biscay bases now, and destroyed all the facilities and accommodations in the towns, we should vitally affect German capacity to carry on the U-boat campaign. It was no good making sporadic attacks; the pressure had to be continued for a considerable period. If the Germans had gone on bombing Plymouth, Liverpool and Glasgow instead of stopping when they did, we should have been placed in a very difficult position indeed.

He could not see that there was any real difference between so-called offensive and defensive bombing. Both were directed against the power of the enemy to carry on the war.

ADMIRAL KING agreed that the bombing of the U-boat bases should be sustained. His impression was that the bombing of anti-submarine targets had so far been sporadic. For example, it appeared that Berlin had had in two raids twice the weight of bombs dropped on Lorient recently.

SIR CHARLES PORTAL agreed that it would be a sound move to destroy completely the four Biscay bases if experience showed this was possible. Attacks would be continued on Lorient, but so far we had no information of the result of the recent concentrated bombardments. It had had a greater weight of bombs dropped on it than Plymouth. In comparing this with the weight on Berlin, regard must be paid to the comparative size of these two targets. Weight in relation to area was much greater at Lorient than Berlin.

U. S. SECRET
BRITISH MOST SECRET

SIR ALAN BROOKE did not think that we could win by defeating the U-boat alone. We should be careful, therefore, not to allot more effort than was absolutely necessary for this purpose. The bombing of Germany contributed directly to the destruction of German power, whereas the bombing of U-boat targets was only an indirect contribution.

GENERAL MARSHALL recalled that in the bombing directive for the Mediterranean the emphasis had been laid on preparations for HUSKY. He asked what would be done from the United Kingdom to support an invasion of Europe.

SIR CHARLES PORTAL said that this point was covered by paragraph 5 of the draft directive. Targets would be selected in accordance with the plan of the Commander-in-Chief, so as to give the best possible support to the operations of the Army. Whenever operations were immediately in prospect, attacks on what might be called the long-term targets, such as industry, had to give way to immediate operational needs.

GENERAL ARNOLD said that no one was keener to go for targets in Germany than the U. S. Air Commanders in the United Kingdom. They had been directed on to U-boat targets by General Eisenhower as a direct means of supporting TORCH. About half the U. S. bomber force in the U. K. had already been withdrawn from the United Kingdom to North Africa, but large increases in its strength were now in prospect. We should soon be able to think in terms of hundreds of bombers where we were now thinking in tens.

GENERAL MARSHALL said that the control of bomber operations by the U. S. Air Forces in the United Kingdom would be in the hands of the British. It would be a matter of command rather than of agreement with the U. S. Commanders. It would be the responsibility of the U. S. Commanders to decide the technique and method to be employed.

After an adjournment,

THE COMMITTEE:
Approved, subject to minor amendments, a revised draft directive prepared by the British Chiefs of Staff (circulated subsequently as C.C.S. 166/1/D).

U. S. SECRET
BRITISH MOST SECRET

3. DRAFT TELEGRAM TO M. STALIN.
   (C.C.S. 165)

SIR ALAN BROOKE suggested that paragraph 5 of the draft telegram prepared for the President and Prime Minister to send to Premier Stalin be amended by changing the first sentence to read, "We have taken the decision to launch wide scale amphibious operations at the earliest possible moment" and to amend the second sentence to read, "the preparations for these operations are now underway and will involve a considerable concentration of forces, particularly landing craft and shipping in North African ports."

These changes were acceptable to the Combined Chiefs of Staff.

SIR JOHN DILL suggested that in paragraph 5 the 5th sentence be terminated with the word "subjected" and that the remainder of the sentence be deleted.

SIR CHARLES PORTAL suggested that paragraph 8 should be strengthened in view of the much greater Allied bomber offensive which will be undertaken against Germany as the result of the increased bomber strength which is in view. The British will increase their heavy bomber strength from 600 to 1,000 and the United States' increase will be from 200 to 900. This will enable the intensity of the bombing attack against Germany to be at least doubled, a fact that M. Stalin should be glad to learn.

ADMIRAL KING suggested that the last two sentences of paragraph 5 be deleted from that paragraph and amalgamated with the redraft of paragraph 8, suggested above by Sir Charles Portal.

It was agreed that the last two sentences of paragraph 5, paragraph 7, and a more positive statement of paragraph 8 be amalgamated into one paragraph.

THE COMMITTEE:
Directed that representatives of the Combined Staffs be directed to revise the draft telegram to M. Stalin in the light of the discussion given above.

U. S. SECRET
BRITISH MOST SECRET

4. ANAKIM.
(C.C.S. 164)

GENERAL MARSHALL suggested that in the remarks on the bottom of page 80 concerning the availability of air forces, the last two words, "Middle East," be deleted and the words, "Mediterranean area" be substituted therefor.

This change was agreed to by the Combined Chiefs of Staff.

SIR ALAN BROOKE stated that he believed the target date of November 1943, given as an assumption in paragraph 2, was probably too early for actual accomplishment, but that it should do no harm to let it stand as a target date to be aimed at.

THE COMMITTEE:
(a) Took note of C.C.S. 164 as amended* and agreed:
  (1) To approve November 15, 1943, as the provisional date for the ANAKIM assault.
  (2) To approve the provisional schedule of forces laid out in paragraph 3 of C.C.S. 164, recognizing that the actual provision of naval forces, assault shipping, landing craft, and shipping must depend on the situation in the late summer of 1943.
  (3) To confirm in July 1943 the decision to undertake or to postpone Operation ANAKIM.

5. BOLERO BUILD-UP.

The Combined Chiefs of Staff were informed that a paper on the subject, being prepared by the British Joint Planning Staff, was not ready for consideration.

GENERAL MARSHALL suggested that there be some general discussion regarding BOLERO prior to receipt of the British paper. He stated that it had already been decided to keep plans for a cross-channel operation up to date on a month-by-month basis in order to be ready at any time to initiate such operations.

SIR ALAN BROOKE agreed with this statement.

* To be subsequently published as C.C.S. 164/1.

U. S. SECRET
BRITISH MOST SECRET

GENERAL MARSHALL then said he wished to discuss the question of organization. He asked what is to be done in England and also how the plans regarding BOLERO are to crystallize

SIR ALAN BROOKE said that the British can absorb American troops at the rate of 120,000 per month. In this connection, GENERAL SOMERVELL said that the number to arrive would be somewhat less than 120,000 per month up to July but considerably more thereafter.

SIR ALAN BROOKE said that one of the greatest difficulties regarding the reception of American troops in England is the lack of sufficient receiving depots for equipment. It would be necessary to construct additional depots. The British have stopped such construction because of the manpower situation and because they have only been committed to receive five additional American divisions, or a total of 427,000 troops. The construction which must be undertaken and the operating force required for new reception depots will require personnel from the United States. These should be included in the earliest possible troop convoys to the U. K.

An area has been reserved in southwestern England for the United States troops which will be next to the area reserved for British troops in southeastern England. These areas will face France. The area to be occupied by the United States troops is being cleared of British forces. Their accommodations, except for some which cannot be moved, such as schools, will be available to the American forces.

He said that the immediate necessity was the appointment of a Commanding General and staff. The British are now engaged in reorganizing their forces from defensive organizations, supplied from fixed bases, to offensive organizations which include their own mobile service elements. It is expected that 12 divisions will be so organized by July and 15 by October. The new offensive organizations will be divorced entirely from the defensive organizations of the British Isles. Each will be under a separate commander. The British offensive forces, together with those being built up by the United States, including air forces, should come under a supreme commander who should be appointed in the near future.

GENERAL MARSHALL stated that General Andrews is now going to

U. S. SECRET
BRITISH MOST SECRET

England to replace General Hartle and undertake the same duties that General Eisenhower performed prior to Operation TORCH. He will have the responsibility of receiving American divisions in England; and, as soon as these divisions are ready, General Andrews will turn them over to the Supreme Commander for assignment to the cross-channel task force. He assumed that although the British contemplated setting up a separate Home Defense force, the cross-channel task force would also have to be on an alert status and considered as available to participate in the defense of the British Isles.

SIR ALAN BROOKE said that there were two types of planning involved with regard to the cross-channel operations; one was for a limited offensive operation which might be expected in 1943, and the other was for the larger task of an all-out invasion of the Continent. In the latter case, the decision must be made as to the direction of the attack once the landing was effected. It must be decided whether such an attack would be aimed at Germany or at occupied France. Plans might well be made to meet both contingencies.

He said that plans must envisage making the maximum use of S.O.E. activities and that these activities must be carefully coordinated with the military operations proposed. This has not always been done in the past.

ADMIRAL KING said he considered that the appointment of a supreme commander was urgent.

GENERAL SOMERVELL said that he had understood Sir Alan Brooke to say that the British could absorb 120,000 troops per month without assistance from the United States. This is contrary to an opinion which General Somervell attributed to Lord Leathers, that assistance would be required from the United States if the flow of troops to England exceeded 70,000 per month. General Somervell said it would be necessary to determine at once which estimate is correct. He also said that he understood it would be necessary for the United States to furnish some locomotives and rolling stock to the British in order to assist in the increased traffic resulting from troop movements.

He pointed out that the speed of sending troops to the U. K. would depend largely upon the success attained in combating the submarine

U. S. SECRET
BRITISH MOST SECRET

menace. He urged that the United Nations concentrate their efforts in this respect.

GENERAL SOMERVELL said that the location of United States troops in England must be made with an eye to training facilities. The troops will need amphibious training for which few facilities are available in southern England. He concluded that, from a supply point of view, an early decision was necessary as to the size of the build-up of United States forces contemplated and the type of operations in which they would be engaged. These decisions are particularly necessary with respect to the allocation of tonnage.

SIR ALAN BROOKE said that any operation in 1943 will of necessity be limited since an all-out offensive across the Channel can hardly be undertaken until 1944. With regard to the rolling stock for the railroads, he pointed out that when an invasion of the Continent is undertaken, the Germans will make every effort to deny our use of their rolling stock. For this reason, the United Nations must be prepared to follow the initial assault with such equipment.

He stated that the British now send their troops from southern England to Scotland or Northern Ireland by brigade groups for amphibious training. He suggested the possibility of United States troops stopping off in Ireland or Scotland for such training on their way to the final assembling area in southwestern England. The greatest difficulty is in the training of armored units, and that as far as possible it would be better if the United States forces could have this training prior to their departure from the United States.

GENERAL MARSHALL said that this can easily be arranged. It must be remembered that the forces used in the TORCH operation were hurriedly gathered together and that the training of the troops, prior to their departure from the United States, had been difficult. The build-up for BOLERO can be accomplished more deliberately and will enable the armored units to participate in major maneuvers and complete their target practice prior to departure. Units will be frozen three months prior to leaving the United States, and this will facilitate their training. He pointed out that firing ranges have been made available for use by units in staging areas en route to ports of debarkation.

U. S. SECRET
BRITISH MOST SECRET

In reply to a question from Lord Louis Mountbatten, he stated that insofar as possible, all units would have had amphibious training prior to their departure from the United States.

LORD LOUIS MOUNTBATTEN said that the British had set up an amphibious training establishment at Appledore on the Bristol Channel. The northern part of this training area has been turned over to the Americans for amphibious training. Flat beaches, changes of tides, and all means of possible defense are available to insure the thoroughness of the training. Another amphibious training establishment will be available in the Clyde area in two months and, in addition, one in northern Ireland which has been started by Admiral Bennett.

GENERAL MARSHALL said that he assumed that the American troops included in the assault waves of a cross-channel attack would have to be rehearsed in amphibious operations, but that the great bulk of American troops would not need such rehearsals.

LORD LOUIS MOUNTBATTEN then pointed out that it would be well to arrange to have American forces use landing craft manned by American crews, with which General Marshall agreed.

GENERAL SOMERVELL stated that the movement of American forces to England must be considered in connection with the escort vessels available for convoys.

ADMIRAL KING agreed that the BOLERO troop movements would constitute an additional requirement for escort vessels.

SIR CHARLES PORTAL said that air forces must be reorganized with BOLERO in view. At present the R.A.F. operates from static bases. Mobile air units must be organized to support cross-channel operations. He suggested that American fighter aircraft should be under the operational direction of the British in the same manner as had already been decided for heavy bombardment aircraft.

SIR CHARLES PORTAL called attention to the fact that a decision must be made as to whether to utilize troop-lift capacity from the United States to Great Britain for ground troops or for the ground echelons of the air force. He also stated that a decision might be forced on the

U S SECRET
BRITISH MOST SECRET

Combined Chiefs of Staff with regard to utilizing some of the shipping engaged in the delivery of munitions to Russia in the build-up of a BOLERO force.

GENERAL SOMERVELL said that a paper was being prepared, designed to show how many troops can be transported from the United States to the U. K. The paper had to be based on a great many assumptions and the figures which it would contain could not be considered as a reliable estimate until certain decisions have been arrived at with reference to other operations, notably HUSKY. Assuming that HUSKY is mounted in August and that an attack will be mounted from England on August 15th, it would be possible to bring in approximately 400,000 troops to England by July 1st. This would give them six weeks to settle down in order to be available for an attack August 15th. The 400,000 troops mentioned included those now in England. Of the total number, approximately 172,000 would be air corps troops and there would be five to six ground divisions. He said that, assuming 150 ship voyages could be made available from British imports, the number could be raised from seven to nine divisions.

SIR ALAN BROOKE stated that these figures bore out his previous estimates that there would be from 18 to 21 divisions available in England in the latter part of the summer.

GENERAL SOMERVELL said that if the attack from England were not to be mounted until September 15th, four additional divisions could be transported from the United States, three in American, and one in British shipping. The rate of four divisions per month could be maintained thereafter inasmuch as most of the overhead personnel would be included in the earlier shipments.

SIR ALAN BROOKE asked what rate of flow could be expected from America monthly, assuming an attack from England in September. Would one division per month be the maximum?

GENERAL SOMERVELL replied that the figure would greatly exceed this as far as shipping was concerned. However, if the troops were to be transported to France, the number would be limited by the port facilities available. For this reason, any plans made should envisage the capture of sufficient port facilities.

U. S. SECRET
BRITISH MOST SECRET

ADMIRAL KING agreed that this should be given careful consideration in planning the operation.

GENERAL MARSHALL suggested that once the operation is initiated, it would probably be necessary to conduct separate operations to gain additional port facilities.

SIR ALAN BROOKE said he thought it would be easier to establish a bridgehead and widen it out by overland operations in order to capture the ports that would be necessary. He said that at least two or three ports would be required before any attempt could be made to advance further inland. He thought that the ports from Calais to Bordeaux were the most desirable. When the British were in France, they operated from Lorient to Calais and that even with these ports, it required a long period of time to build up nine divisions.

GENERAL MARSHALL said that after the direct crossing had been accomplished, he thought it would be desirable to find some method of making a flank attack in order to shorten the operations. In this connection, he had considered the possibilities of Holland and Denmark.

SIR ALAN BROOKE said that before a sufficient force could be built up for a direct attack, the Germans, because of their superior communications, could concentrate against our forces in superior numbers. This will be true unless German divisions are forced to withdraw from France because the Russian "steam roller" had started rolling.

SIR DUDLEY POUND said that Denmark did not offer good opportunities for hostile landings because of the difficulties of air coverage and also because of the lack of ports on her western coast. Holland is undesirable because of her canal system which favors the defense in retarding forward movements.

SIR ALAN BROOKE said that it would be necessary to determine accurately what flow of reinforcements from the United States could be expected.

GENERAL SOMERVELL stated that he would be prepared to present such data within from 8 to 10 hours after a decision concerning Operation HUSKY had been made.

U. S. SECRET
BRITISH MOST SECRET

ADMIRAL KING then suggested that limited operations proposed from England in 1943 be discussed.

The British Chiefs of Staff stated that they had a paper on this subject in the process of preparation and would be prepared to discuss it during the meeting of January 22nd.

SIR ALAN BROOKE brought up the question of what organizational set-up for BOLERO would be.

Both the United States and British Chiefs of Staff agreed that they had not discussed this matter among themselves and had not come to a definite conclusion.

GENERAL MARSHALL said that there were two methods of organization that might be followed: either a Deputy Commander or a Chief of Staff could be set up with an appropriate staff; or a Commanding General could be selected at once and organize his own staff. In either case, the planning and training for these operations should be undertaken at once and carried out on a month-to-month basis, ready at any time to undertake a cross-channel operation if the opportunity was presented.

SIR ALAN BROOKE stated that there was a combined staff in London now which might be a nucleus around which the BOLERO planning organization could be built.

LORD LOUIS MOUNTBATTEN pointed out that any operations undertaken this year would be very small.

SIR ALAN BROOKE considered that regardless of how small the operations might be, they should be tied in with the over-all plan for the all-out invasion of the Continent and designed to further those operations in some way.

THE COMMITTEE:
Agreed that representatives of the Combined Staffs should prepare and submit recommendations to the Combined Chiefs of Staff, to be ready not later than the afternoon of January 22, relative to the command, organization, planning and training set-up necessary for entry of Continental Europe from the U. K. in 1943 and 1944.

U. S. SECRET
BRITISH MOST SECRET

6. REPORT TO THE PRESIDENT AND THE PRIME MINISTER
   Without discussion,

   THE COMMITTEE:
   Directed the Secretariat to prepare a draft report of decisions reached subsequent to the submission of C.C.S. 153/1.

U. S. SECRET
BRITISH MOST SECRET

C.C.S. 66th Meeting

COMBINED CHIEFS OF STAFF

MINUTES of Meeting held at Anfa Camp
on Friday, January 22, 1943, at 1015.

PRESENT

General G. C. Marshall, USA	General Sir Alan F. Brooke
Admiral E. J. King, USN	Admiral of thr Fleet Sir Dudley Pound
Lt. General H. H. Arnold, USA	Air Chief Marshal Sir Charles F. A. Portal

THE FOLLOWING WERE ALSO PRESENT

Lt. General B. B. Somervell, USA	Field Marshal Sir John Dill
Rear Admiral C. M. Cooke, Jr., USN	Vice Admiral the Lord Louis Mountbatten
Brig. General J. E. Hull, USA	Lt. General Sir Hastings L. Ismay
Brig. General A. C. Wedemeyer, USA *	Major General J. N. Kennedy *
Colonel J. E. Smart, USA *	Air Vice Marshal J. C. Slessor *
Commander R. E. Libby, USN	Air Vice Marshal F. F. Inglis **
	Lt. Colonel C. E. R. Hirsch **

SECRETARIAT

Brigadier V. Dykes
Brig. General J. R. Deane, USA
Brigadier E. I. C. Jacob
Lt. Colonel L. T. Grove, USA

* For Part of Meeting   ** For Item 1

U. S. SECRET
BRITISH MOST SECRET

1. DRAFT OF TELEGRAM TO Mr. STALIN.
   (C.C.S. 165/1)
   After several minor amendments had been agreed upon,

   THE COMMITTEE:
   Directed that the draft telegram as amended* be submitted to the President and the Prime Minister for their approval.

2. HUSKY.
   (C.C.S. 161/1)
   SIR ALAN BROOKE said that the British Planners had examined various permutations and combinations with reference to assembling and training the requisite forces for Operation HUSKY and concluded that it could be mounted by August 20th, with the possibility of putting the date forward to August 15th. The British Chiefs of Staff were in favor of Plan A described in C.C.S. 161/1, Enclosure "A", paragraph 5. He said that August 22nd would be the best date because of the favorable state of the moon. The date could be set still earlier if the Tunisian ports were made available to the British for loading.

   The British will require 5 divisions in all for the operation. These would probably be the 5th, 56th, 78th for the first assault; one division in from U. K. for the Catania assault on D + 3; and the New Zealand division for the follow-up. It will be necessary to move the Overseas Assault Force from England to the eastern Mediterranean about March 15th. Once this had been accomplished, the British would be committed to Operation HUSKY to the exclusion of BRIMSTONE.

   GENERAL MARSHALL said that while the U. S. Planning Staff did not have complete data available at this time, the U. S. Chiefs of Staff are of the opinion that as far as the United States forces are concerned, Operation HUSKY could be mounted by August 1st or earlier. He referred to a statement made in paragraph 4 of the outline plan (Enclosure "A" to C.C.S. 165/1) that if the British forces used the Algerian and Tunisian ports in order to be ready by August 1st, the American share of the assault might be delayed beyond August 31st. The United States Chiefs of Staff were of the opinion that the British could utilize all the ports from Bizerte eastward and the United States forces could still be made

---

* Subsequently published as C.C.S. 165/3.

U. S. SECRET
BRITISH MOST SECRET

ready by August 1st. The only use required by the American forces of Bizerte and ports to the eastward would be for refueling purposes. He stated that as far as landing craft is concerned, little difficulty would be encountered. The limiting factor would be the "degree of finished training" that would be necessary. One division to come from the United States is undergoing thorough amphibious training at this time. The remaining divisions to participate are now in North Africa. They have already participated in landing operations, and their further training presents no problem. The question of relieving these divisions which are now being held ready for any eventuality in Spanish Morocco will require careful planning.

SIR ALAN BROOKE said that the British Planners thought that it might be necessary for the British to have ports somewhat further west than Bizerte in order to meet a target date of August 1st.

ADMIRAL COOKE said that the British could train at Bougie and do their loading in the Tunis area. He could see no reason why all the forces could not meet a target date of August 1st. He realized that the Germans might do considerable damage to the ports of Bizerte and Tunis, but he estimated that by blasting processes the ports could be cleared for use by the time the air forces were ready to operate.

SIR ALAN BROOKE pointed out that the British prognostications for the target date were based on an estimate that the Axis forces would be driven from Tunisia by April 30th. If this is accomplished sooner, the target date could be moved forward accordingly.

ADMIRAL COOKE pointed out that there is still uncertainty regarding the character of the beaches in Sicily. They might not be suitable for the new types of landing craft, and this would involve a change of plans. He also indicated that Admiral Cunningham will be presented with some difficulties when landing craft and combat loaders are moved into the Mediterranean. It will be necessary to do this in time for them to be available for training. The American forces will require some of the new type LCA landing craft. These weigh 8 tons empty, 13 tons loaded, and carry 36 men. The davits on the U. S. combat loaders may have to be replaced or adjusted in order to be capable of handling such weight.

LORD LOUIS MOUNTBATTEN said the British are building 30 LCA

U. S. SECRET
BRITISH MOST SECRET

type landing craft per month in England. The number needed by the American forces could either be sent to America from England or the blueprints could be sent to America and the craft could be constructed there. The design is comparatively simple, and he thought that they could easily be manufactured in the United States. If the craft were to be manufactured in England, it would be necessary for the United States to furnish the engines required. The shipping of some 60 LCA to the Mediterranean, however, would not be an easy problem.

SIR ALAN BROOKE said it was apparent that the whole plan might require some changes; there might be some unforeseen and insurmountable difficulties which would necessitate the postponing of the target date too long. He thought that, in this case, we should be prepared with an alternative.

GENERAL MARSHALL stated that he understood the only possible alternative was Operation BRIMSTONE and indicated that he would like to discuss frankly the desirability of undertaking that operation.

SIR ALAN BROOKE said that Operation BRIMSTONE would afford a base for the bombing of the whole of Italy; it would be an easier operation to undertake; and it could be accomplished earlier. It does not assist in clearing the Mediterranean for shipping, and it would not be as great a blow to Italy. However, he felt it essential that consideration of Operation BRIMSTONE, as a possibility, be not delayed so long as to leave us with no alternative for 1943 if it were found that HUSKY could not be accomplished.

GENERAL MARSHALL said it was the opinion of the U. S. Chiefs of Staff that while Operation BRIMSTONE would produce an advantage as far as air attack against Italy is concerned, it would postpone HUSKY. Any operation in the Mediterranean would postpone the BOLERO build-up. He considered BRIMSTONE a minor operation which would result in many military restrictions. Either HUSKY or cross-channel operations will produce great results, whereas BRIMSTONE merely gives an air advantage. At the same time, it jeopardizes the prospects of either HUSKY or cross-channel operations.

GENERAL MARSHALL pointed out that German resistance to Operation BRIMSTONE could not be discounted. In estimating the capabilities of the

U. S. SECRET
BRITISH MOST SECRET

United Nations, it must be assumed that the Germans are aware that Sardinia can be undertaken at an earlier date than HUSKY. They will undoubtedly make their dispositions accordingly. He added that the undertaking of BRIMSTONE would destroy the cover for future operations unless the Germans conclude that we propose to by-pass Sicily entirely and attack southern France. He thought it hardly likely that the Germans would come to such a conclusion.

He said the United States Chiefs of Staff are more concerned with adding to the security of shipping through the Mediterranean and with the immediate effects of our operations on Germany's strength against the Russians than they are with eliminating Italy from the war. He thought that to undertake Operation BRIMSTONE would be to seek the softest spot before turning to the harder spot and in so doing we might make the harder spot harder.

ADMIRAL KING pointed out that the airfields in Sardinia have a relatively small capacity and that they would have to be developed. While the position of Sardinia does bring northern Italy and southern France within range of our fighter aircraft, it is, by the same token, within range of Axis aircraft based in those areas.

GENERAL ARNOLD said that in order to get fighter protection from Sardinia we must capture Corsica.

GENERAL MARSHALL said that the United States Chiefs of Staff are very much opposed to the Operation BRIMSTONE.

SIR ALAN BROOKE said that he agreed with all of these arguments, and he felt that we must go all out for Sicily. At the same time, he felt that there should be an alternative upon which we could fall back in case of absolute necessity.

ADMIRAL KING said that the ideal would be to attack Sicily at the same time the Germans were evacuating Tunis. The longer the attack against Sicily is delayed beyond that date, the stronger will be the defenses of Sicily. He thought it important, therefore, that every effort be made to reduce this lapse of time to the minimum.

LORD LOUIS MOUNTBATTEN said that in his opinion the ideal would

U. S. SECRET
BRITISH MOST SECRET

be to take Sardinia during the time that Tunis was being evacuated by the Axis forces. He felt that the Axis powers would then be giving little attention to the defenses of Sardinia. He thought that the earlier date upon which the Operation BRIMSTONE could be accomplished, the securing of air bases from which to attack northern Italy, and the possibility of conducting Commando raids all along the coast of Italy, combined to make Operation BRIMSTONE very attractive.

GENERAL MARSHALL asked Lord Louis Mountbatten if the training difficulties would be reduced if we were able to attack Sicily at the same time that Tunis was being evacuated by the Axis forces.

LORD LOUIS MOUNTBATTEN said he did not think so inasmuch as the evacuation would have small effect on the fixed defenses of Sicily.

SIR DUDLEY POUND pointed out that if the operation were to be mounted before August 22nd, it should be moved forward to July 25th in order to take full advantage of the favorable stage of the moon.

ADMIRAL KING suggested that for purposes of surprise it might be well to mount the operation at a time other than when the moon was in its best stage.

SIR CHARLES PORTAL pointed out that to avoid undue risk of aerial torpedo attack the periods of the full moon should be avoided and that the assault should be made only when there was moonlight during the early morning hours. There was a period of from 5 to 6 days in each month which would be suitable.

ADMIRAL KING said he thought that July 25th should be set as the target date for planning purposes and that the attack should only be postponed to August if July proved to be impossible.

LORD LOUIS MOUNTBATTEN said that a clear statement should be made by the naval forces as to when their training can be completed. He prophesied that naval training will be the bottleneck.

SIR CHARLES PORTAL agreed with Admiral King that July should be set as the target date in order that we might strive for the best. He added that we should also be prepared for the worst. He pointed out that the critical time on the Russian front is in August and September. If

U. S. SECRET
BRITISH MOST SECRET

the target date for HUSKY had to be postponed beyond September, it would be of little value. He considered that the collapse of Italy would have the most favorable effect on the Russian front. Since this might be accomplished by Operation BRIMSTONE, he thought that we should be prepared to undertake this operation if HUSKY had to be delayed too long. BRIMSTONE in June would be better than HUSKY in September; but a decision to undertake BRIMSTONE must be made by March 1st; otherwise the landing craft would be at the wrong end of the Mediterranean.

GENERAL MARSHALL said he thought there should be no looseness in our determination to undertake Operation HUSKY. He recounted the difficulties regarding the changes and delays in BOLERO in 1942.

SIR ALAN BROOKE and SIR CHARLES PORTAL agreed with this view.

GENERAL MARSHALL said that we must be determined to do the hard thing and proceed to do it. He did not agree with Sir Charles Portal that the elimination of Italy from the war was the most important thing that could be done. To accept this premise might make it absolutely necessary to turn to Operation BRIMSTONE in order that Italy could be eliminated in time. He felt that this should be avoided because Operation BRIMSTONE would neutralize the efforts of the United Nations for 1943. He said that in BRIMSTONE we should be advancing into a salient with limited air support where we might be shot at from three directions. The supply of Sardinia entails an increase in our line of communications and adds a threat to our limited shipping.

SIR DUDLEY POUND said that if Operation BRIMSTONE is undertaken, HUSKY would have to be delayed until the period of bad weather in October or later.

SIR ALAN BROOKE said that Operation BRIMSTONE would not be an easy operation. Fighter support would be inadequate, and it would be necessary to fight our way northward through the entire island. He believed that we should go bald-headed for Sicily. He felt that the capture of Sicily would have more effect on the war. He added, however, that if by March 1st it develops that Operation HUSKY cannot be mounted until too late, it was important for us to have an alternative to turn to in order that we do not remain idle for the entire year.

U. S. SECRET
BRITISH MOST SECRET

The discussion then turned on the Command and Staff organization which would be required for the operation.

ADMIRAL COOKE said that the Combined Staff Planners felt strongly that one man should be made responsible for the whole of the arrangements; otherwise, it was very unlikely that the necessary preparations could be completed within the short time available. A special staff would be required for the purpose.

In the discussion this need was fully accepted, and it was recognized that the Chief of Staff must be carefully selected.

THE COMMITTEE:
- (a) Resolved to attack Sicily in 1943 with the favorable July moon as the target date.
- (b) Agreed to instruct General Eisenhower to report not later than March 1st: (1) whether any insurmountable difficulty as to resources and training will cause the date of the assault to be delayed beyond the favorable July moon; and, (2) in that event, to confirm that the date will not be later than the favorable August moon.
- (c) Agreed that the following should be the Command set-up for the operation:
  - (1) General Eisenhower to be in Supreme Command with General Alexander as Deputy Commander-in-Chief, responsible for the detailed planning and preparation and for the execution of the actual operation when launched.
  - (2) Admiral Cunningham to be the Naval Commander, and Air Chief Marshal Tedder the Air Commander.
  - (3) Recommendations for the officers to be appointed Western and Eastern Task Force Commanders to be submitted in due course by General Eisenhower.
- (d) Agreed that General Eisenhower should be instructed to set up forthwith, after consultation with General Alexander, a special operational and administrative staff, with its own Chief of Staff, for planning and preparing the operation.
- (e) Instructed the Secretaries to draft for their approval the necessary directive to General Eisenhower conveying the above decisions.

U. S. SECRET
BRITISH MOST SECRET

C.C.S. 67th Meeting

COMBINED CHIEFS OF STAFF

MINUTES of Meeting held at Anfa Camp
on Friday, January 22, 1943, at 1430.

PRESENT

General G. C. Marshall, USA	General Sir Alan F. Brooke
Admiral E. J. King, USN	Admiral of the Fleet Sir Dudley Pound
Lt. General H. H. Arnold, USA	Air Chief Marshal Sir Charles F. A. Portal

THE FOLLOWING WERE ALSO PRESENT

Lt. General B. B. Somervell, USA	Field Marshal Sir John Dill
Rear Admiral C. M. Cooke, Jr., USN	Vice Admiral the Lord Louis Mountbatten
Brig. General J. E. Hull, USA	Lt. General Sir Hastings L. Ismay
Brig. General A. C. Wedemeyer, USA	Major General J. N. Kennedy
Colonel J. E. Smart, USA	Air Vice Marshal J. C. Slessor
Commander R. E. Libby, USN	

SECRETARIAT

Brigadier V. Dykes
Brig. General J. R. Deane, USA
Brigadier E. I. C. Jacob
Lt. Colonel L. T. Grove, USA

U. S. SECRET
BRITISH MOST SECRET

1. CONDUCT OF THE WAR IN THE PACIFIC THEATER IN 1943.

    (C.C.S. 168)

    The Combined Chiefs of Staff had before them a memorandum by the Joint U. S. Chiefs of Staff which Admiral King explained with the aid of a map of the Pacific theater.

    GENERAL ARNOLD, in reply to a question by Sir Charles Portal, said that the theoretical radius of action of the B-29 and B-32 was 1,600 miles. This would be sufficient for the bombardment of Tokyo from the Nanchang area. The best bases for the bombardment of Japan were in the Maritime Provinces where there were known to be twenty-five airfields. No details, however, were available regarding their condition.

    THE COMMITTEE:
    Took note of the proposals of the Joint U. S. Chiefs of Staff for the conduct of the war in the Pacific theater in 1943, as set out in C.C.S. 168.

2. PRESS COMMUNIQUE.
    (Previous reference C.C.S. 61st Meeting, Item 4)
    The Combined Chiefs of Staff took note that the President and Prime Minister were themselves preparing the communique for issue to the press at the conclusion of the Conference, and that it would not, therefore, be necessary for them to submit a draft.

3. CONTINENTAL OPERATIONS IN 1943.
    (C.C.S. 167)
    The Combined Chiefs of Staff had before them a report by the British Joint Planning Staff on Continental operations in 1943, C.C.S. 167.

    SIR ALAN BROOKE said that paragraph 2 (c) was somewhat misleading in its present form since there could, in fact, be no half-way house between the limited operations described in (a) and (b) of the paragraph and return to the Continent in full. He proposed that subparagraph (c) should, therefore, be amended to read, "Return to the Continent to take advantage of German disintegration."

    The policy which the British Chiefs of Staff recommended was contained in paragraph 19 of the paper.

U. S. SECRET
BRITISH MOST SECRET

The provision of additional airborne forces from the U. S. would be essential since HUSKY would use up all British resources in this respect.

LORD LOUIS MOUNTBATTEN agreed and emphasized the need for airborne forces to turn the beach defenses. Without these and armored forces to follow up, the assault on the northern coast of France was, in his opinion, quite impracticable. He drew attention to the note at the end of paragraph 5 relating to armored landing craft.

THE COMMITTEE:
Agreed to defer final acceptance of the proposals of the British Chiefs of Staff pending further study.

4. ORGANIZATION OF COMMAND, CONTROL, PLANNING AND TRAINING FOR CROSS-CHANNEL OPERATIONS.
(C.C.S. 169)
The Combined Chiefs of Staff had before them a note by the Combined Staffs, C.C.S. 169.

SIR ALAN BROOKE thought that it would be premature to designate a Supreme Commander for large-scale operations on the Continent at present in view of the limited operations which could be carried out with available resources in 1943. A special staff was, however, necessary for cross-channel operations and should, he thought, be set up without delay.

GENERAL MARSHALL agreed that a Supreme Commander would make a top-heavy organization at present, but thought that it was desirable to put a special staff under a selected Chief of Staff of sufficient standing; such an officer would perhaps suffice for the command of limited operations during the summer. This special staff could work out their plans on the basis of certain forces being available, even though they were not in actual control of the troops themselves.

SIR ALAN BROOKE said that the staff which was at present working on cross-channel operations belonged to various Commanders in the United Kingdom. It would be necessary to take them away from their present Commanders and set them up independently.

U. S. SECRET
BRITISH MOST SECRET

THE COMMITTEE:

(a) Accepted the proposals contained in C.C.S. 169, except for the immediate appointment of a Supreme Commander.

(b) Agreed that a Supreme Commander will ultimately be necessary for the reentry to the Continent, but that he should not be appointed at the present time.

(c) Agreed that a British Chief of Staff, together with an independent U. S.-British staff should be appointed at once for the control, planning and training of cross-channel operations in 1943.

(d) Invited the British Chiefs of Staff to prepare for their approval a draft directive to govern the planning and conduct of cross-channel operations in 1943 in accordance with the decisions to be reached on C.C.S. 167.

(e) Agreed that the above directive should make provision for a return to the Continent with the forces that will be available for this purpose in the United Kingdom month by month.

5. LANDING CRAFT.

LORD LOUIS MOUNTBATTEN gave an account of the British experiences in building up an Assault Fleet. He described how the L.C.I.(L) had been produced and explained the dislocation which had been caused by TORCH. For that operation it had been necessary to stop the entry and training of British crews so that U. S. combat teams could have the use of the training center at Inveraray. As a result, a situation had arisen in which the British were temporarily unable to man all the landing craft at their disposal. The position was now in hand, and there would be no difficulty in manning all the landing craft expected by next August.

He drew attention to the shortage of spare parts which had recently forced him to consider the cannibalization of 25% of the landing craft at his disposal. This position, according to Admiral Cooke, also was now improving; but he emphasized the very great importance of providing ample spares parallel with the production of craft.

He described the organization of the British Assault Fleets. Broadly speaking, there were local forces organized for operations in home waters, western and eastern Mediterranean, and India. Besides these local forces, there was an overseas Assault Force with a lift of 30,000

U. S. SECRET
BRITISH MOST SECRET

personnel, 3,300 vehicles and 200 tanks. The purpose of this Force was to reinforce the local Assault Fleet in whichever theater might be the center of active operations. This Force would be ready to sail for the Mediterranean by March 15th, to take part in HUSKY.

He described three important lessons of amphibious operations which had so far emerged:

(a) For any amphibious campaign involving assaults on strongly defended coasts held by a determined enemy, it is essential that the landing ships and craft shall be organized well in advance into proper assault fleets. These must have a coherence and degree of permanence comparable to that of any first-line fighting formation. Discipline, training, and tactical flexibility are just as necessary for assault fleets as for naval, military and air combat formations. This was the overriding lesson of Dieppe.

(b) No combined operation can be carried out with reasonable hope of success without adequate beach reconnaissance beforehand. He had now organized specially trained beach reconnaissance parties which had already done most valuable work.

(c) Adequate fire support for the assault against a strongly defended coast was most essential. A scale of 100 guns (48 self-propelled in L.C.T. and 52 in the new gun craft to be known as L.C.G.) for each assault brigade had been recommended. He handed around drawings of a type of amphibious close support vessel which had been designed for this purpose. These special assault craft were primarily intended for ROUNDUP, and none could be ready in time for HUSKY.

He then handed around a table* showing the estimated availability of British and American built landing ships and craft. Referring to this table, he pointed out that the main British deficiencies by next August would be in L.S.T. and L.C.I.(L). He urged most strongly that allocations to the British of both these types should be increased to make up these deficiencies. He confirmed that provisions had already been made for manning the full number of all types of craft which had been asked for by next August together with 50 percent spare crews.

* ANNEX

U. S. SECRET
BRITISH MOST SECRET

GENERAL SOMERVELL confirmed that, so far as could be foreseen, sufficient landing craft could be made available for both the U. S. and British portions of HUSKY as now planned.

ADMIRAL KING drew attention to the great diversity of types of British built ships and craft. He asked whether a greater degree of standardization would not be possible. In reply LORD LOUIS MOUNTBATTEN explained that different types had been developed independently by the two navies; improvements had been made as a result of experience. Some of those shown in the table were now out of date.

ADMIRAL COOKE expressed the view that the production of landing craft would be at least as great as the ability of the U. S. and British Navies to man them. He explained the heavy demand for the Pacific where rate of wastage was high and maintenance facilities extremely limited. He confirmed the shortage of spare engines. Spares had been used to fit up new hulls which had come out of production in large numbers.

He explained that the original split of L.S.T. for ROUNDUP, as between U. S. and British, had been in the proportion of 125 to be manned by the U. S. and 75 by the British. Allocations now proposed by the U. S. Navy Department gave a higher proportion to the British, half of the 168 proposed for the European Theater going to the British and half to the U. S.; 117 of these craft would be allocated to the Pacific. He then raised the question of L.C.A., of which the U. S. had none at all. He understood that 96 of these craft were required for the British portion of HUSKY, and he thought that a similar number would be required for the U. S. portion as well.

LORD LOUIS MOUNTBATTEN said that the provision of these craft would need careful examination. It might be found best to send the drawings to America so that they could be built in U. S. yards.

THE COMMITTEE:
(a) Agreed that the question should be reviewed by July 1, 1943, whether the number of L.S.T.(2) to be allocated to the British from the total U. S. production of 390 can be raised from the figure of 120 now proposed by the U. S. Navy Department to 150 which was the full British requirement.

U. S. SECRET
BRITISH MOST SECRET

    (b) Took note that the U. S. Navy Department would investigate whether the follow-up order for 44 L.C.I.(L) can be restored and half of this production allocated to the British.

    (c) Took note that the greatest needs of the British Combined Operations Naval Command were for:

        (1) L.C.M.(3), of which 646 had been asked for by the British by August 1, 1943, but the detailed allocation of which was not yet available.

        (2) Scripps-Ford conversion engines for L.C.A., of which a large additional number would be needed if L.C.A. were built in the United Kingdom for the U. S.

        (3) Spare parts, as a matter of great urgency, for landing craft in the United Kingdom, to be supplied in the first instance on the requisitions already submitted to the U. S. Navy Department by Comamphoreu.

6.   SYSTEM OF COMMAND FOR COMBINED U S. AND BRITISH OPERATIONS
    (C.C.S. 75/3)
    (Previous reference: C.C.S. 45th Meeting, Item 1)

GENERAL MARSHALL said that the intention of the paper under consideration was to lay down general principles for the organization of command where U. S. and British forces were engaged in combined operations under a Supreme Commander. The systems of command employed by the two nations for their own forces differed fundamentally. He recalled that when Field Marshal Wavell had been suddenly called upon to form a combined headquarters at short notice in the Southwest Pacific he had had considerable difficulties in arranging satisfactorily the general organization of his command. Similar cases might occur in the future, and it would be of great assistance to have guiding principles agreed beforehand.

Discussion followed on the precise channels for the communication of orders which would be used in the organization shown in the diagram attached to the paper.

ADMIRAL KING said that in considering the chain of command shown in the diagram, it must be remembered that all Subordinate Commanders act as the agents of the Supreme Commander. The authority of Task Force Commanders was complete in respect of their own task forces. It would not be necessary, however, for the Naval Commander always to transmit

U. S. SECRET
BRITISH MOST SECRET

orders affecting naval forces through the Supreme Commander, and the Task Force Commander to the naval component of the task force. He would be an officer of experience and discretion and would avoid issuing orders which would encroach upon the authority of Task Force Commanders. The channels were not rigid. Taking the example of HUSKY, he explained that the Air Commander with General Eisenhower would have two main functions apart from advising the Supreme Commander. He would arrange for the air bombardment required to soften the defenses of the island, and command the air forces allotted to this task. He would also answer calls for assistance from the task forces. There would be no objection to such calls being passed direct from the Air Commanders in the task forces to the Air Commander at the main headquarters.

    THE COMMITTEE:
    Accepted the basic system of unified command in combined U. S. British operations as set out in C.C.S. 75/3.

U. S. SECRET
BRITISH MOST SECRET

ANNEX

LANDING SHIPS AND CRAFT

Estimated Availability of British Types

TYPE OF SHIP OR CRAFT	Numbers existing December 1, 1942.	Estimated Total Available, allowing for attrition, on	
		April 1, 1943	Aug. 1, 1943
Landing Ships Infantry (Large) White Ensign	4 (a)	5	5
" " Infantry (Large) Red Ensign	10	15	15
" " Infantry (Medium)	2	2	2
" " " (Small)	5	5	5
" " " (Hand hoisting)	13	15	22
" " Headquarter	2	2	2
" " Tank, Class I	3	6	6
" " Stern	2	2	2
" " Gantry	3	4	4
Landing Craft Tank, Mark I	16	4	4
" " " " II	55	43	38
" " " " III	102	109	119
" " " " IV	44	142	233
" " Mechanized, Mark I	125	161	201
" " Infantry (Small)		15	32
" " Assault	274	402 (b)	624 (c)
" " Personnel (Small)	1	195	195
" " " (Medium)	4	55	55
" " Flak (Large)	5	16	26
" " Support (Large)	5	7	12
" " " (Medium)	24	49	69
Landing Barges	380	380	380

NOTE: (a) Two of these are undergoing long repairs.
(b) Includes 30 building in India.
(c) Includes 150 building in India.

U. S. SECRET
BRITISH MOST SECRET

ANNEX

LANDING SHIPS AND CRAFT (Cont'd)

American Built Types to be Manned by British

	April 1, 1943			August 1, 1943		
	Asked for	Allocation proposed by USN Dept.	Short	Asked for	Allocation proposed by USN Dept.	Short
Landing Ships, Tank, Class 2	105	68	37	150	84	66
" " Dock	-	-	-	5	-	5
" Craft, Tank, Mark V	150	150	-	150	150	-
" " Mechanized, Mark III	501	?	?	646	?	?
" " Infantry (Large)	150	150	-	194	150	44
" " Personnel (Large & Ramped)	762	762	-	832	?	?
" " Vehicles	299	299	-	299	299	-
" " Vehicles & Personnel	-	-	-	160	?	?

NOTE: It is hoped that the target figure of 150 for L.S.T. (2) may be completed during 1944, if it cannot be reached in 1943.

Unless adequate spare parts can be provided with high priority, up to 25% of Landing Craft with American engines will have to be cannibalized to keep the remainder running.

U. S. SECRET
BRITISH MOST SECRET

C.C.S. 68th Meeting

COMBINED CHIEFS OF STAFF

MINUTES of Meeting held at Anfa Camp
on Saturday, January 23, 1943, at 1000.

PRESENT

General G. C. Marshall, USA
Admiral E. J. King, USN
Lt. General H. H. Arnold, USA

General Sir Alan F. Brooke
Admiral of the Fleet Sir Dudley Pound
Air Chief Marshal Sir Charles F. A. Portal

THE FOLLOWING WERE ALSO PRESENT

Lt. General B. B. Somervell, USA
Rear Admiral C. M. Cooke, Jr., USN
Brig. General A. C. Wedemeyer, USA
Commander R. E. Libby, USN

Field Marshal Sir John Dill
Vice Admiral the Lord Louis Mountbatten
Lt. General Sir Hastings L. Ismay
Major General J. N. Kennedy
Air Vice Marshal J. C. Slessor
Air Vice Marshal F. F. Inglis

SECRETARIAT

Brigadier V. Dykes
Brig. General J. R. Deane, USA
Brigadier E. I. C. Jacob

U. S. SECRET
BRITISH MOST SECRET

1   BOLERO BUILD-UP.

(C.C.S. 172)

GENERAL SOMERVELL said that his paper had been prepared in collaboration with Lord Leathers, and the figures of U. S. troops to arrive in the United Kingdom in 1943 were dependent on certain assistance being provided by the British. A figure of 50,000 men per division had been taken as a basis of calculation, but this was very high owing to the inclusion of a large overhead in the first half year. The figures would be reduced to about 40,000 in the latter part of the year. In this event, the total number of divisions might rise from fifteen to nineteen by the end of the year. Every means would be used of increasing the number of troops shipped by additional loadings in personnel ships during the summer months and the fitting of more cargo ships for troop carrying.

THE COMMITTEE:

Took note of paper C.C.S. 172.

2   CONTINENTAL OPERATIONS IN 1943.

(C.C.S. 167)

(Previous reference C.C.S. 67th Meeting, Item 3)

GENERAL MARSHALL said that the proposals in the paper by the British Joint Planning Staff were acceptable to the U. S. Chiefs of Staff subject to the following comments:

It appeared that the availability of the British airborne division referred to in paragraph 4 was now doubtful in view of the demands of HUSKY. The dispatch of an American airborne division to the United Kingdom, possibly in June, was, therefore, being considered by the U S Chiefs of Staff. The first airborne division which would be ready for overseas would be required for HUSKY. The chief difficulty lay in the provision of the necessary air transports, but these could be moved across to the U. K more quickly than the personnel, who would have to go by sea.

The U. S. Chiefs of Staff considered it most desirable that any operation of the type mentioned in paragraph 2 (a) of the paper, e g., against the Channel Islands, should be coordinated in time with HUSKY.

As regards the larger operation against the Cotentin Peninsula, for which the target date given in paragraph 19 (b) was August 1st, it

U. S. SECRET
BRITISH MOST SECRET

must be made clear that the plan was only to be based on the U. S. resources available at that time in the United Kingdom. First priority was given to HUSKY, and the U. S. did not wish to accept any additional commitment for operation HADRIAN beyond what was at present envisaged. It was highly improbable that any U. S. landing craft crews would be available for operations from the United Kingdom this summer.

SIR ALAN BROOKE said that, as a result of the decision on HUSKY, paragraph 4 was not now correct. There would only be 11 British divisions and a part of one British airborne division available.

> THE COMMITTEE:
> Approved the proposals contained in C.C.S. 167 subject to the reservations of the U. S. Chiefs of Staff recorded above.

3. REPORT TO THE PRESIDENT AND PRIME MINISTER.
   (C.C.S. 170)

> THE COMMITTEE:
> (a) Approved the draft submitted by the Secretaries, subject to minor amendments agreed in the discussion, and the inclusion of a paragraph on the BOLERO build-up based on C.C.S. 172.*
> (b) Instructed the Secretaries to prepare and submit a final draft forthwith.

4. OPERATION HUSKY--DIRECTIVE TO GENERAL EISENHOWER.
   (C.C.S. 171)

GENERAL MARSHALL proposed certain amendments to the text of the draft directive, which were accepted.**

> THE COMMITTEE:
> Approved the directive as amended and instructed the Secretaries to transmit it to General Eisenhower

5. LANDING CRAFT.

LORD LOUIS MOUNTBATTEN said that the Admiralty had been asked to complete another 160 L.C.A. during the next four months to provide American requirements for HUSKY and training. He might have to send British L.C.A. from Force J (the Channel Assault Force) for the U. S.

* Subsequently published as C.C.S. 172/1.
** Subsequently published as C.C.S. 171/1.

U. S. SECRET
BRITISH MOST SECRET

share of HUSKY, but it was essential that these should be replaced in time to enable cross-channel operations to be undertaken this summer. All L.C.A. engines come from America; and he would, therefore, require 400 Scripps-Ford conversion engines at the rate of 100 a month for the next four months. Each craft had two engines, and 25 percent spares were required. It was of great importance that the Channel Assault Force should be kept in being, even though temporarily short of L.C.A. to make up U. S. requirements. Otherwise, there would be no force available for cross-channel operations. Once broken up, this force would be very difficult to re-form again.

ADMIRAL KING said that no firm promise could be given that this large number of engines would be provided from the U. S. where production resources were already strained. He undertook to see what could be done.

THE COMMITTEE:
(a) Agreed that it was most desirable for the Channel Assault Force to be kept in being for cross-channel operations this summer.
(b) Took note that the U. S. would endeavor to provide the necessary engines for any L.C.A. hulls produced in Great Britain during the coming months.

U. S. SECRET
BRITISH MOST SECRET

C.C.S. 69th Meeting

COMBINED CHIEFS OF STAFF

MINUTES of Meeting held at Anfa Camp
on Saturday, January 23, 1943, at 2130.

PRESENT

General G. C. Marshall, USA	General Sir Alan F. Brooke
Admiral E. J. King, USN	Admiral of the Fleet Sir Dudley Pound
Lt. General H. H. Arnold, USA	Air Chief Marshal Sir Charles F. A. Portal

THE FOLLOWING WERE ALSO PRESENT

Lt. General B. B. Somervell, USA	Field Marshal Sir John Dill
Rear Admiral C. M. Cooke, Jr., USN	Vice Admiral the Lord Louis Mountbatten
Brig. General J. E. Hull, USA	Lt. General Sir Hastings L. Ismay
Brig. General A. C. Wedemeyer, USA	
Colonel J. E. Smart, USA	
Commander R. E. Libby, USN	

SECRETARIAT

Brigadier V. Dykes
Brig. General J. R. Deane, USA

U. S. SECRET

BRITISH MOST SECRET

1. REPORT TO THE PRESIDENT AND PRIME MINISTER.
   (C.C.S. 170/1)
   THE COMMITTEE:
   (a) Agreed, after discussion, to a number of amendments to C.C.S. 170/1.
   (b) Instructed the Secretaries to incorporate these amendments in a final report* to be submitted to the President and Prime Minister.

2. OPERATION HUSKY--DIRECTIVE TO GENERAL EISENHOWER.
   (C.C.S. 171/1/D)
   THE COMMITTEE:
   (a) Agreed to an amendment to the directive to General Eisenhower (C.C.S. 171/1/D) consequent upon the amendments agreed to in C.C.S. 170/2.
   (b) Directed the Secretaries to transmit the amended directive** to General Eisenhower.

3. ASSAULT SHIPPING.
   SIR ALAN BROOKE read a note by Lord Leathers expressing concern at the use of large passenger ships as assault shipping. (A copy of this note is attached as an Annex to these Minutes.)

   ADMIRAL KING said that it was this consideration which had moved him to suggest that the assault in Operation HUSKY should be carried out as far as possible in the larger type of landing craft and not in assault shipping.

   THE COMMITTEE:
   Took note:
   (a) Of the note by Lord Leathers.
   (b) That the British Chiefs of Staff would submit proposals for reducing to the minimum the use of large passenger ships as assault ships.

4. CONCLUSION OF THE CONFERENCE.
   GENERAL MARSHALL, at the conclusion of the conference at Casablanca, expressed his appreciation of the readiness of the British

* Subsequently circulated as C.C.S. 170/2.
** Subsequently circulated as C.C.S. 171/1/D.

U. S. SECRET
BRITISH MOST SECRET

Chiefs of Staff to understand the U. S. point of view and of the fine spirit of cooperation which they had shown during the discussions. He felt sure that the Combined Chiefs of Staff would greatly profit by their contacts with their colleagues and the mutual understanding of each other's problems which had been insured. He paid a tribute to the work of the British 8th Army and expressed his admiration of their energetic prosecution of the operations in Tripolitania. He went on to thank Sir John Dill for accompanying the U. S. Chiefs of Staff to the conference and for paying a visit to India to continue his valuable work as a link between the U. S. and British Staffs.

SIR ALAN BROOKE thanked General Marshall for his words and said that he reciprocated most whole-heartedly General Marshall's expression of the great benefit which had accrued from the conference. Mutual appreciation of each other's problems was only possible through personal contacts. Sir John Dill was performing a great service as a link between the British and U. S. Chiefs of Staff. A great step forward had been taken in agreeing upon a basic strategy for the future prosecution of the war.

SIR CHARLES PORTAL said he was sure he was speaking on behalf of all the British Chiefs of Staff in expressing his appreciation of the great hospitality which had been given by the U. S. Forces and of the excellent arrangements for the conference which had been made by General Patton and the troops under his command.

SIR JOHN DILL thanked the Combined Chiefs of Staff and emphasized the great value of the frank discussions which had been held.

ADMIRAL KING said he fully agreed with Sir Alan Brooke as to the great value of the basic strategic plan which had been worked out at the conference. In his view this was the biggest step forward to the winning of the war. Much had already been done to fill in the details of this plan and more would be done in the future, but the discussions which had been held had enabled a true meeting of minds to take place between the British and U. S. Chiefs of Staff.

GENERAL ARNOLD said that he fully associated himself with these views.

U. S. SECRET
BRITISH MOST SECRET

    GENERAL MARSHALL said that before the conference broke up he would like to pay tribute to the very valuable services performed by the Combined Staff Planners and the Secretariat.

U. S. SECRET
BRITISH MOST SECRET

U. S. SECRET
BRITISH MOST SECRET

ANNEX

I and my advisers are much concerned by the present policy of using large passenger ships as L.S.I. (L)'s.

I know that L.S.I.(L)'s are essential to the success of large amphibious operations; and in the absence of any more suitable shipping, large troopships have had to be converted for this use. Thirteen such ships were employed in the TORCH assault, and 3 were lost. We have now had to select 5 more for conversion.

Apart from the loss of 3 L.S.I.(L)'s in TORCH, we also lost 5 other large troopships in the operation; the total trooping capacity of the 8 ships was over 24,000.

The losses to be expected in future assault operations on a large scale against determined opposition are bound to be much higher. We must realize that further heavy losses of this type of ship would have a crippling effect on our strategy by destroying our ability to carry out large-scale trooping movements, as replacement of this type of ship is impossible.

I wonder whether it would be possible for the U.S.A. to help us out with Combat Loaders, which are replaceable from current production, while the big troopships are not replaceable.

We could, of course, make up to the Americans the loss in their trooping capacity by lending them some of our troopships.

(Signed) LEATHERS

January 23, 1943.

U. S. SECRET
BRITISH MOST SECRET

INDEX

A

Aegean, Opening the, 28
Agenda of the Conference
  Suggested procedure for dealing with the, 20, *249*
Agreements on North Africa coast command, *251*
Agreements reached as to conduct of war in 1943, 16, 18
Aid to Russia, U.S., 17, 22, 72, 75, *149*, *155*, *264*
Aid to China, *145*
Air Command
  Mediterranean, System of, in, 78
  West Africa, Naval and, in, 115, 124
Aircraft
  Requirements of shore-based aircraft for the defense of Trade Communications, United Nations, 54, 57
Air Forces in Tunisia, *140*
Alexander account of 8th Army operation, *136*
Allied
  Manpower, *219*
  Plans relating to Turkey, 23, *257*
Allocation of adequate forces in Pacific, 17, 19
Allocation of resources outlined by General Marshall, *170*
Amphibious operations from the United Kingdom, 122
ANAKIM, 21, *283*
  Burma, Reconquest of, 12
  Forces, Provision of, 80, 82
ANFA Conference
  Meeting, Minutes of, *134*
Annex
  Minutes 61st Meeting, *253*
  Minutes 67th Meeting, *308*
  Minutes 69th Meeting, *317*
Antisubmarine Warfare, *196*
Assault shipping, *315*
Assistance to Russia in relation to other commitments, 109, 117
Atlantic, 45

Axis
  Oil position, 40, 115, 124, *255*

B

Berlin, Raids on, *245*
BOLERO, 113, 121
  Build-up, 21, *311*
    Shipping capabilities for, 129
    Enclosure "A", 130
    Enclosure "B", 131
    Enclosure "C", Assumptions for calculations of U. S. shipping capabilities under plan adopted by C.C.S. for 1943, 132
Bomber offensive from North Africa, The, 44, 120, *268*
Bomber offensive from the United Kingdom, The 21, 86, 88, *279*
Bombing Axis oil sources, 124
British agreement for British efforts against Japan unnecessary, *144*
British responsibility for Turkey, *267*
British will handle Turkish matters, 124
Burma, Operations in, 11
  Reconquest of, 12
Burma Road, The, 11
Business, Future, *275*

C

Calculations of Turkish equipment and needs, *139*
Capture of Dodecanese, 28, *145*
Chiang Kai-shek desires postponement of Operation RAVENOUS, *144*
China
  Communications, Overland, with, 12
  Improvement of air transportation into, 123

NOTE: Numerals in Italics refer to Pages in Minutes of Meetings.
  Numerals in plain type refer to Pages of C.C.S. Papers.

319

U. S. SECRET
BRITISH MOST SECRET   INDEX

Combined Chiefs of Staff
  Final report to The President and Prime Minister summarizing decisions by the, 117
  Memorandum by the, 109
  Minutes of meetings, *169*
  Papers, 1
Combined Strategy, *184*
Command
  Dakar, French West Africa, strategic responsibility and setup for, 249
  Mediterranean, in the, *269*, 119
  Naval and air, in West Africa, 115, 124
  System of
    Air, in the Mediterranean, 78
    Combined U.S.-British Operations for, 1, 306
    Unified command for combined operations, 1
Command, control, planning and training for operations for a reentry to the Continent across the Channel, beginning in 1943, Proposed organization of, 99, 302
Commanders
  Land, naval and air, 2
  Supreme, 2
  Task force, 2
Commitments
  Turkey, Our military, to, 35
Communications
  China, Overland, with, 12
  Defense of trade, United Nations' requirements of shore-based aircraft for the, 54
  Japanese, 11
  Sea, of the United Nations, Minimum escort requirements to maintain the, 45, 57, 109
    Enclosure "A", 50
    Enclosure "B", 51
    Enclosure "C", 52
    Enclosure "D", 53
    Enclosure "E", 54
  Sea, Security of, 117, *155*
Communique, Press, 301
Conclusion of the Conference, 315

Conduct of the War in 1943, 16, 18, *249*
  Pacific Theater, in the 95, *301*
Conference
  Conclusion of the, *315*
  Draft report on the work of the, 102
  Publication of results of the, 252
Continental operations in 1943, 90, *301*, *311*
Convoy, 46
  Escort requirements, Detailed estimate of, 50
  Russian air assistance for P.Q., 230
Coordination of 8th Army and Eisenhower Army, *138*
Craft, Landing, *303*, *312*

D

Dakar, French West Africa, Strategic responsibility and command set-up for, 249
Defeat of the U-Boat, 16, 18
Defensive Requirements of North Africa, *139*
Destroyer (see Fleet Destroyer), 51
Development of the Offensive, 27
Directive
  Allied Expeditionary Force in North Africa, To Commander-in-Chief, General Eisenhower, to *312*, 315
  Operation HUSKY, 125, 127
Dodecanese, Capture of, 28, *145*
Draft--Operation HUSKY, 125
Draft report on the work of the Conference, 102
Draft telegram from the President of the United States and the Prime Minister of Great Britain to Premier Stalin, 84, 282, *293*
Dry cargo import situation, U.K., 45

E

Eastern Theater, 226

NOTE: Numerals in Italics refer to Pages in Minutes of Meetings. Numerals in Plain Type refer to Pages of C.C.S. Papers.

U. S. SECRET
BRITISH MOST SECRET   INDEX

    Situation to be created in, 4, *236*
      Enclosure "A", 4
      Enclosure "B", 7
    Eisenhower, General, Directive to, *312, 315*
      Description of airfields used by Allied Forces, *136*
      Proposal for conduction of forthcoming operation, *135*
      Review of situation on his front, *135*
    Employment of French Forces in North Africa, 223
    Enemy's fighting value, *137*
    Entry of Turkey into the War on the side of the United Nations, 23
    Equipment, Supply of (Turkey), 38
    Escort
      Carriers, United Nations' requirements of, 53
      Convoy, requirements, Detailed estimate of, 50
      Requirements to maintain the sea communications of the United Nations, Minimum, 45
        Enclosure "A", 50
        Enclosure "B", 51
        Enclosure "C", 52
        Enclosure "D", 53
        Enclosure "E", 54
      Requirements, World-wide estimate of, of Fleet Destroyers and ocean-going escort vessels, 52
      Vessels, *243*
    European Theater
      Strategic concept for 1943 in the, *208*
      Strategy in the, *202*

F

Final Report to the President and Prime Minister summarizing decisions by the Combined Chiefs of Staff, 117
Financial and economic assistance for Turkey, 34
Five main lines of action in European theater, 16, *28*

Fleet Destroyers
    Requirements of, and ocean-going escort vessels, World-wide estimate of, 51
French Forces in North Africa, Employment of, 223
Future business, *275*

G

Giraud, General, Meeting with, *259*

H

Hartley Committee, The, 40, 43
HUSKY, Operation, 58, 63, *273*
    Date for the assault, Earliest, 63, 70
    Directive, 125
      Allied Expeditionary Force in North Africa, to Commander-in-Chief, 127
      General Eisenhower, to, *312, 315*
    Draft, 125
    Enclosure "A", 64
    Enclosure "B", Forces Required, 68
    Enclosure "C", Examination of Earliest Date of Assault, 70

I

Iceland, 229
Indian Ocean situation, *177*

J

Japanese
    Communications, 11
    Strategy, *184*
Joint Intelligence Subcommittee' Report, Extracts from, 41

L

Landing Craft, *303, 312*

NOTE: Numerals in Italics refer to Pages in Minutes of Meetings. Numerals in plain type refer to Pages of C.C.S. Papers.

U. S. SECRET
BRITISH MOST SECRET

INDEX

M

Meeting
 ANFA, *134*
 Annex to 61st, Minutes, *253*
 Annex to 67th, Minutes, *308*
 Annex to 69th, Minutes, *317*
 C.C.S., *169*
 General Giraud, with, *259*
 SYMBOL, 117
Mediterranean, 20
 Air command, System of, in the, 78
 Command in the, *269*
 Naval situation in the Western, *245*
 Operations in the, 110, 118, *159*
 Reopening the, 47
Memorandum by the Combined Chiefs of Staff, 109
Military
 Assistance to Turkey, Initial, 25
 Commitments to Turkey, Our, 35
Minutes of Meetings, *134*
 Annex to, 61st, *253*
 Annex to, 67th, *308*
 Annex to, 69th, *317*

N

Naval and air command in West Africa, 115, 124
Naval situation in the Western Mediterranean, *245*
North Africa
 Bomber offensive from, The, 44, *268*
 Employment of French Forces in, *223*
 Situation in, The, *135*, *199*, *208*

O

Offensive
 Bomber, from North Africa, The, 44, *268*
 Bomber, from the United Kingdom, 21, 86, 88, *279*
 Development of the (Turkey), 27
Oil
 Axis, position, 40, 115, 124, *255*

Operation
 ANAKIM, 12, 14, 21, 80, 82, *283*
 BOLERO, 113, 121, *283*, *311*
  Shipping capabilities for, build-up, 129
   Enclosure "A", 130
   Enclosure "B", 131
   Enclosure "C", Assumptions for calculations of U. S. shipping capabilities under plan adopted by C.C.S. for 1943, 132
 HUSKY, 58, 63, *273*
  Alternative "A", 59
  Alternative "B", 59
  Directive, 125
   Allied Expeditionary Force in North Africa, to Commander-in-Chief, 127
  Draft, 125
  Enclosure "A", 64
  Enclosure "B", Forces Required, 68
  Enclosure "C", Examination of Earliest Date of Assault, 70
  Target date, *159*
 SLEDGEHAMMER, *145*
 UNDERBELLY, *146*
Operations
 Burma, January-April, 1943, in, 11, *233*
 Continental, in 1943, 90, *301*, *311*
 Cotentin Peninsula, 122
 Eastern Theater, 6, 8, 19
 European Theater, in the, 18
 Mediterranean, in the, 110, 118, *159*
 Southwest Pacific, in the, 22
 System of command for combined U.S.-British, 1, *306*
 System of unified command for combined, 1
 Turkey, subsequent, 29
 United Kingdom, in and from the, 112, 121, *164*
Organization of command, control, planning and training for cross-channel, 99, *302*
Overland communications with China, 12

NOTE: Numerals in Italics refer to pages in Minutes of Meetings.
Numerals in Plain Type refer to pages of C.C.S. Papers.

322

U. S. SECRET
BRITISH MOST SECRET   INDEX

P

Pacific, The, 47
Pacific Theater
  Conduct of the War in the, 95, 114, 122, *301*
  Far East and, *167*
Plans
  Sprawl, The, 25, 27, 33, 36
  Turkey, Allied, relating to, 23, 257
Polish Forces, potentialities of, 244
Press Communique, *301*
Prime Minister's appraisal of Turkish situation, *150*
Program of Meetings, revised, 253
Proposed organization of command, control, planning and training for operations for a reentry to the Continent across the Channel, beginning in 1943, 99, *302*
Provisional date for ANAKIM assault, 123
Publication of results of the Conference, 252

R

Raids on Berlin, *245*
Recapture of Philippines, discussion of, *193*
Reconquest of Burma, *12*
Reentry to the Continent across the Channel, beginning in 1943, Proposed organization of command, control, planning and training for operations for a, 99, *302*
Report to The President and Prime Minister, 102, 109, *291*, *312*, 315
  Enclosure, Draft Report on the work of the Conference, 102
  Final, summarizing decisions by the Combined Chiefs of Staff, 117
R.A.F. and Army stores dumped into Turkey, 37
Russia
  Assistance to, 17, 22, 72, 75, 155, 264

Russia—continued
  Relation to other commitments, in, 109, 117
  Russian air assistance for P.Q. convoys, 230

S

Sea communications, security of, 117, 155
Shipping
  Assault, *315*
  BOLERO build-up, capabilities for, 129
    Enclosure "A", 130
    Enclosure "B", 131
    Enclosure "C", 132
  Capabilities under plan adopted by C.C.S. for 1943, Assumptions for calculations of U. S., 132
  HUSKY, provision of, *61*
  Situation in North Africa, The, *135*, *199*, 208
  Situation to be created in Eastern Theater, 4
    Enclosure "A", 4
    Enclosure "B", 7
  Pacific and Burma in 1943, *236*
SLEDGEHAMMER, Operation, *145*
Somervell, Lieutenant General, B. B., Note by (BOLERO), 129
Sprawl Plan, 25, 27, 33, 36
Stalin, Premier
  Draft telegram from the President of the United States and Prime Minister of Great Britain to, 84, *282*, *293*
State of German Air Force, *179*
Strategic concept for 1943 in the European Theater, The, 208
Strategic responsibility and command set-up for Dakar, French West Africa, 249
Strategy
  Combined, *184*
  European Theater, in the, *202*

NOTE: Numerals in Italics refer to pages in Minutes of Meetings.
Numerals in Plain Type refer to pages of C.C.S papers.

U S SECRET
BRITISH MOST SECRET   INDEX

Summarizing decisions by the Combined Chiefs of Staff, Final report to The President and Prime Minister, 117
Summary of current conferences by Sir Alan Brooke, *143*
Supplies to Russia, *222*
Supply of equipment (Turkey), 38
SYMBOL, 117
System of
  Command, air, in the Mediterranean, 78
  Command for combined U.S.-British operations, 1, *306*
  Unified command for combined operations, 1

T

Telegram from The President of the United States and the Prime Minister of Great Britain to Premier Stalin, 84, *282*, *293*
Theater
  Eastern, situation to be created in, 4, *226*, *236*
    Enclosure "A", 4
    Enclosure "B", 7
  European
    Strategic concept for 1943 in the, *208*
    Strategy in the, *202*
  Pacific and Far East, 114, 122, *167*
  Pacific, conduct of the War in the, 95, *301*
Turkey, 21, 116, 124
  Aegean, Opening the—Phase I, 28
  Allied plans relating to, 23, *257*
  British responsibility for, *267*
  Commitments, Our military, to, 35
  Conclusions, 32
  Dodecanese, Capture of, 28, *145*
  Entry of, into the War on the side of the United Nations, 23
  Equipment, Supply of, 38
  Financial and economic assistance for, 34
  Military assistance to, Initial, 25
  Military commitments to, Our, 35

Turkey—continued
  Offensive, Development of the, 27
    Phase I—Opening the Aegean, 28
    Phase II—Subsequent operations, 29
  Recommendations, 34
  Stores, R.A.F. and Army, already dumped into, 37
  Subsequent operations
    Phase I, 28
    Phase II, 29
  Summary, 31
  Enclosure "A", 34
  Enclosure "B", 35
  Enclosure "C", 37
  Enclosure "D", 38

U

U-Boat
  Threat, The, 47
  Warfare, 20, *277*
United Kingdom
  Bomber offensive from the, 21, 86, 88, *279*
  Dry cargo import situation, 45
  Operations in and from the, 112, 121, *164*
United Nations
  Aircraft for the defense of trade communications, requirements of shore-based, 54
United States aid to Russia, 17, 22, 72, 75, *155*, *264*
United States Forces for Continental operations, 121
United States troops to U. K., *284*

W

War
  Conduct of, in 1943, 16, 18, *249*, *301*
  U-Boat, The, 20, *277*
Warfare, Antisubmarine, *196*
West Africa
  Naval and air command in, 115, 124
  Dakar, Strategic responsibility and command set-up for, *249*

NOTE: Numerals in Italics refer to Pages in Minutes of Meetings
Numerals in Plain Type refer to Pages of C.C.S. Papers

CASABLANCA CONFERENCE

JANUARY 1943

JOINT CHIEFS OF STAFF

MINUTES OF MEETINGS

Edited and printed in the
Office, U. S. Secretary
Office of the Combined Chiefs of Staff
1943

SECRET

TABLE OF CONTENTS

MINUTES

	PAGE

J.C.S. 50th Meeting (Casablanca) 1
        President's Visit
        Agenda for Coming Conferences
        Further Conferences
        Admiral Glassford's Report

J.C.S. 51st Meeting (Casablanca) 8
        Operation British Eastern Fleet
        Assignment of Heavy Bombers to China
        Procedure to Adopt at Forthcoming Conference
        Operations in the Mediterranean
        Operations in and from the United Kingdom
        Priority Bombing Programs
        Proposed Operations and Commands

J.C.S. 52nd Meeting (Casablanca) 13
        Priority Bombing Program
        Command in England
        Operations in the Mediterranean
        Landing Craft
        General Strategic Policies

J.C.S. 53rd Meeting (Casablanca) 22
        Pacific and Far East Theater
        Attitude of Stalin towards U. S.
        Landing Craft
        Continental Operations
        Operations in Sicily
        U. S. Aid to Russia

J.C.S. 54th Meeting (Casablanca) 27
        Synthetic Rubber Program
        Report of Conversation between the Prime Minister
            and Admiral King
        General Somervell on Tonnage, Visit to Russia, and
            Command of Eisenhower
        Operation in Far East and Mediterranean
        Objections to British Concern in our Strategic Theater
        Strategic Policy Considered in Mediterranean & Far East

SECRET

TABLE OF CONTENTS

	PAGE

J.C.S. 55th Meeting (Casablanca) 32
    Conduct of War in 1943
    Synthetic Rubber Program
    Command Set-up for Dakar-French North-West Africa
    Required Presidential Action
    Planning Staff for HUSKY
    Army and Navy Command Set-up in Mediterranean

J.C.S. 56th Meeting (Casablanca) 37
    Commitments to Turkey
    Dodecanese Operation
    U. S. Aid to Russia
    General Strategic Plan for 1943
    Shipping for Operation in the Pacific
    Proposed Mediterranean Army and Air Command Set-up

J.C.S. 57th Meeting (Casablanca) 41
    Despatches from Eisenhower and Hurley
    Antisubmarine Warfare
    The Bomber Offensive from the United Kingdom
    ANAKIM
    Draft Telegram to M. Stalin
    Assault Date for Operation HUSKY
    Routes through the Levant
    Eviction of Axis from Tunisia
    Training of French Pilots

J.C.S. 58th Meeting (Casablanca) 45
    Draft Reply to M. Stalin
    Operations in the Southwest Pacific
    HUSKY

J.C.S. 59th Meeting (Casablanca) 47
    Continental Operations in 1943
    Shipping Capabilities for BOLERO Build-up
    Operation HUSKY
    Report to the President and Prime Minister

SECRET

TABLE OF CONTENTS

PAGE

Joint Chiefs of Staff Meetings
    (Presided over by the President)
        Minutes of Conference, January 15, 1943 51
            Visit of General Nogues and the Sultan of Morocco
              with the President
            The President's Program
            The British Strategic Concept
            Antisubmarine Warfare
            Operation RAVENOUS
            Command Situation in Europe
            Operations in Tunisia
        Minutes of Conference, January 16, 1943 58
            Strategic Concept for 1943
            Operations in the Mediterranean and on the Continent
            Position of Turkey
            British Strategic Concept
            Aircraft to China
            President's Suggestion of Proposed Plans
            Aid to Russia
            Information from Southern Europe
            Equipment for the French
            Operations in Tunisia
            Supply Situation
            French Shipping in Martinique
            Operations in Pacific

INDEX 67

SECRET

J.C.S. 50th Meeting
(Casablanca)

JOINT CHIEFS OF STAFF

MINUTES OF MEETING

Held on Wednesday, January 13, 1943, at 1500

MEMBERS PRESENT

General G. C. Marshall, USA
Admiral E. J. King, USN
Lt. General H. H. Arnold, USA

SECRETARY

Brig. General J. R. Deane, USA

ADDITIONAL OFFICERS PRESENT

Lt. General B. B. Somervell, USA
Lt. General M. W. Clark, USA
Rear Admiral C. M. Cooke, Jr., USN
Brig. General A. C. Wedemeyer, USA
Commander R. E. Libby, USN

and

Mr. Reilly

SECRET

1. PRESIDENT'S VISIT.

GENERAL MARSHALL and ADMIRAL KING discussed with MR. REILLY certain security measures with reference to the President's visit in North Africa. They decided that his party should come directly to Anfa Camp and not delay at Marrakech. A telegram to this effect was sent to Admiral Leahy.

They then discussed the possibility of the President's visiting Marrakech for a few days and indicated that the Prime Minister might urge such a visit. The Joint Chiefs of Staff felt that security measures were not sufficient in Marrakech and that to make them sufficient would necessitate the sending of additional troops and that would be unsound from a tactical point of view. Mr. Reilly agreed.

The question of the President's visit to the front was then discussed, and GENERAL MARSHALL proposed that he leave here by motor to Rabat where he would see two divisions and speak to certain selected men. He would then proceed to Port Lyautey and see a division there. From Port Lyautey he could proceed to General Clark's headquarters.

ADMIRAL KING suggested that certain selected men might be flown from the Tunisian front to meet the President at General Clark's headquarters.

GENERAL MARSHALL said that he felt the President, on the return trip, should return to Marrakech and remain there long enough to change planes and then have a night flight to Liberia.

MR. REILLY asked if the Liberian trip was necessary, and all agreed that the President would insist upon it.

All agreed that it would be desirable if the President and the Prime Minister went separately after leaving the meetings at Anfa Camp.

2. AGENDA FOR COMING CONFERENCES.

GENERAL MARSHALL raised the question of how to proceed with the business of the coming conferences.

ADMIRAL KING implied that he thought they should first discuss world-wide strategy, our basic strategic concept.

SECRET

GENERAL MARSHALL was concerned as to how he should approach the discussion, feeling that the British had their minds set on the operation BRIMSTONE and that their whole thought would be turned towards this.

ADMIRAL KING then presented some notes regarding what he thought should be discussed initially. He divided the initial discussion into:
- (a) Manpower.
- (b) Munitions and equipment.
- (c) Manpower vs. munitions and equipment.
- (d) That part of the total effort that should be directed against Germany and against Japan.

These suggestions were further subdivided in the notes which he presented to the Chiefs of Staff.

ADMIRAL KING stated that he believed we should discuss world-wide strategy first before getting to specific operations and that we should resist any effort on the part of the British to deviate from this.

GENERAL MARSHALL repeated that he believed that even in the case of world-wide strategy, the British thought would be at all times directed towards Operation BRIMSTONE while he, personally, could not help but have the question of tonnage uppermost in his mind.

GENERAL ARNOLD said that the British were not thinking world strategy but only of the next operation.

The Joint Chiefs of Staff then discussed the question of Operation BRIMSTONE.

GENERAL SOMERVELL said that if we can clear the Mediterranean, he estimated that we could save in five months 1,825,000 tons of shipping; that the blow we can strike anywhere depends on available tonnage; that at the present time, the balance between capital-loaded transport and capital-loaded cargo vessels is such that we can move more troops than supporting cargo; and that if we can institute tank sailings from Haifa or from the eastern Mediterranean to the North African theater, we can save considerable additional tonnage.

He said that, figuring the losses on the same rate that they were sustained in the TORCH Operation, Operation BRIMSTONE could be accomplished with the loss of 46 ships. He also thought that securing Sicily would be essential to opening traffic in the Mediterranean.

SECRET

GENERAL CLARK questioned this, stating that he felt we could protect traffic through the Mediterranean by air coverage from Tunisia.

GENERAL ARNOLD asked what the British losses had been in the Malta operation.

GENERAL CLARK stated that they had suffered a 60 percent loss but that it must be remembered that they had had no fighter coverage.

ADMIRAL KING stated that he thought the basic proposition as far as the Mediterranean is concerned is to open it, thus saving the long voyage around the Cape of Good Hope. He felt that this was much more important than eliminating Italy from the war.

GENERAL CLARK said that Admiral Cunningham felt that traffic between Sicily and Tunisia could be protected once Tunisia is in our hands.

GENERAL MARSHALL asked the effects of the German bombing on Bone and Algiers.

GENERAL CLARK replied that Bone is within reach of German dive bombers and that we had suffered rather severe losses there. He felt, however, that the situation is now much improved because of antiaircraft and fighter protection and also because of the installation of radar equipment. The bombing of Algiers has been considerably lessened since we have employed night fighters to protect it.

ADMIRAL COOKE said that at present it looked as though we would not expel the Germans from Tunisia until spring by which time we would have some 500,000 troops in Africa. The question would then arise as to whether we should use shipping to send some troops elsewhere or to use them directly from North Africa. In any event, we must make our plans at least three months in advance. The capture of Sardinia or Sicily would probably involve some shipping losses, but these would probably be offset by increased safety to subsequent shipping through the Mediterranean.

ADMIRAL KING then asked why we should create such a large excess force in North Africa.

GENERAL CLARK replied that it would not be necessary to do so unless we were going to use them in this area. He pointed out, however,

SECRET

that the occupation of Sardinia or Sicily would be a much more difficult operation than TORCH had been.

ADMIRAL COOKE said that he felt that we could mount an operation against Sardinia largely by using landing craft of the larger types in which we could afford to take some losses. In reply to Admiral King's question regarding the necessity for building up an excess force in North Africa, he stated that some excess was necessary because it would take many more troops to expel the Axis from Tunisia than it would to simply hold North Africa once the Axis powers were driven out; also, that the hazard with regard to Spanish Morocco was greater prior to our capture of Tunisia and more troops would be required to safeguard our interests in that area.

GENERAL CLARK said that it was now evident that the earliest date for an all-out offensive against Tunisia was March 15th and, in view of this, an operation against either Sardinia or Sicily could scarcely be undertaken before summer.

GENERAL MARSHALL asked General Clark what number of troops he thought would be necessary to maintain in North Africa once the Axis forces were expelled.

GENERAL CLARK replied that four divisions would be sufficient. This, including the service troops and the Air Force, would mean a force of about 250,000 men.

GENERAL MARSHALL pointed out that the excess force that we would have after Tunisia had been captured would amount to about three U. S. divisions and the British 1st Army.

GENERAL MARSHALL asked General Clark for his views on the training necessary for the Operation BRIMSTONE.

GENERAL CLARK replied that he thought it should be accomplished in Africa and that it should be completed at the rate of about one division per month after the Army and Navy had completed certain basic training.

GENERAL MARSHALL then asked if the supply of the troops in Sardinia would present any great difficulty.

SECRET

GENERAL CLARK thought it could be accomplished almost entirely by air and landing craft.

GENERAL ARNOLD pointed out that the fighter aircraft based in North Africa could only operate for about one-half hour over Sardinia even with the installation of belly tanks.

GENERAL MARSHALL asked General Clark if he thought it was necessary for the 4th Division to come to North Africa in view of the excess number of troops that would be available here.

GENERAL CLARK replied that if no further offensive operations were contemplated after the capture of Tunisia, it would not be necessary for it to come. He stated, however, that there were still 1½ British divisions to arrive in North Africa and that it was necessary for these to come. He pointed out that in the next few months the German threat to Spain would be critical. Spain is, at the present time, a doubtful quantity. They are waiting to see the results of our Tunisian operations. This being the case, it is necessary for us to maintain a large force available to act against Spanish Morocco. He felt that once the Axis powers had been pushed out of Tunisia, Spain will definitely resist a German invasion and the danger in so far as Spanish Morocco is concerned will be decreased.

GENERAL SOMERVELL asked General Clark if any German troops had come from Sicily, to which GENERAL CLARK replied that he thought not.

ADMIRAL COOKE pointed out that regardless of the decision, whether it be to undertake Operation BRIMSTONE or some other operation, it should be firm and that we should not permit ourselves to be forced into an operation without sufficient time for preparation.

GENERAL SOMERVELL asked General Clark when it was expected that the British would have possession of Tripoli, to which General Clark replied that the operation should be completed on February 1st.

3. FURTHER CONFERENCES

GENERAL MARSHALL suggested that the Joint Chiefs of Staff meet at 0830 and that arrangements be made to meet with the British at 1030, January 16th, to which all agreed.

SECRET

4. ADMIRAL GLASSFORD'S REPORT.

ADMIRAL KING stated that the Glassford Commission had just about completed its work and that their report had been blocked out. He said that it would be sent first to General Eisenhower for approval and then it would be referred to the Combined Chiefs of Staff either at Anfa Camp or in Washington.

He stated that there was one point upon which the entire Commission agreed; i.e., the desirability of giving the French certain tasks to perform and then letting them perform them. He stated that the French are willing to operate under Admiral Pegran who had been made a Vice Admiral. He said that the British had agreed to permit the French to undertake the inshore naval defenses of Gambia as part of French West Africa, but that they were not inclined to permit the French to undertake the air protection of this area.

He suggested that the Joint Chiefs of Staff insist on making the maximum use of French forces by giving them appropriate tasks and then trusting them to accomplish them.

He felt that we would get some opposition in this respect from the British.

SECRET

J.C.S. 51st Meeting
(Casablanca)

JOINT CHIEFS OF STAFF

MINUTES OF MEETING

Held on Thursday, January 14, 1943, at 1030

MEMBERS PRESENT

General G. C. Marshall, USA
Admiral E. J. King, USN
Lt. General H. H. Arnold, USA

SECRETARY

Brig. General J. R. Deane, USA

ADDITIONAL OFFICERS PRESENT

Lt. General B. B. Somervell, USA
Lt. General M. W. Clark, USA
Rear Admiral C. M. Cooke, Jr., USN
Brig. General A. C. Wedemeyer, USA
Commander R. E. Libby, USN

SECRET

ADMIRAL KING stated that the Prime Minister and the First Sea Lord had, in conversation with him, deplored the present state of the British Eastern Fleet, which they said was immobilized because it had been stripped of its destroyers and carriers. Just where the carriers are was not stated. H.M.S. Victorious, which was sent to the United States with nothing but green pilots, cannot be ready before the 1st of February. It is possible that they may have loaned us H.M.S. Victorious and offered us another carrier to further their apparent desire to keep this fleet immobilized. Admiral King feels that the British must make the naval effort to cut the Japanese lines of communications to Rangoon--which they now show no disposition to do. Although it is doubtful that the "limited objective" operations now contemplated are so dependent on the operations of the British Eastern Fleet as China appears to think, nevertheless these operations would greatly facilitate shipping to Calcutta. If the Chinese make movement of the British Eastern Fleet conditional to the undertaking of the contemplated operation, there is no question but that the British should make this move.

GENERAL SOMERVELL said that although the operation might possibly be supported by rail from Bombay, such support would be very slow and probably dangerous to rely upon.

GENERAL MARSHALL said the Chinese feared Japanese seaborne reinforcement via Rangoon and inquired what was needed to counter this threat.

ADMIRAL KING replied that the British Eastern Fleet should be sufficient, particularly as we are keeping the Japanese well occupied elsewhere. He felt that the British should move as many elements of this Fleet as they could cover with their available destroyers. Admiral Helfrich had told Admiral King that he had been urged by the British to go to Australia, where he has two cruisers and two or three destroyers operating under Admiral Carpender.

He had inquired as to what the British Eastern Fleet could be expected to do. Admiral King had replied that he had no information, but that when and if this Fleet moved to Trincomalee, Admiral King would send him back the Dutch ships. Such a move would help to clarify the complicated command set-up in the Southwest Pacific.

SECRET

ADMIRAL KING further remarked that the British Eastern Fleet served no purpose, so far as he could see, basing at Kilindini, but that the British would probably insist that they could not be moved because of a lack of destroyers. He felt that pressure should be brought on them to cover the shipping lines to Calcutta necessary for the projected operation.

With regard to submarines in the Indian Ocean and the Bay of Bengal, the British and Dutch together have a limited number--less than 10. In anticipation of a British demand for additional submarines, ADMIRAL KING is willing to base six at Trincomalee. Before this can be done, a tender should be sent there.

Further discussion developed that U. S. submarines basing at Fremantle could probably operate in the Bay of Bengal as well as in their present operating areas.

GENERAL ARNOLD said that he believed an additional group of heavy bombers should be sent to General Stilwell in order to build up his available heavy bombers to a total of two groups. He believes that these bombers will return more dividends operating in this theater than in the eastern Mediterranean.

ADMIRAL KING remarked that it was of great importance to open up a lower altitude route to China and that an increase in the number of medium bombers assigned this theater would make it possible to attack Japanese shipping in occupied Chinese ports.

In discussing the best line of procedure to adopt at the forthcoming conference, ADMIRAL KING stressed the importance of maintaining the initiative in our hands. He believes that it is essential to agree upon Anglo-American world-wide strategy, the basic concept, before permitting any discussion of details. The United Nations are now in a position to take the initiative in the war; it is essential to fix in the minds of the British the fact that the basic issue must be determined before going into details. The United States now has the principal power; therefore, we should take the lead.

GENERAL CLARK, in reply to a question from General Marshall, said that although it was not possible to dispose landing craft along the Mediterranean coast unknown to the Germans, in his opinion this did

SECRET

not preclude their use for the BRIMSTONE operation, inasmuch as the Axis could not know the objective specifically. While they would undoubtedly be under occasional attack, the real danger is from dive bombers; if disposed west of Algiers, they would be immune from these aircraft. He agreed with Admiral King's impression that there was a number of usable small ports where these craft might be loaded. Installation of additional airfields in North Africa will not disclose our intentions, inasmuch as General Eisenhower has been instructed that these fields should be spotted for general use and not specifically for the operation.

ADMIRAL KING remarked that the British concept of bringing troops from the U. K. and from the U. S. for such an operation was designed for surprise, but that it also resulted in building up a greater excess of troops in North Africa with a corresponding diminution of troops which could be based in the U. K. for projected operations on the Continent. He felt that the British were fully aware of this fact and, in view of their known opposition to any Continental operations, this gave them a good "out."

GENERAL CLARK said that it was his belief that operations against the Brest Peninsula would be very hazardous, would require overwhelming air support, extensive naval support, and immediate and heavy follow up. Such an operation should not be undertaken without adequate preparation. Although many of our troops needed battle training, he believes that they were fully capable of standing up to the German defense. He believed that, if successful, operations against the Brest Peninsula would have far greater results than a successful BRIMSTONE operation.

GENERAL ARNOLD said that maximum air effort from England could seriously limit the German air effort against the Brest Peninsula operation. Current German tactics in opposition to Flying Fortresses was producing a heavy attrition of the German Air Forces. If they persist in these tactics, the German Air Force will be practically eliminated within a year.

GENERAL SOMERVELL stated that it probably would be possible to transport 300,000 U. S. troops to the U. K. by September provided movements to Africa were suspended. He believes this a more accurate figure than the 150,000 estimated by the British. He stated that based on present submarine losses, we shall be able to move fewer troops in 1944

SECRET

than we can in 1943 despite the shipbuilding program, and that unless every possible means--including an effective air offensive against submarine bases, building yards and assembly points, and effective commando raids in force against the bases--is used, we shall be faced with a diminishing effort. If we succeed in opening the Mediterranean, we can probably increase present estimates of 1,000,000 troops moved this year by 150,000. He pointed out that stabilization of the North African situation would not greatly reduce shipping commitments in the Middle East area because of forthcoming commitments in support of Turkey, movement of U. S. troops into Burma, and supply of existing positions. He justified his average turn-around of $2\frac{1}{2}$ months on the basis that in 1943 Pacific troop movements will require approximately the same tonnage as those in the Atlantic.

GENERAL ARNOLD said that he did not believe that the British had ever had a definite bombing program. In view of the large build up with U. S. bombers in the U. K. to a force which will greatly exceed the British bombing force, he felt that the Combined Chiefs of Staff should establish a priority bombing program.

After considerable discussion of the existing command set-up in the European Theater of Operations, it was agreed:
- (a) That the Joint Chiefs of Staff should recommend that the Combined Chiefs of Staff establish a priority bombing program;
- (b) That Air Marshal Harris should operate the bombers in the U. K. (all under his command) under a directive from the Combined Chiefs of Staff setting forth objectives and technique;
- (c) That upon the successful conclusion of the Tunisian operation, it will probably be desirable to establish two separate theaters in Europe (the Mediterranean and the U. K.-French theaters);
- (d) That any operation against the Continent must be a combined operation which must receive the full cooperation and support of the British.

SECRET

J.C.S. 52nd Meeting
(Casablanca)

JOINT CHIEFS OF STAFF

MINUTES OF MEETING

Held at Anfa Camp on Saturday,
January 16, 1943, at 0915.

MEMBERS PRESENT

General G. C. Marshall, USA
Admiral E. J. King, USN
Lt. General H. H. Arnold, USA

SECRETARY

Brig. General J. R. Deane, USA

ADDITIONAL OFFICERS PRESENT

Lt. General B. B. Somervell, USA
Rear Admiral C. M. Cooke, Jr., USN
Brig. General A. C. Wedemeyer, USA
Colonel J. E. Smart, USA

SECRET

GENERAL ARNOLD stated that priority of bombing targets was determined in Britain by a committee composed of RAF officers, RAF Economic Warfare Representatives, plus one United States Army Air Forces Representative. The list of targets so determined was then sent to General Eisenhower for approval and after approval to General Eaker, who selected objectives from this list which weather and other conditions made it possible for him to reach. As to choosing between targets in France or in Germany, the bombers preferred targets in Germany because they encountered considerably less fighter opposition than they did over targets in France. General Eaker already has eight airplanes equipped with the new H2SL device, which is the forerunner of the latest precision bombing by radio beam equipment. It is expected that use of this equipment will permit precision bombing regardless of weather and will enable new low altitude bombing above the overcast when such weather conditions occur. In answer to a question from Admiral King, General Arnold stated that there were eight radio stations in southern England from which the necessary radio beams were transmitted.

With respect to night bombing, GENERAL ARNOLD said that two groups of United States bombers in the United Kingdom were now equipped with flame dampers, but that much more training was required for night bombing than for day bombing in order to keep the losses down to a reasonable figure; therefore, our forces were not yet fully prepared for night bombing.

GENERAL MARSHALL said that it was satisfactory to General Eisenhower to transfer General Andrews to England at any time in order to take command there; it was contemplated that General Brereton would relieve General Andrews of his present command. All that remained to do was to prepare a directive for General Andrews. Under this directive Air Marshal Portal would be given operational control (i.e., designation of objectives and times of attack) over United States Air Forces operating from the United Kingdom.

ADMIRAL KING pointed out that it was essential in framing this directive that "operational control" be clearly defined.

During discussion as to how best to present the views of the Joint United States Chiefs of Staff regarding proposed Mediterranean operations to the Combined Chiefs of Staff, ADMIRAL KING said that the

SECRET

Combined Chiefs of Staff should note that there is now in North Africa a large number of troops--probably sufficient for the contemplated operation. These troops should not sit idle. Timing of the proposed operation is of great importance. He believed that troops in North Africa now not actively engaged in Tunisia could be trained in amphibious warfare, in order to advance the date by which we could undertake either the operations against Sardinia or the operation against Sicily, whichever might be decided upon. Of the two, he felt Sicily was much more decisive and more complete in itself, inasmuch as little was to be gained by the Sardinian operation. If the premise that the Sicilian operation can be done by the troops now in North Africa is accepted, it should be possible to continue the flow of troops to the United Kingdom. On this basis, we could both advance the date of the Sicilian operation and continue our preparations for a Continental operation, continuing to send troops and landing craft to the United Kingdom.

GENERAL MARSHALL said that General Eisenhower had changed his viewpoint as a result of his experiences to date and now felt that it was imperative that we organize for ROUNDUP on a large scale. He now feels that approximately twice the force he originally contemplated will be required. He feels it unsound to count on more than one trip from landing craft used in the first wave, as only a very small proportion of the initial wave is likely to be available for a second trip; therefore, the numbers of landing craft initially provided must be many more than originally conceived.

GENERAL SOMERVELL said that General Patton informed him that losses in small landing craft were about 20 percent in the Casablanca landing.

ADMIRAL COOKE informed the Joint Chiefs of Staff that the British Planners have made detailed studies of both the Sardinia and Sicily operations, which the Joint Chiefs of Staff should see. He felt it essential to bring some additional troops from the United States, even if they were used only as replacements for troops now in North Africa after the latter had been trained in amphibious operations. It is necessary to retain a strong United States force on the border of Spanish Morocco.

The greatest bottleneck appears to be lack of harbor space for assembling landing craft in the Mediterranean. Preliminary investigations

SECRET

indicated that not more than 34 LST's could be accommodated west of Tunisia; the remainder would have to be east of there. These investigations had included eight ports. Admiral Hall was making a survey of the possibilities of accommodating LST's on the west coast.

ADMIRAL KING said that, if necessary, the risk of nesting or banking the landing craft should be accepted.

ADMIRAL COOKE said that, inasmuch as an amphibious division was already here and in view of the possibility of training troops not now operating in Tunisia, he felt the British estimate of a three-month differential between mounting of the Sardinian and Sicilian operations was too large, particularly if the Tunisian operations are not completed before May.

GENERAL ARNOLD questioned the British statement that a Brest operation meant fewer heavy bombers in England because of additional requirement for light and medium bombers.

GENERAL SOMERVELL, responding to a request from General Marshall that he outline the mechanics of the Sicilian operation, said that the key to the situation was to make heavy use of landing craft. We now have available 300-foot, 150-foot, and 105-foot craft which we did not have before. The fact that these can be unloaded over the beaches rapidly materially changes the type of the operation inasmuch as port facilities are not required. He felt that by June it should be possible to lift 90,000 troops in the initial assault. These craft could then return to North Africa for reloading. Allowing for losses, the second wave should be able to expeditiously lift 60,000 troops and some equipment. If the Navy concurs in the use of combat-loaded transports sufficient to lift 32,000 additional troops, the requirement during the following four to six weeks would be reduced to approximately 38,000 troops. This method requires unloading lots of equipment over the beaches, but increases the strength of the first wave by 32,000 troops. Once the landing had been accomplished, supply would be by means of coasters from the United Kingdom and from East Africa in order to permit the use of big ships elsewhere and to reduce losses of cargo.

He agreed with Admiral Cooke regarding the training possibilities, with General Clark regarding possibilities of training in the Casablanca

SECRET

area, and with General Patton as to the expected reaction of Spanish Morocco. He felt that the troops now in the Casablanca area were retrograding and should be actively employed by training them for these operations in order to keep them fit.

Once the landing was accomplished, the landing craft should be removed from the Mediterranean to the United Kingdom, which movement should require about one month. It is essential to keep enough landing craft in the United Kingdom so that training can continue. If we send only fifty LST's to the Pacific, we should be able to accomplish the foregoing; however, if operations in the Mediterranean will prevent operations against the Continent, he felt that they should not be undertaken.

ADMIRAL COOKE said that the LST program should furnish 198 LST's by March 15 and 15 a month thereafter. One hundred were now allocated to the Pacific and 107 to the Atlantic, including British allocations. More than 50 will be required in the Pacific. At least two months were required after completion to make these craft ready for operations. The British now have no crews with which to man 11 craft which will be finished this month and have offered them to us for a month to be used in training. He felt that as many landing craft as the ports would accommodate could be gotten here.

ADMIRAL COOKE cautioned against the tendency to "look back," saying that promising developments in amphibious weapons--the Army amphibious truck, the amphibious tractor, etc.--greatly accelerated unloading. Unloading of LST's and LCI's over the beaches is completely practicable, but he felt it would be disastrous to attempt to do so in the case of combat-loaded transports, which would undoubtedly be sunk by submarines or by air before they could be unloaded.

GENERAL WEDEMEYER said that he believed that, if we subscribed to the British concept, we should disperse our forces in an area which was neither vital nor final. We should examine a proposition to determine how success in the proposed operation would improve our position. The effort could be justified if it resulted in a material saving in shipping. Admiral Cunningham had stated that he would run Mediterranean convoys as soon as Tunisia had been cleared--that Sicily was not essential. He felt the Sicilian operation would require up to 12 divisions

SECRET

The British arguments as to Axis capabilities for moving reinforcements south were, he felt, specious. He believed a ratio of three to seven more nearly accurate than the one to seven ratio which they advanced. Should the Germans move five to ten divisions into Italy, operations in that part of the Mediterranean would, he believed, require a major effort on our part which would vitiate a Continental operation. He felt our best procedure was to continue a heavy bombing offensive against Germany's lines of communication across France, concentrating particularly on eight marshalling yards. After that, we should proceed with an operation against the Brest Peninsula.

ADMIRAL KING said that he understood that Admiral Cunningham would undertake Mediterranean convoys once Tunisia had been cleared, but anticipated heavy losses. He felt we should determine first what constitutes the "General Plan" for the defeat of Germany, and thereafter determine how the Sicilian operation fits into this plan. Perhaps the bridgehead should be at Brest, perhaps elsewhere in northern Europe. The Sicilian operation is opportune but not definitive. It is also essential that we work out a "General Plan" for the defeat of Japan.

ADMIRAL COOKE said that the British view was that Germany could be defeated on land only on the Russian front and that, therefore, it was essential that we assist the Russians by operations this summer. As to Japan, they say they will use the British Fleet after the defeat of Germany but do not say how or where.

GENERAL MARSHALL said that we wanted to keep the German Army engaged with the Russian Army and we wanted to make a landing on the Continent. Can we do that in time to support Russia this summer? Will any other operation destroy our ability to make a Continental landing, our main objective? We must insure that it does not. If we do Sicily, we might not have the means to do anything on the Continent before October. We must determine what must be done to support Russia this summer. If it is essential that we attack, we must determine where. Everything now building up in the United Kingdom is composed of raw troops, which, however, are better than previous unseasoned troops. Some loaders could be moved from the African theater. Although he favored the Continental operation, he believed it impossible before August.

GENERAL WEDEMEYER said that, after the completion of the TORCH operations, approximately 250,000 troops would be required to consolidate

SECRET

from the Atlantic to Tunisia. The British require about the same from Tripolitania to Cairo. They must in addition move troops in behind Turkey. These dispositions will leave no troops for the Central Mediterranean. We do not desire to put more troops there. If we undertake the Sicilian operation, it must be in sufficient strength to assure success. He estimated that almost a million troops would be required in the African theater.

GENERAL SOMERVELL said that the big gain to be expected from the Sicilian operation was a saving of 1,860,000 tons of shipping resulting from opening the Mediterranean; that the Germans could be expected to make a determined effort against Mediterranean convoys from Sicily and elsewhere.

GENERAL ARNOLD said that if an air umbrella was maintained over the convoys (which would require fighter bases every 100 miles along the Mediterranean coast), the losses should be low; but that at night and during bad weather the fighters could offer little protection. The capture of Sicily would remove an imminent threat to these convoys.

ADMIRAL KING pointed out that one of the purposes of taking Sicily was to push the Axis Air back. It would become a base from which to interdict Axis Air from Sardinia and from Italy. Further, it removes the danger of dive bombers. He said that, in considering the likelihood of getting convoys through the Mediterranean with Sicily in Axis hands, the British record in keeping the English Channel open should not be taken too seriously, inasmuch as the type of shipping was materially different. In his opinion, the Sicilian operation was worth the effort; the Sardinian operation is not. He is opposed to the use of combat-loaded transports in either operation. The main question is one of timing--the balance is delicate--but he thinks the operation can be done In response to an objection from General Wedemeyer that up to 12 divisions would be required, he pointed out that adequate forces should be available from those already in North Africa; divisions now occupied in Tunis could be moved to the Spanish Moroccan frontier for rest and rehabilitation; and we should be able to utilize French troops It is essential that we convince the British that they must fully trust the French troops.

GENERAL WEDEMEYER said that we would have seven divisions and the British about four divisions between Tunisia and the Atlantic

SECRET

Placing four French and two U.S. divisions near the Moroccan border would release three U.S. and possibly four British divisions. General Alexander has approximately ten, three of which he needs in Libya and three in Cairo; he should send at least an armored corps to General Wilson in the Turkish rear. He probably could give us two divisions for the Sicilian operation.

ADMIRAL KING proposed that, before the Joint Chiefs of Staff agreed to the Sicilian operation, British concurrence to our plans in the Pacific should be assured. Therefore, the objectives of the Sicilian operation should be specified and the point emphasized that it must be mounted in time to offer real assistance to Russia, remembering that, even if completion of the Tunis operation were delayed, that operation still engaged German forces and contributed toward opening the Mediterranean.

GENERAL ARNOLD said that, in view of the British attitude toward operations on the Continent in 1943 he doubted that any could be mounted this year; therefore, a Mediterranean operation of some sort was a necessity in order to keep the Russians encouraged.

ADMIRAL KING, agreeing, said that this emphasized the necessity of obtaining from the British their general plan, i.e. what they propose to do, when they propose to do it—in particular as to Continental operations.

GENERAL SOMERVELL said that, in order to increase material aid to Russia, effort was being made to add 25 ships per month to shipping to Russia to a total of 150, and that this shipping apparently can come only from savings resulting from opening the Mediterranean. The British have already taken from Indian Ocean shipping to the Army there, 52 ships for civilian trade. He feels it essential that additional ships for Russia must come from British shipping.

ADMIRAL KING recommended that we obtain from the British their general plan and let them take the initiative in the discussion of operations in their strategic sphere. We must also present to them our general plan for the Pacific, a large consideration of which must be the possibility of war between Russia and Japan. As to that, Russia will not force the issue; however, it is vital to Japan that she seize the Maritime Provinces in order that she may be secure. The key to our successful

SECRET

attack on the Japanese homeland is the geographical position and the manpower of China; if we attempt to beat our way up through the Netherlands East Indies, we shall make extremely slow progress. England can best operate against Japan in Burma, Thailand, and Indo-China, and should leave to the United States the "managing" of China.

In response to a question as to the ability of the United Nations promptly to direct their forces against Japan in the event of the defeat of Germany, ADMIRAL KING remarked that Great Britain might send her Fleet and could use some Indian divisions, but could do little else until the European situation was stabilized. Therefore, unless the U. S. and Britain make some definite move toward the defeat of Germany, Russia will dominate the peace table.

SECRET

J.C.S. 53rd Meeting
(Casablanca)

JOINT CHIEFS OF STAFF

MINUTES OF MEETING

Held at Anfa Camp on Sunday,
January 17, 1943, at 0930.

MEMBERS PRESENT

General G. C. Marshall, USA
Admiral E. J. King, USN
Lt. General H. H. Arnold, USA

SECRETARY

Brig. General J. R. Deane, USA

ADDITIONAL OFFICERS PRESENT

Lt. General B. B. Somervell, USA
Rear Admiral C. M. Cooke, Jr., USN
Brig. General A. C. Wedemeyer, USA
Commander R. E. Libby, USN

SECRET

ADMIRAL KING read a despatch, summarizing the situation in the Aleutian Islands and in the South Pacific, which said, among other things, that 30 Japanese aircraft had been shot down.

GENERAL ARNOLD remarked that British estimates placed the current Japanese airplane strength at 2,500 first-line aircraft, about 500 below the number estimated by our Intelligence Services. Both British and our estimates of current Japanese strength indicate a rapid decline in their air strength. Continued attrition at present rates will seriously affect future Japanese operations.

ADMIRAL COOKE reported that the Combined Staff Planners had agreed upon the Pacific concept for 1943 except as concerned operations in Burma, which they believe could not be mounted this year. Admiral Cooke feared that if the operation is not planned for 1943 China may drop out of the war; therefore, in his opinion it is essential that the operation be planned to commence not later than November, 1943. He had informed the Combined Planners that it was not the intention of the United States to undertake all the operations set forth in the plan simultaneously, although some part of the Gilberts-Marshalls-Truk operation might be initiated during the progress of the Rabaul operation, which is estimated to require from two to five months. The British Planners proposed to furnish specific information as to what they proposed in Burma, both now and in the future, for the information of the Combined Chiefs of Staff. The British contention is that sufficient naval forces and landing craft cannot be made available. Admiral Cooke disagreed and had told the British Planners that by the time the operation was to be mounted, he felt that sufficient landing craft would be available.

In answer to General Marshall's question as to the effect failure to do Operation RAVENOUS would have on Operation ANAKIM, **ADMIRAL COOKE** stated that our air activity would be greatly hampered inasmuch as one of the purposes of Operation RAVENOUS was to establish airfields in the region for our prospective use. As he understood the British proposals, they were that nothing be done until November, 1944. Although he had agreed to list forces required for the ANAKIM operation, he would prefer not to have this list appear in the plan.

ADMIRAL KING remarked that we should certainly include Operation ANAKIM in the Pacific plan. Whether or not it is carried out fully will depend upon the situation then existing, but at any rate it should be planned. General Brooke had said that two African divisions were being shifted to the Indian Theater and preparations for the utilization of the Indian troops were in hand; Vice Admiral Mountbatten had said that landing craft were being provided in India; there must be some objective for these moves. He proposed to ask Admiral Pound to base part of the Eastern Fleet at Ceylon and would release the Dutch cruisers and destroyers now operating through Sicily to support the Eastern Fleet if they moved there; he would also arrange that six U. S. submarines now operating from Fremantle cover the northern end of the Straits of Malacca. He feels it essential to get some British naval activity under way in the Bay of Bengal. Since the Japanese Fleet is now largely contained in the Pacific, it is unlikely that they can detach much naval strength for operations in the Bay of Bengal. He suggested that the Pacific situation should be discussed with the Combined Chiefs of Staff at this morning's meeting when the United States Chiefs of Staff should insist that Operation RAVENOUS be carried out and that Operation ANAKIM be initiated not later than November 1, 1943. This operation is essential because of its importance to China and because the geographical position and manpower of China is the key to the defeat of Japan, just as the geographical position and manpower of Russia is the key to the defeat of Germany. Therefore, it is impossible to omit these operations from our Pacific concept. Even if the question is not to be settled at this time, he felt it necessary to keep the British fully aware of the Pacific. The British proposal to do nothing in Burma until the end of next year he characterized as fantastic. The diminishing prospect of being able to use any air bases in Russia was a further reason which compelled us to operate in Burma.

GENERAL WEDEMEYER said that the British were firmly convinced that Germany would be defeated in 1943 and were, therefore, reluctant to take any resources away from the United Kingdom, in hopes that they would be able to conduct a successful Channel operation. He personally felt it essential that such an Operation RAVENOUS be done now when possible. The further they go with the operation, the less danger they will suffer from malaria when the rainy season starts. He felt it essential that the British be pressed to do everything they possibly could now.

GENERAL MARSHALL said that we were still faced with the Chinese reluctance to do anything. To carry out Operation RAVENOUS, the Chinese

SECRET

must start first. The target date for the completion of the deployment was March 1st. It would soon be too late to meet this date.

GENERAL MARSHALL informed the Joint Chiefs of Staff that Stalin had informed the President that he desired no U. S. personnel in Russia. The reconnaissance and survey contemplated by General Bradley could not now be carried out. Stalin does not wish to see General Marshall. The Russians will accept planes and materiel but no U. S. or British survey parties.

GENERAL SOMERVELL said that he and Admiral Mountbatten had discussed the British landing craft situation in detail since the last meeting. The principal contribution by Great Britain to the landing craft pool was some 600 L.C.A. (armored craft). Mountbatten concluded that 150 of these would be required for the Sicilian operation, leaving 450 in the United Kingdom for training and other purposes. Lord Mountbatten had not fully understood the decision of time required to rehabilitate landing craft--he had been talking about small craft whereas we had been talking about landing ships. He had had no knowledge that the engineers' amphibious force had completed repairs here in North Africa of landing craft utilized in the Operation TORCH. British training and combined operations were dislocated by the TORCH Operation and were now three months in arrears, but by August Admiral Mountbatten felt confident that he could man all available landing craft.

In Lord Mountbatten's opinion, any land attack must be led by L.C.A.'s, the tactics being to seek out a "soft spot" by a reconnaissance in force, and then to pour forces through the "soft spot" once found. It is apparent that more landing craft will be available than Lord Mountbatten had believed. Probably we can armor a considerable number of our smaller landing craft by September, but the number we could build by June would be insignificant. However, the British capacity in that direction should suffice.

GENERAL SOMERVELL said that he had reviewed with Lord Mountbatten certain plans for operations on the Continent. Planning for the Brest Peninsula had been investigated by considering four lines of opposition which might be reached, i.e., initial and expanded positions. For each line, more forces were required than could be supplied by the available ports. Therefore, it was concluded that the Brest plan was

SECRET

impracticable from a supply standpoint. The situation is becoming absolutely impossible if the report that the Germans had mined all the docks in the proposed area is true. On the other hand, operations at Cherbourg would be possible; the same factors which would make it relatively easy to hold, once captured, would make exploitation and expansion very difficult. Lord Mountbatten was in favor of capturing the Channel Islands both as stepping stones toward a prospective continual operation and as a base from which to operate against sea-borne supply to German submarine bases on the French coast. Lord Mountbatten stated he could capture the Channel Islands without help from the United States.

With respect to Sicily, discussion revealed that the batteries there were 4.6 inch and that the most feasible means of reducing them would be by parachute attack. These parachute troops would probably have to be carried in U. S. transport planes. Use of the L.C.A.'s would require moving them by combat-loaded transports. It was agreed that it was preferable that the landing craft should start from North Africa, and that it was not essential to use armored boats if full advantage was taken of the possibility of surprise. It is probable that all troops encountered in Sicily would be either first-class German troops or Italian troops heavily leavened with German troops so that they would be effective. There does not appear to be room in the Island for more than two additional divisions

ADMIRAL KING, pointing out that the key to the European situation was Russia, suggested coordinating all supply to Russia under one head and under one code name, placing one officer in general charge. This officer would then have the task of emphasizing the necessity for air action against German airfields in northern Norway.

After some discussion, it was agreed that the Russians would undoubtedly ask for additional heavy bombers, ostensibly for this purpose, and that the airfields could not be rendered ineffective by means other than a combined operation against them.

SECRET

J.C.S. 54th Meeting
(Casablanca)

JOINT CHIEFS OF STAFF

MINUTES OF MEETING

Held at Anfa Camp on Monday,
January 18, 1943, at 0930.

MEMBERS PRESENT

General G. C. Marshall, USA
Admiral E. J. King, USN
Lt. General H. H. Arnold, USA

SECRETARY

Brig. General J. R. Deane, USA

ADDITIONAL OFFICERS PRESENT

Lt. General B. B. Somervell, USA
Rear Admiral C. M. Cooke, Jr., USN
Brig. General J.E. Hull, USA
Brig. General A. C. Wedemeyer, USA
Colonel J. E. Smart, USA
Commander R. E. Libby, USN

SECRET

GENERAL MARSHALL read a despatch which said that the proposed freeze on 55 percent of the synthetic rubber program would reduce the high octane gasoline program by 5,000,000 barrels, the airplane program by 10,000 airplanes, and would delay the escort vessel program from two to three months. He recommended that the Joint Chiefs of Staff present a memorandum to the President and ask him to instruct Mr. Nelson not to authorize Mr. Jeffers' proposed procedure.

ADMIRAL KING remarked that he doubted that the President would agree to freeze the synthetic rubber program at the 20 percent level, inasmuch as political questions were involved.

ADMIRAL KING, recounting his conversation with the Prime Minister the previous evening, said that Mr. Churchill had committed himself to undertake ANAKIM in 1943 and that he was agreeable to Operation RAVENOUS, concerning which there still remains the question of Chinese cooperation. They had thoroughly discussed the submarine situation; and Mr. Churchill appeared agreeable to giving highest priority to bombing the submarine bases, building yards, and assembly points, although he said the United States must help. The Prime Minister objected to our "putting the cart before the horse" with respect to Pacific operations, and said we had refused to give the British accurate information as to our landing craft program and as to our dispositions in the Pacific. He appeared greatly concerned over our stand with respect to Pacific operations. With respect to the Burma operation, Admiral King had tried to explain to the Prime Minister his concept regarding the geographical position and manpower of China. The President was anxious to get additional airplanes to General Chennault, which could not be supplied unless the upper Burma Road is opened. Admiral King understands the purpose of RAVENOUS to be to open this upper Burma Road in order to improve communications to China. He feels that Chiang Kai-shek should be urged to move at once.

GENERAL SOMERVELL said that the tonnage question had been under discussion; that in view of the message the President had received from Stalin, General Marshall ought not to go to Moscow; that Mr. Hopkins had informed him that command of the 8th Army would pass to General Eisenhower as soon as this Army got into the Tunisian battle, Alexander becoming Eisenhower's Deputy Commander-in-Chief for the period of the actual battle, but that this proposal must come from the British.

SECRET

GENERAL MARSHALL, referring to the Burma operation, said that Sir John Dill believed General Wavell could move even if the Chinese did not; General Wavell might possibly be better off in this case in view of the limited logistic facilities available to his forces. He believed the Generalissimo might reverse his present stand provided he receives reassurances from the Prime Minister rather than from General Wavell-- that the deal was not completely closed. Two cargo ships have already sailed for General Stilwell, and the remainder will depart shortly. Troop ships are sailing today.

GENERAL WEDEMEYER said if the Ramgarh force were to come down at this time, building the road as they progressed, it would greatly facilitate later coordinated action. Any landing fields that Wavell can establish by this movement will be of great assistance to a later advance. As to the Mediterranean operation, he said the British Planners now tended to urge Sardinia in lieu of Sicily, contending that Sardinia would accomplish as much toward the security of Mediterranean shipping as will Sicily. If the First Sea Lord's statements in the minutes of yesterday's meeting are correct, General Wedemeyer does not believe we are justified in undertaking either operation.

ADMIRAL COOKE pointed out the necessity of discussing with the British Chiefs of Staff, points in which the President is intimately concerned, in order that his stay here need not be prolonged. He objected to the British tendency to go into detail and to concern themselves with operations in our strategic theater which were really not their concern. The Kiska operation is an example. They argue that after we have seized Rabaul, the Combined Chiefs of Staff should then dictate future operations and their timing. Admiral Cooke objects to this. They have rightly kept us in the dark as to certain of their operations in their own theater, and should accord us the same privilege. They insist that we set forth in detail the forces we propose to employ, and, yet, do not use the same system in listing their forces as we do. As far as the Planners are concerned, the main point at issue seems to be: "Shall we defeat Germany first?" or: "Shall we bring the war to a successful conclusion expeditiously?" The British desire to assemble in the United Kingdom sufficient landing craft to move on to the Continent should Germany crack. Admiral Cooke objects to having forces static in the United Kingdom instead of employing them actively against Japan, and has

SECRET

made landing craft allocations on that basis. These craft are badly needed in the Pacific for General MacArthur and for our planned operations. Because of shortage in naval ships and landing craft, the British demur at the Burma operation. Admiral Cooke thinks that we can make landing craft available by that time and that some auxiliary aircraft carriers will also be available. We have allocated nothing in landing craft not scheduled to be completed before the 15th of March. It is difficult to specifically allocate forces in advance for each separate operation in the Pacific. All that can be done practically is to allocate our production to areas and not to specific campaigns. Although deliveries have been delayed, he believes present allocations to be sufficient for planned operations. As a matter of actual fact, the British cannot use in the United Kingdom as many landing craft as are already allocated there.

ADMIRAL COOKE reiterated that he saw no reason why the British should examine our proposed Pacific campaign in detail, and that if they insist on doing so, we should pin them down as to what forces they will contribute toward the defeat of Japan. He felt that we should take the position that details of our operations were not a proper subject for the Agenda of these meetings as it was essential that we get on with combined considerations.

ADMIRAL KING said that we felt it necessary to take action to secure Mediterranean communications and that the British were anxious to do something quickly in order to satisfy the Russians. He feared that if we undertook the Sardinia operation, we would be asked to do the Sicilian operation later. As to our Pacific strategy, we should stand on the paper we have submitted. The British have always been opposed to our Pacific proposals; nevertheless, in spite of our Pacific operations, we can bring against Germany, either in Sicily or on the Brest Peninsula, everything that the British are willing to do. They have not yet clarified their own position as to what they propose on the Continent. The Burma operation is at present a long-range concept. He expects the British to make an issue of the shipping to the Pacific and to attempt to continue to sit in review on our operations. Inasmuch as the Prime Minister has committed himself to RAVENOUS and to ANAKIM and to putting the maximum practicable air force into China, Admiral King feels that no effort should be spared to carry out these operations as planned.

SECRET

The President and the Prime Minister should inform the Generalissimo that RAVENOUS is not the all-out Burma campaign, that this will be set up at a later date, and that by this time naval forces will be made available. With respect to the Mediterranean, Admiral King is utterly opposed to the Sardinian operation, but feels that the Sicilian operation should be undertaken since troops and means will be available, since Sicily is the strategic location, and since the alternative--sending excess troops from the Mediterranean Theater to the United Kingdom--accomplishes no real result.

SECRET

J.C.S. 55th Meeting
(Casablanca)

JOINT CHIEFS OF STAFF

MINUTES OF MEETING

Held at Anfa Camp on Tuesday,
January 19, 1943, at 0930.

MEMBERS PRESENT

General G. C. Marshall, USA
Admiral E. J. King, USN
Lt. General H. H. Arnold, USA

SECRETARY

Brig. General J. R. Deane, USA

ADDITIONAL OFFICERS PRESENT

Lt. General B. B. Somervell, USA
Rear Admiral C. M. Cooke, Jr., USN
Brig. General J.E. Hull, USA
Brig. General A. C. Wedemeyer, USA
Colonel J. E. Smart, USA
Commander R. E. Libby, USN

SECRET

ADMIRAL KING informed the Joint Chiefs of Staff that 11 destroyers had been transferred from escort duty in the Sea Frontiers for use as ocean escorts, in order to improve the position with respect to ocean escorts.

The Joint Chiefs of Staff discussed C.C.S. 155, the draft memorandum of "Conduct of the War in 1943," and agreed upon certain modifications which they would present to the Combined Chiefs of Staff. During the discussion, ADMIRAL KING remarked that he saw no objection to continuing in the Mediterranean beyond Sicily if such operations required no more resources than were then present in the Mediterranean Theater.

GENERAL MARSHALL read a revised draft of the memorandum to the President from the Joint Chiefs of Staff concerning the synthetic rubber program which was approved and which is attached hereto as Annex "A."

ADMIRAL KING outlined his proposals as to the command set-up in West Africa which he favored as a result of his conversations with Admiral Glassford. He would propose to the Combined Chiefs of Staff that Vice Admiral Collinet, now in command of the naval forces at Dakar, assume the status of a Naval District Commander and that the limits of his command extend from the northern boundary of Sierra Leone to Cape Bojador. Vice Admiral Collinet, in his status of Naval District Commander, would operate directly under Vice Admiral Pegram who, from his headquarters at Freetown, would have command of the West African Sea Frontier. Admiral King pointed out that Gambia, lying in Vice Admiral Collinet's district, would be under his command. Admiral King foresaw some difficulty with the British concerning control of air activity in the French district, and said that the British probably would insist on putting in their own aircraft because they did not trust the French. He urged the necessity of placing full trust and confidence in the French Army, Navy, and Air Forces and in equipping these forces as rapidly as may be.

GENERAL MARSHALL agreed, saying that he thought it impracticable to go halfway with the French. They must either be trusted completely or not at all. He had every reason to believe that certain French divisions, when equipped, would be excellent. He felt the objections to placing full trust in the French were more with respect to technical equipment than anything else. He foresaw difficulties as to control, i.e., command, but felt that these problems could be handled as they arose.

SECRET

During a discussion as to when the President would be able to leave, it was concluded that Presidential action would be required upon the following four items:
  (a) Approved strategy.
  (b) Attitude toward the French.
  (c) Aid to Russia.
  (d) Turkey.

GENERAL MARSHALL said that the President had not disagreed to the proposal of the Prime Minister that operations in support of Turkey be entirely British. The President would be interested in the proposals concerning aid to Russia, but General Marshall believed he should be informed that the Joint Chiefs of Staff were opposed to "destroying ourselves" in the attempt to get ships to Murmansk against extremely strong opposition. In reply to a statement by Admiral King that the President wanted Turkey in the war as a passive rather than an active belligerent, in order that the United Nations might utilize her air bases to attack the Axis and her territory to expedite supplying Russia, General Marshall said that this passive attitude on the part of Turkey was purely a diplomatic question; if and when they enter the war, it will be a military matter to see to it that they do not advance.

ADMIRAL KING remarked that he expected that political problems concerning the French would delay the President longer than would the business of the Combined Chiefs of Staff.

The Joint Chiefs of Staff next considered C.C.S. 156, "Suggested Procedure for Dealing with the Agenda of the Conference." ADMIRAL COOKE said that it was important to set the target date for Operation HUSKY, and that the plan should be set up well in advance of preparation and training of the forces involved. In view of the complicated nature of the operation, it is essential to indicate, insofar as we can, who will provide the forces in specific areas. One of the difficulties with TORCH has been that the plans were not adequate, and that many changes had been made while the operation was being mounted. A planning staff, not preoccupied with the battle in Tunisia, should be set up now for this operation.

He said that item 2 could produce no more than a study which would result in an approximation of what additional losses will result

SECRET

in convoys caused by escort requirements for HUSKY. With respect to command organization in the Mediterranean, Admiral Cooke had informed the Combined Planners as to the proposed command arrangements on which the Combined Chiefs of Staff must reach general agreement concerning spheres of influence, etc.

ADMIRAL KING said he proposed a western Mediterranean area under command of a United States Navy Flag Officer who will operate directly under Admiral Cunningham. Western North Africa would be included in this command. The British had approved this proposal.

GENERAL MARSHALL reviewed the proposed army command set-up in the Tunisian area, and said that it was highly desirable that, after completion of the Tripoli operation, the French occupy that country. When the Axis had been cleared from North Africa, General Alexander will cease to be Deputy Commander-in-Chief; the 8th Army will probably move to the rear of Turkey. He agreed that it was necessary to establish a planning staff for HUSKY, and to determine where and when training for this operation should be set up.

"ANNEX A"

January 18, 1943

MEMORANDUM FOR THE PRESIDENT:

1. The U. S. Joint Chiefs of Staff have received information that Mr. Nelson has recommended the outright allotment of all materials and equipment necessary for the construction of 55 percent of the entire synthetic rubber program and that Justice Byrnes is about to render a decision in the matter. In the fall Mr. Nelson made such an allotment for 20 percent of materials and equipment necessary for the rubber program. The Joint Chiefs of Staff gave their approval to this allotment even though it was realized that it might interfere with other strictly military programs. We are convinced, however, that the effect of the proposed increase to 55 percent of the program will have serious effects on the high octane gas, escort vessel and aircraft programs.

2. Just prior to our departure from the United States a memorandum to you was prepared by the Joint Chiefs of Staff which remained undelivered by reason of Admiral Leahy's illness. In this memorandum we called attention to the fact that an extension of the present allocation

SECRET

beyond 20 percent would bring about a loss in delivery in 1943 of approximately 5,000,000 barrels of high octane gas, over 10,000 aircraft, and two to three months delay in the completion of the escort vessel program, all vital to the war effort. We are convinced that the result would very seriously jeopardize the effective prosecution of the war. For instance, the most serious doubt at the present moment is whether or not sufficient escort vessels can be provided during the next five months: (1) to permit the Russian convoys to be stepped up from 42 days to 28-- which now appears practically impossible; (2) to enable the HUSKY (S) Operation to be mounted; and (3) to permit HUSKY to be mounted without necessitating the running of the Freetown convoys without escort--as TORCH compelled us to do, resulting in heavy losses. A delay of a month in the present escort program would have most serious consequences. The dangers of reductions in high octane gas (already a shortage) and planes on the eve of heavy operations are evident.

We, therefore, recommend that Justice Byrnes be issued instructions in accordance with the telegram suggested below:

> TELEGRAM TO BYRNES, WASHINGTON: "Proposed extension of freeze in rubber program from 20 to 55 percent of total will have serious effects on other programs whose successful completion is necessary for the effective prosecution of the war. Over-riding priorities will not be granted to more than 20 percent of the rubber program above escort vessels, aircraft, high octane gas, and other items in the number one group of the military program of the Chiefs of Staff."

For the Joint Chiefs of Staff:

(Signed) G. C. MARSHALL,
Chief of Staff, U. S. Army.

SECRET

J.C.S. 56th Meeting
(Casablanca)

JOINT CHIEFS OF STAFF

MINUTES OF MEETING

Held at Anfa Camp on Wednesday,
January 20, 1943, at 0900.

MEMBERS PRESENT

General G. C. Marshall, USA
Admiral E. J. King, USN
Lt. General H. H. Arnold, USA

SECRETARY

Brig. General J. R. Deane, USA

ADDITIONAL OFFICERS PRESENT

Lt. General B. B. Somervell, USA
Rear Admiral C. M. Cooke, Jr., USN
Brig. General J.E. Hull, USA
Brig. General A. C. Wedemeyer, USA
Colonel J. E. Smart, USA
Commander R. E. Libby, USN

SECRET

The Joint Chiefs of Staff discussed certain possibilities in connection with the proposed movements of the President.

GENERAL MARSHALL gave some background information on the Lend-Lease situation with respect to Turkey. It is proposed that the Prime Minister will proceed to Cyprus to meet Turkish authorities there. It is hoped that he can induce Turkey to enter the war on the side of the United Nations. Our objection to the proposed method of handling Lend-Lease commitments is that we are, in fact, surrendering control of U. S. allocations to Turkey since we have no assurance of where the material is ultimately sent. He remarked, however, that the main purpose of bringing pressure to bear on Turkey was to ultimately permit the operation of American bombers from Turkish soil; since the object at stake was so important, we could afford to make concessions concerning the method of allocating material to this theater. He felt that, in any event, the Combined Chiefs of Staff should have an opportunity to see requests submitted to the C.M.A.B. by the British, in order that after General Brooke and General Marshall had determined what they were shortly to undertake to provide Turkey, the C.M.A.B. could inform the Combined Chiefs of Staff as to the practicability of these proposals.

ADMIRAL KING said that in addition to our present commitments to furnish equipment to the French in North Africa, to Russia, and to China, and supplying our own needs, we were apparently about to undertake additional commitments to Turkey. He inquired what we should do in order to insure that Turkey understood the real source of this material. He wonders if a U. S. representative should not accompany the Prime Minister in order to handle American interests and point up the fact that the United States is directly involved. If Britain assumes responsibility for processing bids for supplying Turkey, they should properly deal with the Combined Munitions Assignments Board. In Admiral King's opinion, these requests should go through the Combined Chiefs of Staff. He is opposed to permitting the British to go direct to the Combined Munitions Assignments Board, obtain a decision from that Board, and then inform the Joint Chiefs of Staff what had been done. His main concern is to insure that all material allocated for this purpose is put to use against the enemy.

ADMIRAL COOKE was of the opinion that if requests from Turkey were to continue, they should process their own. He felt, however, that for initial bargaining the proposed arrangement was satisfactory.

SECRET

GENERAL MARSHALL said that he thought the British might undertake operations in the Dodecanese concurrently with our operations against Sicily, utilizing landing craft assigned to the Middle East for this purpose. It was brought out in subsequent discussion that the Middle East at present has landing craft sufficient only to train one brigade troop, and that the U. S. could not supply additional landing craft for Dodecanese operations while the Sicilian operation was in progress. If the Dodecanese operation is undertaken as a follow-up to Sicily, one result would be that the residual landing craft earmarked for the U. K. would never reach there.

GENERAL SOMERVELL, discussing C.C.S. 162, "U. S. Aid to Russia," said that since the paper was prepared, Lord Leathers had withdrawn his concurrence to it as a joint paper because he did not have first-hand knowledge of the U. S. production back-log. He did, however, accept General Somervell's figures. U. S. calculations of loss rate for dry cargo shipping are 2.6 percent. This figure is based upon the actual loss rate during 1942. The British figure of 1.9 percent is an attempt at forecasting expected losses for 1943, and U. S. authorities believe it too low. General Somervell recommended changing the first sentence of paragraph 14 to read: "Supplement British assistance, in accordance with U. S.-British agreement of November 13, 1942." He believes that the Russian Protocol should be regarded in the same status as any other operation; that it should not be sacrosanct, but susceptible of reduction if such be necessary because of other operations of equal importance The President is beginning to believe that it may be well to have a showdown with Stalin concerning the necessity of suspending Murmansk convoys, particularly since other means of supply to Russia are still available. General Somervell pointed out the importance of the last sentence in C.C.S. 162 and suggested that the particular attention of the Combined Chiefs of Staff be invited to this sentence.

ADMIRAL KING, summarizing the general strategic plan for 1943, pointed out that our main reliance in Europe was placed on Russia. Therefore, he felt that no effort should be spared to place in Russian hands every possible tool of war. The question was not one of placating Stalin but of implementing the Russians to our own interest. He agreed with General Marshall that it was not wise to attempt to continue Murmansk convoys when the loss becomes prohibitive.

SECRET

GENERAL SOMERVELL and ADMIRAL COOKE informed the Joint Chiefs of Staff that necessary shipping for operations in the Pacific had already been allocated. They agreed that no accurate determination of the effect on loss rate produced by the new Air and Escort program could be determined before June because of the necessity of integrating the effect over an appreciable time.

GENERAL MARSHALL, disqussing the proposed Army and Air Command set-up in the Mediterranean, informed the Joint Chiefs of Staff that he had received a draft plan for subdividing the North African and European Theaters, and that General Andrews was working on the proposal. General Marshall said he had discussed with Sir John Dill the question of Britain's control over U. S. heavy bombers in England in operations which might involve heavy losses; the U. S. Commander would always have the right to appeal. He believes British Command is logical until such time as our forces outnumber the British and until we have demonstrated the efficacy of our day-bombing methods. When this time arrives, a reexamination of the command arrangements will be in order.

SECRET

J.C.S. 57th Meeting
(Casablanca)

JOINT CHIEFS OF STAFF

MINUTES OF MEETING

Held at Anfa Camp on Thursday,
January 21, 1943, at 0900.

MEMBERS PRESENT

General G. C. Marshall, USA
Admiral E. J. King, USN
Lt. General H. H. Arnold, USA

SECRETARY

Brig. General J. R. Deane, USA

ADDITIONAL OFFICERS PRESENT

Lt. General B. B. Somervell, USA
Rear Admiral C. M. Cooke, Jr., USN
Brig. General J.E. Hull, USA
Brig. General A. C. Wedemeyer, USA
Colonel J. E. Smart, USA
Commander R. E. Libby, USN

SECRET

GENERAL MARSHALL read a despatch from General Eisenhower reporting an enemy attack in Tunisia which resulted in some disorganization of the French defense lines, and said that Eisenhower was proceeding to his advance command post; Admiral Cunningham would be senior officer at Algiers until his return. General Marshall also read a despatch containing a report by General Hurley which emphasized the absence of German air from the Russian front.

ADMIRAL KING informed the Joint Chiefs of Staff that they could expect Admiral Pound to propose a modification of the phrasing of the paper on "Conduct of the War in 1943" concerning antisubmarine warfare. Admiral King said that Admiral Pound had discussed with him recommendations he felt should be made to the Combined Chiefs of Staff regarding this subject, but that these recommendations were largely a summary of actions which had already been taken.

GENERAL ARNOLD said that the British were constantly raising objections to our proposals that bombing of submarine targets be intensified on the ground that the manufacturing points of certain items essential to submarine construction were extremely difficult targets.

GENERAL MARSHALL remarked that he had been given to understand that a British Captain had been given the task of surveying the general antisubmarine warfare situation, and that he felt it essential that some similar procedure with regard to this important problem be adopted by us.

The Joint Chiefs of Staff next considered C.C.S. 160, "Minimum Escort Requirements to Maintain the Sea Communications of the United Nations." It was agreed that the paper could be accepted as a premise for verification at a future date, noting that this was only one phase of a parallel study of the over-all antisubmarine position which was now being completed in the United States.

The Joint Chiefs of Staff next considered C.C.S. 166, "The Bomber Offensive from the United Kingdom."

GENERAL MARSHALL did not clearly understand the meaning of paragraph 6 and suggested that we get the British to explain the meaning of this paragraph. It appeared to General Marshall that the Prime Minister had probably instigated the paper.

SECRET

ADMIRAL KING said that he understood the paragraph to imply that before laying waste to whole cities in occupied territory, it would be necessary to obtain the approval of the British Cabinet because of the political implications of such an act.

GENERAL SOMERVELL suggested elimination of the word "synthetic" in paragraph 2 (d) of the paper, pointing out that the two tetraethyl plants in Germany were vital objectives.

Discussing C.C.S. 164, ANAKIM, it was agreed that it probably would be necessary to supply supplementary forces required from the Pacific. It was further agreed that it is essential that it appear in the minutes of the Combined Chiefs of Staff meeting that the LSD may not be ready in time for this operation, and that it is probable that United States forces will have to be shifted to the theater in October.

The Joint Chiefs of Staff considered C.C.S. 165, "Draft Telegram to M. Stalin," but took no action.

ADMIRAL KING remarked that he was dissatisfied with the late date proposed for operation HUSKY He felt it indicative that nothing would be done on the Continent during 1943. He agreed with General Marshall's assertion that the Prime Minister was anxious to mount BRIMSTONE and that the late date for HUSKY may have been influenced by this desire. He feels BRIMSTONE to be "doing something just for the sake of doing something"; that even if BRIMSTONE is accomplished, HUSKY will have to follow, thus further deferring Continental operations.

GENERAL MARSHALL said that in his opinion any forces deployed in Sardinia were in an extremely vulnerable position in case the Germans advanced through Spain; that the Axis might permit us to occupy Sardinia with little opposition, in order that they might occupy Spain and completely flank our forces in the Mediterranean. On the other hand, they would be forced to resist strongly in Sicily.

ADMIRAL COOKE said that it should be reemphasized that the entire problem for either operation will be one of training and that the British are fully cognizant of the difficulties of the Sicilian operation, partly as a result of their exhaustive study of Operation BRIMSTONE. They have considered and evaluated the difference in air coverage obtainable between

SECRET

Sicily and Sardinia, but, even so, appear to favor the Sardinian operation. Our calculations for HUSKY are based upon completion of operations in Tunisia by April 1. The British insist that LCA(L) must be used for the assault stage. They admit to having 400 of these craft and probably have more. We have none. We should ascertain from them how many they will give us for the assault. The disadvantage is that they can be carried only by British combat-loaded transports, inasmuch as our davits cannot handle them. They have a radius of approximately 50 miles. He agreed with a suggestion by General Somervell that their radius might be increased by installing auxiliary tanks, with a slight loss of personnel capacity.

GENERAL SOMERVELL, summarizing the capacity of various routes through the Levant, said that none of them looked very promising. Turkish railways are inadequate. All routes require a large number of heavy trucks and rolling stock. He said that the route via the Persian Gulf, expected to have a capacity of 10,000 tons per month but so far only able to handle from 4,000 to 5,000 tons per month, would improve as soon as the necessary personnel (due at the end of January) arrived.

COLONEL SMART suggested that, inasmuch as the final eviction of the Axis from Tunis and Bizerte might take on the characteristics of another Dunkirk, it might be advisable to delay this eviction until such time as we were prepared to mount Operation HUSKY in order to take advantage of the confusion and disorganization resulting from the Axis evacuation of Tunisia.

GENERAL ARNOLD said that he had settled the question of training French pilots with General Eisenhower; that training of one fighter group and one bombardment group in the rear areas was now in hand. There is an adequate number of fighter aircraft already in Africa; the question is one of deploying them in the correct spots.

SECRET

J.C.S. 58th Meeting
(Casablanca)

JOINT CHIEFS OF STAFF

MINUTES OF MEETING

Held at Anfa Camp on Friday,
January 22, 1943, at 0900.

MEMBERS PRESENT

General G. C. Marshall, USA
Admiral E. J. King, USN
Lt. General H. H. Arnold, USA

SECRETARY

Brig. General J. R. Deane, USA

ADDITIONAL OFFICERS PRESENT

Lt. General B. B. Somervell, USA
Rear Admiral C. M. Cooke, Jr., USN
Brig. General J.E. Hull, USA
Brig. General A. C. Wedemeyer, USA
Colonel J. E. Smart, USA
Commander R. E. Libby, USN

SECRET

1. C.C.S. 165/1--DRAFT REPLY TO M. STALIN.

The Joint Chiefs of Staff agreed upon certain modifications to be proposed to the Combined Chiefs of Staff.

2. C.C.S. 168--OPERATIONS IN THE SOUTHWEST PACIFIC.

GENERAL MARSHALL questioned the desirability of declaring our intention to clear the Aleutians of the enemy. He said that the British have been informed of the magnitude of the Kiska operation, and that this gave them a yardstick by which they might attempt to judge the magnitude of other operations in the Pacific Theater. He felt it essential that they understand that we will not commit ourselves to become involved in any large-scale operation in Alaska.

> After some discussion, it was agreed:
> To change the paper to read, "make the Aleutians as secure as may be," and to issue it as C.C.S. 168.

3. C.C.S. 161/1--HUSKY.

The Joint Chiefs of Staff discussed this paper by the Combined Staff Planners with a view to determining how it might be possible to mount the operation earlier than proposed in the paper. ADMIRAL KING remarked that it appeared that it would be necessary to utilize combat-loaded transports; that the British, although maintaining that convoys could be passed through the Mediterranean without occupying Sicily, still were reluctant to send assault convoys by this route, which prevented training and loading combat-loaded transports in the United Kingdom. Considerable work remains to be done as to reconnaissance of beaches.

> It was agreed:
> That the Joint Chiefs of Staff would inform the Combined Chiefs of Staff that they did not favor a late HUSKY, and were unalterably opposed to Operation BRIMSTONE at any time.

The Joint U. S. Chiefs of Staff believe that Operation HUSKY can be mounted by the 1st of August without undue difficulty although the necessary documents are not available here to sustain this belief. ADMIRAL KING remarked that we should meet this date and should do whatever has to be done to accomplish it.

ADMIRAL COOKE pointed out that if the Italian Fleet had not been driven into the Adriatic before the operation was launched, it would be necessary to provide two naval covering forces; but that the British hoped to have dealt with the Italian Fleet before the operation was scheduled.

SECRET

J.C.S. 59th Meeting
(Casablanca)

JOINT CHIEFS OF STAFF

MINUTES OF MEETING

Held at Anfa Camp on Saturday,
January 23, 1943, at 0900.

MEMBERS PRESENT

General G. C. Marshall, USA
Admiral E. J. King, USN
Lt. General H. H. Arnold, USA

SECRETARY

Brig. General J. R. Deane, USA

ADDITIONAL OFFICERS PRESENT

Lt. General B. B. Somervell, USA
Rear Admiral C. M. Cooke, Jr., USN
Brig. General J. E. Hull, USA
Brig. General A. C. Wedemeyer, USA
Colonel J. E. Smart, USA
Commander R. E. Libby, USN

SECRET

1. C.C.S. 167--CONTINENTAL OPERATIONS IN 1943.

GENERAL SOMERVELL remarked that he believed the number of U. S. divisions should properly be stated as five instead of four, on the basis of 40,000 men per division. One of these divisions will probably be airborne. He pointed out that the British reservation concerning the Metropolitan Air Force was introduced for the first time in this paper, and that this was the first intimation that there might be any difficulty with respect to air.

ADMIRAL KING remarked that if the provisions with regard to the U. S. furnishing assault craft were interpreted literally, it might cut into what we were able to furnish in the Pacific.

GENERAL MARSHALL said that we must, in accepting the paper, note the reservation that we would furnish only the resources remaining after mounting HUSKY and filling Pacific requirements, and that we see no prospect of providing U. S. crews or the totals of assault shipping and landing craft set forth in this paper by August 1st.

It was agreed:
(a) That in regard to paragraph 4, other commitments must be first met;
(b) That on our basis of calculation, the number of U. S. divisions would be five in lieu of four;
(c) That of these five U. S. divisions, one will probably be airborne.

2. C.C.S. 172--SHIPPING CAPABILITIES FOR BOLERO BUILD-UP.

GENERAL SOMERVELL explained the basis on which this paper had been produced, emphasizing that it made provision for sending 16,000 troops from the U. S. in combat-loaded transports, and that these had been computed on the basis of one trip only so that the transports might be held as long as necessary without detriment to other calculations. A balance of combat loaders to give 23,000 troop lift remains for the Pacific.

3. C.C.S. 171--OPERATION HUSKY.

After discussion, it was agreed:
(a) That the first paragraph should include, "with the target date as the period of the favorable July moon. Code designation, HUSKY";

SECRET

    (b) Under paragraph 1 of the command set-up, the words, "responsible for," should be replaced by "charged with";

    (c) The directive should provide for immediate preparation of cover plans;

    (d) An overall code designation for all Mediterranean operations should be made.

4.   C.C.S. 170--REPORT TO THE PRESIDENT AND PRIME MINISTER.

During the discussion of this paper, the question arose as to what duties General Eisenhower would perform during the carrying out of Operation HUSKY. GENERAL MARSHALL said that he would be responsible for all of Africa, for issuing directives to Air Marshal Tedder having no immediate application to HUSKY, etc. He felt the command relationship to be a formal one in view of the preponderance of British forces.

ADMIRAL KING said that this was in accordance with the general principle that immediate command vested in the nation having a preponderance of forces; but that the principle should not be rigidly applied and, in fact, C.C.S. 75/3 should be revised by inserting the qualification that this would be a normal, rather than a required arrangement under these circumstances.

CASABLANCA CONFERENCE

JANUARY 1943

JOINT CHIEFS OF STAFF

MINUTES OF MEETINGS

(Presided Over By The President)

	PAGE
Minutes of Conference, Janaury 15, 1943	51
Minutes of Conference, January 16, 1943	58

SECRET

JOINT CHIEFS OF STAFF

MINUTES OF CONFERENCE

Held at Anfa Camp, January 15, 1943, at 1000.

PRESENT

The President
General Marshall
Admiral King
Lt. General Arnold
Mr. Harry Hopkins
Mr. Averill Harriman
Brig. General Deane

SECRET

1. **VISIT OF GENERAL NOGUES AND THE SULTAN OF MOROCCO WITH THE PRESIDENT.**

The PRESIDENT asked as to the advisability of his seeing General Nogues and possibly the Sultan of Morocco. GENERAL MARSHALL and ADMIRAL KING both stated they felt that General Eisenhower was in a better position to advise the President on this subject and he would no doubt do so when he arrived at Anfa Camp. Admiral King, however, questioned whether or not General Nogues merited the honor of visiting the President of the United States.

2. **THE PRESIDENT'S PROGRAM.**

GENERAL MARSHALL explained that it had at first been thought the President would stay here for about four or five days; then leave by motor for Rabat and Port Lyautey, where he would visit three divisions and interview certain selected officers and men; then proceed by air to Oran, observe the troops there and also visit a hospital. From Oran, it was planned that he should go to Marrakech, change planes at the airfield there and then return to the United States. He stated that, in view of the fact that the conference would probably last about ten days, these plans would of necessity have to undergo some change. He said that it is not desirable for the President to visit Marrakech and he should refuse any invitation of the Prime Minister to do so.

GENERAL MARSHALL explained that Marrakech is inland, that its airfield is entirely open. No one knows how many Axis agents may be included in the civilian populations. He also said that it would be unwise to have the President of the United States in a city that contained about one and one-half French divisions which have recently been hostile to us and only one regiment of American troops.

GENERAL MARSHALL suggested that if the Prime Minister desired to visit Marrakech, he might do so with Mr. Hopkins; and this would furnish good cover for the real location of the President.

It was decided that the President would remain here and that if there was any indication that his presence here had become known, he would immediately start on the inspection tour which had been previously planned to start at the conclusion of his stay in Africa, except that, when he returned to the Marrakech airport, he would change planes and leave the Marrakech airport as though returning to the United States.

SECRET

Actually, he would return to the Anfa Camp in time to be here to finish up such business as might be necessary in connection with the conference.

In discussing the protection available at Anfa Camp, GENERAL ARNOLD brought out the fact that there was a French squadron equipped with our P-40 airplanes; and, at the request of the President, he explained something of our program for equipping French air units.

3. THE BRITISH STRATEGIC CONCEPT.

GENERAL MARSHALL gave the President a brief summary of the British Chiefs of Staff concept regarding the prospects in the European theater. They believe that we should first expand the bombing effort against the Axis and that operations in the Mediterranean offer the best chance of compelling Germany to disperse her air resources. He explained that the British are now in favor of an attack against Sicily rather than Sardinia and that this change of attitude was probably inspired by the Prime Minister.

At the same time, the United Nations should try to bring Turkey in on our side. Continued aid should be given to the Russians. A balance will have to be struck between these various commitments because they are mutually conflicting.

They also feel that we must be in a position to take advantage of any weakness developing in Germany by being prepared for operations across the English Channel.

GENERAL MARSHALL said that both Lord Mountbatten and General Clark agreed that there must be a long period of training before any attempt is made to land against determined resistance. General Clark had pointed out many of the mishaps that occurred in the landing in North Africa which would have been fatal had the resistance been more determined. General Clark was also apprehensive about our ability to maintain a surprise because of the necessity of locating landing craft along the northern coast of Africa prior to initiating operations. General Marshall stated that General Clark felt that, while this presented some difficulties, they could be overcome.

GENERAL MARSHALL stated that the British are extremely fearful of any direct action against the Continent until a decided crack in the German efficiency and morale has become apparent. The British point out

SECRET

that the rail net in Europe would permit the movement of seven divisions a day from east to west, which would enable them to reinforce their defenses of the northern coast of France rapidly. On the other hand, they can only move one division from north to south each day in order to reinforce their defense of southern Europe.

GENERAL MARSHALL said that General Clark had expressed the opinion that operations in the Mediterranean could be mounted more efficiently from North Africa. His reasons are that the lines of communication would be shorter there, that the troops in North Africa have had experience in landing operations, and that there will be an excess number of troops available for the operation once the Axis have been forced out of Tunisia, and finally that training will be more effective if undertaken in close contact with the enemy.

GENERAL MARSHALL stated that, while the British wish to build up a strong force in the United Kingdom for possible operations against Germany in case a weakness develops, it must be understood that any operation in the Mediterranean will definitely retard BOLERO.

ADMIRAL KING pointed out that the line of communication is the bottleneck in any operations in the Mediterranean.

MR. HOPKINS asked if the British Chiefs of Staff felt that the lines of communication are sufficient. GENERAL MARSHALL said that the two critical factors in the decision as to whether the operation is to be in the north or the south were: (1) the safety of the line of communications and (2) the fact that there will be an excess of veteran soldiers available in North Africa to mount an operation.

In discussing Turkey, GENERAL MARSHALL said that the British 8th Army would be prepared to send a considerable force there or near there. The aim of the United Nations should be to have Turkey resist Axis aggression and at the same time permit and protect our use of their airfields.

The PRESIDENT said that the question of bringing Turkey into the war is one for the diplomats to settle. In conducting negotiations, he stated that he and the Prime Minister should be given information as to how much military support the United Nations should be prepared to offer Turkey in order to accomplish what is desired. He stated that he did not

SECRET

want to be in the position of overpromising anything to the Turkish Government. (The Joint Staff Planners have been directed to investigate how much aid it would be necessary for us to furnish Turkey in order to enable them to provide effective resistance to an Axis invasion.)

It was agreed that, regardless of whether Turkey came into the war on the side of the United Nations, we should assemble sufficient force to the east of the Turkish boundary to enable the United Nations to reinforce Turkey as soon as she did become involved in the war. This can probably be accomplished by using part of the British 8th Army.

4. ANTISUBMARINE WARFARE.

GENERAL MARSHALL then pointed out that both the American and the British Chiefs of Staff agreed that effective measures must be taken against the Axis submarines. He said that Admiral King had pointed out that the most effective targets would be at the places where the submarines are assembled. He agreed with the statement, which he attributed to Sir Charles Portal, that we must keep hammering on one link in the chain, whether it be the factories which manufacture component parts, the submarine assembly yards, submarine bases, or submarines along the sea lanes.

5. OPERATION RAVENOUS.

GENERAL MARSHALL informed the President of the British attitude concerning the Operation RAVENOUS.

ADMIRAL KING stated that he had the impression that the British were coming around to the idea that it would be a profitable gamble.

GENERAL MARSHALL explained that there were hazards, particularly from Japanese action against the southern flank, but that if the operation was successful, it would secure favorable results far out of proportion to the risks involved. The most important benefit to be hoped for would be a decrease in the Japanese pressure in the southern Pacific by forcing the Japanese to divert their attention to the Burma theater; and, even in the event of failure, it would almost certainly result in a junction of the Chinese forces now in Burma with those from Yunnan; and, if a retirement became necessary, a trained Chinese army would withdraw into China.

GENERAL MARSHALL then spoke of the Generalissimo's refusal to mount the operation. One reason given by the Generalissimo is the failure

SECRET

to secure British cooperation in assembling naval forces in the Bay of Bengal, which he felt was a definite British commitment.

It was agreed that an effort should be made to obtain firm British support for the operation before requesting the President to discuss the matter further with the Generalissimo.

The PRESIDENT added that for psychological reasons he thought it would be advisable to double General Chennault's force in China and also to bomb Japan proper. GENERAL ARNOLD replied that he agreed that it would be wise to increase General Chennault's force and expressed great confidence in his ability to operate effectively against the Japanese. He stated, however, that the difficulty of supplying gasoline, spare parts, and other maintenance necessities prevented doing this at this time. He indicated that this was one of the most urgent reasons for opening the Burma Road.

MR. HOPKINS asked General Marshall what he thought the prospects of success in Operation RAVENOUS were.

GENERAL MARSHALL replied that he thought they were better than fifty-fifty. He said the British presented all sorts of difficulties which must be overcome but that he personally did not feel any of them were insurmountable. The tactical operations involved would not be of long duration, but it would be necessary to build an improved road rapidly before the rainy season set in. He felt that our engineers could do this, but the British were inclined to doubt it. The British also feared the effects of malaria, but GENERAL MARSHALL pointed out that their malaria preventive methods did not approach the effectiveness of ours.

ADMIRAL KING stated that he thought it was most essential to undertake Operation RAVENOUS, particularly for its effect on the Japanese in the South Pacific. He stated that they are operating on interior lines, and it was difficult to understand why they did not make some serious thrusts at Midway or other points on our line of communications.

6. COMMAND SITUATION IN EUROPE.

GENERAL MARSHALL stated that he had learned that the Prime Minister was concerned over the effectiveness of our bombing operations in Europe. The utilization of our bombing force is tied up with the question of command. At the present time General Eisenhower controls the

SECRET

Air Force, both in North Africa and in England. We are cooperating with the British in selecting the bombing objectives, but we are not subject to their orders. GENERAL MARSHALL said that he felt the time had come when we should establish a separate United Kingdom theater. He stated that he had sent General Andrews to Cairo to give him some experience in an active theater of operations and that he now proposed to put him in command of the American troops in the United Kingdom.

GENERAL MARSHALL stated that so far as operational direction of bombing, i.e., time and mission, our bombers in England should be subject to British command. So far as technique, etc., they should not be permitted to dictate our procedure.

7. OPERATIONS IN TUNISIA.

GENERAL MARSHALL indicated that there may be a change in the British command in the operations in Tunisia. He said that Admiral Cunningham agreed that the command had not been well handled. Instances occurred in which trained United States combat teams loaned to the British were broken up, thus reducing their effectiveness. There had also been instances of the misuse of British parachute troops. This situation is now being corrected.

SECRET

JOINT CHIEFS OF STAFF

MINUTES OF CONFERENCE

Held at Anfa Camp, January 16, 1943, at 1700.

PRESENT

The President
General Marshall
Admiral King
Lt. General Arnold
Lt. General Somervell
Rear Admiral Cooke
Brig. General Wedemeyer
Mr. Harry Hopkins
Mr. Averill Harriman
Brig. General Deane

SECRET

ADMIRAL KING informed the President that the Joint Chiefs of Staff have been attempting to obtain the British Chiefs of Staff's concept as to how the war should be won. He said that the British have definite ideas as to what the next operation should be but do not seem to have an over-all plan for the conduct of the war.

GENERAL MARSHALL stated that the Planners are making a study of what is required in the Pacific in order to maintain constant pressure on the Japanese and keep the initiative in that theater. The Combined Chiefs of Staff have been particularly concerned with the strategic concept for 1943. They have had discussions on the Burma operations and also whether an immediate operation should be planned for the Mediterranean or for the Continent or both. He stated that the Planners had been instructed to estimate the earliest possible date that an operation against Sicily could be mounted in order that the Chiefs of Staff could determine what residue of force would be available for operations on the Continent and if such operations would be advisable this year.

GENERAL MARSHALL stated that the most critical factors in the coming operations are the availability of landing craft, the time necessary for amphibious training, and the availability of escort vessels.

He stated that there will be excess troops available in North Africa when the Axis powers have been expelled from North Africa and that this is one of the chief reasons why Operation HUSKY appears to be attractive.

The British have estimated that the operations against Sicily cannot be mounted prior to August, but feel that there is a possibility of moving this date up to some time in July.

GENERAL MARSHALL said that the question being determined is whether we can undertake an operation against the Continent together with Operation HUSKY or separately and at a later date. The British maintain a spearhead in the United Kingdom for an operation against the Continent in the event of a crack in German morale. This includes enough landing craft to move four brigade groups; and, additionally, the British are putting motors in approximately 1,000 barges which they will use, together with other small craft, to bring in troops following the spearhead.

SECRET

The PRESIDENT asked how many troops were in England at this time, to which GENERAL MARSHALL replied that there were one trained division and about 140,000 to 150,000 men. He said that by next summer we can have six to nine divisions in the United Kingdom, and the British will have thirteen.

GENERAL MARSHALL quoted Sir Charles Portal as saying a crack in Axis morale may come at any time because of the explosive elements existing in the populations of the occupied countries. Sir Charles Portal feels that, if such an explosion comes, it will start in the interior of Germany but will finally reach the front-line troops who will desire to return to their families. In this case, an occupation of the Continent would be comparatively simple.

GENERAL MARSHALL said that training for amphibious operations is the most critical factor which we have to face. The training must be of much higher quality than that given for TORCH. He quoted General Eisenhower as saying that he believed that there must be an invasion on the Continent but that it would require a minimum of 12 divisions, which is double previous estimates. General Eisenhower also feels that there is a need for more training. Other limiting factors to any proposed operation are the necessities of combating the submarine menace and for the delivery of supplies to Russia.

An operation against Sardinia can be accomplished about six weeks earlier than one against Sicily, but the results will have little effect in improving the shipping situation through the Mediterranean. The only positive result to be received from the capture of Sardinia would be the ability to bomb Italy and perhaps the southern coast of France.

GENERAL ARNOLD pointed out that there would be much better air coverage for Operation HUSKY than could be given to Operation BRIMSTONE. The PRESIDENT asked where the Germans had the best defense.

GENERAL MARSHALL replied that their defense in Sicily was better than that in Sardinia and that by summer it might be expected that the Germans would have six to eight divisions there. General Marshall said that the Combined Chiefs of Staff were all agreed on the necessity of placing adequate troops in rear of Turkey to be prepared to reinforce her for a resistance to Axis invasion.

SECRET

The PRESIDENT remarked that Turkey's entry into the war was a diplomatic question, to which GENERAL MARSHALL replied that he felt that the concentration should be made regardless of whether Turkey came into the war or not.

ADMIRAL KING said that, in our endeavors to obtain a definite strategic concept from the British Chiefs of Staff, it had become apparent that they intended using the geographic and manpower position of Russia to the maximum. This necessitates making every effort to maintain the flow of supplies to Russia and also to divert German air and ground troops from the Russian front. He added that the British make no mention of where or when a second front on the Continent should be established. The PRESIDENT said that we now have a Protocol with the Russians which involves a certain delivery of munitions to them and that this shall probably be continued on the same scale when the present Protocol expires.

ADMIRAL KING stated that British convoys by the northern route are set up for 30 ships every 42 days. With an additional 12 destroyers this could be improved to a rate of 30 ships each 27 days. He stated that he did not believe we should base our plans too largely on a contemplated German crack-up. It now appeared that a real ROUNDUP operation is not feasible before April 1944 because of British lack of enthusiasm.

GENERAL MARSHALL said that the British would undertake an Operation SLEDGEHAMMER if they saw signs of a break in German morale. This would be followed by a makeshift ROUNDUP operation. He said the British feel that they cannot gather the means for a real thrust against the Continent in 1943, and that Admiral Pound states that no operation should be undertaken after August. It is apparent that British cooperation cannot be obtained unless there are indications of the Germans weakening.

ADMIRAL KING stated that, if the operations on the Mediterranean and on the Russian front caused the Germans to withdraw their forces from France, the British would be willing to seize this opportunity to invade the Continent.

GENERAL MARSHALL informed the President that the British were not interested in occupying Italy, inasmuch as this would add to our burdens without commensurate returns.

SECRET

The PRESIDENT expressed his agreement with this view.

GENERAL MARSHALL stated that in his opinion we may be able to obtain a decision from the Combined Chiefs of Staff concerning the operations in the Pacific by January 17th and that the Joint Chiefs of Staff had come to the conclusion that Operation HUSKY should be undertaken, but they had not yet informed the British to this effect.

The PRESIDENT stated that from the political point of view he thought it would be extremely wise to send more airplanes to China. He felt that they could be used to great advantage there; and if periodic bombing raids over Japan could be undertaken, they would have a tremendous morale effect on the Chinese people. GENERAL ARNOLD stated that he agreed with this view but wished to see for himself whether or not an increased air force in China could be supplied.

The PRESIDENT then stated that he thought it was desirable to set up additional transport planes to insure a supply of a larger air force in China.

GENERAL MARSHALL said that transport planes now allocated to China are sufficient and that we must be extremely careful about making additional allocations. He pointed out that, in addition to China, we would receive demands for transport planes from Russia. We would need a considerable number for the Operation HUSKY and also for General MacArthur's forces in the Pacific.

The PRESIDENT suggested the possibility of preparing two or three plans and making all preparations to carry them out, but leaving the decision as to the objective until a later date.

ADMIRAL COOKE pointed out that, if plans were made for Operation HUSKY, the objective could readily be changed to either the Dodecanese, Crete, or Sardinia.

The PRESIDENT said he would like to have some flexibility to the plans in case it became apparent that Turkey might enter the war. In that case we could then adopt the objective which would fit in best with this development.

GENERAL MARSHALL stated he did not feel that the Operation HUSKY would interfere with Turkey's entering into the war, but rather that a success in Sicily might be an added inducement to her to join with us.

SECRET

The **PRESIDENT** then directed the discussion to Russia. He said that he had received information that the Russians did not desire any of our personnel and also indicated that they would not welcome General Bradley's mission to make a survey of the available air facilities in Siberia.

He asked General Somervell about the supply situation to Russia.

GENERAL SOMERVELL replied that the Persian port is capable of handling 15 ships per month. The road and rail facilities are capable of handling about 10,000 tons per day, which are sufficient to handle the freight from 40 ships per month; and efforts are now being made to expand the port facilities to make this possible. He then went on to describe to the President several overland routes to Russia, all of which are limited by the availability of truck transportation.

The **PRESIDENT** asked what might happen if Turkey remained neutral but permitted our transporting munitions and bombs through her territory.

GENERAL SOMERVELL replied that certain routes could be made available by this means; but, if they were used, it would be necessary to establish a truck assembly plant in that area. He added that he thought this should be done and that all available routes into Russia should be used.

The **PRESIDENT** asked General Somervell if truck bodies could be manufactured in the Near East, to which **GENERAL SOMERVELL** replied that lumber would have to be obtained from India.

MR. HARRIMAN stated that, until a truck assembly plant could be constructed, the one now at Cairo could be used.

ADMIRAL KING stated that the last convoy to Murmansk arrived without loss of any of its 16 cargo ships, but that one destroyer had been sunk and another damaged. He stated that we could help Russia more if they would help us to do so.

The **PRESIDENT** asked if we were getting as much information from southern Europe as are the British. **GENERAL MARSHALL** replied that he would have this investigated. (A message was sent to G-2, Allied Force Headquarters, asking for a report as to the amount of intelligence received out of southern Europe by U. S. Intelligence agencies and how our efforts in this regard compared with those of the British.)

SECRET

GENERAL MARSHALL then informed the President that the British had agreed to transfer their Valentine tanks from the 6th Armored Division to the French as soon as the British had received our Sherman tanks. He also stated he thought it necessary to equip the best French divisions rapidly.

GENERAL MARSHALL then informed the President regarding a decision which had been made by General Eisenhower concerning the Tunisian operations. A drive towards Sfax, which had been planned for January 24th, has been called off. This was necessary because the British 1st Army on the north could not attack until March 15th and General Alexander could not attack Rommel's forces on the south until February 15th. It was decided that the attack against Sfax might be premature and expose them to an attack from the north by German Tunisian forces and from the south by Rommel. Instead, General Eisenhower is to hold his 1st Armored Division in the vicinity of Tebessa prepared to assist either Alexander's forces in the south or the 1st British Army in the north; and the attack against Sfax will be made by infantry units at a later date, to be coordinated by General Eisenhower and General Alexander.

The PRESIDENT then asked General Somervell about the general supply situation. GENERAL SOMERVELL replied that the greatest shortages in North Africa were in road machinery and motor transportation. Both of these are now being sent to North Africa. The machinery is needed to improve the railroads and also for the construction and improvement of airfields. Efforts are also being made to bring in needed locomotives.

The PRESIDENT then asked about the civilian supply situation. GENERAL SOMERVELL replied that it was being handled satisfactorily, except that valuable cargo space was being utilized by some of the civilian agencies in the United States in sending unnecessary and ridiculous items.

The PRESIDENT then informed the Chiefs of Staff that Admiral Robert in Martinique had received a message from Laval to sink his ships immediately upon receiving evidence that the United States intended action against Martinique. Laval required Robert to give him an answer at once. Robert informed Laval within four hours that he would comply with his orders. This definitely eliminates the possibility of our obtaining the use of French shipping now in Martinique.

SECRET

ADMIRAL COOKE then informed the President that the British were becoming conscious of the fact that the United States was engaged in a war in the Pacific and described his discussions with the British Staff Planners, who recognized the necessity for adequate means being provided to handle the Pacific situation. He stated, however, that he did not feel that the British Chiefs of Staff were as yet convinced of this necessity. The Chiefs of Staff feel that we should maintain the status quo and simply hold, whereas the Planners recognize that a constant pressure must be kept on the Japanese and that every effort must be made to keep China in the war. The Planners admit the possibility of the Chinese dropping out of the war.

The PRESIDENT then discussed the proposed operations in Burma. GENERAL MARSHALL informed him that just as he felt that we had convinced the British that Operation RAVENOUS should be undertaken, the Generalissimo had declined to participate. The reason given by the Generalissimo is that the British refuse to place a naval force in the Bay of Bengal to interrupt the Japanese line of communications. The Generalissimo feels that a definite commitment to this effect had been made by the Prime Minister in a talk last year before the Pacific Council. GENERAL MARSHALL said that the Prime Minister probably had the ANAKIM operation in mind.

ADMIRAL COOKE stated that the British have no intention of undertaking an operation to recapture Burma in the present dry season.

GENERAL MARSHALL pointed out that the Chinese, particularly General Hsiung, had been loud in their complaints about failures to assist them; and now that we offer them assistance, they refuse our help.

SECRET

INDEX

A

Admiral Glassford's report, 7
Agenda
  For coming conferences, 2
  Suggested procedure for dealing with the, 34
Aid to Russia
  Balance of commitments to Russia and Turkey, 53
  Coordination of supply, 26
  General Somervell's discussion of, 39
  Through Continental landing, 18
Aid to Turkey, 55
Air forces in China, 56, 62
Aircraft over Tunisia, 6
Aleutian Islands, 23
  Operations in, 46
Algiers, Air situation at, 4
Allocation for shipping in the Pacific, 40
Allocation of forces and production, Discussion of, 30
Amphibious weapons, 17
ANAKIM, Operation
  C.C.S. 164, Discussion of, 43
  Affect of RAVENOUS on, 23
  Initiation of, 24
  Prime Minister's agreement, 28
Andrews General—proposed for command of troops in United Kingdom Theater by General Marshall, 57
Anfa Camp, Protection available, 53
Annex "A" to J.C.S. 55th Meeting Minutes—Memorandum for the President, 35
Antisubmarine warfare survey, 42, 55
Approach to the discussion
  Admiral King's, 3
  General Marshall's, 3

B

BOLERO build-up
  Shipping capabilities for, 48
Bombing in occupied territory and political implications, 43
Bombers to General Stilwell, 10
Bone, Air situation at, 4

Brest Peninsula
  Operations against, 26
BRIMSTONE, 3, 6
  Comparison of, with results of Brest Peninsula operation, 11
  Deception of land craft, 11
  Training, 5
British
  Convoys, 61
  Eastern Fleet, 9
    At Ceylon, 24
  Possession of Tripoli, 6
  Strategic concept of conduct of war, 39, 53, 61
Burma
  Admiral King's concept of, explained to Prime Minister, 28
  British can operate against, regardless of China, 29
  Plan for operation, 23
Burma Road, Reason for opening, 56
Byrnes, Telegram to, 36

C

Channel Islands
  Lord Mountbatten's plan for capture, 26
Chennault General, Air forces under, 56
China
  Air forces in, 56
  Transport planes to, 62
Chinese reluctance to begin RAVENOUS, 24, 28
Civilian supply situation, 64
Clearing the Mediterranean, 3
Combined Staff Planners
  Pacific concept for 1943, 23
  Requirements in Pacific, 59
  Strategic concept of war in Pacific, 59
Command
  Army and Air, in Mediterranean, 40
  Discussion of, in European theater, 12
  England, in, 14
  Set-up in Tunisia proposed by General Marshall, 35

67

Command—continued
  Set-up in West Africa proposed by Admiral King, 33
  Tunisian set-up following Tripoli operation, 35
Command situation in Europe, 56
Communications, Mediterranean, 54
Conduct of the war in 1943, Discussion of, 33
Conferences
  Agenda for coming, 2
  Further, 6
  Suggested procedure for dealing with the Agenda of the, 34
Continental invasion, Forces for, 60
Continental landing, 18
  As aid to Russia, 18
  Operations in 1943, 48
Convoys
  British, 61
  Continuing, in Mediterranean, 18
Cooke, Admiral, C. M., Jr.
  Date suggested for Operation HUSKY, 34
Craft, landing, 17
  Assembly in U. K., 29
  Contribution by British, 25
  Discussion of, by General Marshall and Lord Mountbatten, 25
  For India, 24

D

Decisions reached concerning command set-up in European theater, 12
Defeat of
  Germany, Key to, 24
  Japan, Key to, 24
Destroyers transferred to ocean escorts, 33
Discussion
  Admiral King's
    Approach, Method of, 2
    Procedure, Method of, 2
  General Marshall's
    Approach, Method of, 2
    Procedure, Method of, 2
Dodecanese, plans for, 62

E

Eastern Fleet, British, 9
  At Ceylon, 24

Eighth Army command to Eisenhower, 28
Europe
  Bombing operations effectiveness in, 56
  Command situation in, 56
European theater
  Decisions as to command set-up, 12
Expelling the Germans from Tunisia, 4

F

Fighter aircraft over Tunisia, 6
Forces
  Allocation of, Discussion of, 30
  Continental operations, for, 60
  Listing of, by U. K. and U. S., 29
Fourth Division to North Africa, 6
French
  Pilots, Training of, 44
  Ships at Martinique to be sunk, 64
Further conferences, 6

G

German threat to Spain, 6
Glassford, Admiral, report, 7

H

High octane gas production affected by synthetic rubber program, 36
HUSKY, Operation
  Agreement following discussion, 48
  Calculations for, 44
  Date proposed objectionable to Admiral King, 43
  Discussion of mounting, 46
  Target date suggested by Admiral Cooke, 34

I

Information from Southern Europe, 63

J

Japan
  Operations against, 56
  Supplies to, 56
Japanese air strength, 23
Joint Chiefs of Staff
  Opposition to shipping via Murmansk, 34

Joint Chiefs of Staff—continued
  Presidential movements, Discussion of proposals of, 38
  Recommendations for instructions to Justice Byrnes regarding synthetic rubber freeze, 36
  Synthetic rubber material allotments recommendation of Mr. Nelson approved by, 35

K

King, Admiral E. J.
  Appraisal and observation of United Nations' ability to take initiative and United States' power to lead, 10
  Approach to the discussion, His, 3
  Attitude toward Sardinian and Sicilian operations, 31
  Mediterranean command proposal, 35
  Summary of general strategic plan for 1943, 39
  U. S. representative to accompany Prime Minister to Turkey proposed by, 38
  West Africa command set-up proposals, 33
Kiska operation, President's objection to British interest in, 29

L

Landing craft
  Assembly in U. K., 29
  Contribution by British, 25
  Discussion of, by General Marshall and Lord Mountbatten, 25
  Disposition following Sicilian landing, 17
  For India, 24
Landing on the European Continent, 18
  As aid to Russia, 18
Lend-Lease to Turkey, 38
Levant, Capacity of routes through, 44
Listing of forces by U. K. and U. S., 29

M

Marrakech, Conditions in, 52

Marshall, General G. C.
  Agreement to Admiral King's proposal for full trust in French, 33
  Approach to the discussion, 3
  Tunisian command set-up following the Tripoli operation, 35
  Turkish Lend-Lease situation revealed by, 38
Martinique, Laval's message to Admiral Robert, 64
Mediterranean
  Army and Air command in, 40
  Clearing and opening, 3
  Command proposal by Admiral King, 35
  Communications, 54
  Continuation of convoys by British, 18
  Memorandum for the President, Annex "A" to J.C.S. 55th Meeting Minutes, 35
  Minutes of Meetings, 1
Modifications to C.C.S. 155, 33
Morale of the Axis, 60

N

Nelson recommendation for synthetic rubber material allotments, 35
Nogues, General, Visit with the President, 52
North Africa
  Supply situation, 64
  Training in, for landings, 53
  Troops in, 19
Norway, Bombing of airfields, 26

O

Objections to British concern in our strategic theater, 29
Operation
  Aleutians, 46
  ANAKIM
    Prime Minister's agreement, 28
    Relation to RAVENOUS, 23
  BOLERO build-up, Shipping capabilities for, 48
  Brest Peninsula, 26
  BRIMSTONE, 3, 6
    Comparison of, with results of Brest Peninsula operation, 11

Operation—continued
  BRIMSTONE—continued
    Deception of landing craft, 11
    Training, 5
  Burma, 23
    Admiral King's concept explained to Prime Minister, 28
    British can operate against regardless of Chinese, 29
  Continental, in 1943, 28
  HUSKY
    Agreement following discussion, 48
    Calculations for, 44
    Date proposal objectionable to Admiral King, 43
    Discussion of mounting operation, 46
    Target date suggested by Admiral Cooke, 34
  Kiska
    President's objection to British interest in, 29
    Southwest Pacific, Operations in the, 46
  Norway
    Bombing of airfields, 26
  Pacific
    Concept for 1943, 23
    Prime Minister's objection to operation, 28
    Shipping, 40
  RAVENOUS
    Chinese reluctance to begin, 24, 65
    Prime Minister's agreement, 28
    Prospects for success, 56
    Purpose of, 28
    Relation to ANAKIM, 23
  ROUNDUP
    Date feasible, 61
    Forces needed, 15
  Sicilian
    Date for, 59
    Mechanics and key to, 16
  SLEDGEHAMMER
    British will undertake, 61
  TORCH
    Available troops following completion, 18
    United Kingdom, in and from the, 11
Operations
  Continental and HUSKY combined, 59
  Landing barges for, 59
  Japan, Against, 56
  Sardinian, Advantages of success, 60
  Tunisia, In, 59

P

Pacific
  Allocation for shipping, 40
  British recognizance of necessary Allied action, 65
  Concept for 1943, 23
  Prime Minister's objection to operation, 28
Peace table, Domination of, 21
Possession of Tripoli by British, 6
President, The
  Action required prior to departure, 34
  Memorandum for, Annex "A" to J.C.S. 55th Meeting Minutes, 32
  Objection to British interest in U. S. strategic theater, 29
  Report to, and Prime Minister, 49
  Visit, 2
  Visit of General Nogues and the Sultan of Morocco with, 52
President's Program, The, 52
Prime Minister's
  Agreement to Operations ANAKIM and RAVENOUS, 28
  Objection to Pacific operation, 28
  Report to President and, 49
Priority bombing program, 12
Protection available at Anfa Camp, 53

R

RAVENOUS, Operation
  British attitude concerning, 55
  Chinese reluctance to begin, 24, 65
  Effect on ANAKIM, 23
  Initiation of, 24
  Prime Minister's agreement, 28
  Prospects of Success, 56
  Purpose of, 28
  Report to the President and Prime Minister, 49
  Resources to be furnished following mounting HUSKY, 48
Robert, Admiral, Message regarding ships from Laval, 64
ROUNDUP, Operation
  Feasible date for, 61
  Forces needed for, 15
Russia
  Aid to
    Continental landing, 18
    Coordination of, 26
    Opposition of Joint Chiefs of Staff to shipping via Murmansk, 34

Russia—continued
  Aid to—continued
    Pacific plan, 20
    Rejection of U. S. and British personnel, 25, 63
    Supply to, 63

S

Sardinia
  Advantages of capture, 60
  Mounting and operation against, 5
  Operation favored over Sicily, 29
Sfax, British drive on, canceled, 64
Shipping capabilities for BOLERO build-up, 48
Shipping for operations in Pacific, 40
Sicily
  Date for operations against, 59
  Means of reducing fortifications, 26
  One of purposes of capture, 19
  Strength in, 26
Situation in the air at Algiers and Bone, 4
SLEDGEHAMMER, Operation
  British to undertake, 61
Somervell, General B. B.
  Aid to Russia discussed by—C.C.S. 162, 39
  Outline of mechanics of Sicilian operation, 16
Southwest Pacific, Operations in, 46
Spain, German threat to, 6
Stalin rejects U. S. and British personnel, 25
Strategic policies, General, 17
Submarines
  Bombing of, 28
  Indian Ocean, In, 10
  U. S. loan of six, 10
Sultan of Morocco, Visit with the President, 52
Summarizing of general strategic plan for 1943 by Admiral King, 39
Supplies to General Stilwell, 29
Supply situation
  Civilian, 64
  In North Africa, 64
  To Russia, 63
Synthetic rubber program, 28
  Effects on military programs including high octane gas and plane production, 36
  Material allotment recommended by Mr. Nelson, 35

T

Tanks of British to French, 64
Telegram to Byrnes, Washington, 36
Theater, European
  Decisions reached at discussion of command set-up in, 12
TORCH, Operation, Available troops following completion of, 18
Training
  In North Africa for landings, 53
  Of French pilots, 44
Transport planes for China, 62
Tripoli, British possession of, 6
Troops
  Movement of, 12
  North Africa, for maintaining, 5, 19
  To General Stilwell, 29
  To United Kingdom, 11, 60
Truck assembly plant, 63
Tunisia
  Expelling the Germans from, 4
  Operations in, 57
Turkey
  Aid to, 55
  British 8th Army Force for, 54
  Lend-Lease situation with respect to, 38
  Passive belligerency, 34
  U. S representative to accompany Prime Minister to Turkey proposed, 38

U

United Kingdom, Operations in and from the, 11

V

Visit of General Nogues and the Sultan of Morocco with the President, 52

W

West Africa, Command set-up as proposed by Admiral King for, 33

www.ingramcontent.com/pod-product-compliance
Lightning Source LLC
Chambersburg PA
CBHW060453300426
44113CB00016B/2575